A CENTURY OF DIPLOMATIC BLUE BOOKS
1814 - 1914

A CENTURY OF
DIPLOMATIC BLUE BOOKS
1814 - 1914

Lists Edited, with Historical Introductions

by

HAROLD TEMPERLEY

and

LILLIAN M. PENSON

NEW   YORK

BARNES & NOBLE, INC.

Publishers · Booksellers · Since 1873

Published by Frank Cass & Co. Ltd.,
10 Woburn Walk, London W.C.1
by arrangement with Cambridge University Press.

Published in the United States
in 1966
by Barnes & Noble, Inc.
105 Fifth Avenue, New York, N.Y. 10003.

First Edition   1938
New Impression   1966

Printed in Great Britain

To
SIR STEPHEN GASELEE
Librarian and Keeper of the Papers of
the Foreign Office

*Nam nec historia debet egredi ueritatem, et honeste
factis ueritas sufficit.*

PLINIUS MINOR.

CONTENTS

PREFACE

This work on Blue Books was originally designed for a very simple purpose. The date of presentation of a White Paper or a Blue Book, whether to the House of Lords or to the House of Commons, is seldom printed on the paper itself, nor is it recorded in the volumes in which the papers are bound. Yet the date of the publication of a paper, particularly of a State Paper on foreign affairs, is most important for historians and even for general readers. Since the days of Canning Blue Books have been published in order to meet the ebb and flow of public opinion. Unless the exact date of such a paper is known, there is no way of discovering its importance, and its connection with popular opinion, or of estimating the national reaction to its publication. At present these dates can be found only by the tedious process of searching through the Journals of the House of Commons or of the House of Lords, and these Journals are by no means available in every library. In consequence the date itself and its significance are often overlooked, even by historians. The first aim of this book, therefore, was to give a list of the titles of Foreign Office Blue Books from Castlereagh to Grey, and to add the dates on which they were laid before Parliament.

It was soon found that a mere list of titles and dates was not enough, and that the addition of certain other features would make the book not only useful to the technical historian, but even attractive in some sense to the general reader. The different methods by which a paper is laid, whether by command, by order of the House, or in reply to Address, all involve constitutional points of considerable interest. Thus a detailed study of replies to Addresses shows that, during the whole period which began with Palmerston and ended with the Midlothian campaign, independent pressure from Parliament succeeded in extracting a number of papers from ministers which they would have preferred to refuse. This is a most important aspect of the activity and enterprise of the Commons. Yet it has been, and still is, almost a concealed chapter of English Parliamentary life.

The next important problem in connection with Blue Books is to consider how far documents were suppressed or mutilated, and how this practice varied from Foreign Minister to Foreign Minister. It has been possible to indicate the extent and character of such omissions in the case of a number of Blue Books, though clearly to do this exhaustively would be a task enormous in itself and one quite beyond the capacity of any individual editors. What it was possible to do, however, was to give a general sketch of the Blue-Book policy of each successive Foreign Minister, underlining his more important achievements in publication and showing the character of his suppressions. These general surveys led to some interesting and apparently novel conclusions. Castlereagh is revealed as bridging the gap between the time when the Government could refuse to publish papers and the time when it could no longer do so. Canning stands out from the canvas as the designer of a new system, clearly formulating a policy of publicity, and succeeding to an extent unrivalled by any of those who came after him. Palmerston himself, despite his power, became the victim of this policy of publication, and, unlike Canning, was unable to refuse the demands of the Commons when he wished to do so. The period of Palmerston is, indeed, the Golden Age of Blue Books; they abounded in number and fullness and the public had good measure pressed down and running over. Aberdeen and Peel, Malmesbury and Derby were not so anxious to publish freely, but the current was too strong for them. The spate of Blue Books on foreign affairs in the Russell-Palmerston period (1859–65) has seldom been exceeded in volume and, perhaps, never in exuberance. Gladstone's policy was more restrained, and though his Blue Books were numerous, he revealed more to the House by his occasional indiscretions. In the Disraeli period public opinion forced the unwilling hands of Derby and Salisbury, and drove them to follow the lavish tradition of the Palmerstonian age.

The curious fact emerges from this study that the advent of
a more democratic era resulted in a restriction on the publications on foreign affairs in some important ways. This tendency
is evident in Gladstone's second administration, but is much
more marked in the long period dominated by Salisbury, and
is most fully developed in the time of Sir Edward Grey. It is
clearly a matter of great interest, and ultimately of much
importance, to enquire why pressure from independent
members of Parliament gradually disappeared, and why
ministers took advantage of this fact to become more secretive
and restrained in their publications on foreign policy. Judged
by a Blue-Book test Sir Edward Grey took the public into his
confidence very much less than did Palmerston. This undoubtedly is a constitutional development of no common
interest. It is literally true to say that as Parliament became
more democratic its control over foreign policy declined, and,
while Blue Books on domestic affairs expanded and multiplied
at the end of the nineteenth century, those on foreign affairs
lessened both in number and in interest.

In compiling the list of Blue Books, the Editors have cast
their net widely; for some papers whose bearing on foreign
affairs is indirect are particularly important for the study of
diplomatic history. Each entry is annotated to show the date
on which the paper was laid before Parliament, and the
reason for its presentation, i.e. by command of the Crown or
in reply to an Address from one or other of the Houses of
Parliament. The date of the Address as well as that of presentation is given, and it will often be found that both serve
as a guide to Parliamentary debates. The introductions describe
the publication policy of successive Secretaries of State. This
information is complete for the periods of Castlereagh and
Canning (1814–27). It is reasonably complete for that of
Palmerston, Russell and Clarendon (1830–70). The work
which the Editors have done in conjunction with Dr G. P.
Gooch, on *British Documents on the Origins of the War*, has
enabled them to read the whole of the Foreign Office archive

material from 1897 to 1914, and in the course of these and other researches they have also studied in some detail the period 1870 to 1897.

The conclusion is that while the Blue Books are much fuller at some periods of the century than at others, it remains true that total reliance on them at any period would be a cardinal error. Much was always omitted and texts were frequently curtailed. Generally, though not always, the fact that the documents had been 'cut' was shown by the heading 'Extract', though no indication was given of the nature of the excisions. A study of the introductions given in this book will serve as a preliminary guide to the character of the material which the Blue Books supply, and give some knowledge of the sources from which it can be supplemented. Generally speaking the Blue Books are always valuable and indeed essential to historical students, but they are never in themselves enough. The Editors hope that, in publishing this work and in giving materials for study, they may be paving the way for further intensive research in a relatively new field.

ACKNOWLEDGEMENTS

The Editors acknowledge gratefully the help given them in the preparation of this book. They wish to express their appreciation of valuable suggestions made by Sir Stephen Gaselee, K.C.M.G., Librarian of the Foreign Office, and of the facilities afforded them by Mr C. Clay, Librarian to the House of Lords. They would also record their thanks to the officials of the Public Record Office, of the Cambridge University Library and of the British Museum. They are greatly indebted to Miss Agatha Ramm, M.A., for her help in the preparation of the volume for the press.

H. T.
L. M. P.

June 1938

TECHNICAL NOTE ON BLUE BOOKS

In estimating the value of Blue Books, the purpose of publication has constantly to be borne in mind; and here the distinction between theory and practice is important. In theory the object of presenting papers was, and is to-day, to give Parliament the information needed, and at times demanded, to provide a basis for judgment on foreign affairs. In practice presentation meant publication; that is, revelation not only to constituents and the British public but to the Governments of foreign states. In the early years of the century, when publication on a large scale was new, the laying of papers was to a greater extent than later an instrument of policy. Canning of set purpose incited public opinion to support his policy in South America, and Palmerston deliberately cultivated a reputation for publicity. It is true that the tables were sometimes turned. Leakages to the Press from foreign sources or open publication abroad embarrassed several Secretaries of State; but they made others suffer more often than they suffered themselves. The fact is that the policy inaugurated by Canning and Palmerston could not easily be abandoned, and no other European state has rivalled Britain in her wealth of publications. In the middle period of the century tradition was reinforced by party controversy and both Liberals and Conservatives published freely in answer to their opponents. The mass of papers on the Eastern Question in 1875–85 is perhaps the most conspicuous result. Between 1885 and 1914 the situation again altered. By this time party organisation had been tightened; successful pressure was less often exerted in Parliament itself, and virtually all Blue Books were the result of the initiative of the Crown. Moreover differences of party no longer affected to an appreciable degree the conduct of foreign affairs. After 1885 there was no publication reflecting on the policy of political opponents such as those on Egypt and Tunis in 1881–4. The result is that the Blue Books of the immediately pre-war era are disappointing to the historical student. It is true that French and German publication stimulated the laying of papers on Egypt and Africa, and that, in view of British public opinion, the affairs of the Near East continued to be well documented.

By about the year 1880 publication had become formalised and governed by rules. The growth of a regular system of consulting foreign powers before documents affecting them were published prevented Blue Books from being used, as in the days of Canning and Palmerston, as instruments of policy. Successive governments, of both political colours, resisted proposals that treaties should be laid before ratification: while unfinished negotiations were withheld by common consent. Perhaps the best proof of the growing formality of procedure is the change that took place in the use of motions for Addresses. Originally a method by which the legislature extracted documents from the executive—a method frequently successful in the earlier half of the period—it had become merely a formal opening for a debate by about 1880. Motions for Addresses came to be moved by responsible ministers as well as by members of the opposition, and in either case their withdrawal at the end of the debate was foreseen from the beginning. In this period the distinction between papers presented by command and those which resulted from an Address became of no importance, whereas, between 1822 and 1880, the difference was a vital one. Thus it may be seen that the hey-day of Blue-Book publication, which opened with Canning, ended about 1880. The years 1870 to 1890 were transitional from this point of view, but political controversy made 'the 'seventies' prolific. From 1890 to the eve of the Great War Blue Books were plentiful in number, but the proportion of diplomatic correspondence which they contained was far slighter than before. In this period the most important material in Blue Books, apart from the texts of treaties, is often scattered amongst miscellaneous papers and needs careful search for its discovery.

The field covered by the entries given in the list is thus designedly a large one. In the early part of the century, and again towards its close, there is much useful material in the

Slave Trade papers, and these have been included except when they are specifically concerned with British affairs alone (*v. infra*, p. 38, note). Similarly commercial papers have often a diplomatic importance. Attention is called to those which concern the Suez Canal (e.g. No. 950) and the navigation of the Danube (e.g. No. 827). Again some naval papers are included (e.g. No. 1178), and, particularly in the latter part of the century, colonial Blue Books (e.g. Nos. 306, 1150–1157a). A few Indian papers are listed (e.g. Nos. 243–243c, 559), but here, as in the case of the colonial Blue Books, the list is necessarily not exhaustive. Another class of paper occasionally entered is administrative in character. Reports on the Diplomatic Service are obviously relevant (e.g. Nos. 768, 791, 791a, 816), and care has been taken also to include the paper of 1904 which refers to the Committee of Imperial Defence (No. 1643). Generally, the list aims at completeness for papers whose bearing on foreign affairs is direct, and contains also a selection of others, in which students of diplomatic history may find material of special interest.

In the early part of the century some entries have been added from *British and Foreign State Papers* (*B.F.S.P.*). This series, begun by Mr Lewis Hertslet in 1825, was originally intended only for distribution to ambassadors and ministers. Shortly after its inception, however, the volumes were released for general sale.* Normally the material printed here was selected from papers already published, but from time to time other documents were included and it is useful to see what these were.†

The list of Blue Books is based on the bound set of Parliamentary Papers laid before the House of Commons. Where, however, Blue Books of importance were laid before the House of Lords alone, their names have been added and references made to the House of Lords set.

---

* Cp. Sir Edward Hertslet, *Recollections of the Old Foreign Office* [1901], 145–7. Sir E. Hertslet became editor of the series in 1870. In 1896 the work was taken over officially by the Foreign Office.

† Cp. *infra*, p. 46.

The practice of binding the Blue Books of each session in a series of volumes began in the year 1802, and is therefore applicable to the whole period covered by the present work. The listing of the entries in the order in which the papers are bound in the House of Commons set will make its use easy for those students who work in reference libraries, such as the Cambridge University Library, the Bodleian or the British Museum. The bound set of the House of Lords is not nearly so accessible, and this has therefore been quoted only for papers which are not to be found in the House of Commons series. Care has been taken, however, to provide for students who are accustomed to use Blue Books in unbound form. From the year 1801 papers ordered to be printed by the House of Commons received a sessional number, and this is always given (cp. No. 8, where the number is entered below the title in clarendon type). In the early part of the period no number was given to papers which were laid by command of the Crown. A separate system was begun in 1836.* The numbers were distinguished from those of sessional papers by the fact that they were placed in square brackets (cp. No. 243c). In 1870, 'C.' was added before the number, and in 1900 the 'C.' became 'Cd.' (cp. Nos. 769, etc.). Command papers, unlike sessional papers, are numbered continuously from session to session, a new series starting only in 1870, 1900, and later in 1919 ('Cmd.'). A further means of identification is provided from the session 1864, when command papers dealing with foreign affairs were frequently given short titles—e.g. *North America No. 1 (1864)* (cp. No. 650). This short title, where it exists, has been added after the title of each paper. Further facilities of reference are provided in the Index.

The distinction between sessional papers and command papers is no mere matter of numbering. The former class includes all Blue Books which were laid in pursuance of an Act of Parliament (cp. No. 94), or as the result of an order of the House (cp. No. 9), or in response to an Address (cp. Nos. 8, etc.). Procedure by Address is by far the most important

---

* It was not until 1839 that the system was applied to diplomatic Blue Books.

from the present point of view. Frequently in the first half of our period, less often as the century advanced, an Address asking for papers was moved in one or other of the Houses of Parliament. Frequently, again, it was successful. Blue Books which resulted from this procedure thus represent successful pressure brought to bear upon the Government by Parliament. Care has been taken to distinguish such papers in every case (even where, as happened occasionally, papers technically laid by command resulted from an Address), and the dates of the Addresses are given as well as the dates on which the papers were laid. The moving of an Address was often the occasion for a debate on foreign affairs, and these dates themselves give a valuable guide to *Hansard*. It is to be noted that in the second half of the period Blue Books dealing with foreign affairs were generally, though not always, laid before both Houses of Parliament, even when they resulted from an Address in one House. Palmerston had laid it down as a principle as early as 1847 that it was 'a good rule to present to both Houses Papers moved for by address to the Crown in either House', and this practice was frequently followed (cp. Nos. 449, 449 a, 476, etc.). It was not, however, the rule until a much later date (cp. Nos. 376–8, 453, etc.). In 1853, there were complaints from the Speaker that papers returned to an Address were laid in print as if they were presented by command. This had two disadvantages. It deprived the House of the right of decision as to what should be printed and circulated, and it ran the risk of causing charges of libel, the latter being the immediate cause of the complaint. A compromise was reached in the end; but in fact all papers of a substantial size continued to be laid in print.

Blue Books laid by command of the Crown owed their origin normally not to demand in Parliament but to the Government itself, although sometimes evidence of a desire for information preceded the presentation. Almost from the beginning of our period command papers were laid in print, and from the first they were intended to give an explanation of Government action. It is important to note that from the earliest times the information contained in the Blue Books reached a wider public than Parliament. Regular machinery for sale did not exist, indeed, until 1835, but before that date there were various methods by which publicity was secured. Papers were printed in the appendices to the *Journals* and (down to 1829) in *Hansard*. Officers of the House of Commons sold a number of copies, this being one of the perquisites of office. Some copies were distributed without charge—apart from those circulated to members of Parliament; extracts appeared in the *London Gazette*, and in the daily press. While therefore access to Blue Books was easier after 1835, the difference was one of degree and not of principle. In 1881 it was stated as a traditional rule that 'All papers should be easily accessible to the public'. So much was this the case that, even after a regular system of sale had been instituted, important papers which became ready for presentation during the Recess were published at once in the *London Gazette* so that the public should not have to wait for them (cp. Nos. 798, 798*a*, 940). In 1896 this procedure was made unnecessary by a standing rule that all such papers should be distributed at once to members and delivered at the sales office for the public. Blue Books which were circulated in this way were laid formally on the opening day of the session.

BIBLIOGRAPHICAL NOTE

For a general introduction to Parliamentary Papers reference should be made to J. Redlich, *The Procedure of the House of Commons* (trans. by A. E. Steinthal, London, 1908)—largely historical in character; Sir T. Erskine May, *A Treatise on the Law, Privileges, Proceedings and Usage of Parliament* (13th edition, London, 1924); *Manual of Procedure in the Public Business of the House of Commons, prepared by the Clerk of the House* [Sir Courtenay Ilbert] (3rd edition, London, 1912). Attention is called to the periodic issue of Indexes to Parliamentary Papers of which an analysis is given in *Bulletin of the Institute of Historical Research*, xi, No. 31 [June 1933], 24–30.

Much detailed material of value can be obtained from Professor H. Bellot's article on ·'Parliamentary Printing, 1660–1837', *Bulletin of the Institute of Historical Research*, xi, No. 32 [Nov. 1933], 85–98. Reference is made there to a number of Parliamentary Papers dealing with publication. Among such papers may be mentioned as of special value the 'Report from the Select Committee on Publication of Printed Papers', *A. & P.* 1837, xiii, 286, pp. 97–201, and the 'Report from the Select Committee on Publications', *A. & P.* 1908, x, 358, pp. 849–990—Sir Courtenay Ilbert's evidence (pp. 971–7) is of particular interest.

ERRATUM

p. 356, No. 1177. *For* [*v. supra*, Nos. 729, 935 *a*]
read [*v. supra*, No. 860 *a*]

ABBREVIATIONS USED IN
LIST OF BLUE BOOKS

L/C. = Laid by Command of the Crown.
HC. = House of Commons.
HL. = House of Lords.

> **Example:** *L/C.* HC. 3 Feb., HL. 5 Feb. 1813 = Laid by Command before the House of Commons on 3 February 1813 and before the House of Lords on the 5th.
>
> Where the paper was laid before both Houses on the same day, the abbreviations HC. and HL. are omitted (cp. No. 3).

R–A. = Returned to an Address to the Crown from one House of Parliament.

> **Example:** *R–A.* (*HC. 28 Ap.*), HC. 5 May 1814 = Returned in the House of Commons on 5 May 1814 to an Address made in the Commons on 28 April.
>
> Where the paper was laid before both Houses on the same day, the abbreviations HC. and HL. are omitted (cp. No. 39). Where it was laid before the other House on a different day this is separately indicated (cp. No. 177).

O.T.B.P. = Ordered to be printed by one House of Parliament.

> This occurs most frequently with papers returned to an Address (as they were sometimes laid in MS.) and with reports from Select Committees. Where the order to be printed was made on the same date as the laying of the paper, the abbreviation is omitted (cp. No. 185).

THE BLUE-BOOK POLICY OF CASTLEREAGH

1812–22

THE year 1814, with which this annotated list of documents really begins, is important as marking a relative change in Blue-Book policy. The British Government had not been wholly indifferent to the claims of publicity during the eighteenth century. For instance, a certain amount of relevant material was given to the public in connection with the negotiations ending in the peace of Paris (1760–3), and again over the Falkland Islands' crisis (1770). But the Government had not in that period made up their mind whether to issue propaganda pure and simple or to give the texts of documents. Thus they sometimes inspired pamphleteers like Dr Johnson to defend the British policy in regard to the Falkland Islands, and sometimes published relevant State Papers as in the case of the Peace of Paris. Towards the end of the eighteenth century, however, the publicity of parliamentary debates did much to satisfy the public's thirst for information in foreign affairs. But a systematic publication of State Papers was hardly pursued before 1814. The man who came nearest to satisfying the public's demands was Canning during his first period as Secretary of State for Foreign Affairs (1807–9). It was remarked then by Lord Malmesbury, than whom there was no more experienced diplomat, that Canning published papers more frequently than any previous Foreign Minister.* He did so because he had a definite popular policy. His aim was to excite feeling against Napoleon. And the publication for example of the course of the negotiations at Erfurt certainly achieved that end. But this was in time of war, and it is not certain that Canning would have pursued this same policy during the period of peace negotiations.

* Lord Malmesbury, *Diaries and Correspondence* [1844], IV, 404, quoted by Algernon Cecil, *Cambridge History of British Foreign Policy* [1923], III, 550. Malmesbury called it a '*new* habit'.

On 4 March 1812 Castlereagh became Secretary of State for Foreign Affairs and, almost from the moment of his accession to power, was occupied with building up the Allied coalition against Napoleon, and with all sorts of delicate diplomatic transactions which it was not at all desirable to reveal to the public at the time, or even at all. Then, during 1814–15, the transactions leading to the Congress at Vienna produced a great outburst of popular feeling in England and confronted Castlereagh with an unparalleled situation.

According to Professor Webster, 'Castlereagh's position was extraordinarily difficult throughout the whole of his career from 1814 to 1822 because he was prosecuting a policy which made no appeal to the vast majority of his countrymen', and again, 'Throughout his career, therefore, Castlereagh was impatient of Parliamentary criticism and of public opinion generally.'* The fact is that Castlereagh was, or at least soon became, the 'most European' of British statesmen. He wanted to let off France easily, a wise decision. But the British public, having triumphed over France after a long and cruel war, were not particularly anxious to spare her feelings or to return her colonies or to lessen her war indemnity. Castlereagh found out that there were great advantages in round-table conferences with the diplomats of the military monarchies, Austria, Prussia and Russia. But with these latter the British public had no sympathy. They detested their political principles and, like the United States after the late war, were only too anxious to retire from Europe and its entanglements altogether. Castlereagh knew that such withdrawal was impossible at once and that close intercourse with Europe was desirable, as long as it could be maintained without prejudice to British interests. The British public did not understand his attitude at all and he was neither very ready nor very desirous to explain it. Of course, it was impossible for him to avoid giving them information at times. But it was also impossible always to give it frankly, impartially and fully during, or even after, the peace negotiations. His

* v. *Cambridge Historical Journal* [1924], vol. I, no. 2, 159.

normal policy was to anticipate criticism by publishing documents concerning transactions already partially known and likely to be more fully revealed. In a certain number of instances, his own partial publication of documents misled the public as to the real nature of the events which the papers purported to relate. The whole history of the nineteenth century shows how suppression of some documents can mislead the British public as to the meaning of others. But it is as possible to excuse Castlereagh on the ground that he was treading a new path, as it is impossible to make the same plea for his successors—who had his experience before them.

It may be well, however, to begin by mentioning two instances in which Castlereagh published State Papers with a freedom which almost satisfied the public. These were in regard to the Slave Trade (Nos. 58, 62 b, v, 66 p, etc.), and to the United States (Nos. 1, 2, etc.). The two subjects were connected, because the Right of Search and the question of International Tribunals were necessary to make the abolition of slavery effective, and both caused difficulties with the United States and, incidentally, with France. The ardent humanitarian feeling about the Slave Trade was one with which Castlereagh certainly sympathised, and he was the true inaugurator of the vast Blue-Book literature published on the subject during the nineteenth century. On the other hand he, quite intelligibly and rightly, took care to exclude from these publications the traces of sharp diplomatic quarrels with the United States and France on this subject.

As regards the United States, from the time of the dispute which led to the war of 1812 and onwards, it was advisable to publish papers on a liberal scale. European diplomats have since found that, whether they publish their version of events or not, the United States will always do so. On the other hand a number of delicate Anglo-American questions were left open after the peace of 1813 and Castlereagh deserves great credit for the tactful selection of the papers laid before the public. John Quincy Adams, the American Secretary of State of Monroe, in particular was a difficult man to handle and over the Rush-Bagot agreement of 1817 concerning armaments on the Great Lakes Castlereagh's silence, as regards the British share in the transactions, was of great service. Professor Webster even goes so far as to say the result of publication might have been 'disastrous'. Whether war would in fact have resulted from publication is necessarily a matter of opinion. But silence was probably better than speech.

Having thus mentioned the two cases where papers were published with relative freedom, we may mention those in regard to which Castlereagh was clearly secretive. The first is in regard to the only question, apart from the Slave Trade, in which public opinion in England continually influenced Castlereagh at Vienna. This was in regard to Poland, which had been cut into three parts a generation earlier by Russia, by Austria and by Prussia. Burke had protested against the original partitions and British public feeling most unreasonably expected Castlereagh to do what Lloyd George did a century later, that is to resurrect Poland and make her one nation again. Castlereagh knew well enough that he could not get his three Allies to agree to any such proposal, and that the mere suggestion would make it impossible to sign peace at Vienna. What he really wanted to do was to reestablish the old partitions of Polish territory, and to prevent Russia from obtaining the lion's share of them, as she ultimately did. What however he revealed to the British public was that he had made protests to the powers against the partition of Poland. And that was about all he told them.

This policy of discretion was one which any statesman would probably have pursued at a peace conference, when confronted by the strong liberal and humanitarian wave of sentiment in England. It is more difficult to excuse him over the problem of Murat, Napoleon's Marshal, who had been made the King of Naples. The story is one of the most complicated even in European diplomacy. To put it in a word, Castlereagh had agreed with his Allies to depose Murat in any case. But, on Napoleon's return from Elba, Murat rallied to his side and proclaimed the Union of Italy. He failed altogether and was promptly overthrown. In the

British publications the Allied design of deposing Murat, whatever happened, was concealed, and stress laid on the other aspects of the case.*

Whatever opinion may be held on this transaction over Naples, a similar concealment in connection with Sicily is incapable of defence. Castlereagh was not wholly to blame, for Lord William Bentinck, while in Sicily during the British occupation, had compelled the exiled King of Naples to grant a constitution to his Sicilian subjects. It was liberal, academic, generous and as unsuitable for peasants in Sicily as it was dear to the hearts of Whigs in England. Castlereagh told Metternich that he could not openly allow it to be abolished, and ultimately arranged that a harmless paper constitution, without any real check on the King, should remain in Sicily. Metternich was induced, with difficulty, to agree to this and to the mention of the detested word 'Parliament'. Castlereagh then arranged that a series of dispatches should be written for publication by the British Minister at Naples, explaining the Sicilian Constitution. Austria was not mentioned in this connection: 'You will explain to Prince Metternich', wrote Castlereagh in a private letter to Stewart, 'that in framing my dispatches on the Sicilian question my object has been not to bring into view the Austrian policy in any of those documents which we might possibly deem it necessary to bring before Parliament.'†

This transaction was one which was intended to mislead the British public, and is described by Professor Webster as 'by far the worst incident in Castlereagh's relations to Parliament'. But it is only fair to say that it was probably regarded by Castlereagh as a comparatively negligible incident affecting a remote province in Italy whose inhabitants cared little for constitutions. What brought the matter ultimately into high relief was that Naples revolted against

* v. infra, No. 56, also Hans[ard] Deb[ates], xxxi, 59–154, and B.F.S.P., ii, 226–305. Compare the letter to Wellington of 24 March 1815 with the full dispatch given in C. K. Webster, British Diplomacy, 1813–15, [1921], 314. See also Cambridge History of British Foreign Policy, i, 484–90. These throw light on Castlereagh's methods of 'editing'.

† Castlereagh to Stewart, 6 Sept. 1816 (F.O. 7/125), quoted by Professor Webster, Camb. Hist. Journ. [1924], vol. i, no. 2, 162, note 1.

its Absolute King in 1820, and that Austria ultimately sent an army to suppress the newly granted Constitution of Naples. Castlereagh, bound by his pledges, did not intervene or protest. This attitude caused great indignation in England and Castlereagh attempted to satisfy public opinion in an interesting way by declaring publicly his dissent from the despots of Europe.

During the whole period since 1814 Castlereagh had been striving for 'diplomacy by conference', that is to settle the affairs of Europe by causing its chief statesmen to meet at periodic intervals, and to settle their differences in informal and formal conferences round a table. From the Congress of Aix-la-Chapelle onwards,* it had however become increasingly clear that the three despotic Powers (Austria, Prussia and Russia) wished to use their concert with England for purposes that Castlereagh did not desire. They were not satisfied with the obligations to protect the frontiers of Europe as settled at Vienna, and to repress Bonapartism in France. They wished to use these pledges for the purpose of justifying collective interference in the internal affairs of other nations and of repressing constitutions everywhere. Castlereagh had already on 5 May 1820 formulated the attitude of England in a famous State Paper.† He confined it to the two obligations mentioned above and pronounced that England must act in accordance with the views of her 'strongly popular and national government' in all other cases. He thus conveyed a strong hint that the British Government would have to repudiate the sentiments of their Allies, and publicly separate from them, if they did not abandon the attempt to extend the obligations of Vienna beyond what England had agreed to.

Austria's intention to intervene in Naples and her subversion of its constitution were justified by the three Allies on the grounds of their union. This had to be repudiated publicly by Castlereagh. He had to say openly that England could neither justify, nor support, the extension of the

* *v.* Temperley and Penson, *Foundations of British Foreign Policy*, 34–46.

† A very jejune abstract was published by Canning on 22 Ap. 1823 (*v. infra*, No. 119; *v.* also No. 356). *v.* Text in Temperley and Penson, *Foundations of British Foreign Policy*, 48–63.

treaty obligations of the Alliance to include the suppression
by the Great Powers of a constitution in a sovereign international state. Accordingly, in Professor Webster's words,
'the result was the famous circular of 19 January 1821
[*v.* No. 95], a document almost as frank and outspoken as any
of Canning's. It produced a great effect on public opinion in
[Great] Britain and Europe.' It did so certainly, for the time
being. But Castlereagh 'had no wish to exploit the situation.
He was anxious on the contrary to resume his relations with
the other Great Powers.'* He wanted to prevent a war between
Russia and Turkey, which was threatening to break out. His
only method of doing this was to summon another Congress
(that which ultimately met at Verona) and to use Prussia and
Austria to restrain the Tsar in the name of the Concert of
Europe. Castlereagh died before this Congress met, and left
the heritage to Canning. The latter soon inaugurated a
strong publicity campaign against the three Eastern Powers,
and, in doing so, formulated the first systematic policy of
publicity as regards State Papers (*v. infra*, pp. 30–7).

Castlereagh must be regarded as bridging a gap between
two periods, rather than as formulating any definite policy in
relation to Blue Books. It is most important to avoid criti-
cising him for not doing so. His situation at the Congress
of Vienna, in relation to the British public, was the most
formidable that any British statesman had yet encountered,
and he had little previous experience to help him. That he
was not incapable of popular appeal is shown by his circular
of January 1821. But his conduct after that date seems to
show that he was not fully conscious of the effects of his own
action in that case. His period of power covers a transitional
period, in which neither the defects nor the advantages of
publicity were fully realised. But it is certainly possible to
argue that, up till the year 1820, a policy of discretion was
even more advantageous to England than any policy of
publicity could have been. Castlereagh's death closes the
epoch, for, after that date, a policy of publicity was certainly
inevitable, though it might have followed somewhat different
lines from those which Canning laid down.

* *Camb. Hist. Journ.* [1924], vol. I, no. 2, 162.

SESSION 24 NOVEMBER 1812 TO 22 JULY 1813

VOLUME XIV (1812–13)

Correspondence and Treaties with Foreign Powers

Session 4 November 1813 to 30 July 1814

Volume XIV (1813–14)

Miscellaneous and Treaties with Foreign Powers

16   Supplementary convention;—30 September 1813 [signed at London].   PAGE 155

              R–A. (HC. 8 Nov.), HC. 10 Nov. 1813.

17   Another convention with Russia;—6 July 1813 [signed at Peterswaldaw].   PAGE 165

              L/C. 8 Nov. 1813.

18   Treaty with France; signed at Paris 30 May 1814 [*v. infra*, No. 577].   PAGE 225

              L/C. 6 June 1814.

*JOURNAL OF THE HOUSE OF COMMONS**

VOLUME LXIX (1813–14)

Appendix

19   Convention between His Britannic Majesty and His Majesty the King of Prussia; signed at Reichenbach, the 14th June 1813.
                                               PAGE 671

              L/C. 8 Nov. 1813.

20   Supplementary convention between His Britannic Majesty and His Majesty the King of Prussia, to the Treaty of Concert and Subsidy of the 14th June 1813; signed at London, the 30th of September 1813.   PAGE 681

              R–A. (HC. 8 Nov.), HC. 10 Nov., *R–A. (HL. 8 Nov.)*, HL. 11 Nov. 1813.

21   Treaty of Union, Concert, and Subsidy between His Britannic Majesty and His Majesty the Emperor of All the Russias; signed at Chaumont, the 1st March 1814 [*v. infra*, No. 33].   PAGE 682

              L/C. 2 May 1814.

22   do. between His Britannic Majesty and His Imperial and Royal Apostolic Majesty The Emperor of Austria; signed at Chaumont the 1st of March 1814.   PAGE 683

              L/C. 2 May 1814.

23   do. between His Britannic Majesty and His Majesty the King of Prussia; signed at Chaumont the 1st of March 1814.
                                               PAGE 684

              L/C. 2 May 1814.

---

* In the copy of vol. XIV (1813–14) of the set of Parliamentary Papers in the British Museum the texts of the six documents given here from the *Journal* have been added. They are marked as having been 'received after these Volumes were made up'.

VOLUME XIII (1814–15)

Miscellaneous Papers

39   Papers relative to the person and family of Napoleon Buonaparte.

PAGE 151

R–A. (HC. 5 Ap.), 7 Ap. 1815.

39a   1. Dispatch from Viscount Castlereagh to Earl Bathurst, Paris, April 13, 1814.

39b   2. Treaty between the High Allied Powers and Napoleon Bonaparte concluded at Paris on the 11th of April 1814.

39c   3. Dispatch from Viscount Castlereagh to Earl Bathurst, Paris, April 27, 1814.

40   Memorandum. Substance of three Conventions Supplementary to the Treaties of Chaumont and Paris, concluded at London, the 29th of June 1814, on the part of His Majesty, the Emperors of Austria and Russia, and the King of Prussia. [November 10, 1814.]   PAGE 163

L/C. HC. 14 Nov.; R–A. (HL. 14 Nov.), HL. 16 Nov. 1814.

41   Convention between His Britannic Majesty and His Majesty the King of Sweden [signed at London, 13 August 1814].

PAGE 165

L/C. 9 June 1815.

42   Convention between Great Britain and the United Netherlands [signed at London, 13 August 1814].   PAGE 171

L/C. 9 June 1815.

43   Overture from Buonaparte [correspondence of M. de Caulaincourt and Viscount Castlereagh, Ap. 1815].   PAGE 181

L/C. 22 May 1815.

44   Correspondence on Alliance against France [Viscount Castlereagh and Earl Clancarty, Ap.–May 1814].   PAGE 185

L/C. 22 May 1814.

45   Declaration of the Allies, dated Vienna, March 13, 1815.

PAGE 189

L/C. 7 Ap. 1815.

46   Counter-Declarations on the part of Their Majesties the Emperors of Austria and Russia, and the King of Prussia.   PAGE 193

L/C. HC. 26 May, HL. 30 May 1815.

56   Papers relative to Naples, 1814–15.   PAGE 333
> *R–A.* (*HL. 2 May*), HL. 23 May; *R–A.* (*HC.
> 2 May*), HC. 24 May 1815.

57   Papers respecting the Papal Authority, 1814–15.   PAGE 451
> *R–A.* (*HC. 15 June*), HC. 4 July 1815.

58   Papers shewing the present State of the Slave Trade, 1813–15.
>   PAGE 463
> *L/C.* HC. 4 Ap., HL. 5 Ap. 1815.

Session 1 February to 2 July 1816

Volume XVII (1816)

Treaties

59   Class A. Treaties of Accession and Subsidy, between Great Britain and other Powers, in virtue of the Treaty of Alliance between Great Britain, Austria, Russia and Prussia; signed at Vienna, the 25th March 1815.   PAGE 1

Treaties of Accession:

> Baden, 13 May 1815; Bavaria, 15 Ap.; both at Vienna. Denmark, 1 Sept., at Paris. Hanover, 7 Ap.; Hesse (Grand Duke), 23 May; Netherlands, 28 Ap.; Portugal, 8 Ap.; Sardinia, 9 Ap.; Saxony, 27 May; all at Vienna. Switzerland, 20 May, at Zurich. Wurtemburg, 30 May; Princes and Free Towns of Germany, 27 Ap.; both at Vienna.
>   *L/C.* 2 Feb. 1816.

Treaties of Subsidy:

> Baden, 19 May 1815; Bavaria, 7 June; both at Brussels. Denmark, 14 July; Hanover, 26 Aug.; Hesse (Grand Duke), 15 July; all at Paris. Sardinia, 2 May, at Brussels. Saxony, 14 July, at Paris. Wurtemburg, 6 June, at Brussels.

> Princes and Free Towns of Germany:

> Anhalt-Dessau, Bernbourg and Cœthen, 10 July; Brunswick-Luneburg, 28 Aug.; Frankfort on the Maine, 1 Aug.; Hesse (Elector), 15 July; Holstein-Oldenburgh, 5 Sept.; Hohenzollern-Hechingen and Sigmaringen, 1 Aug.; Lubeck, Hamburgh and Bremen, 21 July; Mecklenburgh-Schwerin, 29 July;

[*BRITISH AND FOREIGN STATE PAPERS (B.F.S.P.)*

VOLUME IV (1816–17)

SESSION 28 JANUARY TO 12 JULY 1817

VOLUME XIII (1817)

Estimates and Accounts

VOLUME XVII (1817)

Miscellaneous Papers

Session 27 January to 10 June 1818

Volume XVII (1818)

Miscellaneous Papers

76 Constitutional Chart of the United States of the Ionian Isles as agreed on and passed unanimously by the Legislative Assembly on the 2nd May 1817.　　　　　　　　　　　　　　PAGE 1

　　132　　　*R–A. (HC. 3 Mar.)*, HC. 18 Mar. 1818.

Volume XVIII (1818)

Miscellaneous Papers

77 Treaty between His Britannic Majesty and His Catholic Majesty [*re* Slave Trade; signed at Madrid, 23 Sept. 1817].　　PAGE 1

　　　　　L/C. 28 Jan. 1818.

78 Additional Convention to the Treaty of 22 January 1815 between His Britannic Majesty and His Most Faithful Majesty [*re* Slave Trade; signed at London, 28 July 1817].　　　　PAGE 33

　　　　　L/C. HC. 11 Feb., HL. 19 Feb. 1818.

79 Treaty between His Britannic Majesty and the King of the Netherlands [*re* Slave Trade; signed at The Hague, 4 May, 1818].
　　　　　　　　　　　　　　　　　　　　PAGE 69

　　　　　L/C. 1 June 1818.

Session 21 January to 13 July 1819

Volume XVIII (1819)

Miscellaneous Papers

80 Red River Settlement.　　　　　　　　　　　　PAGE 1

　　584　　　*R–A. (HC. 24 June)*, HC. 12 July 1819.

81 Slaves, Papers relating to the treatment of, in the Colonies; viz. Colonial Acts passed in 1818.　　　　　　　　PAGE 289

　　414　　　*R–A. (HC. 7 Ap.)*, HC. 8 Ap., O.T.B.P. 7 June 1819.

Session 21 April to 23 November 1820

Volume XI (1820)

Estimates and Accounts 1820

Session 23 January to 11 July 1821

Volume XXII (1821)

Miscellaneous Papers

Volume XXIII (1821)

Miscellaneous Papers

SESSION 5 FEBRUARY TO 6 AUGUST 1822

VOLUME XXII (1822)

Slave Trade, etc.

HOUSE OF LORDS SESSIONAL PAPERS

VOLUME CXLI (1822)

Accounts and Papers

[BRITISH AND FOREIGN STATE PAPERS (B.F.S.P.)

VOLUME IX (1821–2)

THE BLUE-BOOK POLICY OF CANNING*

1822–7 †

WITH Canning we come to a man with modern conceptions as regards the public and Parliament. It was noted during his first period at the Foreign Office (1807–9) that he published papers with unusual freedom. He went to the Foreign Office for the second time in 1822, just as the Congress of Verona began to sit. He took an early opportunity of instructing our representative Wellington to dissociate himself from the other members, 'if there be a determined project to interfere by force or by menace in the present struggle in Spain...to any such interference, *come what may*, His Majesty will not be a Party'. The Congress of Verona broke up, with England dissenting from its measures. France acted on her own, with the moral support of Austria, Russia and Prussia, went to war with Spain, put down the Constitution, and liberated the King.

Henceforward Canning seems to have been of opinion that England should not attend at Conferences at all. At the Congress of Laybach differences of opinion between England and the Neo-Holy Alliance had been proclaimed in the face of all Europe. After Verona 'the differences of opinion with respect to the affairs of Spain had given occasion to long and perilous discussions'.‡ It was better, therefore, to have no Congresses.

It seems, however, if we examine it closely, that not the least 'perilous' part of the 'discussions' on this occasion was caused by Canning's publication of State Papers at a critical moment. By the middle of March 1823, it was clear that France was going to war with Spain. Canning took the bold

---

* Appointed Secretary of State for Foreign Affairs on 16 September 1822.
† Reprinted by permission from *Camb. Hist. Journ.* [1924], vol. i, no. 2: a few dates are added.
‡ F.O. 185/95. Canning to Sir William A'Court, 23 April 1824.

step of appearing at the Bar of the House of Commons with his papers in his hand.

'It was not', he explained, 'a usual practice of government to lay documents on the table of the House, upon which they did not intend to call for some proceeding, but in the present instance it was intended to depart from the customary usage....In most cases in which documents relative to negotiations had been laid before parliament, the negotiations had terminated in a declaration of war, and, on all such occasions, government had availed itself of the opportunity of stating to parliament what had been the course of policy which had led to the issuing of the declaration of war. The late negotiations, however, had not so terminated, and the statement he intended to make was merely meant to supply the place of a declaration of the government.'*

This was an ominous utterance. In a dispatch to France of 31 March (which he ordered to be read to Chateaubriand, in itself a strong step), Canning intimated the three conditions on which England would observe neutrality in the event of a war with Spain. (1) If France did not show aggressive designs on European Spain, or (2) on Spanish America, (3) if France did not violate the territorial integrity of Portugal. This was really an ultimatum if any of these conditions were infringed. Its character was more strongly marked by the publicity. For France declared war on 6 April, and the papers, including this dispatch of 31 March, were actually published on 14 April, only five days after it had been read to Chateaubriand.† Clearly Canning's idea was to mobilise British public opinion behind him against France to face any of these three contingencies, and in this he entirely succeeded.

A further object was to discredit the Congress System, and he published a series of dispatches relating to Verona, including an extract from the famous 'come what may' instruction. He also, to Wellington's intense annoyance, published the Duke's Memorandum of 30 October 1822, which showed that England had definitely dissociated herself from France and the Neo-Holy Alliance in their proceedings against Spain.‡ Canning's aim in publishing all these papers is quite clear.

---

* *Hans. Deb.* N.S. VIII, 801–2, 10 April 1823. I use the term 'Neo-Holies' to designate Austria, Prussia and Russia.

† *v. infra*, No. 118 a.   ‡ *v. infra*, No. 118.

He wished to work up feeling in England against France and the Neo-Holy Alliance and Congress System by revealing their illiberal views at the psychological moment.

This publicity not only angered Wellington, but this 'new diplomacy' horrified the statesmen of the Continent. Yet nothing could have been smoother than Canning's phrases when protests arrived. Wellington's Memo. of 30 October had been published *in toto* because Chateaubriand had quoted extracts from it in his speech of 25 February 1823. Other dispatches had been published for the same reason. A few days later he published several more, on the grounds that Chateaubriand had again quoted from State Papers, that the *Moniteur* had hinted at assurances from France about Portugal 'which I presume it must be peculiarly agreeable to Mr de Chateaubriand to have placed in a clear and satisfactory light'.* He had also, in response to stimulation from Parliament, published the separate article in the Spanish Treaty with England in 1814, by which Spain bound herself not to revive the Family Compact in favour of France.† The diplomats were in no way convinced by these explanations, but they recognised that a new and formidable weapon was being wielded by the new minister.

In October 1823, on the fall of Cadiz, Canning asked Polignac the intentions of France as to Spanish America and the revolted colonies. He embodied the discussion in a Memorandum, in which he compelled Polignac to disclaim on behalf of France 'any attempt by force or menace' against the Spanish revolted colonies. Great pressure was next put on Canning to join in a Congress on the Spanish American question. He at once used the argument that it would be 'exceedingly hazardous' to do so. The debates on the Congress of Verona had roused very angry feelings against the Continent. We could not agree with the Neo-Holy Alliance about the Spanish colonies. 'To have protested a third time in the face of the world, and to have been a third time perfectly passive after such protest, would have placed the

---

* F.O. 146/55. Canning to Sir C. Stuart, 21 April 1823, No. 34.
† *v.* p. 74 of the Additional Papers, whose title is given in *infra*, No. 119.

British Government in a point of view almost ridiculous,'
especially when 'it was considered how much more extended
and immediate is the concern of England with all Colonial
questions, than that of any other Power in Europe.'* In a
word he could not face Parliament and explain to it that
England was going into another Congress. He finally refused·
to join the proposed Congress in a dispatch of 30 January
1824. When Parliament met he published (4 March) both
this paper and the Polignac Memorandum.†

The Continental diplomats were horrified again, Chateaubriand objected to the publication of the Polignac Memorandum, and Metternich complained secretly to Wellington
that Canning was a revolutionary, sacrificing institutions and
stable customs to 'a search after a vain popularity'. Wellington
was now thoroughly aroused and, as he thought it hopeless
to remonstrate with Canning, wrote a letter of protest to the
Prime Minister: ‡

> The consequence of producing these papers [on Spanish
> America] at present is, that Parliament must form a judgment
> upon the whole subject, which must have its influence hereafter,
> whatever form it may assume, and however disadvantageous,
> whenever the final decision is to be made; and that the decision
> of the government cannot be independent, as it ought to be.
> But this is not all. Foreigners who have witnessed and are
> aware of the caution and reserve with which we are in the habit
> of communicating papers of this description to Parliament, will
> see in this act a desire to throw it [the question of the British
> recognition of the Spanish colonies] out of our own hands.

Here is outlined sharply the difference between the old
school and the new. Canning would have answered that he
did not wish to be independent of Parliament and of the
mercantile interest and of the country, that he thought it a

---

* F.O. 185/95. Canning to A'Court, 23 April 1824. This is only a stronger
statement of previous arguments.

† v. infra, No. 131. He suppressed, however, from the latter an important
statement made to Polignac. When the latter suggested a Congress Canning
told him he would not join it unless the United States were invited. This was
a method of refusing, as he well knew the United States would not join.
The mere suggestion horrified France and Austria. v. Temperley and Penson,
Foundations.

‡ 5 March 1824. Wellington to Liverpool, Desp. Corr. and Mem. [1867],
II, 229.

good thing for foreigners to see that a minister was supported by public opinion and that, if publication of papers led to that end, it was an eminently desirable one. Of one thing there can be no doubt. The publication of these papers at this moment did excite public opinion and produced a rain of petitions from the merchants in favour of recognition. It was this demonstration of mercantile and popular support, in reality stimulated by himself, which enabled Canning to overbear his colleagues and to carry the recognition of Buenos Ayres, Columbia and Mexico in the Cabinet in December 1824.

It would be impossible to trace in similar detail the methods pursued by Canning in publishing papers in other cases. Those in fact already mentioned are the most important and typical instances. The root idea of Canning's policy of publicity was that the public and the private aspects of diplomacy must be the same. If he remonstrated strongly with a power in private, as he did with France on 31 March 1823, he took care that his remonstrance should see the light, moreover, that it might be supported by the nation, and that the other governments should see that the remonstrance was real and not 'a little dust in the eyes of Parliament'.

This conception led to results which greatly distressed Metternich. During the autumn of 1824 Metternich became much alarmed that the Tsar Alexander would go to war with the Turks over Greece, and he was much pressed by the Russian Church and people to do so. The only way he could see of stopping him was to assemble a new Congress, a word and a system odious to Canning. On 16 October Metternich therefore proposed a Congress for, he said, the 'moral solidarity' of the rest of Europe could be used as an argument with the Tsar to repress the ardour of the people of Russia. Anyhow, time, he said, would be gained.* To his intense astonishment Canning replied as follows:

We have 'this decisive objection'; that in lending ourselves to an undertaking which we ourselves believed to be utterly useless, we must either assign to the Parliament and people of this country reasons for our conduct, by which in fact it is not

* F.O. 7/66. Wellesley to Canning, 16 October 1824. v. F.O. 7/67 for Canning's reply of 5 December, No. 29, Confidential.

actuated, and must express hopes of success, which in fact we do not feel; or by declaring frankly our real motives for engaging in so unpromising a negotiation must betray the secret of Prince Metternich's dispatch (16 October) and therewith destroy the illusion by which the Emperor of Russia was to be fortified against the warlike impulsion of his people.

In the silent recesses of a Cabinet, it may be possible to employ arguments which you do not openly avow, and to leave to the event to explain and to justify to the world the consideration by which you have been guided; but in the broad daylight of Parliament, no British Minister could venture on a declaration, by which the truth should be knowingly either altered or concealed, and on the other hand, to avow openly that we only entered into a negotiation for the purpose of enabling the Emperor of Russia to manage the feelings of his people, would be as disrespectful to His Imperial Majesty's person as it would be destructive of the advantage we designed for him.

It does not seem possible to explain the advantages or disadvantages of the connection of a parliamentary minister with public opinion more clearly than this.

It will, perhaps, be interesting to give some instances in which Canning withheld knowledge of public transactions from Parliament. The most famous instance is the interviews Canning had with Rush in August and September 1823, in which he tried to get the United States to unite with England in a joint declaration against European aggression in Spanish America. He failed to get Rush to agree, but as he called the United States 'confessedly the leading power' in America he greatly encouraged them, and thus did something (not willingly) towards the formulation of the 'Monroe doctrine'. Of all this there is no trace in the published papers, and very little in the official records. Canning intended to keep the whole affair private, until the definite negotiation was achieved. He was so successful that we should know very little about it even now, but for the Diaries of Adams and Rush.*

Similarly, in 1825, some important negotiations about

* An important dispatch on the subject, which Canning tried to turn into a private letter, has been preserved, v. F.O. America 41, Nos. 18–20, 3–20 November, Addington to Canning. v. Paulin and Paxson, *Guide to Materials in London Archives for History of U.S.A. since 1783* (Carnegie Institute, Washington, 1914), 54 n.

Cuba took place both with the United States, France and Mexico and Columbia. France was forced by Canning in July to give formal assurances to England disclaiming any aggressive designs*. Further, Canning attempted to negotiate with France and with the United States a Tripartite Agreement of disinterestedness on Cuba. The attempt failed, and there is no trace of it in British published papers though there is some in the American.

Two other important negotiations relating to France were also kept secret. In July 1824 the indiscretions of the French Ambassador in Portugal became so serious that Canning obtained from France a written disavowal of one of his actions, and a formal written assurance against aggressive designs. But these intrigues continued, and finally, by strong pressure on the Portuguese Government, Canning got Subserra (the head of the Pro-French party) turned out of the Ministry. This latter incident could not be published, but the French assurances, and some dispatches indicating the friendly feeling of the new Portuguese Ministry, might have been. Probably Canning thought that the assurances were good enough this time without the support of British public opinion.

We may conclude with giving two instances in which Canning's publicity idea was, to his intense annoyance, practised against him. The protocol of 4 April 1826, by which Russia separated from the Neo-Holy Alliance and came into line with England, was known to the public a week after it was signed. † The same is true of the Treaty over Greece of 6 July 1827, reinforcing the protocol, to which France was also a signatory. ‡ Neither document in the nature of things could have been withheld for long, but Canning in each case wanted to prepare public opinion before he gave it the documents. In each case a foreign Power (probably Russia) saved (or rather gave) him trouble by a surreptitious communication to the Press. Leakages to the Press have always been a diplomatic resource and one to which neither Metternich nor

---

* *France, Archives Étrangères*, Angleterre, tome 618, Villèle to Polignac, 9 July 1825.

† *v. infra*, No. 159.

‡ *v. infra*, Nos. 158–60; *v.* also p. 46.

France nor Russia were strangers. The peculiarity of Canning is that he had no connection with the Press, except by supplying them with public documents, in which he was very liberal. Whether any Minister in modern days could thus refuse all private information to the Press is doubtful. In his own day Canning was certainly successful, and his well-timed revelations of State Papers were calculated with an unerring sense of their effect on the public and on his diplomatic opponents. One sees his ideas in a flash in a passage like this:

'I trust', writes he to his cousin, Stratford Canning, 'that this Emperor of Russia [Alexander] will recover from his *pet* and that we shall be again on terms of good understanding with Russia. I trust and am inclined to believe that the measures which we have adopted towards the New States of America will not permanently disturb that understanding, but if it should do so (and we must be prepared for everything in this Mortal World) *there are nice papers for Parliament, whenever an account of our transactions with the Holy Alliance shall come to be rendered.'*

HAROLD TEMPERLEY

* F.O. 352/10, Stratford Canning Papers. George Canning to Stratford Canning. Private, 23 February 1825, last set of italics my own.

Note on Slave Trade Correspondence. This was (*a*) with the British Commissioners at Sierra Leone, Havannah, etc. and (*b*) with Foreign Powers. It was systematised under these headings and regularly published in Parliamentary Papers from 1822 onwards. After 1837, however, they are with few exceptions relegated to special slavery volumes. The correspondence with the Commissioners is generally òmitted here, but Treaties and other details relating to the foreign, as distinguished from the British, aspects of slavery are retained.

SESSION 4 FEBRUARY TO 19 JULY 1823

VOLUME XIX (1823)

Spain, France and Portugal; the Slave Trade, etc.

Volume XIV (1823)

Accounts and Papers

123   Account of the sums received from France in respect of the Pecuniary Indemnity payable under the Convention No. 5 of the 15th November 1815: and of the Appropriation thereof.
PAGE 125

497   *Pursuant to Order (HC. 23 June)*, HC. 25 June 1823.

[*BRITISH AND FOREIGN STATE PAPERS (B.F.S.P.)*

Volume X (1822–3)

124   Correspondence respecting the political and commercial relations of Russia and Turkey, 1823.   PAGES 850–64

125   Spanish Decree relative to blockade of Spanish Main, etc. Sept.–Dec. 1822. [Includes Protest by Admiral Rowley.]
PAGES 938–45]

Session 3 February to 25 June 1824

Volume XXIV (1824)

Miscellaneous

126   Class A. Correspondence with Foreign Powers, relating to the Slave Trade, 1823, 1824.   PAGE 127
L/C. 15 June 1824.

127   Additional Articles to the Convention with His Most Faithful Majesty for the prevention of the illicit traffick in Slaves [signed at Lisbon, 15 Mar. 1823].   PAGE 605
L/C. HC. 4 Feb., HL. 5 Feb. 1824.

128   Convention of commerce with the King of Prussia [signed at London, 2 Ap. 1824].   PAGE 613
    L/C. 31 May 1824.

129   Treaty with the King of the Netherlands, respecting territory and commerce in the East Indies [signed at London, 17 Mar. 1824].   PAGE 619
    L/C. 9 June 1824.

130   Declarations of Sweden respecting British Commerce in the ports of that country [signed at Stockholm, 24 Ap. 1824].
    PAGE 635
    L/C. 31 May 1824.

131   Communications with France and Spain, relating to the Spanish American Provinces [includes the Polignac Memorandum 9 Oct. 1823].   PAGE 641
    L/C. 4 Mar. 1824.

132   Convention between His Majesty and the Emperor of Austria, for the definitive settlement of the Austrian Loan [signed at Vienna, 17 Nov. 1823].   PAGE 655
    L/C. HC. 4 Feb., HL. 5 Feb. 1824.

SESSION 3 FEBRUARY TO 6 JULY 1825

VOLUME XXV (1825)

Slave Trade, etc.

133   Extracts of all Correspondence...with the Naval Officers and the Governor of the Mauritius, etc. [contains Treaty of 1817 between Governor Farquhar and King of Madagascar and of additional articles of October 1820].   PAGE 739
    244   *R–A.* (*HC. 28 Mar.*), HC. 25 Ap. 1825.

    [Cp. Additional Articles to the Treaties concluded in 1817 and 1820...signed at Tamatave, 31st May 1823.
    B.F.S.P., XIII (1825–6), 332–3.]

VOLUME XXVI (1825)

Commerce and Navigation, Slave Trade, etc.

VOLUME XXVII (1825)

Slave Trade, etc.

139a   Class B. Correspondence with Foreign Powers relating to the
       Slave Trade, 1824–25.   PAGE 463
       L/C. HC. 27 May, HL. 31 May 1825.

*JOURNAL OF THE HOUSE OF COMMONS**

VOLUME LXXX (1825)

Appendix

140   Convention between His Majesty, the Emperor of Russia, and the
       United States of America, for carrying into effect His Imperial
       Majesty's award on the First Article of the Treaty of Ghent
       [signed at St Petersburg, 30 June/12 July 1822].   PAGES 938–9
       L/C. 22 Mar. 1825.

[*BRITISH AND FOREIGN STATE PAPERS (B.F.S.P.)*

VOLUME XII (1824–5)

141   Note of Mr Secretary Canning to the Chevalier de Los Rios of
       25 March 1825.†   PAGES 909–15

141a   Note of the Conde de Ofalia to Sir W. à Court, relative to the
       Spanish American Provinces.   PAGES 958–62]

[*BRITISH AND FOREIGN STATE PAPERS (B.F.S.P.)*

VOLUME XIII (1825–6)

142   Message from the President of the United States to Congress
       31 Jan. 1826 with correspondence with the British Government
       re boundary of the United States on the Pacific Ocean.
                                                          PAGES 498–520

* The text of the document, given here from the *Journal*, was subsequently included
in vol. xxvi (1825) of the set of Parliamentary Papers in the British Museum.
† The peculiar case of this 'Note' is explained *infra*, p. 567, *App.* II.

SESSION 2 FEBRUARY TO 31 MAY 1826

VOLUME XXIX (1826)

Slave Trade; Treaties

Session 21 November 1826 to 2 July 1827

Volume XXV (1826–7)

State Papers

Volume XXVI (1826–7)

State Papers

HOUSE OF LORDS SESSIONAL PAPERS

Volume CCXX (1826–7)

Accounts and Papers

THE BLUE-BOOK POLICY OF DUDLEY*

1827–8

THE publications of the session of 1828 may be considered as a legacy of Canning though the influence of Huskisson is also clear. They fall into three groups. The publication of the Commercial Treaties with Mexico and Brazil (Nos. 157, 157 a) completed Canning's policy of recognition of Latin America. The papers dealing with the United States deal partly with Boundary questions (Nos. 161, 162), and partly with the grave question of commercial intercourse between the United States and the British West Indies (No. 164). This question was one which greatly interested Canning and Huskisson alike, and the publication was apparently meant to put the United States in the wrong. The papers relating to Greece (Nos. 158–60) are, in fact, merely tardy official confirmations of documents whose texts had already been unofficially published. No one ever discovered who communicated the Greek Treaty (Nos. 158, 160) to the Press. France suspected England, England Russia, and Russia both her co-signatories. The publication here was, therefore, an enforced one. In later years, the British Government did not usually follow this example. On two occasions they adopted the plan of not publishing such papers in Blue Books, but printing in the *B.F.S.P.* papers which had seen the light in a way which they considered irregular (*v. infra*, Nos. 168, 206–206 b).

---

* John Ward, Viscount Dudley and Ward, appointed Secretary of State for Foreign Affairs on 30 April 1827, Earl of Dudley October 1827, remained until 1 June 1828.

SESSION 29 JANUARY TO 28 JULY 1828

VOLUME XXVI (1828)

Slave Trade

156   Honduras Indians; Report of the Commissioners of Legal Inquiry on their state.   PAGE 1
     522   *L/C.* HC. 10 July 1828.

156a   Madagascar; Correspondence between His Majesty's Government and the Sovereign Chief of Madagascar; 1826–7 [*v.* also *supra*, No. 133].   PAGE 31
     297   *R–A.* (*HC. 29 June 1827*), HC. 1 May 1828.

156b   Correspondence relating to the Slave Trade, 1827....Class B. Correspondence with Foreign Powers.   PAGE 281
     542   *R–A.* (*HC. 25 Ap.*), HC. 8 July, HL. 10 July 1828.

VOLUME XXVII (1828)

State Papers

157   Treaty of Amity, Commerce and Navigation, between His Majesty and the United States of Mexico [signed at London, 26 Dec. 1826].   PAGE 1
     L/C. 31 Jan. 1828.

157a   Treaty of Amity and Commerce between His Majesty and the Emperor of Brazil [signed at Rio de Janeiro, 17 Aug. 1827].   PAGE 15
     L/C. 31 Jan. 1828.

158   Treaty for the Pacification of Greece between His Majesty, the Most Christian King, and the Emperor of All the Russias [signed at London, 6 July 1827].   PAGE 27
     L/C. 31 Jan. 1828.

159   Protocol relative to the Affairs of Greece [signed at St Petersburg, 4 Ap. 1826].   PAGE 35
     L/C. 31 Jan. 1828.

THE BLUE-BOOK POLICY OF
ABERDEEN*

1828–30

FROM the session of 1829 onwards Wellington's influence was all powerful. As has already been indicated (*supra*, p. 33) he hated publicity in the matter of State documents. He told Metternich once that it was most inconvenient when 'ces habitans de Westminster' began to discuss foreign policy. For as soon as a negotiation was revealed the Government were no longer master of its future course. Aberdeen was not so hostile as Wellington to publicity as such, but seems to have followed the dictates of the master. As regards Portugal the Government published some papers (No. 168) apparently under pressure. They contain however some singular omissions. These laid perhaps undue stress on the abstention of Canning from interference in the internal affairs of Portugal. Lady Canning and Stapleton thereupon issued a pamphlet in which they sought, also by omissions, to prove that Canning supported the Constitution.† The true facts are that by sending troops to Portugal to defend her territory against Spanish incursions, Canning acted in accordance with our Treaty obligations to Portugal. Once there, the troops tended to support the Constitutionalist party; but this was not Canning's motive for sending the troops. Other Portuguese papers were published surreptitiously by Dom Miguel himself (No. 168 *note*); while some were extracted by Address from Parliament (*v. infra*, Nos. 182–182 c). In general, nothing did more to discredit the Wellington Government than its foreign policy in Portugal, except its attitude towards Charles X of France just before his fall. Palmerston asserted that Wellington had favoured Charles X's absolutist designs, but the British Government preserved a judicious silence in

---

* George Gordon, Earl of Aberdeen was appointed Secretary of State for Foreign Affairs on 2 June 1828.

† *v.* Temperley, *Foreign Policy of Canning* [1925], 457 and note 2.

print. Over the question of Algiers, and its occupation by the French in 1830, Aberdeen thought that he had obtained satisfactory assurances that this occupation would be only temporary. He omitted to publish the documents at the time and thus lost an opportunity of pinning the French down to a public pledge. In later years the publications on the subject (Nos. 205, 248, 289) were too late to affect the issue.

As regards Greece the publications of Aberdeen were full enough. He had a real interest in Greece but, in this case, the Russian Government forced his hand by publishing in the Press documents suiting their case. The best remedy against this was a full and early official publication of relevant documents, which was in fact adopted.

Session 5 February to 24 June 1829

Volume XXIV (1829)

Hayti, Mexico, etc.

165   Communications received at the Foreign Office, relative to Hayti.   PAGE 1

    18   *R–A.* (*HC. 10 June 1828*), HC. 17 Feb. 1829.

166   Copy of a Letter from H. G. Ward, Esq., to Mr. Secretary Canning, on the subject of the Culture of Sugar, etc. in Mexico [13 Mar. 1826].   PAGE 167

    345   *R–A.* (*HC. 18 Ap. 1828*), HC. 19 June 1829.

Volume XXVI (1829)

State Papers

167   Convention between His Majesty and the Catholick King, for the final settlement of the Claims of British and Spanish subjects under the Convention concluded at Madrid, the 12th of March 1823, signed at London 28th October 1828.   PAGE 1

    L/C. 9 Feb. 1829.

168   Papers respecting the Relations between Great Britain and Portugal, 1826–9.   PAGE 13

    R–A. (*HC. 1 June*), 19 June 1829.

    [Cp. Papers under the same title but with the dates 1825–9, including, as No. 2, Protocol of a Conference in London, respecting the Infant Dom Miguel as Regent of Portugal, 12 Jan. 1828. They contain other papers, with letters of Aberdeen from 1828 to 1829, and were published in Paris under the title of Exposé des Droits de Sa Majesté Très Fidèle, 1830.

    B.F.S.P., XVI (1828–29), 491–531.]

169   Class B. Correspondence relative to the Slave Trade with Foreign Powers.   PAGE 319

    L/C. 19 May 1829.

VOLUME XXXIII (1830)

State Papers. Slave Trade

177   Class B. Correspondence with Foreign Powers relating to the
Slave Trade (1829).   PAGE 205
> R–A. (*HC. 16 Feb.*), HL. 30 June, HC. 2 July
> 1830.

HOUSE OF LORDS SESSIONAL PAPERS

VOLUME CCLXXII (1830)

Accounts and Papers

178   Convention of Commerce and Navigation between his Brittanick
Majesty and the Emperor of Austria. Signed at London,
December 21, 1829.   PAGE 552
> *L/C.* HL. 30 Mar., HC. 1 Ap. 1830.

SESSION 26 OCTOBER 1830 TO 22 APRIL 1831

VOLUME XVI (1830–1)

State Papers

179   Correspondence between Great Britain and the United States,
relative to Commercial Intercourse between America and the
British West India Colonies [December 1829 to November 1830].
                                                       PAGE 263
> *L/C.* 16 Nov. 1830.

SESSION 14 JUNE TO 20 OCTOBER 1831

VOLUME XIX (1831)

Colonies and Slaves

VOLUME XX (1831)

State Papers

THE BLUE-BOOK POLICY OF
PALMERSTON*

1830–4, 1835–41

PALMERSTON was deeply under the influence of Canning and in no direction more so than in the policy of strengthening his hand by popular support by publishing papers at moments convenient for England and inconvenient for other Powers. There is, however, this important difference between the two men. Canning was prepared to refuse and did, in fact, refuse publication of papers when he thought it inadvisable. Palmerston, with a weaker majority and a more critical opposition, was seldom able to do so. He admitted that papers must be produced when a treaty was signed,† but Canning had not always produced the papers as well as the treaty. Just before Palmerston became Foreign Minister in 1830 he complained of Wellington's 'delicacy' about 'not producing every document'.‡ Shortly before that he had admitted that 'There may be many occasions, on which it may be the duty of the Government to resist the production of papers, and when it would be inexpedient for the House to press for such production'. He added that Government ought either to take their stand on a denial of any information whatever, or to give it in its fullest shape; for 'to give imperfect information, mutilated extracts, and fragments of correspondence, from which the most important parts have been cut off, is to make a mockery of Parliament, under pretence of submitting to its jurisdiction'.§ Such a standard may be laid down out of office but cannot be maintained. For no Government, even the British under Palmerston, could afford to publish their documents intact.

Palmerston generally sought to make a merit of publicity and claimed that he had thrown the fullest light into diplo-

---

* Henry Temple, Viscount Palmerston was appointed Secretary of State for Foreign Affairs on 22 November 1830. Arthur Wellesley, Duke of Wellington was appointed Secretary of State for Foreign Affairs on 15 November 1834; Palmerston was reappointed on 18 April 1835.

† *Hans. Deb.* 3rd Ser. XXII, 328, 17 March 1834.
‡ *Hans. Deb.* N.S. XXV, 188–9, 10 June 1830.
§ *Hans. Deb.* N.S. XXIII, 76–7, 10 March 1830.

matic dark corners. He made the important qualification
that papers ought not generally to be published until
transactions are complete.* But he described his own policy
between 1830 and 1841 as follows: 'Whatever may be said
for or against our foreign policy, it must be admitted that
there have been few Governments that have afforded more
full information respecting all important transactions in which
we were concerned.' He mentioned negotiations with Belgium,
Greece, United States, Naples, and added 'upon those which
we carried on with Russia respecting the affairs of Persia and
Affghanistan, and with China, we afforded Parliament the
fullest information...'. †

To take the subjects in the order named: as regards Belgium
and Greece, Palmerston published fairly full details, though
in each case taking care to save the face of France. The
United States certainly published more information at times
than Palmerston did, and thus outdid him at his own game.
In respect to the South American States he occasionally
refused information (as on 19 March 1839, over the blockades
of Mexico and Buenos Ayres).

With Russia Palmerston was much concerned. In the case
of the 'Vixen' and its voyage to Circassia that strange
character, David Urquhart, was involved. Indeed in consequence of this and other incidents he was relieved of his
duties in the diplomatic service. All save one of the papers
were produced in response to Addresses and unwillingly (Nos.
184–184 c, 187, 222, 225, 236, and 236 a). Further publication
took place on Urquhart in 1848 (v. infra, No. 381). Poland was
a burning question and, in response to Addresses, Palmerston
produced some papers (Nos. 197, 198) but refused others.
His correspondence with Talleyrand (1831) and with Russia
(1831–32) was not published until 1861 (Nos. 590 and 590 a).

Mehemet Ali's attack on Turkey brought the Sultan to the
verge of ruin during 1832–3. Yet Palmerston delayed papers
until 1839 (No. 255). The Treaty of Unkiar Skelessi (whereby
Turkey entered into alliance with Russia) was signed on
8 July 1833. No British Blue Book recorded its text in that

* Hans. Deb. 3rd Ser. xix, 578, 11 July 1833.
† Hans. Deb. 3rd Ser. lxxi, 809–10, 15 August 1843. Cp. also infra, p. 567 App. ii.

year though it was known to the British Government. It was not communicated till 1836 (No. 222). But, for some time, there was a good deal of doubt as to whether a correct text was secured, and Palmerston had indicated its general purport in Parliament. Full information was, however, given in the Levant papers on the crisis from 1839 to 1841 (Nos. 272–272 b, 275, 283). As regards Afghanistan there were certainly some suppressions.* As regards China (Nos. 260–260 d) the same is true, despite Palmerston's assertion to the contrary. When some diplomatic correspondence on China (1839–41) came up for sale in the open market in 1858 the Foreign Office took measures to prevent its being revealed to the public on the ground that important secrets were involved. †

The biggest case of suppression was, however, in reference to the Falkland Islands. These had been occupied and abandoned by Great Britain. They were reoccupied owing to the fact that the Argentine Republic sent a mission to annex them in 1832. A furious controversy as to ownership followed which was ultimately settled by England's superior force. No papers were published by Palmerston until 1841. These (No. 282) were not on diplomatic matters; but the deficiency was amply made up by the Argentine Government. Their publications (v. Nos. 206–206 b) were abundant and included British correspondence from 1771 to Palmerston. But Palmerston clearly did not think his case in this matter would gain by publicity—an unusual attitude for him. In the Slave Trade, Palmerston, though publishing much, was unable to satisfy the zeal for information and several times yielded to Addresses (e.g. Nos. 207, 223, 229–34).

On the whole, however, Palmerston may claim to have made good his boast of publicity. Blue Books were issued on a greater scale than had occurred in England before, and they had a very important effect on British policy.‡

* The whole case of Palmerston's suppressions is strongly argued by Mr Anstey in two speeches, v. Hans. Deb. 3rd Ser. xcvi, 304, 309, 8 February, and 1147, 1154, 1209–14, 23 February 1848.

† v. F.O. 83/299. E. Hammond to A. Panizzi, 11 May 1858.

‡ Palmerston's policy as regards the Levant Correspondence is described separately, v. infra, pp. 79–82.

SESSION 6 DECEMBER 1831 TO 16 AUGUST 1832

VOLUME XXVI (1831–2)

Finance Accounts

VOLUME XXX (1831–2)

The Church

VOLUME XXXII (1831–2)

Colonies

186   New Brunswick: Award of the King of the Netherlands, relative
to the Boundary Line between New Brunswick and the United
States.   PAGE 241
   688   *R–A. (HC. 26 July)*, HC. 3 Aug. 1832.

VOLUME XXXIV (1831–2)

Customs and Excise, etc.

187   Russian Ukase: Copy of Ukase of the 23d November 1831,
increasing Duties on Articles imported into Russia.   PAGE 477
   447   *R–A. (HC. 23 Mar.)*, HC. 15 May 1832.

VOLUME XLVII (1831–2)

Slaves

188   Slave Trade: Class B. Correspondence with Foreign Powers.
                                                            PAGE 681
    L/C. 11 Aug. 1832.

VOLUME XLVIII (1831–2)

State Papers

189   Treaty relative to the Netherlands, signed at London, November
15, 1831.   PAGE 1
    L/C. 2 Feb. 1832.

189a Maps of Luxemburg and Limburg, annexed to the above Treaty.
                                                            PAGE 19
    L/C. 2 Feb. 1832.

190   Convention relative to the Belgick Fortresses, signed at London,
November 14, 1831.   PAGE 27
    L/C. HL. 14 May, HC. 15 May 1832.

191   Convention between His Majesty and the Emperor of All the Russias, signed at London, November 16, 1831 [*re* Russian Dutch Loan].   PAGE 35
       L/C. HC. 27 June, HL. 28 June 1832.

192   Netherlands. Convention signed at Mayence, March 31, 1831, referred to in the Ninth Article of the Treaty relative to the Netherlands, signed at London, November 15, 1831, and of the Tariff annexed to that Convention; with Translation.
                                                        PAGE 41
       742   *L/C.* HL. 15 Aug., HC. 16 Aug. 1832.

193   Frankfort: Copy of the Frankfort Tariff referred to in the Fifth Article of the Treaty of Commerce and Navigation between His Majesty and that Free City, signed at London, May 18, 1832; with Translation.   PAGE 121
       R–A. (HC. 9 Aug.), HL. 15 Aug., HC. 16 Aug. 1832.

193*a*   Treaty of Commerce and Navigation between His Majesty and the Free City of Frankfort: signed at London, May 13, 1832.
                                                        PAGE 165
       L/C. 16 July 1832.

194   Greece: Convention relative to the Sovereignty of Greece, between His Majesty, the King of the French and the Emperor of all the Russias on the one part, and the King of Bavaria on the other, signed at London, May 7, 1832.   PAGE 173
       L/C. 2 Aug. 1832.

195   Protocols of Conferences held in London relative to the Affairs of Greece.   PAGE 183
       L/C. HC. 3 Aug., HL. 4 Aug. 1832.

196   Slave Trade: Convention between His Majesty and the King of the French, for the more effectual suppression of the Traffick in Slaves, signed at Paris, November 30, 1831.   PAGE 369
       L/C. 20 Jan. 1832.

197   Poland: Copy and Translation of the Manifesto of The Emperor of Russia, 14/26 February 1832, and of the Organic Statute to which it refers.   PAGE 375
       719   *R–A. (HC. 28 June),* HC. 10 Aug. 1832.

198   Copy and Translation of the Constitutional charter of the Kingdom of Poland [15/27 Nov. 1815].   PAGE 387
       720   *L/C.* HC. 10 Aug., O.T.B.P. 11 Aug. 1832.

SESSION 29 JANUARY TO 29 AUGUST 1833
VOLUME XXIII (1833)
Finance Accounts

VOLUME XLII (1833)
State Papers. Belgium

VOLUME XLIII (1833)
State Papers

HOUSE OF LORDS SESSIONAL PAPERS

VOLUME CCCXXIV (1833)

Accounts and Papers

[BRITISH AND FOREIGN STATE PAPERS (B.F.S.P.)

VOLUME XX (1832–3)

* This was referred to by Palmerston on 13 February 1838, *Hans. Deb.* 3rd Ser. XL, 1057–9, as having been published in '1831 or 32' by the Lords.

† *v. infra,* p. 64 n.

BRITISH AND FOREIGN STATE PAPERS
VOLUME XXII (1833–4)

206*b*   Correspondence between Great Britain and Buenos Ayres relative to the Falkland Islands. [Includes British correspondence from 1771 and dispatch of Palmerston dated 8 Jan. 1834.]*
PAGES 1366–94]

SESSION 4 FEBRUARY TO 15 AUGUST 1834
VOLUME XLIV (1834)
Colonies, East India Co., Slave Trade, etc.

207   Correspondence relating to the Slave Trade: Class B. Correspondence with Foreign Powers.   PAGE 649
471   R–A. (*HC. 17 June*), 8 July 1834.

VOLUME XLIX (1834)
Trade, Customs and Excise, etc.

208   Extract from Despatch [from Lord Howard de Walden to Viscount Palmerston, dated Lisbon, 20 April 1834] transmitting, Decree equalising Duties on Imports from all Countries.
PAGE 395
318   L/C. HC. 22 May 1834.

VOLUME LI (1834)
Miscellaneous Accounts

209   State Papers: Treaty between His Majesty, the Queen Regent of Spain, the King of the French, and the Duke of Braganza, Regent of Portugal; signed at London, April 22, 1834.
PAGE 299
L/C. 9 July 1834.

* These papers were published by the Argentine Government in the first instance and merely reprinted by the British. For the whole incident, which the British Government certainly deplored, *v.* A. F. Kirkpatrick, *History of the Argentine Republic* [1931], App. IV.

SESSION 19 FEBRUARY TO 10 SEPTEMBER 1835

VOLUME LI (1835)

Slave Trade and State Papers

SESSION 4 FEBRUARY TO 20 AUGUST 1836

VOLUME XXXIX (1836)

Colonies: Malta, etc.

VOLUME L (1836)

State Papers

221   Papers relating to the Proclamation of the [Spanish] Constitution of 1812.*   PAGE 633

    609   *L/C.* HC. 19 Aug., O.T.B.P. 20 Aug. 1836.

222   Copy of Treaty of Constantinople, called the Treaty of Unkiar Skelessi.†   PAGE 635

    85   *R–A. (HC. 19 Feb.)*, HC. 7 Mar., O.T.B.P. 8 Mar. 1836.

> [Cp. Correspondence between Great Britain and Russia relative to the Treaty of Unkiar Skelessi [Mr Bligh and Count Nesselrode, Oct., Nov. 1833].
> *B.F.S.P.*, XXIV (1835–6), 1292–3.]

Session 31 January to 17 July 1837

Volume LIV (1837)

State Papers

223   Slave Trade: Class B.   Correspondence with Foreign Powers.   PAGE 377

    R–A. (HC. 24 June), 15 July 1837.

224   Additional Article to the Treaty of 4 May 1818, between Great Britain and the Netherlands for the Prevention of the Traffic in Slaves; signed at the Hague, 7 February, 1837.   PAGE 531

    L/C. HL. 17 Mar., HC. 8 Ap. 1837.

225   Vixen: Papers relating to Seizure and Confiscation by Russia.   PAGE 535

    R–A. (HC. 8 June), HL. 4 July, HC. 5 July 1837.

226   Russell, J. W.: Imprisonment at Panama; Correspondence with the Government of New Granada.   PAGE 573

    L/C. 15 July 1837.

* A motion for laying of dispatches from Mr Villiers announcing the proclamation of the Constitution of 1812 at Malaga, Saragossa, Cadiz, etc., and the recent events at Madrid was proposed as an amendment to the Borough Boundaries Bill on 16 August 1836. *C.J.* xci, 820. The amendment was negatived.

† The Address was carried on 19/20 February 1836. A motion for Correspondence relative to the Treaty of St Petersburg of 29 January 1834, for Correspondence with Turkey and Russia relative to this treaty of Unkiar Skelessi and for British remonstrances to Russia as to her conduct towards Poland was negatived on 20 February 1836. *C.J.* xci, 64.

Session 15 November 1837 to 16 August 1838

Volume XXXIX (1838)

Colonies: Canada

227 North American Boundary: (A.) Correspondence relating to the Boundary between the British Possessions in North America and the United States of America, under the Treaty of 1783.

PAGE 1

L/C. 26 Mar. 1838.

227*a* do. (B.) Proceedings and Correspondence relating to the Pretensions of the States of Maine, Massachusetts and New Hampshire, and to the question of Jurisdiction within the disputed Territory, from 1831–1837. PAGE 123

L/C. 16 Aug. 1838.

[Cp. Message of the President of the United States to Congress transmitting correspondence with Great Britain relating to the North Eastern Boundary of the United States 1832–6.

B.F.S.P., XXIV (1835–6), 1166–83.]

Volume XLI (1838)

East India Company

228 China: Papers relative to the Establishment of a [British] Court of Judicature in China. [1835–7.] PAGE 351

L/C. HC. 10 May 1838.

[*v.* also Bill for the purpose, vol. 1, 1838, p. 1.]

Volume L (1838)

Slavery

229 Slave Trade: Class B. Correspondence with Foreign Powers.

PAGE 287

R–A. (*HC. 23 Dec. 1837*), HL. 9 Ap., HC. 10 Ap. 1838.

VOLUME LII (1838)

Slavery: State Papers

235   French Fishermen: Memorials, etc., received by Her Majesty's
       Government, complaining of the Aggressions of French Fisher-
       men on the British Coast.   PAGE 201
                R–A. (HC. 5 Ap.), 20 July 1838.

236   Vixen: Further Papers relating to the Seizure and Confiscation
       of the 'Vixen', by the Russian Government.   PAGE 221
                L/C. HL. 18 May, HC. 21 May 1838.

236a   do. (B).   PAGE 237
                R–A. (HC. 18 June), HC. 21 June 1838.

237   Spain: Papers relative to the Services rendered by the British
       Auxiliary Legion to Spain, or to the Spanish Army, 1836–1837.
                                                           PAGE 245
                R–A. (HC. 13 Mar.), HC. 26 Mar. 1838.

238   Slave Trade: Convention between Her Majesty, the King of the
       French, and the King of the Two Sicilies, for the more effectual
       Suppression of the Slave Trade [signed at Naples, 14 Feb. 1838].
                                                           PAGE 255
                L/C. HC. 1 June, HL. 7 June 1838.

238a   Convention between Her Majesty, the King of the French, and
       the Grand Duke of Tuscany, for the more effectual Suppression
       of the Slave Trade. Signed at Florence 24 Nov. 1837.
                                                           PAGE 263
                L/C. HL. 22 Mar., HC. 26 Mar. 1838.

238b   Convention between His Late Majesty, the King of the French,
       and the Hans Towns, for the more effectual Suppression of the
       Slave Trade [signed at Hamburg, 9 June 1837].   PAGE 269
                L/C. HL. 1 Dec., HC. 4 Dec. 1837.

239   Greece: Convention of Commerce and Navigation between Her
       Majesty and the King of Greece [signed at London, 4 Oct. 1837].
                                                           PAGE 275
                L/C. 29 Jan. 1838.

240   Netherlands: Convention of Commerce and Navigation between
       Her Majesty and the King of the Netherlands. Signed at the
       Hague 27 Oct. 1837.   PAGE 285
                L/C. HL. 1 Dec., HC. 4 Dec. 1837.

241   Peru-Bolivian Confederation: Treaty of Amity, Commerce, and
       Navigation between His Late Majesty and the Peru-Bolivian
       Confederation. Signed at Lima 5 June 1837.   PAGE 295
                L/C. HL. 1 Dec., HC. 4 Dec. 1837.

HOUSE OF LORDS SESSIONAL PAPERS

VOLUME XVII (1838)

Accounts and Papers

SESSION 5 FEBRUARY TO 27 AUGUST 1839

VOLUME XL (1839)

East Indies

VOLUME XLVII (1839)

Trade, etc.

VOLUME XLVIII (1839)

Slave Trade

245   Slave Trade: Class B. Correspondence with Spain, Portugal, Brazil, Netherlands and Sweden, relative to the Slave Trade from May 1838 to February 1839.   PAGE 213

    [181]   *L/C.* 7 May 1839.

VOLUME XLIX (1839)

Slave Trade

245*a*   Class C. Correspondence with Foreign Powers, Parties to the Conventions between Great Britain and France, upon the Slave Trade.   PAGE 1

    [182]   *L/C.* 7 May 1839.

245*b*   Class D. Correspondence with Foreign Powers, not Parties to Conventions, giving Right of Search of Vessels suspected of Slave Trade.   PAGE 39

    [183]   *L/C.* 7 May 1839.

245*c*   Class B (Further Series). Correspondence with Spain, Portugal and Brazil, relative to the Slave Trade.   PAGE 265

    [189]   *L/C.* 24 June 1839.

245*d*   Class C (Further Series). Correspondence with Foreign Powers, Parties to the Conventions between Great Britain and France.   PAGE 415

    [190]   *L/C.* 24 June 1839.

245*e*   Class D (Further Series). Correspondence with Foreign Powers, not Parties to Conventions, etc.   PAGE 421

    [191]   *L/C.* 24 June 1839.

VOLUME L (1839)

Admiralty Court, Slave Trade, etc.

* Papers relative to affairs of Belgium were laid by command in the House of Commons on 23 August 1839 and in the Lords on the 26th. In the latter they were ordered to be printed, but no printed copy can be traced.

HOUSE OF LORDS SESSIONAL PAPERS

VOLUME XI (1839)

Accounts and Papers

258   Correspondence relative to the Expulsion of British Subjects from the Convent of La Meilleraye, by the Government of France, in 1831.   PAGE 93
R–A. (HL. 22 July), HL. 6 Aug. 1839.

SESSION 16 JANUARY TO 11 AUGUST 1840

VOLUME XXXII (1840)

Colonies: Canada

259   North American Boundary: Part I. Correspondence relating to the Boundary between the British Possessions in North America and the United States of America, under the Treaty of 1783.
PAGE 457
[257]   *L/C.* 27 July 1840.

259*a*   Part II.   PAGE 631
[257]   *L/C.* 27 July 1840.

VOLUME XXXVI (1840)

China

260   Correspondence relating to China [1834–9].   PAGE 5
[223]   *L/C.* HC. 5 Mar., HL. 6 Mar. 1840.

260*a*   Additional Correspondence relating to China [Oct., Nov. 1839].
PAGE 469
[224]   *L/C.* HL. 16 Mar., HC. 17 Mar. 1840.

260*b*   Additional Papers relating to China [1833, 1839].   PAGE 483
[230]   *L/C.* HC. 26 Mar., HL. 27 Mar. 1840.

260c Additional Papers relating to China [Nov.–Dec. 1839].
                                                    PAGE 497

    [234]   L/C. HC. 30 Mar., HL. 31 Mar. 1840.

260d Papers and Despatches on the Subject of Hostilities between the
      Chinese and British Subjects employed in the Opium Trade,
      1830–33.   PAGE 575

    156   *Pursuant to Order (HC. 13 Feb.),* HC. 23 Mar.,
                    O.T.B.P. 24 Mar. 1840.

260e Memorials addressed to Her Majesty's Government by British
      Merchants interested in the Trade with China.*   PAGE 637

    [262]   L/C. HL. 3 Aug., HC. 4 Aug. 1840.

VOLUME XLIII (1840)

Revenue, Population and Commerce

261   Return of Revenue, Population, Trade, etc., of Turkey. In
      Tables of Revenue, Population and Commerce, etc., of the
      United Kingdom and its Dependencies:—Part VIII., 1838.
                                                    PAGE 372

    [275]   L/C. 10 Aug. 1840.

VOLUME XLIV (1840)

Trade, etc.

262   Papers relative to the Sulphur Monopoly in Sicily [Sept. 1837–
      Ap. 1840].   PAGE 447

    [243]   L/C. 12 May 1840.

263   Correspondence relative to the continuance of Monopolies in the
      Dominions of Turkey. 1839–40.   PAGE 541

    [247]   R–A. *(HC. 25 Feb.),* HC. 15 Ap. 1840.

---

* There are references to another Chinese Paper in *C.J.* xcv, 169, 190, 241, but
this is not strictly diplomatic.

VOLUME XLVI (1840)

Slavery

264   Class B. Correspondence with Foreign Powers, 1840.

PAGE 415

[266]   L/C. 10 Aug. 1840.

VOLUME XLVII (1840)

Slavery

264*a*   Class B. Correspondence with Foreign Powers (Further Series, 1840).   PAGE 1

[271]   L/C. 10 Aug. 1840.

264*b*   Class C. Correspondence with Foreign Powers, Parties to the Conventions between Great Britain and France, upon the Slave Trade.   PAGE 159

[267]   L/C. 10 Aug. 1840.

264*c*   do. do. Further Series.   PAGE 195

[272]   L/C. 10 Aug. 1840.

264*d*   Class D. Correspondence with Foreign Powers, not Parties to Conventions giving Right of Search of Vessels suspected of the Slave Trade, 1839–40.   PAGE 219

[268]   L/C. 10 Aug. 1840.

264*e*   do. do. Further Series, 1840.   PAGE 445

[273]   L/C. 10 Aug. 1840.

VOLUME XLVIII (1840)

State Papers

265   Port Mahon: Papers relative to the temporary Occupation by the French Government of King's Islet in the Port of Mahon 1837–9.   PAGE 1

[216]   L/C. HC. 13 Feb. 1840.

VOLUME XLIX (1840)

State Papers

MEHEMET ALI, 1839

The Levant Correspondence

As regards Russia, then generally regarded as the enemy of England, the omissions are numerous. Suggestions by Ponsonby from Constantinople that Russia had stirred up Mehemet Ali to attack the Sultan are deleted from various dispatches (No. 272 Lev[ant Correspondence] i, Nos. 9, 16, 18, 26). One dispatch of 12 February 1839 is omitted altogether. Next all references to Russia's inability to undergo a war are omitted (Lev. i, Nos. 50, 122). Interviews with the Russian Emperor are cut out of the part of a dispatch published (Lev. i, No. 419), or omitted altogether as in a dispatch from Clanricarde of 9 August. As the Emperor expressed himself as pro-British and anti-French and more so in each case than Nesselrode, the effect is misleading. An important dispatch from Palmerston to Granville (Lev. i, No. 82) of 29 June has the crucial passage omitted, which declared that the object of Russia was to weaken Turkey. The passage showing that Marshal Soult was anti-Russian is also omitted (Lev. i, No. 101). An important incident at the end of June 1839 when Beauvale wrote from Vienna (in conjunction with Metternich) to advocate the introduction of a Russian Squadron into the Mediterranean is much obscured by omissions (Lev. i, Nos. 108–9). Palmerston's refusal, as yet, to admit this suggestion is much minimised (Lev. i, No. 111).

The good influence of Austria and Metternich in trying to unite Russia with England and England with France is, on the whole, rather depreciated (Lev. i, Nos. 28, 107, 109, 202, 207). On the other hand a dispatch of 2 August in which Lord Beauvale declares that Metternich has 'escaped' him is omitted altogether. A published dispatch (Lev. i, No. 288 of 22 August) omits the great credit ascribed to the Austrian representative at Constantinople for promoting the European aspect of things with the Turks. Finally a published dispatch (Lev. i, No. 393 of 16 November) omits the passage declaring that Metternich believes that no settlement with Mehemet Ali will be more than a truce. This is an important light on Austrian policy.

Prussia is not much mentioned and the fact that she is described as 'a satellite of Austria' is not disclosed in one dispatch referring to her (*Lev.* 1, *No.* 304).

The treatment of France is of course the most important, and with respect to omissions may be regarded as the test case. Most references to King Louis Philippe are omitted, particularly an important one reported on 27 January 1840. When his views are quoted they are described, with some inaccuracy, as those of the French Government. Bulwer (30 August) insists strongly on Soult's ignorance of the East and on the weakness of his Ministry (*Lev.* 1, *No.* 270). The fact that the King was more pacific than the Ministry is obscured by omissions (*Lev.* 1, *Nos.* 313, 315, 317). The extreme friction between Russia and France is largely concealed in the same way (e.g. *Lev.* 1, *No.* 357).

A good many of the dispatches of Ponsonby are devoted to the internal difficulties of Turkey and intrigues at Constantinople. But, as he invariably ascribes the disturbances to Russian influence, it was difficult to insert many of them in the Blue Books. Generally speaking it may be said that Russia came to terms with Palmerston from 22 November 1839 onwards (*Lev.* 1, *No.* 401) and thereafter Anglo-Russian relations were good. Palmerston therefore exerted himself to keep anything anti-Russian out of the Blue Books; but he was less solicitous about offending France.

The crucial question, however, is whether the Blue Book gives an accurate account of the breach with France. Guizot remarked later that 'France would not have quarrelled about the treaty of the 15th July [1840] if they had had *fair warning* that it would be signed without them if not with them. Guizot assured him [Cowley] that the warning was not given.'* Palmerston wrote a private letter on this subject, using *Levant Correspondence* for his text. He quotes first (*Lev.* 1, *No.* 281)

---

* Bulwer, *Life*, II, 425–33. Letters of Hobhouse 7 July, of Palmerston 27 July 1843.

to show that he warned Sebastiani on 10 September 1839 that we would, if necessary, 'act in concert with a less number than four' Great Powers to check Mehemet Ali. He desired that Soult should see the dispatch in which this conversation was recorded. A similar warning was given on 23 September and, though the published version omits references to the French King, it preserves the warning.* Also the French Ambassador was asked to repeat the conversation to Soult. In an instruction to Granville of 29 October (*Lev.* I, *No.* 358) obscure hints on the same subject are given. Palmerston states in his letter that a copy of this dispatch was given to Soult, but there is no instruction to that effect in the dispatch itself. A letter from Palmerston of 5 January 1840 (*Lev.* I, *No.* 430) informed Sebastiani that Austria, Great Britain, Prussia and Russia had come to agreement and hoped for the concurrence of France. A sketch of the proposed Four-Power (or Five-Power) Convention was given by Palmerston to Sebastiani, as is shown by a reference in Granville's dispatch of 24 January (*Lev.* I, *No.* 458) and as is still more clear in the unpublished version. In March Sebastiani was recalled and Guizot came to London as French Ambassador. Palmerston recorded a conversation with Guizot in a dispatch to Paris of 12 March 1840 (*Lev.* I, *No.* 611) in which he intimated that England would act with other Powers if necessary,† and even discussed the possibility of war with France. On 3 April (*Lev.* I, *No.* 533) Granville reported that no change in French views was to be expected and on the 15th (*Lev.* I, *No.* 546) he repeated that France would never agree to coerce Mehemet Ali. On 17 April (*Lev.* I, *No.* 547) Granville reported Thiers as declining to join a Conference of Five Powers, the object of which was to drive Mehemet Ali out of Syria. The reason he gave for refusal was that a French refusal to join in coercion, after the Conference met, would be a more marked separation than a refusal beforehand.

* *Lev.* I, *No.* 313. This is one of the rare cases in which a material change is made on publication and the fact not indicated by the paper being described as an extract (cp. *infra*, pp. 499–500).

† The argument is slightly misrepresented in the Blue Book. In a passage omitted from it Palmerston expressed the fear that Austria might not act with the others.

After this Palmerston did not think it necessary to consult France further and did not do so. On 15 July he concluded a Four-Power Treaty to drive Mehemet Ali from Syria. This aim was successful and was executed by the British fleet before the end of the year. France was humiliated because she was left out, and thought of going to war. At such a time she naturally complained that she had not been consulted.

In this rather lengthy survey Palmerston argued that France had had fair warning that the Four-Power Treaty would be signed without France and that she would be left out of the European Concert. That is a matter purely for diplomats or historians to settle. But what is of real interest for our purpose is that Palmerston relied solely on a Blue Book to prove his case. There were serious omissions in this Blue Book, which have already been mentioned. Much was omitted in deference to national susceptibilities. Ponsonby's Russophobia, Austria's timidity and Prussia's subservience to her are all glossed over. They were friends, so this deference was paid to them. But the great essential facts as to the quarrel with France and Palmerston's justification for it are made clear. Reference to the original documents does not show any new arguments of substance or omissions that really mattered from the point of view of this conclusion. It was not the first time that a Blue Book was used to reveal the facts as to British policy in a great diplomatic crisis. That had been done under Canning and against France (*v. supra*, No. 131). But it is not often that a Blue Book stands the test so well as Palmerston's *Levantine Correspondence* does. Certainly neither the origins of the Crimean War, nor—much later—the diplomatic crisis of Agadir, are so fully shown in the Blue Books of the day.*

* This account is reproduced, by permission of Messrs Longmans & Co., from Temperley, *England and the Near East. The Crimea* [1936], 429–32 (note 196).

Session 26 January to 22 June 1841

Volume XXIX (1841)

Affairs of the Levant

272   Correspondence relative to the Affairs of the Levant. Part I.
Table of Contents [1839].   PAGE 1
    [322]   *L/C.* HL. 6 Ap., HC. 21 June 1841.

272*a* do. Part I with numerical list of Papers.   PAGE 21
    [304]   *L/C.* HL. 6 Ap., HC. 21 June 1841.

272*b* do. Part II [1840].   PAGE 737
    [323]   *L/C.* 21 June 1841.

Volume XXX (1841)

Slave Trade

273   Class B. Correspondence with Foreign Powers, 1840.
                                                             PAGE 373
    [331]   *L/C.* HC. 17 June, HL. 21 June 1841.

273*a* Class C. Correspondence with Foreign Powers, Parties to the
Conventions between Great Britain and France, upon the
Slave Trade.   PAGE 645
    [332]   *L/C.* HC. 17 June, HL. 21 June 1841.

273*b* Class D. Correspondence with Foreign Powers, not Parties to
Conventions, giving Right of Search of Vessels suspected of the
Slave Trade.   PAGE 727
    [353]   *L/C.* HC. 17 June, HL. 21 June 1841.

VOLUME XXXI (1841)

State Papers

Session 19 August to 7 October 1841

2nd Session. Volume III (1841)

Colonies and Emigration

282   Papers relative to the Falkland Islands.   PAGE 251
       3   *L/C.* HC. 26 Aug., O.T.B.P. 27 Aug., HL. 27 Aug. 1841.

2nd Session. Volume VIII (1841)

Affairs of the Levant, State Papers, etc.

283   Correspondence relative to the Affairs of the Levant. Part III.
                                   PAGE 1
      [337]   *L/C.* HC. 24 Aug., HL. 27 Aug. 1841.

284   Turkey: Correspondence respecting the Operation of the Commercial Treaty with Turkey, of August 16, 1838.   PAGE 483
      [341]   *L/C.* HC. 24 Aug., HL. 27 Aug. 1841.

285   Hans Towns: Convention of Commerce and Navigation between Her Majesty and the Hans Towns, signed at London, 3 August, 1841.   PAGE 517
      [343]   *L/C.* HC. 30 Aug., HL. 6 Sept. 1841.

THE BLUE-BOOK POLICY OF ABERDEEN*

1841–6

THE policy of publicity, to which Palmerston had committed England, was followed in the main by Aberdeen. The year 1842 contained an abundant legacy of the Palmerstonian policy in the shape of papers, and in fact it seems to have proved difficult to stop the flow. Palmerston conducted or inspired an active campaign against Aberdeen in the pages of the *Morning Chronicle*.† He complained, for instance, that 'the despatches of the Foreign Office are like the touches of a torpedo' (etc.); he spoke of 'their benumbing influence' and 'deathlike appearance' (9 August 1845). But he did not complain that Aberdeen withheld or concealed information in this period, as he had done during his previous Secretaryship under Wellington. On the other hand, information was not as spontaneously given as it had been under Palmerston. A mild process of extraction was applied by the Commons to which the Government readily submitted. This took place in the case of Syrian papers (Nos. 309–309 a), and over Tahiti (No. 320) in 1843. In the case of Turkey, where executions for apostasy took place (No. 327), and of Tunis, where a British subject was mishandled (No. 326), Aberdeen yielded to the demand for papers unwillingly. Sir Stratford Canning took a very prominent part in preventing further executions for apostasy in Turkey, and some omissions in the Blue Book (No. 327) rather disguised that fact. Aberdeen had no desire to interfere in Turkey's internal affairs or to emphasise Stratford's success in doing so.‡ But it may be said, in general, that Aberdeen pursued a policy of publicity although without enthusiasm.

* Appointed Secretary of State for Foreign Affairs on 2 September 1841.
† He lost control of this organ in the year 1848.
‡ *v.* Temperley, *England and the Near East. The Crimea* [1936], 227–8.

Session 3 February to 12 August 1842

Volume XXVIII (1842)

Colonies: Canada, etc.

286 Supplementary Reports relating to the Boundary between the British Possessions in North America and the United States, under the Treaty of 1783; with Map and Section. PAGE 1
  413 *L/C.* 8 Aug. 1842.

Volume XXX (1842)

East Indies

287 Papers relative to the Execution of the Treaty of 1824 by the Netherland Authorities in the East Indies. PAGE 123
  [352] *L/C.* 3 Feb. 1842.

Volume XLIII (1842)

Slavery

288 Class B. Correspondence with Foreign Powers, from January 1 to December 31, 1841. PAGE 1
  [403] *L/C.* HC. 25 July, HL. 26 July 1842.

Volume XLIV (1842)

Slavery

288*a* Class C. Correspondence with Foreign Powers, Parties to Conventions under which Vessels are to be tried by the Tribunals of the Nation to which they belong, from January 1 to December 31, 1841. PAGE 1
  [404] *L/C.* HL. 1 Aug., HC. 3 Aug. 1842.

288*b* Class D. Correspondence with Foreign Powers, from January 1
to December 31, 1841.   PAGE 173
[405]   *L/C.* HL. 1 Aug., HC. 12 Aug. 1842.

VOLUME XLV (1842)

State Papers

288*c* African Slave Trade: Treaty between Great Britain, Austria,
France, Prussia and Russia, for the suppression of the African
Slave Trade, signed at London, December 20, 1841.   PAGE 1
[363]   *L/C.* 21 Feb. 1842.

289   Algiers: Copy of Despatch relating to the French Occupation
of Algiers [Aberdeen, 28 Jan. 1842].   PAGE 25
94   *L/C.* 7 Mar., HC. O.T.B.P. 8 Mar. 1842.

290   Claims of British merchants: Copies and Extracts from the
Correspondence between Her Majesty's Government and Her
Majesty's Mission at Brussels, relative to the Claims of British
merchants, arising out of the Destruction, in October, 1830, of
the Entrepot at Antwerp. [1834–42.]   PAGE 27
[369]   *R–A.* (*HC. 23 Feb.*), HC. 23 Mar. 1842.

291   Republick of Bolivia: Treaty of Amity, Commerce and Navigation, between Her Majesty and the Republick of Bolivia, signed
at Sucre, September 25, 1840.   PAGE 55
[416]   *L/C.* HC. 2 May, HL. 10 May 1842.

292   Treaty between Her Majesty and the Republick of Bolivia for
the Abolition of the Traffic in Slaves, signed at Sucre, September
25, 1840.   PAGE 69
[417]   *L/C.* HC. 2 May, HL. 10 May 1842.

293   *Straits of the Dardanelles and the Bosphorus:* Convention between
Great Britain, Austria, France, Prussia, Russia and Turkey,
respecting the Straits of the Dardanelles and of the Bosphorus,
signed at London, July 13, 1841.   PAGE 95
[350]   *L/C.* 3 Feb. 1842.

294   Mexican Republic: Treaty between Her Majesty and the
Mexican Republick, for the Abolition of the Traffic in Slaves,
signed at Mexico, February 24, 1841.   PAGE 103
[407]   *L/C.* 1 Aug. 1842.

295   Persia: Treaty of Commerce between Her Majesty and the Shah of Persia, signed at Tehran, October 28, 1841.   PAGE 125

    [354]   *L/C.* HC. 11 Feb., HL. 14 Feb. 1842.

296   Poland: Copies of certain Ukases, bearing date the 15th and 18th days of September 1841, issued by the Russian Government, and relating to the Administration of the Kingdom of Poland.
    PAGE 129

    [408]   *R–A.* (*HC. 30 June*), HC. 4 Aug. 1842.

297   Portugal: Treaty between Her Majesty and the Queen of Portugal, for the Suppression of the Traffic in Slaves, signed at Lisbon, July 3, 1842.   PAGE 143

    [414]   *L/C.* HL. 9 Aug., HC. 12 Aug. 1842.

297 *a*   Treaty of Commerce and Navigation between Her Majesty and the Queen of Portugal, signed at Lisbon, July 3, 1842.
    PAGE 185

    [415]   *L/C.* HL. 9 Aug., HC. 12 Aug. 1842.

298   Sardinia: Treaty of Navigation between Her Majesty and the King of Sardinia, signed at Turin, September 6, 1841.   PAGE 201

    [351]   *L/C.* 3 Feb. 1842.

299   Sound Dues: Final Arrangements between Great Britain and Denmark, respecting the Sound Dues; viz. Agreement signed at Elsinore, August 13, 1841, and Declaration signed at Copenhagen, October 7, 1841.   PAGE 209

    [349]   *L/C.* 3 Feb. 1842.

300   Sulphur Question: Papers relative to the Sulphur Question with the Government of Naples, 1840–2 [*v. supra*, No. 262].
    PAGE 225

    [365]   *R–A.* (*HC. 14 Feb.*), HC. 7 Mar. 1842.

301   Republic of Texas: Treaty of Commerce and Navigation between Her Majesty and the Republic of Texas, signed at London, November 13, 1840.   PAGE 239

    [393]   *L/C.* 30 June 1842.

302   Convention between Her Majesty and the Republic of Texas, containing arrangements relative to Publick Debt, signed at London, November 14, 1840.   PAGE 245

    [394]   *L/C.* 30 June 1842.

303   Treaty between Her Majesty and the Republic of Texas, for
      the Suppression of the African Slave Trade, signed at London,
      November 16, 1840.   PAGE 249

      [395]   L/C. 30 June 1842.

304   Turkey: Correspondence respecting the Operation of the Com-
      mercial Treaty with Turkey, of August 16, 1838 [v. supra,
      No. 284].   PAGE 261

      [418]   L/C. HC. 2 May, HL. 10 May 1842.

305   Republic of Uruguay: Treaty between Her Majesty and the
      Oriental Republic of the Uruguay, for the abolition of the
      Traffic in Slaves, signed at Montevideo, July 13, 1839.
                                                            PAGE 297

      [391]   L/C. HC. 10 June, HL. 13 June 1842.

                SESSION 2 FEBRUARY TO 24 AUGUST 1843

                    VOLUME XXXIII (1843)

                         Colonies

306   *Falkland Isles:* Copies or extracts of correspondence relating to
      the Falkland Isles, since the last Papers laid before the House
      upon the 27th August 1841* [v. supra, No. 282].   PAGE 1

      160   R–A. (HC. 31 Mar.), HC. 3 Ap., R–A. (HL. 9 May),
                    HL. 22 June 1843.

                    VOLUME XXXVII (1843)

                        Affghanistan

307   Letter from the Governor-General of India, dated 9 May 1843.
                                                            PAGE 13

      [495]   L/C. HL. 17 Aug., HC. 24 Aug. 1843.

      * This paper and No. 282 *supra* are administrative and financial, but the papers
      given *supra*, Nos. 206 *a* and *b*, which were not published by either Palmerston or
      Aberdeen, are diplomatic.

VOLUME LVIII (1843)

Slave Trade

308   Class B. Correspondence with Foreign Powers, from January 1
to December 31, 1842.   PAGE 347
      [483]   L/C. 25 July 1843.

VOLUME LIX (1843)

Slave Trade

308 a   Class C. Correspondence with Foreign Powers, Parties to
Conventions under which Vessels are to be tried by the Tri-
bunals of the Nation to which they belong, from January 1 to
December 31, 1842.   PAGE 1
      [484]   L/C. 25 July 1843.

308 b   Class D. Correspondence with Foreign Powers, not Parties to
Conventions giving Right of Search of Vessels suspected of the
Slave Trade, from January 1 to December 31, 1842.
                                                        PAGE 337
      [485]   L/C. 25 July 1843.

VOLUME LX (1843)

State Papers

309   *Syria:* Correspondence relative to the Affairs of Syria, Part I
[1841–3].   PAGE 1
      [455]   R–A. (*HC. 28 Feb.*), HC. 6 Ap. 1843.

309 a   Correspondence relative to the Affairs of Syria, Part II [1841–2].
                                                        PAGE 139
      [456]   R–A. (*HC. 28 Feb.*), HC. 6 Ap. 1843.

310   France: Convention between Her Majesty and the King of the
French, for the mutual surrender, in certain cases, of Persons
fugitive from justice, signed at London, February 13, 1843.
                                                        PAGE 487
      [444]   L/C. 14 Mar. 1843.

VOLUME LXI (1843)

State Papers

314*c* North American Boundary: Correspondence relating to the Boundary between the British Possessions in North America and the United States of America, under the Treaty of 1783 [*v. supra*, Nos. 259–259*a*].   PAGE 95

   [442]   *L/C.* HC. 13 Mar., HL. 14 Mar. 1843.

314*d* Map to illustrate the Boundary established by the Treaty of Washington of the 9th August 1842, between Her Majesty's Colonies of New Brunswick and Canada and the United States of America.   PAGE 267

   [451]   *R–A. (HC. 27 Mar.),* HC. 3 Ap. 1843.

315 German Customs Union: Copies and Extracts of Despatches from Her Majesty's Ministers abroad, having reference to the recent modifications in the Tariff of the German Customs Union.   PAGE 271

   [445]   *L/C.* HC. 15 Mar., *R–A. (HL. 30 Mar.),* 3 Ap. 1843.

316 Chile: Treaty between Her Majesty and the Republic of Chile, for the Abolition of the Traffic in Slaves, signed at Santiago, January 19, 1839.   PAGE 289

   [452]   *L/C.* 6 Ap. 1843.

316*a* Additional and Explanatory Convention between Her Majesty and the Republic of Chile, for the Abolition of the Traffic in Slaves, signed at Santiago, August 7, 1841.   PAGE 317

   [453]   *L/C.* 6 Ap. 1843.

317 Portugal: Additional Article to the Treaty concluded at Lisbon, July 3, 1842, between Her Majesty and the Queen of Portugal, for the Suppression of the Traffic in Slaves, signed at Lisbon, October 22, 1842.   PAGE 321

   [425]   *L/C.* HC. 2 Feb., HL. 6 Feb. 1843.

318 Russia: Treaty of Commerce and Navigation between Her Majesty and the Emperor of all the Russias, signed at St. Petersburgh, January 11, 1843.   PAGE 325

   [426]   *L/C.* HC. 2 Feb., HL. 6 Feb. 1843.

319 Servia: Treaties and Hatti-Sheriffs relating to Servia.   PAGE 337

   [464]   *L/C.* HC. 19 May, HL. 30 May 1843.

HOUSE OF LORDS SESSIONAL PAPERS

VOLUME VI (1843)

Commercial Treaties, etc.

SESSION 1 FEBRUARY TO 5 SEPTEMBER 1844

VOLUME XLVIII (1844)

Slave Trade

VOLUME XLIX (1844)

Slave Trade

VOLUME LI (1844)

State Papers

329*a* Supplementary Treaty between Her Majesty and the Emperor
of China, signed at Hoomun-Chae, October 8, 1843, with other
documents relating thereto.   PAGE 341

[534]   *L/C.* HL. 1 Ap., HC. 2 Ap. 1844.

329*b* Instructions under Her Majesty's Royal Sign Manual, Com-
missions providing for the temporary Exercise of the Duties of
Chief Superintendent of British Trade in China; Orders in
Council, and Ordinance passed and issued in virtue of the
Powers conferred upon Her Majesty by the Act of the 6th and
7th Vict., *c.* 80.   PAGE 359

[556]   *L/C.* 17 May 1844.

329*c* Statement of the Foreign Trade with China, and Account of the
Inland or Transit Duties of the Chinese Empire.   PAGE 369

[570]   *L/C.* HL. 8 July, HC. 10 July 1844.

330   Hanover: Treaty of Commerce and Navigation between Her
Majesty and the King of Hanover, signed at London, July 22,
1844, with various Documents annexed thereto.   PAGE 383

[584]   *L/C.* 9 Aug. 1844.

330*a* Mecklenburg-Schwerin and Mecklenburg-Strelitz: Treaties of
Commerce and Navigation between Her Majesty and the Grand
Dukes of Mecklenburg-Schwerin and Mecklenburg-Strelitz,
signed at Schwerin, May 1, 1844.   PAGE 467

[590]   *L/C.* 5 Sept. 1844.

331   Netherlands Postage Convention: Postage Convention between
the General Post Office of the United Kingdom of Great Britain
and Ireland, and the General Post Office of the Kingdom of the
Netherlands, dated October 14, 1843.   PAGE 475

[526]   *L/C.* HC. 14 Feb., HL. 19 Feb. 1844.

332   Oldenburg: Treaty of Commerce and Navigation between Her
Majesty and the Grand Duke of Oldenburg, signed at London,
April 4, 1844.   PAGE 515

[549]   *L/C.* 30 Ap. 1844.

Session 4 February to 9 August 1845

Volume XLIX (1845)

Slave Trade

333 Class D. Correspondence with Foreign Powers, not Parties to Treaties or Conventions giving a mutual Right of Search of Vessels suspected of the Slave Trade, from 1 January to 31 December, 1844. PAGE 405

  [635] *L/C.* HC. 10 June, HL. 13 June 1845.

Volume L (1845)

Slave Trade

333*a* Class B. Correspondence with Foreign Powers, Parties to Treaties under which captured Vessels are to be tried by Mixed Tribunals, 1844. PAGE 1

  [633] *L/C.* HC. 10 June, HL. 13 June 1845.

333*b* Class C. Correspondence with Foreign Powers, Parties to Treaties and Conventions under which captured Vessels are to be tried by the Tribunals of the Nation to which they belong, 1844. PAGE 503

  [634] *L/C.* HC. 10 June, HL. 13 June 1845.

Volume LI (1845)

State Papers

334 *China:* Ordinances passed in the year 1844 by the Chief Superintendent of British Trade in China, with the advice of the Legislative Council of Hong-Kong, in virtue of the Powers conferred upon Her Majesty by the Act of the 6 and 7 Vict., *c.* 80. PAGE 1

  [637] *L/C.* 17 June 1845.

VOLUME LII (1845)

State Papers

* Cp. motion on commercial relations with Spain, *L.J.* LXXVII, 747, 15 July 1845.

Session 22 January to 28 August 1846

Volume LI (1846)

Slave Trade

Volume LII (1846)

State Papers

* A motion in the Lords for an Address for Correspondence with France relating to intervention in the Affairs of Rio de la Plata was withdrawn on 19 February 1846. *L.J.* LXXVIII, 79.

351*a* Postage Convention between the General Post Office of the United Kingdom of Great Britain and Ireland, and the General Post Office of the Duchy of Brunswick, dated 8th July 1845.

PAGE 33

[678]   *L/C.* 29 Jan. 1846.

351*b* Convention between Her Majesty and the King of Denmark, regulating the Communication by Post between the British and Danish Dominions, signed at London, June 26, 1846. PAGE 39

[744]   *L/C.* HL. 13 Aug., HC. 28 Aug. 1846.

351*c* Additional Articles to those agreed upon between the Post Office of Great Britain and the Post Office of France, for carrying into execution the Convention of the 3rd April 1843.   PAGE 55

[679]   *L/C.* 29 Jan. 1846.

351*d* Additional Articles, as above, signed at Paris, March 25, 1846, and at London, March 30, 1846.   PAGE 63

[702]   *L/C.* HC. 5 May, HL. 8 May 1846.

351*e* Additional Articles, as above, signed at London, 14th March 1846.   PAGE 71

[714]   *L/C.* HC. 19 June, HL. 25 June 1846.

351*f* Postage Convention between the General Post Office of the United Kingdom of Great Britain and Ireland, and the General Post Office of the Kingdom of Hanover, dated 8th July 1845.

PAGE 75

[677]   *L/C.* 29 Jan. 1846.

352 Convention between Her Majesty and the King of Prussia, for the Establishment of International Copyright, signed at Berlin, May 13, 1846.   PAGE 99

[715]   *L/C.* 22 June 1846.

353 Correspondence relative to the Negotiation of the Question of disputed Right to the Oregon territory, on the North-West Coast of America, subsequent to the Treaty of Washington, of August 9, 1842.   PAGE 109

[695]   *R–A.* (*HL. 17 Mar.*), 7 Ap. 1846.

353*a* Treaty between Her Majesty and the United States of America, for the settlement of the Oregon boundary, signed at Washington, June 15, 1846.   PAGE 185

[722]   *L/C.* 17 July 1846.

THE BLUE BOOKS OF PALMERSTON'S THIRD PERIOD AT THE FOREIGN OFFICE*

1846–51

ABERDEEN's last session as Foreign Secretary was in 1846. He ended triumphantly with a series of documents, culminating in the papers detailing the successful settlement of the Oregon Boundary. These were laid by command during the session; there had been no pressure by Parliamentary Addresses. Even Palmerston could have no better record than this, and his third term as Foreign Secretary (1846–51) shows him less certain in his publicity policy than during his first. He had to pass through difficult times and was not always at one with his public as he had once been.

The year 1847 began badly with a publication in *The Times* (4 January 1847) of Castlereagh's correspondence with the Tsar on Poland in 1814. H. U. Addington, the permanent Under-Secretary for Foreign Affairs, declared that the dispatches were in substance authentic though not copies of the originals. They were, therefore, printed for the Cabinet† and then published, in response to an Address in Parliament (*v.* No. 359). These just anticipated the publication of Castlereagh's private papers by the Marquis of Londonderry. Palmerston therefore suggested that the Foreign Office should censor them as these papers were 'in some degree of a public character'. Londonderry replied tartly, refusing to agree.

In 1848 there were further storms. The whole Blue-Book policy of Palmerston was arraigned by Mr Anstey in the Commons on 8 February 1848, and again on 23 February 1849. The *cause célèbre* of David Urquhart (*v. supra*, Nos. 225, 236 and 236*a*) was revived (*v.* No. 381) but Palmerston successfully resisted the publication of papers showing why

* Henry, Viscount Palmerston, was reappointed Secretary of State for Foreign Affairs on 6 July 1846. For his dismissal *v.* note on p. 123.

† *v.* F.O. 83/299. Hertslet 8 January 1847, H. U. Addington to Palmerston 4 January 1847, and subsequent correspondence of Palmerston with Londonderry beginning 31 January 1847.

Urquhart was relieved of his duties. He argued that the Crown's prerogative to dismiss its servants without cause assigned was not to be questioned by Parliament.

Palmerston was less communicative in regard to the affairs of Latin America than before. Thus it needed an Address to get him to publish a series of extracts (from 1824 to 1847) illustrating the policy of the British Government to Foreign Loans and British bondholders (v. No. 362). This particular publication was very nearly a perversion of the truth. For it tended to disguise the fact that Palmerston had bullied several countries a good deal in private in the interests of British bondholders. Spain had been the chief victim, but Spanish American States had suffered too.* Palmerston also directly refused information, as when he declined to lay papers on the Anglo-French blockade of the Rio de la Plata (14 February 1848).

The session of 1847–8 involved Palmerston in other difficulties. His unwisdom in advising Spain to adopt a liberal ministry and liberal principles had diverse and important results. Sir Henry Bulwer was handed his passports; Palmerston himself was impelled to publish an abundance of Parliamentary papers very near to the events described (Nos. 379–379e), and to face a fierce debate on them in the Commons.† His publication on Switzerland in 1847 (No. 380) was in the best Palmerstonian tradition. Those on Italy and Rome generally represented (Nos. 375, 377) his well-known view that Austrian rule in Italy was a weakness to her and that it would be better for her to surrender Lombardy to the Italian ruler of Piedmont. This was repeated *ad infinitum* in publications in 1849 (Nos. 391–394 c). It was much disapproved by Queen Victoria and by most of his colleagues, but doubtless did him good with the public.†

On the other hand, while Palmerston urged Austria to abandon her dominion in Italy, he pressed her to retain it in Hungary. This attitude was incomprehensible to British patriots who were anti-Austrian everywhere and always, because Austria was opposed to constitutions and constitutionalism. Palmerston admitted that, but none the less, in his

---

* v. Temperley and Penson, *Foundations of British Foreign Policy*, 300–2.
† Cp. Temperley and Penson, *Foundations of British Foreign Policy*, 164.

great speech of 21 July 1849, declared that Austria was 'an essential element' in the balance of European power, and that she must retain Hungary. In May 1849 Russia sent an army to assist Austria against the Hungarian rebels. Palmerston was urged to produce papers showing his attitude. He was asked to produce 'any communications which have passed involving naval or military aid or interference on the part of this country'.* He refused and said there were no such papers to produce. The fact is that he had not protested to Russia against her action in sending military aid to enable Austria to subdue the revolt in Hungary.† Palmerston was anti-Russian and for this reason he thought it better for Austria to have Russian aid in the reconquest of Hungary. He feared that, with so large a proportion of Slavs in her population, Hungary, independent and anti-Austrian, would become a satellite of the Slav Colossus.

Once we grasp Palmerston's doctrine that expediency demanded that Austria should retain and reconquer Hungary, even with Russian aid, the puzzle is solved. During the whole of 1848 only two brief notes referring to Hungary got into the Blue Books. The British Ambassador at Vienna (Lord Ponsonby) continually denounced Kossuth and the Hungarian revolutionaries, but Palmerston carefully excised all these passages from the Vienna dispatches as published. When, however, Blackwell, the British agent in Hungary, sent reports favourable to Kossuth and the Hungarian Revolution, suggesting British intervention on their behalf, these were also cut out. Remonstrances by Hungarian patriots on the 'perjured House of Lorraine-Habsburg' were also carefully suppressed. Palmerston tried to use public opinion to force Austria out of Lombardy, but he lent no countenance to the agitation for separating Hungary from Austria or establishing an independent Hungarian Republic.‡

---

* Hans. Deb. 3rd Ser. cvii, 786–817.

† v. the instruction to the British Ambassador at St Petersburgh in Temperley and Penson, Foundations of British Foreign Policy, 172.

‡ Sproxton, Palmerston and the Hungarian Revolution [1919], 60–1, 62 and note, 63 and note, 72 and note. Dr Temperley went through most of these Blue Books with the author and can confirm his statements. Cp. Temperley and Penson, Foundations of British Foreign Policy, 170–1.

Palmerston considered that Hungary and Austria must continue their uneasy union. He meant to do nothing, and did nothing, to imperil that. But he had hoped for a generous amnesty and for a substantial restoration of the old Hungarian parliament and constitution. He viewed with the deepest indignation the shooting of the thirteen generals, the execution of the hundred patriots, the floggings of noble women, the imprisonments, the persecutions. He was the more indignant because the suburbs of London and the towns of the North were indignant too. When, late in 1850, Kossuth came to England Palmerston, to the Queen's horror, listened with complacence to delegations and petitions which denounced the Emperors of Russia and Austria as 'odious and detestable murderers and assassins'. Then General Haynau or 'General Hyena', the man who had ordered executions and barbarities, first in Italy and then in Hungary, came to England. The manly hearts of the draymen of Messrs Barclay and Perkins were offended by the presence of this persecutor of bravery and innocence. They set upon him, maltreated him and tore his long yellow moustaches.* The Austrian Government protested indignantly. Palmerston, again to the Queen's disgust, hinted, in the midst of his apologies, at the 'impropriety' of such a man visiting England. The Hungarian papers were then published—both those relating to our policy in Hungary from 1847 to 1849 (No. 419) and those concerning General Haynau (No. 419 b). Palmerston had steered a very clever course between supporting Austria on the one hand, and Hungary on the other. But there were limits to the possibilities of publicity and also to the power of Palmerston to impose policies on the Queen and on Lord John Russell. He had nearly fallen over the Pacifico incident (No. 414) in 1850 but recovered himself with the *Civis Romanus sum* speech. The Queen had pointed out that General Haynau was entitled to the same protection in England that Palmerston claimed for Englishmen abroad. But it was not over Don Pacifico or

---

* What is remarkable is that General Haynau went later to live in Hungary as a country gentleman among the people whose relatives he had executed or imprisoned. It is still more remarkable that he was kindly received.

General Haynau that Palmerston was destined to fall. He fell in the end over his mistake in recognising the *coup d'état* of Napoleon without consulting Queen or Cabinet. About this there was no information in any Blue Book.

In so turbulent a period the private members and the majority of the Commons both exerted pressure on Palmerston to secure publicity. The chief instances of success in such demands are Nos. 373 *a*, 373 *c*, 395, 395 *c*, 403 *c*, 421–421 *c*, 437 (anti-slavery or anti-piracy); Nos. 376, 418 (American); Nos. 377, 416 (Papal); Nos. 378, 419 *b* (Austrian). Nos. 370, 413, 417 and 417 *a* exhibit humanitarian and missionary influences; while No. 381 was the result of the old personal quarrel between Palmerston and Urquhart. The extinction of the Republic of Cracow by Austria led to the re-publication of the extract from Castlereagh's famous State Paper of May 1820* (No. 356), which Canning (No. 119) had published in 1823.

* *v.* Temperley and Penson, *Foundations of British Foreign Policy*, 48–63.

Session 19 January to 23 July 1847

Volume LXVI (1847)

Slave Trade

354   Class B. Correspondence on the Slave Trade with Foreign Powers, Parties to Treaties under which Captured Vessels are to be tried by Mixed Tribunals [1 Jan.–31 Dec. 1846].   PAGE 1

     [855]   L/C. 20 July 1847.

354a   Class C. do., with Foreign Powers, Parties to Treaties and Conventions, under which Captured Vessels are to be tried by Tribunals of the Nation to which they belong [1 Jan.–31 Dec. 1846].   PAGE 339

     [856]   L/C. 20 July 1847.

354b   Class D. do., with Foreign Powers, not Parties to Treaties or Conventions, giving a mutual Right of Search of Vessels suspected of the Slave Trade [1 Jan.–31 Dec. 1846].   PAGE 425

     [857]   L/C. 20 July 1847.

Volume LXVII (1847)

Slave Trade

354c   Minutes of Evidence taken before the Duc de Broglie and the Right Hon. Stephen Lushington, D.C.L., March and April 1845, relative to the Right of Search.   PAGE 1

     [851]   L/C. HC. 23 July 1847.

Volume LXVIII (1847)

Portugal

355   Protocol of a Conference relating to the Affairs of Portugal held at the Foreign Office on 21 May 1847.   PAGE 1

     [823]   L/C. HC. 3 June, HL. 4 June 1847.

Volume LXIX (1847)

State Papers

Volume LXX (1847)

State Papers

HOUSE OF LORDS SESSIONAL PAPERS

VOLUME XVIII (1847)

State Correspondence, etc.

Session 18 November 1847 to 5 September 1848

Volume XLVIII (1847–8)

East India; China

Volume LXIV (1847–8)

Slave Trade

373*b* Treaty between Her Majesty and the Republic of the Equator, for the Abolition of the Traffic in Slaves, signed at Quito, 24th May 1841.   PAGE 85
[885]   L/C. HL. 23 Nov., HC. 25 Nov. 1847.

373*c* Correspondence between the Governments of Great Britain and the United States, relative to the General Abolition of Slavery in Texas, and throughout the World.   PAGE 125
136   R–A. (*HC. 15 Feb.*), HC. 29 Feb.,O.T.B.P. 1 Mar. 1848.

373*d* Class B. Correspondence on the Slave Trade with Foreign Powers, Parties to Treaties under which captured Vessels are to be tried by Mixed Tribunals [1 Jan. 1847–31 Mar. 1848].
                                                                  PAGE 487
[976]   L/C. HL. 18 July, HC. 19 July 1848.

373*e* Class C. do., with Foreign Powers, Parties to Treaties and Conventions under which captured Vessels are to be tried by Tribunals of the Nation to which they belong [1 Jan. 1847–31 Mar. 1848].   PAGE 859
[977]   L/C. HL. 18 July, HC. 19 July 1848.

373*f* Class D. do., with Foreign Powers, not Parties to Treaties or Conventions, giving a Mutual Right of Search of Vessels suspected of the Slave Trade [1 Jan. 1847–31 Mar. 1848].
                                                                  PAGE 927
[978]   L/C. HL. 18 July, HC. 19 July 1848.

VOLUME LXV (1847–8)

State Papers

374   Convention between Her Majesty and the King of Hanover for the establishment of International Copyright, signed at London, August 4, 1847.   PAGE 1
[889]   L/C. HL. 23 Nov., HC. 2 Dec. 1847.

374*a* Accession of the Grand Duke of Oldenburg to the above Convention. Signed at Hanover, December 28, 1847.   PAGE 11
[898]   L/C. 3 Feb. 1848.

375   *Italy:* Communication from the Austrian Government as to the Territorial Arrangements and Political Condition of Italy, together with the Reply of the British Government.   PAGE 19
[903]   L/C. HC. 10 Feb., HL. 11 Feb. 1848.

376   Correspondence respecting the Mosquito Territory.   PAGE 27
      [966]   *R–A.* (*HC. 3 Ap.*), HC. 3 July 1848.

377   *Papal States:* Representation made to the Roman Government
      by the Allied Powers in 1831, advising it to adopt certain Reforms
      and Improvements.   PAGE 179
      [918]   *R–A.* (*HC. 28 Feb.*), HC. 14 Mar. 1848.

378   Papers relative to the Claim of Mr. Rayson on the Austrian
      Government.   PAGE 185
      [905]   *R–A.* (*HC. 10 Feb.*), HC. 11 Feb. 1848.

379   *Spain:* Papers relative to certain Restrictions imposed by the
      Spanish Government on the Importation of Foreign Woollen
      and Cotton goods.   PAGE 211
      [920]   *L/C.* 20 Mar. 1848.

379*a* Correspondence between the British Government and the
      Government of Spain.   PAGE 221
      [935]   *L/C.* 5 May 1848.

379*b* Appendix to the above.   PAGE 233
      [936]   *L/C.* HC. 9 May, HL. 11 May 1848.

379*c* Papers relative to the Affairs of Spain, and Correspondence
      between Sir Henry Bulwer and the Duke of Sotomayor.
                                                      PAGE 237
      [946]   *L/C.* HC. 26 May, HL. 30 May 1848.

379*d* Despatch from Sir Henry Bulwer to Viscount Palmerston dated
      London, May 30, 1848.   PAGE 309
      [950]   *L/C.* 5 June 1848.

379*e* Correspondence between Viscount Palmerston and M. De
      Isturiz, relating to the Removal of Sir Henry Bulwer from
      Madrid.   PAGE 325
      [954]   *L/C.* HC. 6 June, HL. 16 June 1848.

380   *Switzerland:* Correspondence relative to the Affairs of Switzerland
      [1842–8].   PAGE 353
      [897]   *L/C.* 20 Dec. 1847.

381   Correspondence between Mr. Urquhart and Mr. Backhouse in
      the Years 1836, 1838 and 1839 (The Portfolio).   PAGE 681
      [959]   *R–A.* (*HC. 3 Ap.*), HC. 22 June 1848.

HOUSE OF LORDS SESSIONAL PAPERS

VOLUME XIX (1847–8)

State Correspondence, etc.

382   Further Communication from the Austrian Government as to
the Territorial Arrangements and Political Condition of Italy.
[*v. infra*, No. 394.]   PAGE 149

L/C. HL. 22 Aug. 1848.

382*a*   Copies and Extracts of Correspondence relative to the Intervention of the King of Sardinia in the Affairs of Lombardy.
[*v. infra*, No. 394*a*.]   PAGE 153

R–A. (*HL. 11 Ap.*), HL. 5 May 1848.

SESSION 1 FEBRUARY TO 1 AUGUST 1849

VOLUME LV (1849)

Slave Trade

383   Class B. Correspondence with British Ministers and Agents in
Foreign Countries and with Foreign Ministers in England,
relating to the Slave Trade [1 Ap. 1848–31 Mar. 1849].

PAGE 317

[1128]   L/C. HL. 30 July, HC. 31 July 1849.

VOLUME LVI (1849)

State Papers

384   Circular addressed by Viscount Palmerston to Her Majesty's
Representatives in Foreign States, respecting Debts due by
Foreign States to British subjects.   PAGE 1

[1049]   R–A. (*HC. 2 Ap.*), HC. 16 Ap. 1849.

385   Treaty of Friendship and Commerce between Her Majesty and
the Sultan of Borneo, signed May 27, 1847.   PAGE 5

[1014]   L/C. HL. 1 Feb., HC. 2 Feb. 1849.

386 Treaty of Friendship, Commerce, and Navigation between Her Majesty and the Republick of Guatemala, signed at Guatemala, February 20, 1849. PAGE 13

[1085] L/C. 18 June 1849.

387 *Moldavia and Wallachia:* Act between Turkey and Russia relative to the Principalities of Moldavia and Wallachia. PAGE 25

[1106] L/C. HL. 31 July, HC. 1 Aug. 1849.

388 *Schleswig and Holstein:* Preliminaries of Peace and Convention of Armistice concluded between the King of Denmark and the King of Prussia, Berlin, July 10, 1849. PAGE 33

[1105] L/C. HL. 30 July, HC. 31 July 1849.

389 *Slave Trade:* Additional Articles to the Treaty concluded at the Hague, May 4, 1818, between Great Britain and the Netherlands, for the Suppression of the Slave Trade, signed at the Hague, August 31, 1848. PAGE 49

[1013] L/C. HL. 1 Feb., HC. 2 Feb. 1849.

389a Treaty containing the Accession of Belgium to the Treaty signed at London, December 20, 1841, for the Suppression of the African Slave Trade, signed at London, February 24, 1848, with a Protocol relating thereto. PAGE 57

[1091] L/C. 28 June 1849.

390 *Naples and Sicily:* Account of all Ordnance Stores returned from that Department to any Contractor in the year 1848, for the Purpose of being sent to Sicily; with Correspondence between the Board of Ordnance and other Departments, with reference to the Transaction in question. PAGE 69

182 *Pursuant to Order (HC. 12 Mar.), R–A. (HC. 26 Mar.),* HC. 27 Mar., O.T.B.P. 28 Mar. 1849.

390a Despatch from Viscount Palmerston to the Hon. W. Temple, dated 26th January 1849, relative to a supply of Ordnance to the Provisional Government of Sicily. PAGE 73

[1045] R–A. (HC. 26 Mar.), HC. 27 Mar. 1849.

390b Correspondence relative to Atrocities alleged to have been committed by the Neapolitan Army in Sicily. PAGE 77

[1044] R–A. (HC. 27 Feb.), HC. 29 Mar., HL. 2 Ap. 1849.

390c Correspondence relating to Sicilian Affairs, 1814–1816 [*v. supra,* No. 71]. PAGE 193

[1058] R–A. (HL. 27 Ap.), 4 May 1849.

Session 31 January to 15 August 1850

Volume LV (1850)

Piracy; Slave Trade

Volume LVI (1850)

State Papers

398   *Liberia:* Treaty of Friendship and Commerce between Her
      Majesty and the Republic of Liberia, signed at London,
      November 21, 1848.   PAGE 21
         [1132]   *L/C.* 31 Jan. 1850.

399   *Prussia and Denmark (Schleswig and Holstein):* Extract of a Des-
      patch from the Earl of Westmorland, enclosing the Treaty of
      Peace between the King of Prussia and the King of Denmark,
      signed at Berlin, 2 July 1850.   PAGE 29
         [1258]   *R–A. (HC. 26 July)*, HC. 12 Aug., HL. 13 Aug.
                           1850.

400   *United States of America:* Convention between Her Majesty and
      the United States of America, relative to the Establishment of
      a Communication by Ship-Canal between the Atlantic and
      Pacific Oceans; signed at Washington, 19 April 1850.   PAGE 37
         [1264]   *L/C.* 15 Aug. 1850.

401   *Greece:* Correspondence respecting the Demands made upon
      the Greek Government, and respecting the Islands of Cervi and
      Sapienza [Oct. 1842–Aug. 1849].   PAGE 43
         [1157]   *L/C.* 22 Feb. 1850.

401 *a* Further Correspondence [18 Jan.–17 May 1850].   PAGE 407
         [1179]   *L/C.* 17 May 1850.

401 *b* do. [2 Ap.–22 May 1850].   PAGE 799
         [1209]   *L/C.* HC. 24 May, HL. 27 May 1850.

401 *c* do. [28–31 May 1850].   PAGE 827
         [1211]   *L/C.* 14 June 1850.

401 *d* do. [13, 14 June 1850].   PAGE 833
         [1226]   *L/C.* HC. 18 June, HL. 21 June 1850.

401 *e* do. [20, 22 June 1850].   PAGE 839
         [1230]   *L/C.* 24 June 1850.

401 *f* Correspondence respecting Mr. Finlay's claim upon the Greek
      Government [Aug. 1848–Oct. 1849].   PAGE 847
         [1233]   *L/C.* HC. 11 Ap., HL. 12 Ap. 1850.

402   *Spain:* Correspondence relating to the Renewal of Diplomatic
      Relations between Great Britain and Spain [30 Mar., 23 Ap.
      1850].   PAGE 859
         [1207]   *L/C.* 13 May 1850.

SESSION 4 FEBRUARY TO 8 AUGUST 1851

VOLUME LVI (1851)

Piracy; Slave Trade, Part I

403 Paper relating to the Piracies committed in the Indian Archipelago, and to the Measures adopted by the Netherlands Government, in the Years 1816 to 1845, for their Repression. PAGE 1

[1390] L/C. HC. 9 July, HL. 10 July 1851.

403a Additional Papers respecting the Operations against the Pirates on the North-West Coast of Borneo. PAGE 123

[1351] L/C. HC. 28 Ap., HL. 1 May 1851.

403b Copy of Instructions to Commander Farquhar, referred to in his Letter to Rear-Admiral Sir F. Collier, dated 25 August 1849; together with Copies of subsequent Despatches from the Admiralty to Sir F. Collier on the same subject. PAGE 145

53 Pursuant to Order (HC. 11 Feb.), HC. 14 Feb., O.T.B.P. 17 Feb. 1851.

403c Copies or Extracts of Despatches from the Officer commanding the 'Nemesis' War Steamer, and Officer commanding the British Forces; and also, from Sir Raja Brooke, of Sarawaak, respecting their Military Operations against alleged Pirates on the River Moratatias, and other Places in the Eastern Archipelago, in March and April 1849. PAGE 149

378 R–A. (HC. 8 Ap.), HC. 4 June, O.T.B.P. 6 June 1851.

VOLUME LVI (1851)

Slave Trade, Part II

404 Class B. Correspondence with British Ministers and Agents in Foreign Countries, and with Foreign Ministers in England, relating to the Slave Trade [1 Ap. 1850–31 Mar. 1851]. PAGE 1

[1424–II] L/C. 7 Aug. 1851.

VOLUME LVII (1851)

State Papers: Treaties and Conventions, Correspondence, etc.

412   *Sweden and Norway:* Convention between Her Majesty and the King of Sweden and Norway for the Regulation and Improvement of the Communications by Post between Great Britain and Sweden and Norway, signed at London, August 24, 1850.

PAGE 73

   [1299]   *L/C.* 4 Feb. 1851.

413   Correspondence respecting the British Protestant Chapel at Florence.   PAGE 97

   [1354]   *R–A. (HC. 5 May)*, HC. 8 May, HL. 9 May 1851.

414   *Greece:* Correspondence respecting the Mixed Commission appointed to investigate the Claims of M. Pacifico upon the Government of Greece, in regard to the Loss of Documents connected with his Claims upon the Portuguese Government.

PAGE 105

   [1415]   *L/C.* 7 Aug. 1851.

415   *Netherlands:* Laws of the Netherlands Government relaxing Restrictions on Trade with Holland and her Colonial Possessions.   PAGE 129

   [1385]   *R–A. (HC. 12 June)*, HL. 26 June, HC. 30 June 1851.

416   *Rome:* Correspondence respecting the Affairs of Rome, 1849.

PAGE 149

   [1363]   *R–A. (HC. 14 Ap.)*, 26 May 1851.

417   *Turkey:* Correspondence respecting the Condition of Protestants in Turkey, 1841–1851.   PAGE 271

   [1392]   *R–A. (HC. 27 Mar.)*, HC. 15 Ap., HL. 14 July 1851.

417*a*   Despatches from Her Majesty's Ambassador at Constantinople, communicating the Tariff settled between Great Britain and Turkey on the 31st October 1850, to be in force from January 1, 1847 to March 13, 1855.   PAGE 379

   [1350]   *R–A. (HC. 1 Ap.)*, HC. 15 Ap., HL. 2 May 1851.

418   Correspondence respecting the Light Dues levied on the Shipping of the United States in the United Kingdom.   PAGE 407

   [1320]   *R–A. (HC. 13 Feb.)*, HC. 28 Feb. 1851.

VOLUME LVIII (1851)

State Papers: Hungary

419   Correspondence relative to the Affairs of Hungary, 1847–1849.
PAGE 1
[1323]   *L/C.* 15 Aug. 1850.

419*a*   Correspondence respecting Refugees from Hungary within the Turkish Dominions.   PAGE 407
[1324]   *L/C.* 28 Feb. 1851.

419*b*   Correspondence respecting the Assault committed upon Marshal Haynau, on the occasion of his Visit to the Brewery of Messrs. Barclay and Perkins.   PAGE 547
[1319]   *R–A.* (*HC. 17 Feb.*), HC. 21 Feb. 1851.

VOLUME LIX (1851)

State Papers: Roman Catholics

420   Correspondence respecting the Relations existing between Foreign Governments and the Court of Rome [Dec. 1850–Feb. 1851].   PAGE 1
[1341]   *R–A.* (*HC. 18 Feb.*), 27 Mar. 1851.

420*a*   Further Correspondence [Mar., Ap. 1851].   PAGE 341
[1359]   *L/C.* 15 May 1851.

420*b*   do. [2 June 1851].   PAGE 411
[1379]   *L/C.* HC. 12 June, HL. 16 June 1851.

420*c*   do. No. IV [26 Ap. 1851: enc. 1743–1851].   PAGE 417
[1407]   *L/C.* HC. 31 July, HL. 1 Aug. 1851.

420*d*   Return of the Number of Addresses which have been presented to Her Majesty on the Subject of the recent Measures taken by the Pope for the Establishment of a Roman Catholic Hierarchy in this Country; with Statement of the Places, Corporations or Persons from whom the same have been received.... PAGE 649
84   *R–A.* (*HC. 5 Feb.*), HC. 24 Feb., O.T.B.P. 28 Feb. 1851.

420e   Copy of an Address presented to Her Majesty from Her Majesty's Roman Catholic Subjects in England, disclaiming any Intention of trenching upon the Royal Prerogative in the recent Appointment of a Roman Catholic Hierarchy, with the Number of Signatures attached.   PAGE 741

    236   R–A. (*HC. 15 Ap.*), HC. 28 Ap., O.T.B.P. 29 Ap. 1851.

SESSION 3 FEBRUARY TO 1 JULY 1852*

VOLUME XXXI (1852)

Colonies

421   *Borneo:* Letter from Mr. Wise, dated 26 April 1852, and Reply thereto.   PAGE 429

    [1537]   R–A. (*HC. 1 July*), HC.   1852,† R–A. (*HL. 9 Dec. 1852*), HL. 17 Feb. 1853.

421a   Correspondence respecting Mr. Burns.   PAGE 445

    [1462]   R–A. (*HC. 23 Mar.*), HC. 29 Mar. 1852, R–A. (*HL. 9 Dec. 1852*), HL. 17 Feb., O.T.B.P. 18 Mar. 1853.

421b   Further Correspondence respecting Piracy on the Coast of Borneo.   PAGE 473

    [1538]   R–A. (*HC. 30 June*), HC.   1852,† R–A. (*HL. 9 Dec. 1852*), HL. 17 Feb., O.T.B.P. 18 Mar. 1853.

421c   Further Papers respecting Mr. Burns.   PAGE 543

    [1536]   R–A. (*HC. 25 June*), HC.   1852,† R–A. (*HL. 9 Dec. 1852*), HL. 18 Mar. 1853.

* Granville George Leveson-Gower, Earl Granville, was appointed Secretary of State for Foreign Affairs on 26 December 1851. James Howard Harris, Earl of Malmesbury, was appointed Secretary of State for Foreign Affairs on 22 February 1852. After the fall of Palmerston in December 1851 there was no striking development in Blue-Book policy until Aberdeen became Prime Minister in December 1852.

† The date on which these papers were laid is not recorded in *C.J.* There is an entry on 1 July, the last day of the session, recording a resolution asking 'that all Papers presented to the House and ordered to be printed, shall, notwithstanding the Dissolution, be delivered to the Members of the present House of Commons'. *C.J.* CVII, 372.

VOLUME LIV (1852)

State Papers: Treaties and Conventions, etc.

VOLUME LV (1852)

State Papers: Austria, Rome, Turkey, Slave Trade

THE BLUE-BOOK POLICY OF CLARENDON*

1853–8

FOR a short period under the Aberdeen Government, Lord John Russell was Foreign Secretary. But, as he found this post incompatible with the leadership of the Commons, Lord Clarendon soon received the Foreign Office. He survived both Russell and Aberdeen and was continuously Foreign Secretary till 1858. Palmerston, though in the Government, was at the Home Office and a little in disgrace as a result of his fall in 1851. At first Aberdeen, as his private correspondence shows, exercised some influence over Clarendon. He pruned the dispatches considerably, and his influence is probably to be seen in the meagre output of diplomatic Blue Books during the session of 1853. As the autumn drew to its close the prospect of war with Russia came in sight, and Palmerston's influence over Clarendon grew. His resignation and return to the Government in December increased his power: war came early in 1854 and with it a spate of Blue Books. These were partly due to the fact that the Russians began publishing their own distorted version of affairs in the Press. Thus Clarendon writes to Aberdeen: 'I am afraid that the Petersburg [sic] Gazette will render it necessary to produce Seymour's despatches relating his confidential conversations with the [Russian] Emperor. I shall dislike doing this because we engaged to consider them secret but how shall we be able to resist the demand for them?' They were produced within the next week (17 March 1854, v. infra, No. 462).†

Clarendon, as this extract indicates, was more susceptible to popular pressure than Aberdeen. But, in any case, Palmerston with the advent of war was all powerful. In principle,

* Lord John Russell was appointed Secretary of State for Foreign Affairs on 28 December 1852. George, Earl of Clarendon was appointed on 21 February 1853 and held office until 27 February 1858.

† Brit. Mus. Pte Aberdeen Papers, Add. MSS. 43789, f. 14. Clarendon to Aberdeen, 11 March 1854.

though not always in detail, Clarendon was a Palmerstonian. He had almost as much direct connection with the Press. He had frequent interviews with the Editor of *The Times* and supplied him with much information. And, not being as strong as Palmerston, he was more and not less susceptible to public opinion and popular pressure. It is impossible to analyse as a whole the mass of information laid before Parliament in connection with the Crimean War, but certain points may be selected in detail. The British statement of the Origins of the War was contained in *Eastern Papers*, Parts 1–7 (*v. infra*, Nos. 460–463). These are a representative collection, but as Clarendon explained a little later there are 'excisions' to avoid hurting 'national susceptibilities'.* In this case, care was observed in relation to France. She was not friendly to us in 1852, but was our ally in January–March 1854 when all these seven papers saw the light. The volume of *Eastern Papers*, I (*infra*, No. 460), suppresses statements made by M. de la Valette, French Ambassador at Constantinople. What is suppressed is that de la Valette made it clear that a refusal of French demands about the Holy Places by Turkey 'involves war'.† When the papers were intended to show that Russia caused the war in 1854, it would not do to show that France threatened it in 1853.

Eastern Papers, II (*infra*, No. 460 a), omits some more comments unfavourable to France but also more surprisingly omits some comments unfavourable to Russia. The British Archives show that both the Tsar and Nesselrode admitted ignorance as to the provisions of the Treaty of Kutchuk-Kainardji (1774), though they so frequently used its clauses as an argument in the dispute. But Clarendon refrained from quoting these dispatches in public.‡ On the whole, Stratford de Redcliffe, the British Ambassador at Constantinople, does

---

* *v. The Times* of 6 May 1856. For details of some of these excisions *v.* H. Temperley, *England and the Near East. The Crimea* [1936], 312*, 326*, 339*, 346*, 362*, 364*, 372*, 379*, 478 (note 570).

† *v.* No. 460. *Eastern Papers*, I, No. 41 of 14 August 1852, and No. 48 of 1 October. Cp. the original dispatches of Colonel Hugh Rose, Nos. 50 and 92, under these dates in F.O. 78/893 in 894 respectively.

‡ F.O. 65/427. From Seymour to Clarendon, No. 263 of 31 May 1853; No. 292 of 16 June; No. 314 of 24 June.

not benefit by some of these omissions, obviously because he had differences with his home Government. Some omissions are made in his dispatch of 15 September 1853, in which he explained how he obtained naval protection for the British Embassy at Constantinople against a possible Turkish insurrection. He did this by smuggling up two British steamers 'under cover of steam communications',* and persuaded the French Ambassador to do the same. This action was a piece of sharp practice but not a violation of the Straits Convention of 1841, for all the four vessels were of the 'light' variety. But under Palmerston's lead, Clarendon had used another argument to Russia, viz. that a state of war had existed since July 1853, when Russian troops had crossed the Turkish frontier and occupied the Principalities. That action, he argued, rendered the Straits Convention no longer operative. As the Clarendon-Palmerston argument was not that used or believed by Stratford, Clarendon found it expedient to suppress this part of his dispatch.

Eastern Papers, III (No. 460 *b*), is concerned with the final stages before the War and like IV (No. 461) is not particularly important. *Eastern Papers*, v (No. 462), contains the famous conversations between Seymour and the Tsar. These, being published at a moment of excitement, were much misinterpreted and their meaning was distorted for the time and for posterity. The British public regarded the Tsar as tempting England by a share of the spoils to acquiesce in the partition of Turkey.† Sir Hamilton Seymour had indeed expressed suspicions of the Tsar's sincerity, but the British Government suppressed all references to these in the Blue Books. They had no intention of attacking the Tsar in this particular and only published his conversations because the Russian Government had already revealed some of them. The British Government did not question his sincerity in January and February 1853

---

* The published part of the dispatch is in No. 460 *a*, *Eastern Papers*, II, No. 114, of 15 September 1853. The suppressed passages have been published by V. J. Puryear, *England, Russia and the Straits question*, Univ. of California Press [1931], 445–6.

† *v.* further on this point Temperley and Penson, *Foundations of British Foreign Policy*, 134–5.

as shown in *Eastern Papers*, v (No. 462), but they maintained by their publication of documents in *Eastern Papers*, I–II (Nos. 460, 460 *a*), that he had gone back on his pledges of disinterestedness in July when his troops entered the Principalities. *Eastern Papers*, VI (No. 462 *a*), contains a Memorandum by Nesselrode referring, among other things, to a conversation between Aberdeen and the Tsar in 1844.* A letter from Aberdeen to Nesselrode was suppressed. But in neither this nor the preceding case do suppressions materially alter the sense. The construction put on these documents by the public was quite unwarranted and apparently unintended by the Government. But war propaganda, once assumed, becomes fixed in the popular mind as historic truth.†

It is unnecessary to detail the numerous documents published during 1854–5. Many of them dealt with the Vienna Conference of 1855 and, as Austria was a neutral, considerable excisions had to be made in the documents illustrating the course of the negotiations. Palmerston became Prime Minister in 1855. He took care not to allow anything to appear in writing in connection with his negotiations with Austria and France about presenting an ultimatum to Russia in January 1856.‡ The documents accompanying the Peace of Paris of 1856 (Nos. 509–509 *b*, 512, 523–523 *d*) are, however, fairly full. The protocols of the Conference of Paris (No. 509 *a*) were published owing to Clarendon's insistence and despite French opposition. The Triple Alliance, by which Austria, France and Great Britain agreed to defend Turkey against Russia (*v*. No. 523 *b*), signed on 15 April, was published on 2 May, owing to a premature disclosure. But it is curious that Palmerston had wished to make one of the articles of the Treaty secret.§ The insertion of secret articles in a Treaty and their

---

* *v.* Temperley and Penson, *Foundations of British Foreign Policy*, 134–5; and G. B. Henderson, 'The Seymour Conversations, 1853', *History*, XVIII, 244–7, October 1933.

† *Eastern Papers*, VII, *No.* 450, contains no very notable omissions.

‡ *v.* Temperley, *Journal of Modern History*, December 1932, 391–2. The ultimatum to Russia was presented by Austria alone, after a document had been drawn up and initialled by her and by France. Palmerston knew of its contents but did not initial it. He evidently feared questions in Parliament.

§ *v.* Temperley in *Journal of Modern History*, December 1932, 528. But for Article II there read Article III.

suppression in the version published at the time are exceedingly rare in English history.* It is difficult in fact to see how Parliament can be bound by the articles of a Treaty it has never seen.

Some very serious disputes took place between England and Russia during the autumn of 1856, which concerned the execution of the Treaty of Paris. It was during a recess of Parliament, so Palmerston alluded to them in speeches on the platform but published no papers until the crisis was over. Even then he only published the protocol settling the dispute (No. 532). Subsequently in the middle of the year very serious disputes arose between France and Russia on the one side and England and Austria on the other. This was in relation to Turkey and the Principalities and practically all information was withheld. Much information was, however, given in papers connected with Italy and Naples (e.g. Nos. 514, 530). Clarendon was more critical of the misgovernment of Naples than Palmerston himself.†

Clarendon produced a considerable amount of information referring to purely Turkish matters, that is as distinct from Russian. When the Kars papers came out (Nos. 523 *e*, 523 *f*) it was found that Stratford de Redcliffe had not answered a letter of General Williams, the defender of that fortress. It was held that this omission had been deleterious to the defence and it was fiercely criticised in Parliament. The publication also revealed the sordid tale of Turkish intrigue and corruption ending in the sacrifice of gallant men and the surrender of the fortress (Nos. 523 *f*, 523 *g*). A further publication emphasised Stratford's efforts to induce the Sultan to grant equality of status to Christians and to promote reform on western lines (Nos. 523, 523 *a*), and this timely revelation redeemed the reputation of the great British Ambassador. But no mention of the Franco-Russian attempts to bully Turkey over the Principalities in the middle of 1857 was made in the Blue Books.

---

* The Declaration between the United Kingdom and France respecting Egypt and Morocco, signed at London, 8 April 1904, contained secret articles. These were not published at the time but were revealed in 1911. *v.* Gooch and Temperley, *British Documents on the Origins of the War*, II, 385–98, and *infra*, pp. 498–9.

† *v.* Temperley and Penson, *Foundations of British Foreign Policy*, 58.

As regards Replies to Addresses the influence of the independent member is found in the following: Anti-American, Nos. 443 *a*, 508 *e*; Anti-Chinese, Nos. 526 *e*, *f*, *ij*, 533 *c*, *e*, *f*, *g*; Anti-Papal and Italian, Nos. 449, 449 *a*, 453, 485, 498; Anti-Russian, Nos. 467, 511; Anti-Austrian, Nos. 442, 476; Technical and mainly commercial, Nos. 455, 458–9, 481, 501–3, 516, 524, 543–4, 547 *d*, *e*, 549 *a*, *b*. The Ionian Isles (Nos. 441 and 441 *a*) were a case in which the bad relations of government and subjects were revealed owing to Parliamentary insistence.

The ministry, of which Palmerston had been head for three years, seemed stronger than ever in 1858. It ended suddenly and abruptly. Napoleon III only just escaped assassination at the hands of Orsini, an Italian political refugee from London. The bombs used for the purpose, like Orsini himself, had come from England. This circumstance raised at once an acrid controversy, and a French dispatch (No. 547 *b*) assumed so sharp a tone that Clarendon refused to give any direct answer to it (Nos. 547 *a*–547 *c*). None the less the majority in Parliament considered that Palmerston and Clarendon had truckled to France and turned them out of office. Stratford de Redcliffe happened to be in England at the time. He remarked with some humour that the White Paper which showed that he had not answered a dispatch had led to criticism of himself in the Crimea, but the White Paper revealing that Clarendon had not answered one had produced the fall of the Government.

Clarendon was to be Foreign Minister again on two occasions. But he never had so long a spell of office again and it may be useful here to quote his Apologia for publicity. In giving evidence before a Royal Commission three years later he declared: 'as to there being one set of Despatches written for the Minister really to act upon, and another set of Despatches to be laid before Parliament and the public;...such a notion is utterly and entirely without foundation....No important documents, nothing of that kind is ever sent in private letters.'*

---

* Clarendon's standpoint as to private letters is thus expressed in a letter to Stratford de Redcliffe: 'Private letters are only of use as commentaries upon despatches and to communicate matters which should be known without being publicly recorded.' (19 December 1856. *Pte Clar. Papers.*)

'I know that foreign Governments rather complain of our Blue Books,' he admitted, 'and to a certain extent they may curtail some of the communications that are made to our foreign Ministers. I should be extremely sorry to see our system of publication of diplomatic papers in any way curtailed or different from what it is.' He summed up thus: 'I believe that it is an immense advantage to this country that our despatches and diplomatic transactions should be known, because if they have the approbation of Parliament and of the country, the Government then has the whole weight of public opinion in its favour, and it is that which gives such strength to our policy and to our opinions in foreign countries....'* Clarendon, like Palmerston in 1843,† perhaps protested too much in his own favour. But in principle and in general he was for publicity in diplomacy.

* Diplomatic Service Select Committee (1861). Clarendon, §§ 990, 991, 1032. *v. infra*, No. 584.

† *v. supra*, p. 57.

Session 4 November 1852 to 20 August 1853

Volume XXXIX (1852–3)

Slave Trade Treaties, etc.

Volume LVII (1852–3)

Finance

Volume LXI (1852–3)

Navy

440 *b*   Correspondence between Lord Wodehouse and Sir James Brooke, on alleged Discrepancy between his 'Vindication' and his Deposition of 1849.   PAGE 333

281   L/C. HC. 18 Mar. 1853.

440 *c*   Further Papers.   PAGE 335

[1612]   L/C. HC. 4 Ap. 1853.

440 *d*   Correspondence respecting Piracy in the Eastern Archipelago, and the Proceedings of Sir James Brooke.   PAGE 343

[1599]   R–A. (*HC. 14, 20 Dec. 1852*), HC. 22 Feb., HL. 8 Mar. 1853.

Volume LXII (1852–3)

Colonies; Ionian Islands

441   *Ionian Islands:* Copies of the Correspondence between Sir John Pakington, Bart., Secretary for the Colonies, and Sir Henry Ward, Lord High Commissioner of the Ionian Islands, since February 1852...including the Correspondence with the banished Members of the Legislative Assembly of the Ionian Islands, respecting the Terms proposed to them for their Liberation from Exile; and, of the Protest by the same respecting the Prorogation of the newly-elected Assembly at its first meeting.
                                                        PAGE 571

226   R–A. (*HC. 2 Dec. 1852*), HC. 11 Mar. 1853.

441 *a*   Copies or Extracts of Papers relating to the Discontinuance of the Payment of Salary to the Chevalier Mustoxidi; and Papers and Documents relating to the removal of Ionian Judges.
                                                        PAGE 755

772   R–A. (*HC. 3 May*), HC. 14 July 1853.

Volume CII (1852–3)

State Papers, Slaves

442   Further Correspondence respecting the expulsion of Messrs. Edward, Wingate and Smith from the Austrian Dominions [*v. supra*, No. 435].   PAGE 1

[1577]   R–A. (*HC. 7 Dec.*), HC. 20 Dec. 1852.

442 *a* Correspondence respecting the arrest of Mr. Harwood by the Austrian Authorities, 1852–1853.   PAGE 19

[1597]   *L/C.* HL. 21 Feb., HC. 22 Feb. 1853.

443   *Chile:* Convention between Her Majesty and the Republic of Chile for the Reciprocal Abrogation of Differential duties; signed at Santiago de Chile, 10 May, 1852.   PAGE 273

[1586]   *L/C.* 10 Feb. 1853.

443 *a*   *Cuba:* Correspondence between the United States, Spain and France, concerning alleged Projects of Conquest, and Annexation of the Island of Cuba.   PAGE 279

[1664]   *R–A. (HC. 11 Ap.),* HC. 1 Aug. 1853.

444   *Denmark:* Papers relative to the Succession to the Throne of Denmark.   PAGE 369

[1675]   *L/C.* 20 Aug. 1853.

445   Treaty of Friendship, Commerce and Navigation between Her Majesty and the Republic of the Equator, signed at Quito, 3 May, 1851.   PAGE 381

[1649]   *L/C.* HL. 4 July, HC. 5 July 1853.

446   *Greece:* Treaty relative to the Succession to the Crown of Greece, signed at London, 20 November, 1852.   PAGE 391

[1587]   *L/C.* 10 Feb. 1853.

447   *Peru:* Treaty of Friendship, Commerce and Navigation between Her Majesty and the Republic of Peru, signed. at London, 10 April, 1850.   PAGE 403

[1540]   *L/C.* 11 Nov. 1852.

447 *a*   Convention between Her Majesty and the Republic of Peru for the Regulation of the Mail Communication between Great Britain and Peru, signed at Lima, 13 August, 1851.   PAGE 417

[1541]   *L/C.* 11 Nov. 1852.

448   Accession of the Duke of Anhalt to the Convention concluded 13 May, 1846, between Great Britain and Prussia, for the Establishment of International Copyright; signed at Berlin, 8 February, 1853.   PAGE 429

[1598]   *L/C.* HC. 22 Feb., HL. 28 Feb. 1853.

VOLUME CIII, PART I (1852–3)

Consuls; Slave Trade

455   Return of all Consuls-General, Consuls, and Salaried Vice-Consuls, with the amount of their salaries; of the Fees received by them in the Years 1849, 1850, 1851 and 1852 respectively, and of any other Salary or Emolument; specifying whether the Consulate is a Trading Consulate or not, and the Country of which each Consul is a Native.   PAGE 1

    0.1   *R–A. (HC. 12 Ap.)*, HC. 19 Aug. 1853.

VOLUME CIII, PART II (1852–3)

Slave Trade

456   Class B. Correspondence with British Ministers and Agents in Foreign Countries, and with Foreign Ministers in England [1 Ap. 1851–31 Mar. 1852].   PAGE 1

    0.3   *L/C.* HC. 7 Dec., HL. 13 Dec. 1852.

VOLUME CIII, PART III (1852–3)

Slave Trade

456*a*   Class B. Correspondence with British Ministers and Agents in Foreign Countries, and with Foreign Ministers in England [1 Ap. 1852–31 Mar. 1853].   PAGE 203

    0.5   *L/C.* 19 Aug. 1853.

Session 31 January to 12 August 1854

Volume XXXIX (1854)

Finance

Volume LXV (1854)

Trade and Navigation

Volume LXIX (1854)

Miscellaneous

VOLUME LXXI (1854)

Eastern Papers

460   Correspondence respecting the rights and privileges of the Latin
        and Greek Churches in Turkey [May 1850–July 1853]. Part I.
                                                              PAGE 1
        [1698]   *L/C.* 31 Jan. 1854.

460*a*   do. [July 1853–Jan. 1854]. Part II.   PAGE 417
        [1699]   *L/C.* 31 Jan. 1854.

460*b*   do. [16 Jan.–7 Feb. 1854]. Part III.   PAGE 811
        [1709]   *L/C.* 10 Feb. 1854.

461   Instructions [23, 24 Feb. 1854] of the British and French
        Governments for the joint protection of British and French
        Subjects and Commerce. Part IV.   PAGE 823
        [1721]   *L/C.* 28 Feb. 1854.

462   Communications respecting Turkey made to Her Majesty's
        Government by the Emperor of Russia, with the answers
        returned to them, January to April, 1853 [Seymour Conversa-
        tions]. Part V.   PAGE 833
        [1736]   *L/C.* 17 Mar. 1854.

462*a*   Memorandum by Count Nesselrode delivered to Her Majesty's
        Government, and founded on Communications received from
        the Emperor of Russia subsequently to His Imperial Majesty's
        Visit to England in June, 1844. Part VI.   PAGE 863
        [1737]   *L/C.* 17 Mar. 1854.

463   Correspondence respecting the rights and privileges of the Latin
        and Greek Churches in Turkey [15 Jan.–27 Mar. 1854].
        Part VII.   PAGE 871
        [1744]   *L/C.* 28 Mar. 1854.

464   Protocol signed at Vienna on 9 April 1854, by the Representa-
        tives of Austria, France, Great Britain, and Prussia. Part VIII.
                                                         PAGE 965
        [1756]   *L/C.* 27 Ap. 1854.

464*a*   do., signed on 23rd May 1854 by the same. Part IX.
                                                         PAGE.971
        [1782]   *L/C.* 1 June 1854.

464b Additional Article to the Treaty between Austria and Prussia, dated 30 April 1854. Part X.   PAGE 981

        [1794]   R–A. (*HC. 22 June*), 30 June 1854.

465 Correspondence respecting the rights and privileges of the Latin and Greek Churches in Turkey. Part XI.   PAGE 987

        [1826]   L/C. 12 Aug. 1854.

466 Convention between Austria and the Sublime Porte, signed at Boyadji Keny, on the 14th June 1854. [Occupation of the Principalities.] Part XII.   PAGE 997

        [1828]   L/C. 12 Aug. 1854.

VOLUME LXXII (1854)

State Papers

467 *Treaty of Adrianople:* Despatch [31 Oct. 1829] from the Earl of Aberdeen to Lord Heytesbury, respecting the Treaty of Peace between Russia and Turkey concluded at Adrianople on the 14th September 1829.   PAGE 1

        347   R–A. (*HL. 26 June*), HL. 26 June, R–A. (*HC. 30 June*), HC. 4 July, O.T.B.P. 5 July 1854.

468 Treaty between Her Majesty and the Argentine Confederation for the Free Navigation of the Rivers Parana and Uruguay, signed at San José de Flores, July 10, 1853.   PAGE 7

        [1773]   L/C. 15 May 1854.

469 Papers relative to Borneo, and the Commission of Inquiry respecting Sir James Brooke.   PAGE 15

        [1771]   L/C. 8 May 1854.

470 Convention between Her Majesty and the Free Hanseatic City of Hamburgh, for the Establishment of International Copyright, signed at Hamburgh, August 16, 1853.   PAGE 83

        [1700]   L/C. 31 Jan. 1854.

471 *France:* Convention between Her Majesty and the Emperor of the French, relative to the Military Aid to be given to Turkey, signed at London, 10 April, 1854.   PAGE 95

        [1757]   L/C. HC. 27 Ap., HL. 23 May 1854.

472   Treaty between Her Majesty, the Emperor of the French, and
      the Sultan, relative to the Military Aid to be given to Turkey,
      signed at Constantinople, March 12, 1854.   PAGE 101
      [1775]   *L/C.* 23 May 1854.

473   Treaty of Friendship, Commerce and Navigation between Her
      Majesty and the Republic of Paraguay, signed at Assumption,
      March 4, 1853.   PAGE 119
      [1701]   *L/C.* 31 Jan. 1854.

474   *Russia and Turkey:* Treaties, Political and Territorial, between
      Russia and Turkey, 1774–1849.   PAGE 131
      [1735]   *L/C.* 17 Mar. 1854.

475   Her Majesty's Declarations, Proclamations and Orders in
      Council, etc. with reference to the Commencement of Hostilities
      against the Emperor of All the Russias.   PAGE 213
      [1762]   *L/C.* 28 Ap. 1854.

476   *Servia:* Memorandum addressed by the Servian Government to
      the Sublime Porte, respecting the Occupation of that Principality
      by Austrian troops [5/17 Ap. 1854].   PAGE 237
      [1800]   *R–A. (HC. 22 June),* HC. 6 July, HL. 7 July
      1854.

477   *Spain:* Decrees signed by the Queen of Spain on the 22nd March,
      1854, respecting Slavery in the Island of Cuba.   PAGE 245
      [1784]   *L/C.* HC. 8 June, HL. 9 June 1854.

478   *Greece and Turkey:* Correspondence respecting the Relations
      between Greece and Turkey [Mar. 1853–May 1854].
                                                        PAGE 289
      [1781]   *L/C.* 1 June 1854.

479   Correspondence respecting the condition of Protestants in
      Turkey [Mar. 1853–Mar. 1854].   PAGE 587
      [1752]   *R–A. (HL. 10 Mar.),* 4 Ap. 1854.

480   *Denmark, Sweden and Norway:* Correspondence relative to the
      Neutrality of Denmark, Sweden and Norway [2 Jan.–20 Jan.
      1854].   PAGE 601
      [1711]   *L/C.* 16 Feb. 1854.

481   Correspondence with the Peruvian Government respecting the
      importation of Guano, 1852–53.   PAGE 611
      [1740]   *R–A. (HC. 14 Feb.),* HC. 20 Mar. 1854.

VOLUME LXXIII (1854)

Slave Trade

SESSION 12 DECEMBER 1854 TO 14 AUGUST 1855

VOLUME LV (1854–5)

State Papers

488   Convention between Her Majesty and the King of the Belgians for the Establishment of International Copyright, signed at London, 12 August 1854.   PAGE 9

[1872]   L/C. HL. 29 Jan., HC. 1 Feb. 1855.

489   *France:* Convention between Her Majesty and the Emperor of the French additional to the Convention of 3 April, 1843, relative to Post Office arrangements, signed at Paris, 12 December 1854.   PAGE 23

[1857]   L/C. 23 Jan. 1855.

490   Convention between Her Majesty and the Emperor of the French relative to the Establishment of a line of Electric Telegraph between Bucharest and Varna, signed at London, 1 February 1855.   PAGE 31

[1886]   L/C. 1 Mar. 1855.

491   Convention between Her Majesty and the Emperor of the French relative to Supplies to be furnished to the Turkish Army, signed at London, 24 January 1855.   PAGE 37

[1887]   L/C. 1 Mar. 1855.

491 a   Convention between Her Majesty and the Emperor of the French respecting Prisoners of War, signed at London, 10 May 1854.   PAGE 43

[1862]   L/C. 12 Dec. 1854.

492   *Turkey:* Convention between Her Majesty, the Emperor of the French and the Sultan, for the Guarantee of a Loan to be raised by the Sultan, signed at London, 27 June 1855.   PAGE 49

[1961]   L/C. 17 July 1855.

493   Declaration exchanged between the British and French Governments relative to the Turkish Loan, signed at London, 27 July 1855.   PAGE 57

[1968]   L/C. 31 July 1855.

494   *Eastern Papers:* Papers relating to the Negotiation at Vienna on the Eastern Question [Dec. 1854–Ap. 1855]. Part XIII.

PAGE 63

[1924]   L/C. HL. 8 May, HC. 9 May 1855.

494a   Abstract of the above papers.   PAGE 155

251   HC. O.T.B.P. 17 May 1855.

494b   Paper relating to the Negotiation at Vienna on the Eastern Question. Part XIV.   PAGE 199

[1939]   L/C. HL. 12 June, HC. 13 June 1855.

494c   Abstract of the above Paper.   PAGE 211
       310   HC. O.T.B.P. 14 June 1855.

494d   Communications with the Austrian Government [3 Ap.–19 June
       1855]. Part XV.   PAGE 217
       [1959]   *L/C.* 12 July 1855.

494e   Instructions [22 Feb. 1855] to Lord John Russell on proceeding
       to Vienna. Part XVI.   PAGE 265
       [1964]   *L/C.* 24 July 1855.

495   *Sardinia:* Acts and Conventions relative to the Co-operation of
       His Majesty the King of Sardinia in the War, signed at Turin,
       26 January 1855.   PAGE 271
       [1895]   *L/C.* 15 Mar. 1855.

495a   Convention between Her Majesty and the King of Sardinia for
       the Reciprocal Opening of the Coasting Trade, signed at Turin,
       9 August 1854.   PAGE 285
       [1905]   *L/C.* 29 Mar. 1855.

496   *Turkey:* Convention between Her Majesty and the Sultan, for
       the Employment of a body of Turkish Troops in the British
       Service, signed in the English and Turkish languages at Con-
       stantinople, 3 February 1855.   PAGE 291
       [1906]   *L/C.* 29 Mar. 1855.

497   *Tuscany:* Convention between Her Majesty and the Grand Duke
       of Tuscany for the Reciprocal Opening of the Coasting Trade,
       signed at Florence, 30 Dec. 1854.   PAGE 297
       [1884]   *L/C.* 26 Feb. 1855.

498   Correspondence relating to the recent case of the imprisonment
       of Miss Cunninghame at Florence [23 Sept.–21 Dec. 1853].*
                                                             PAGE 303
       0.10   *R–A. (HC. 13 Feb.),* 24 Mar. 1854.

499   *U.S.A.:* Convention between Her Majesty and the United States
       of America, extending the Term allowed for the Operations of
       the Mixed Commission established under the Convention of
       8 February, 1853, for the Mutual Settlement of Claims, signed
       at Washington, 17 July 1854.   PAGE 361
       [1860]   *L/C.* 12 Dec. 1854.

* For the case of Miss Cunninghame, *v.* B. Kingsley Martin, *The Triumph of Lord
Palmerston* [1924], 152–3 n.

500   Treaty between Her Majesty and the United States of America relative to Fisheries, Commerce and Navigation, signed at Washington, 5 June 1854.   PAGE 367

     [1861]   *L/C.* 12 Dec. 1854.

501   Copy of the present Postal Engagements agreed to between the United States and England, and of the correspondence for the Modification of the present Agreements.   PAGE 375

     0.35   *Pursuant to Order (HC. 16 May)*, HC. 11 Aug. 1854.

502   Correspondence respecting the Sound Dues [3 July 1854].
                                                                     PAGE 507

     0.2   *R–A. (HC. 16 Feb.)*, HC. 7 Mar. 1855.

503   Correspondence with the French Government relating to the Channel Fisheries [Ap. 1852–Mar. 1855].   PAGE 561

     0.6   *R–A. (HC. 8 June)*, HC. 13 July 1855.

504   Copies and Extracts of dispatches from Her Majesty's Ministers at Foreign Courts, on the subject of admitting British Shipping to the Coasting Trade [1853–5].   PAGE 581

     0.9   *L/C.* 14 Aug. 1855.

504*a*   Abstract of Reports of the Trade of Various Countries and Places, for the year 1854, received by the Board of Trade (through the Foreign Office) from Her Majesty's Ministers and Consuls.   PAGE 601

     [2007]   *L/C.* HL. 9 Aug., HC. 10 Aug. 1855.

VOLUME LVI (1854–5)

Slave Trade

505   Class B. Correspondence with British Ministers and Agents in Foreign Countries, and with [Foreign] Ministers in England, relating to the Slave Trade [1 Ap. 1854–31 Mar. 1855].
                                                                     PAGE 179

     0.4   *L/C.* 30 July 1855.

505*a*   Copies of Treaties with Native Chiefs of the Sherbro Country for the Suppression of the Slave Trade.   PAGE 899

        406   *L/C.* HC. 13 July, HL. 17 July, O.T.B.P. HC. 20 July 1855.

HOUSE OF LORDS SESSIONAL PAPERS

VOLUME XVII (1854–5)

War with Russia

506　Circular addressed by Her Majesty's Ambassador at Constantinople to Her Majesty's Consuls in Turkey, dated 20th November 1854. PAGE 215

R–A. (HL. 20 Ap.), HL. 7 May 1855.

SESSION 31 JANUARY TO 29 JULY 1856

VOLUME LVIII (1856)

Diplomatic Service, etc.

507　Names of all Persons employed in the Diplomatic Service as Ambassadors, Envoys, Ministers, Chargés d'Affaires, Secretaries of Embassy, or Secretaries of Legation, Paid Attachés, and the Countries where so employed; stating the Period of Absence of each Officer in each year, during the last Ten Years, from his post. PAGE 361

166　*R–A. (HC. 27 Feb. 1855),* HC. 18 Ap., O.T.B.P. 21 Ap. 1856.*

VOLUME LX (1856)

State Papers (United States)

508　Correspondence with the United States, respecting Central America. PAGE 1

[2052]　*L/C.* 24 Ap. 1856.

508a　Further Correspondence [24 May, 26 June 1856]. PAGE 317

[2107]　*L/C.* 26 June 1856.

* A similar return was made to the House of Lords on 21 July 1856, containing particulars of dates of appointment and promotion. *House of Lords Sessional Papers,* XXII (1856), 105.

VOLUME LXI (1856)

State Papers

511 *Danish Succession:* Copy of the Protocol of Warsaw, relative to the Danish Succession, and of the Renewal of that Document by Russia in 1852. PAGE 173

    58   *R–A.* (*HC. 18 Feb.*), HC. 21 Feb., O.T.B.P. 22 Feb. 1856.

512 Declaration exchanged between the British and French Governments, relative to the Division of Trophies and Booty, signed at Paris, July 10, 1855, with the Accession of the Ottoman and Sardinian Governments thereto, signed at London, November 15, 1855. PAGE 177

    [2010]   *L/C.* 31 Jan. 1856.

513 *France:* Convention between Her Majesty and the Emperor of the French relative to the Reciprocal Transmission of Printed Papers by Post, signed at Paris, December 10, 1855. PAGE 183

    [2012]   *L/C.* 31 Jan. 1856.

514 *Italy:* Correspondence with Sardinia, respecting the state of Affairs in Italy [1856]. PAGE 193

    [2093]   *L/C.* 5 June 1856.

515 *Japan:* Convention between Her Majesty and the Emperor of Japan, signed at Nagasaki in the English and Japanese Languages, October 14, 1854. PAGE 207

    [2014]   *L/C.* 31 Jan. 1856.

515*a* Correspondence respecting the late Negotiation with Japan. PAGE 215

    [2077]   *L/C.* 2 May 1856.

516 Treaty between Austria, Modena, and Parma, signed at Milan, July 3, 1849; and Accession of the Pope thereto, signed at Portici, February 12, 1850, relative to the Navigation of the River Po. PAGE 237

    0.11   *R–A.* (*HC. 4 June*), HC. 20 June 1856.

517 *Netherlands:* Convention between Her Majesty and the King of the Netherlands, for the Reciprocal Admission of Consuls of the one Party to the Colonies and Foreign Possessions of the other, signed at the Hague, March 6, 1856. PAGE 251

    [2081]   *L/C.* 6 May 1856.

518 Convention between Her Majesty and the King of Prussia, additional to the Convention concluded at Berlin, May 13, 1846, for the Establishment of International Copyright; signed at London, June 14, 1855. PAGE 263

    [2013]   *L/C.* 31 Jan. 1856.

519   *Sardinia:* Convention between Her Majesty and the King of
      Sardinia respecting the Advance of a Million sterling, contem-
      plated by the Convention of January 26, 1855, signed at Turin,
      June 3, 1856.   PAGE 271
      [2100]   *L/C.* 12 June, HL. 16 June 1856.

520   Correspondence relative to the Sound Dues.   PAGE 277
      [2099]   *L/C.* HC. 10 June, HL. 12 June 1856.

521   *Sweden and Norway:* Treaty between Her Majesty, the Emperor
      of the French, and the King of Sweden and Norway, signed at
      Stockholm, November 21, 1855.   PAGE 327
      [2009]   *L/C.* 31 Jan. 1856.

522   *Swiss Confederation:* Treaty of Friendship, Commerce and
      Reciprocal Establishment, between Her Majesty and the Swiss
      Confederation, signed at Berne, September 6, 1855. PAGE 333
      [2041]   *L/C.* HL. 11 Mar., HC. 13 Mar. 1856.

523   *Turkey (Eastern Papers):* Firman and Hatti-Sherif, by the Sultan,
      relative to Privileges and Reforms in Turkey. Part XVII.
                                                       PAGE 343
      [2040]   *L/C.* HC. 10 Mar., HL. 11 Mar. 1856.

523*a* Correspondence respecting Christian Privileges in Turkey.
      Part XVIII.   PAGE 353
      [2069]   *L/C.* 24 Ap. 1856.

523*b* Treaty between Her Majesty, the Emperor of Austria, and the
      Emperor of the French, guaranteeing the Independence and
      Integrity of the Ottoman Empire, signed at Paris, April 15,
      1856 [*v. infra*, No. 975 *ij*].   PAGE 441
      [2076]   *L/C.* 2 May 1856.

523*c* Convention between Her Majesty, the Emperor of the French,
      and the King of Sardinia, on the one part, and the Sultan on
      the other, extending the term previously stipulated for the
      Evacuation of the Ottoman Empire; signed at Constantinople,
      May 13, 1856. [Ratifications exchanged at London, 16 Jan.
      1856.]   PAGE 447
      [2112]   *L/C.* 3 July 1856.

523*d* Convention containing the Accession of the Ottoman Porte and
      Sardinia to the Convention concluded between Great Britain
      and France, May 10, 1854, relative to Joint Captures; signed at
      London, November 15, 1855.   PAGE 453
      [2011]   *L/C.* 31 Jan. 1856.

VOLUME LXII (1856)

Slave Trade

152

VOLUME XII (1857)

China

VOLUME XVIII (1857)

State Papers

2ND SESSION 30 APRIL TO 28 AUGUST 1857

VOLUME XLIII (1857)

State Papers

VOLUME XLIV (1857)

Slave Trade

THE BLUE-BOOK POLICY OF MALMESBURY*

1858–9

MALMESBURY showed marked reluctance to publish the decisions made by the Great Powers at a Conference held at Paris in the summer of 1858 for the settlement of the Principalities of Moldavia and Wallachia. A Convention was ultimately signed on 19 August 1858. Malmesbury, as well as Cowley, the British Ambassador at Paris, successfully protested against the publication of the protocols of the Conference. Walewski, the French Foreign Minister, was in favour of publicity perhaps because the protocols had in fact been published pretty accurately in a Brussels newspaper.†️ Malmesbury, in supporting the prohibition, went back on the more liberal policy of Clarendon who had insisted on publishing the protocols of the Conference of 1856 (v. supra, No. 509 a). Even the text of the Convention was not published until 3 February 1859 (v. No. 554).‡️ Otherwise there is little to note except that Parliament by Address extracted a copy of Treaties, political and territorial, with Austria from 1815 to 1848 (No. 552), and 'Copies of such Parts of all Treaties and Conventions now existing and still obligatory, as contain an Engagement of Guarantee' (No. 562). In publishing the latter Malmesbury included the Treaty of Alliance of 1856 (v. supra, No. 523 b) between Austria, France and Great Britain in the list, although Austria and France were in fact at war with one another.

* Appointed Secretary of State for Foreign Affairs on 28 February 1858.
† Cp. Malmesbury, *Memoirs of an Ex-Minister* [1885], 442, 444, where private letters are printed of 30 July and 8 August 1858; cp. also F.O 27/1257, from Cowley, No. 1087 of 19 August 1858.
‡ The protocols are printed in *B.F.S.P.*, XLVIII, 81–132 (Protocols 1–19), XLIX, 454–9 (Protocols 20–2), v. infra, Nos. 554 a and b.

Session 3 December 1857 to 2 August 1858

Volume XXXIV (1857–8)

Finance: Banking, Revenue, etc.

540 Sums paid or advanced by way of Loan, Subsidy or otherwise, to any Foreign State, from the Year 1854 up to the present Time, arranged Alphabetically, showing the Total Amount now owing by each.   PAGE 145

  320 *Pursuant to Order (HC. 4 May)*, HC. 7 June, O.T.B.P. 8 June 1858.

540*a* *Sardinian Loan*: Total Sums issued up to the 31st December 1857, out of the Consolidated Fund, and advanced to His Majesty the King of Sardinia, by virtue of the Acts 18 Victoria, cap. 17, and 19 and 20 Victoria, cap. 39; and also of the Sums received from the Sardinian Government for Interest and Sinking Fund in respect thereof in the same Period. PAGE 409

  80 *Pursuant to Act*, 11 Feb., O.T.B.P. HC. 15 Feb. 1858.

Volume LIX (1857–8)

State Papers: Naples and Sardinia

541 Papers relative to the Imprisonment of the Engineers, Watt and Park, at Salerno [Nov. 1857].   PAGE 1

  [2296] *L/C.* HC. 10 Dec., HL. 12 Dec. 1857.

541*a* Correspondence respecting the 'Cagliari' [July 1857–Mar. 1858].   PAGE 7

  [2341] *L/C.* 26 Mar. 1858.

541*b* Appendix to the above Correspondence. PAGE 155

  [2347] *L/C.* 26 Mar. 1858.

541*c* Further Correspondence [Ap. 1858]. PAGE 399

  [2361] *L/C.* 22 Ap. 1858.

VOLUME LX (1857–8)

State Papers

  * This paper is missing from the set of Parliamentary Papers in the British Museum, but is available in the set in the Cambridge University Library.

VOLUME LXI (1857–8)

Slave Trade

1ST SESSION 3 FEBRUARY TO 19 APRIL 1859

VOLUME XXVII (1859)

Slave Trade; State Papers

* Papers laid on this subject in later sessions are omitted, as they are not diplomatic
in character.

553   *Brazil:* Convention between Her Majesty and the Emperor of
      Brazil for the Settlement of outstanding Claims by a Mixed
      Commission, signed at Rio de Janeiro, 2 June 1858.   PAGE 71
         [2455]   *L/C.* 3 Feb. 1859.

554   *Moldavia and Wallachia:* Convention between Great Britain,
      Austria, France, Prussia, Russia, Sardinia, and Turkey, relative
      to the Organisation of the Principalities of Moldavia and
      Wallachia, signed at Paris, 19 August 1858.   PAGE 81
         [2454]   *L/C.* 3 Feb. 1859.

      554*a* [Protocols of Conferences between Austria, France, Great Britain,
            Prussia, Russia, Sardinia, and Turkey, relative to the Organisa-
            tion of the Principalities of Moldavia and Wallachia. May–
            August, 1858.
               B.F.S.P., XLVIII (1857–8), 81–132.

      554*b* Protocols of Conferences...relative to the Organisation of the
            Principalities of Moldavia and Wallachia. April–September,
            1859.
               B.F.S.P., XLIX (1858–9), 454–9.]

555   Correspondence with Her Majesty's Chargé d'Affaires in Peru
      as to Price of Guano.   PAGE 107
         [2464]   *L/C.* HL. 10 Feb., HC. 11 Feb. 1859.

555*a* Correspondence with the Agent of the Peruvian Government
      respecting the same.   PAGE 113
         [2492]   *L/C.* 15 Ap. 1859.

556   Correspondence respecting the Charles et Georges. [Mozam-
      bique, Portugal.]   PAGE 119
         [2468]   *L/C.* 18 Feb. 1859.

556*a* Further Papers [30 Mar. 1859].   PAGE 201
         [2488]   *L/C.* 7 Ap. 1859.

557   *Russia:* Treaty of Commerce and Navigation between Her
      Majesty and the Emperor of All the Russias, with three separate
      Articles thereunto annexed, signed at St Petersburgh, 12 January,
      1859.   PAGE 205
         [2453]   *L/C.* 3 Feb. 1859.

THE BLUE-BOOK POLICY OF PALMERSTON AND RUSSELL 1859–65 AND OF RUSSELL AND CLARENDON 1865–6*

THE features of this period are broadly the same as those of the years 1853–8, of which the Blue-Book policy has already been described (*v. supra*, pp. 127–33). But publication was even more abundant, and perhaps more courted, by Russell than by Palmerston. Even over so delicate a question as that of Schleswig-Holstein not much was hidden. The chief unpublished document is a report by Mr Ward, Minister to the Hansa Towns, which was considered by Palmerston to be too pro-German in tone.† But Professor Aage Friis, the chief Danish authority, is of opinion that any omissions deal chiefly with Danish internal affairs which Russell probably thought of no interest to the British public. Over Italy and Poland there was also abundance of information published freely. None the less, the majority of the House was at times critical of foreign policy. The hand of the Government was often forced, and there is abundant evidence of strong pressure for publication in certain directions. It is impossible to go into the reasons in detail, but the main lines of interest shown by the Commons are summarised here.

Africa: *Abyssinia*, Nos. 698, 712; *Dahomey*, No. 633; *Lagos*, No. 602 *a*; *Madagascar*, No. 640; *Réunion*, No. 644.

America: *United States*, Nos. 627 *m, p, q, r*; *Brazil*, Nos. 679, 679 *a*, 702 *a*; *Peru*, Nos. 668, 670.

Asia: *Afghanistan*, No. 559‡; *China*, Nos. 563, 566–566 *b*, 579 *a*, 652 *a, d, f, g*; *Japan*, Nos. 580 *b*, 597 *a*.

---

* Lord John Russell was appointed Secretary of State for Foreign Affairs on 18 June 1859; the 4th Earl of Clarendon was appointed Secretary of State for Foreign Affairs on 3 November 1865.

† The report (dated May 1857) was originally asked for in the House of Commons on 27 April 1858. *Hans. Deb.* 3rd Ser. CXLIX, 1799. The late Sir Adolphus Ward, son of the above Minister, used to say that his father received a private letter of Palmerston, saying that he could not put his report in a Blue Book but had sent it to the Prince Consort 'who, I am sure, will enjoy it'.

‡ On the circumstances in which this paper was laid cp. F. R. Flournoy, *Parliament and War* [1927], 20–2, and note 4.

Europe: *Austria*, No. 586; *France and Savoy*, Nos. 567 *a*, *b*; *Ionian Islands*, Nos. 598, 637, 686; *Italy*, Nos. 611, 613, 614, 618, 706; *Papacy*, No. 568 *g*; *Poland*, Nos. 643, 643 *d*; *Russia*, No. 646; *Turkey*, Nos. 581, 624 *a*, 654, 654 *a*.

Technical and Commercial: Nos. 558, 558 *a*, 570, 572, 577 *a*, 589 *a*, 591, 631 *k*, 634, 638 *a*, 662 *b*, 668 *a*, 669 *b*.

This list of demands for information, which had to be met, shows clearly that the private member or the independent element in Parliament was still very powerful and that it was stimulated rather than satiated by the Government's liberality in publishing papers.

2ND SESSION 31 MAY TO 13 AUGUST 1859

VOLUME XV (1859)

Finance; Revenue; Public Offices, etc.

558   Return of Ambassadors, Envoys, etc. Appointed since 1st January 1856, stating Salaries, Date of Appointment, previous Service, etc.   PAGE 165

    194   *R–A.* (*HC. 19 July*), HC. 11 Aug., O.T.B.P. 12 Aug. 1859.

558*a*   Return of Consuls General, Consuls, Interpreters, Secretaries, etc. Appointed since 1st January 1856, stating Salaries, Date of Appointment, previous Service, etc.   PAGE 291

    195   *R–A.* (*HC. 19 July*), HC. 11 Aug., O.T.B.P. 12 Aug. 1859.

VOLUME XXV (1859)

East India

559   Correspondence of Sir Alexander Burnes with the Governor General of India, during his Mission to Cabul, 1837 and 1838. And Correspondence of the Governor General of India with the President of the Board of Control and with the Secret Committee of the East India Company, from the 1st day of September 1837 to the 1st day of October 1839, relative to the Expedition to Affghanistan, or of such part thereof as has not been already Published [*v. supra*, No. 243 *a*].   PAGE 7

    I   *Pursuant to Order* (*HC. 13 July 1858*), HC. 24 Mar., O.T.B.P. 8 June 1859.

VOLUME XXXII (1859)

State Papers: Italy, Portugal, etc.

560   *Italy:* Correspondence respecting the Affairs of Italy, January to May, 1859.   PAGE 1

    [2524]   *L/C.* HL. 7 June, HC. 9 June 1859.

560*a*   Further Correspondence [Feb.–June 1859].   PAGE 443

    [2527]   *L/C.* 10 June 1859.

560 b *Prussia (Neutrality):* Copy of a Despatch addressed by Her Majesty's Principal Secretary of State for Foreign Affairs to Her Majesty's Minister at Berlin, dated the 22nd day of June, with reference to the Neutrality of Prussia, with regard to the War in Italy.   PAGE 559

117   R–A. (*HC. 22 July*), HL. 19 July, HC. 25 July, O.T.B.P. 26 July 1859.

560 c Further Despatch [7 July 1859] from Lord John Russell to Lord Bloomfield.   PAGE 565

[2550]   L/C. 28 July 1859.

560 d *Italy:* Instructions given to each Officer sent by the British Government to the Head Quarters of the Armies in Italy, of Austria, Sardinia, and France, together with any Correspondence that has passed between the Government of England and those Countries, relative to such Mission.   PAGE 571

46   R–A. (*HC. 9 June*), HC. 30 June, O.T.B.P. 1 July 1859.

561   Convention between Her Majesty and the King of Portugal relative to Communication by Post, signed at Lisbon 6 April 1859.
                                                        PAGE 575

[2533]   L/C. HL. 7 June, HC. 30 June 1859.

562   *Treaties and Conventions (Engagements of Guarantee):* Copies of such Parts of all Treaties and Conventions now existing and still obligatory, as contain an Engagement of Guarantee.

[Belgium, Greece, Neuchâtel and Valengin, Portugal, Prussia, Savoy, Chablais and Faucigny, Sweden and Norway, Switzerland, Turkey, and the United States.]* [*v. infra,* Nos. 813, 813 a and 1530.]   PAGE 593

[2574]   R–A. (*HC. 9 Aug.*), 11 Aug. 1859.

VOLUME XXXIII (1859)

China and Japan

563   Correspondence relative to the Earl Elgin's Special Missions to China and Japan, 1857–59.   PAGE 1

[2571]   R–A. (*HC. 15 July*), 11 Aug. 1859.

* A supplementary paper containing the additional article of the Treaty with Honduras of 27 August 1856 (*v. supra,* No. 535) was laid before the House of Lords on 20 March 1860, and was printed in the *House of Lords Sessional Papers,* XVIII (1860). It was included in the later returns of guarantees laid before both Houses in 1871 and 1899 (*v. infra,* Nos. 813, 813 a and 1530).

VOLUME XXXIV (1859), SESSION 2

Slave Trade

564   Class B. Correspondence with British Ministers and Agents in Foreign Countries, and with Foreign Ministers in England, relating to the Slave Trade [1 Ap. 1858–31 Mar. 1859].

PAGE 281

[2569–I]   *L/C.* 11 Aug. 1859.

HOUSE OF LORDS SESSIONAL PAPERS

VOLUME XIII (1859)

State Correspondence, etc.

565   Despatch from Count Cavour relative to the Neutrality of Parma, in reply to the Earl of Malmesbury's Despatch to Sir J. Hudson, dated June 7, 1859.*   PAGE 569

R–A. (HL. 15 July), HL. 19 July 1859.

565a   Correspondence respecting the alleged Annexation of the Duchies of Central Italy by the Sardinian Government.   PAGE 573

R–A. (HL. 15 July), HL. 19 July 1859.

SESSION 24 JANUARY TO 28 AUGUST 1860

VOLUME XLVIII (1860)

China: Hong Kong

566   Correspondence respecting Affairs in China [23 Ap.–23 Nov. 1858].   PAGE 1

94   *R–A. (HC. 14 Feb.)*, HC. 20 Feb., O.T.B.P. 21 Feb. 1860.

566a   Papers relating to Hong Kong.   PAGE 21

161   *R–A. (HC. 6 Mar.)*, HC. 16 Mar., O.T.B.P. 21 Mar. 1860.

---

* The Earl of Malmesbury's dispatch was included in the papers laid before both Houses on 10 June 1859. *v. supra*, No. 560 a.

VOLUME LXVII (1860)

State Papers: Italy, Savoy, and Nice

VOLUME LXVIII (1860)

State Papers: Italy, etc.

VOLUME LXIX (1860)

State Papers: China, Japan, Syria

VOLUME LXX (1860)

Slave Trade

* A motion for an Address for these papers was defeated in the House of Lords and withdrawn on 3 August 1860. The papers were nevertheless laid on the same day that they were presented to the Commons.

HOUSE OF LORDS SESSIONAL PAPERS

VOLUME XXII (1860)

Miscellaneous Subjects

583   Return of the Date of all Communications between the Secretary of State and Her Majesty's Ambassador at Paris on the Subject of the Annexation of Savoy and Nice to France, from the Accession to Office of the present Ministry up to this Time.

PAGE 395

29   R–A. (*HL. 14 Feb.*), HL. 16 Feb., O.T.B.P. 20 Feb. 1860.

583 a   Copies or Extracts from the Despatches of Her Majesty's Minister in Tuscany in 1855, 1856, and 1857, referring to the Condition and Administration of the Roman States.   PAGE 445

369   R–A. (*HL. 30 July*), HL. 2 Aug., O.T.B.P. 13 Aug. 1860.

SESSION 5 FEBRUARY TO 6 AUGUST 1861

VOLUME VI (1861)

Diplomatic Service

584   Report from the Select Committee appointed to inquire into the Constitution and Efficiency of the present Diplomatic Service; together with the Proceedings of the Committee, Minutes of Evidence, Appendix, and Index.*   PAGE 1

459   HC. O.T.B.P. 23 July 1861.

VOLUME LXIV (1861)

Slave Trade

585   Class B. Correspondence with British Ministers and Agents in Foreign Countries, and with Foreign Ministers in England, relating to the Slave Trade [1 Ap.–31 Dec. 1861].   PAGE 89

[2823–I]   L/C. 10 May 1861.

* A report from a Select Committee on 'the Consular Service and Consular Appointments' was presented to the House of Commons on 27 July 1858. *A. & P.* [1857–8], VIII, 482, p. 1.

VOLUME LXV (1861)

State Papers: Austria, etc.

VOLUME LXVI (1861)

State Papers: China, Japan

VOLUME LXVII (1861)

State Papers: Ionian Islands, Italy, Sardinia, Turkey

598*a* Papers relating to the Mission of the Rt. Hon. W. E. Gladstone to the Ionian Islands in the year 1858.   PAGE 17

    [2891]   *L/C.* HC. 2 Aug., HL. 6 Aug. 1861.

599 *Italy:* Further Correspondence relating to the Affairs of Italy. Part VII.   PAGE 109

    [2757]   *L/C.* 5 Feb. 1861.

599*a* do. [June 1860–Mar. 1861]. Part VIII, including Despatches from Rear Admiral Mundy relating to Affairs at Naples.   PAGE 305

    [2787–8]   *R-A. (HL. 1 Mar., HC. 5 Mar.),* 11 Mar. 1861.

599*b* do. [Jan., Mar. 1861]. Part IX.   PAGE 341

    [2804]   *L/C.* 22 Ap. 1861.

599*c* Correspondence respecting the Assumption of King Victor Emmanuel of the Title of King of Italy.   PAGE 353

    [2799]   *L/C.* HC. 8 Ap., HL. 9 Ap. 1861.

599*d* Despatches relating to the Affairs of the Duchy of Modena, from Her Majesty's Ministers accredited to the Courts of Central Italy, 1855–1858.   PAGE 359

    [2886]   *R-A. (HL. 22 July),* 2 Aug., O.T.B.P. HL. 6 Aug. 1861.

599*e* Papers respecting the Affairs of Southern Italy [1861].   PAGE 375

    [2864]   *L/C.* HL. 9 July, HC. 12 July 1861.

599*f* Copies or Extracts of Decrees of the King of Naples of the 1st and 15th days of March and of the 1st day of May 1860; together with all the Despatches of the English Minister at Naples enclosing the same.   PAGE 407

    85   *R-A. (HC. 1 Mar.),* HC. 5 Mar., O.T.B.P. 6 Mar. 1861.

599*g* Convention between Her Majesty and the King of Sardinia for the Establishment of International Copyright, signed at Turin, 30th November 1860.   PAGE 433

    [2758]   *L/C.* 5 Feb. 1861.

599*h* Correspondence respecting Changes in the Italian Tariffs in 1859 and 1860; and Extract of a Despatch from Lord John Russell to Mr. Elliott of the 21st June 1860.   PAGE 443

    [2812]   *R-A. (HC. 9 Ap.),* HC. 3 May, HL. 6 May 1861.

600   *Turkey:* Convention between Her Majesty and the Sultan for the Establishment of a Telegraphic Cable between Malta and Alexandria, signed at Constantinople, April 21st, 1861.

                                              PAGE 479

      [2856]   *L/C.* HL. 27 June, HC. 1 July 1861.

600*a*   Treaty of Commerce and Navigation between Her Majesty and the Sultan, signed at Kanlidga, April 29, 1861.   PAGE 485

      [2869]   *L/C.* 22 July 1861.

600*b*   Reports received from Her Majesty's Consuls relating to the Condition of Christians in Turkey.   PAGE 499

      [2810]   *L/C.* 3 May 1861.

600*c*   Correspondence with Her Majesty's Embassy at Constantinople on the subject of Financial or Administrative Reforms in Turkey [1858–61].   PAGE 599

      [2884]   *R–A. (HL. 12 July),* 2 Aug., O.T.B.P. HL. 6 Aug. 1861.

VOLUME LXVIII (1861)

State Papers: Syria

601   Convention between Great Britain, Austria, France, Prussia, Russia, and Turkey respecting Measures to be taken for the Pacification of Syria; signed at Paris, 5th September, 1860, with Protocols relating thereto.   PAGE 1

      [2759]   *L/C.* 5 Feb. 1861.

601*a*   Convention between the above Powers prolonging the Occupation of Syria to 5th June 1861; signed at Paris, 19th March 1861.

                                             PAGE 11

      [2835]   *L/C.* 27 May 1861.

601*b*   Correspondence relating to the Affairs of Syria, 1860–1.

                                             PAGE 17

      [2800]   *L/C.* HC. 8 Ap., HL. 9 Ap. 1861.

601*c*   do. [Mar.–June 1861]. Part II.   PAGE 551

      [2866]   *L/C.* 15 July 1861.

601*d*   Maps to the above.   PAGE 695

      [2866–I]   *L/C.* 15 July 1861.

Session 6 February to 7 August 1862

Volume LXI (1862)

Slave Trade

Volume LXII (1862)

State Papers: United States of North America

603*c*   Correspondence respecting the Withdrawal by the Government of the United States of Mr. Bunch's Exequatur as Her Majesty's Consul at Charleston. [*North America No. 4 (1862)*.]   PAGE 575

    [2912]   *L/C.* 6 Feb. 1862.

603*d*   Correspondence respecting the Seizure of Messrs. Mason, Slidell, M'Farland, and Eustis, from on board the Royal Mail Packet 'Trent', by the Commander of the United States Ship of War 'San Jacinto'. [*North America No. 5 (1862)*.]   PAGE 607

    [2913]   *L/C.* 6 Feb. 1862.

603*e*   Correspondence respecting the Steamers 'Nashville' and 'Tuscarora' at Southampton. [*North America No. 6 (1862)*.]

                                                      PAGE 649

    [2914]   *L/C.* 6 Feb. 1862.

603*f*   Papers relating to the Imprisonment of Mr. Shaver at Fort Warren, in Boston Harbour. [*North America No. 7 (1862)*.]

                                                      PAGE 685

    [2926]   *L/C.* 14 Feb. 1862.

603*g*   Papers relating to the Blockade of the Ports of the Confederate States. [*North America No. 8 (1862)*.]   PAGE 697

    [2931]   *L/C.* 24 Feb. 1862.

603*h*   Despatch from Lord Lyons respecting the Obstruction of the Southern Harbours. [*North America No. 9 (1862)*.]   PAGE 831

    [2933]   *L/C.* 28 Feb. 1862.

603*ij*   Extract of a Despatch from Lord Lyons respecting Political Arrests in the United States.   PAGE 835

    [2979]   *L/C.* 6 May 1862.

603*k*   Despatch from Lord Lyons respecting the Reciprocity Treaty. [*North America No. 10 (1862)*.]   PAGE 839

    [2993]   *L/C.* 27 May 1862.

603*l*   Papers respecting the 'Emily St. Pierre', of Liverpool. [*North America No. 11 (1862)*.]   PAGE 867

    [3015]   *L/C.* 26 June 1862.

603*m*   Further Correspondence relating to the Civil War in the United States of North America. [*North America No. 12 (1862)*.]

                                                      PAGE 887

    [3063]   *L/C.* 7 Aug. 1862.

VOLUME LXIII (1862)

State Papers: Belgium, China, Canton, Denmark, etc.

604   *Belgium:* Convention between Her Majesty and the King of the Belgians, additional to the Convention of October 19, 1844, relative to Communication by Post; signed at London, July 5, 1862.   PAGE 1
   [3032]   *L/C.* 14 July 1862.

605   *China:* Correspondence on the Employment of British Officers by the Government of China.   PAGE 7
   [3057]   *R–A. (HL. 28 July),* 4 Aug. 1862.

605*a*   Papers relating to the Rebellion in China, and Trade in the Yang-Tze-Kiang River.   PAGE 15
   [2976]   *R–A. (HC. 8 Ap.),* 1 May 1862.

605*b*   Maps referred to at pages 48, 111, 114, and 158 of the above Papers.   PAGE 179
   [2976–I]   *R–A. (HC. 8 Ap.),* 1 May 1862.

605*c*   Further Papers relating to the Rebellion in China.   PAGE 191
   [2992]   *L/C.* 27 May 1862.

605*d*   Further Papers [Feb.–July 1862].   PAGE 211
   [3058]   *L/C.* 4 Aug. 1862.

605*e*   Correspondence respecting the Evacuation of Canton.   PAGE 269
   [2919]   *L/C.* HC. 7 Feb., HL. 10 Feb. 1862.

606   *Denmark:* Convention between Her Majesty and the King of Denmark, for the mutual Surrender of Criminals; signed at London, April 15, 1862.   PAGE 277
   [3000]   *L/C.* 30 May 1862.

607   *France:* Reports respecting the Strength of the Naval and Military Forces of France.   PAGE 283
   [3001]   *L/C.* HC. 2 June, HL. 16 June 1862.

608   Convention between Her Majesty and the Emperor of the French, relative to Joint Stock Companies; signed at Paris, April 30, 1862.   PAGE 325
   [2987]   *L/C.* 19 May 1862.

609   *Princess Alice's Marriage:* Treaty between Her Majesty and the
      Grand Duke of Hesse, for the Marriage of Her Royal Highness
      the Princess Alice Maud Mary with His Grand Ducal Highness
      the Prince Frederick William Lewis Charles of Hesse.
                                                    PAGE 331
         [2905]   *L/C.* 6 Feb. 1862.

610   Accession of the Grand Duke of Hesse to the Conventions
      concluded 13 May 1846, and 14 June 1855, between Great
      Britain and Prussia, for the Establishment of International
      Copyright.   PAGE 341
         [2908]   *L/C.* 6 Feb. 1862.

611   *Italy:* Papers relating to the Affairs of Italy.   PAGE 347
         [2961]   *R–A.* (*HC. 17 Mar.*), 4 Ap. 1862.

612   Correspondence respecting Southern Italy.
                                                    PAGE 355
         [2965]   *L/C.* HL. 10 Ap., HC. 11 Ap. 1862.

612*a* Papers respecting the Affairs of Southern Italy.   PAGE 369
         [2973]   *L/C.* HC. 28 Ap., HL. 2 May 1862.

613   Correspondence relative to the Prosecution of Mr. G. Watson
      Taylor, in the Island of Elba, for an alleged Act of Sedition, and
      the Plunder of the Island of Monte Christo by Followers of
      General Garibaldi, in the Steamer 'Orwell'.   PAGE 377
         [3002]   *R–A.* (*HC. 16 May*), HC. 5 June 1862.

614   Correspondence respecting the Seizure of the British Steamer
      'Orwell' in 1860, by the Followers of General Garibaldi.
                                                    PAGE 419
         [2969]   *R–A.* (*HC. 31 Mar.*), HC. 11 Ap. 1862.

615   Correspondence respecting Arrests in Brescia.   PAGE 455
         [3016]   *L/C.* 26 June 1862.

616   Papers respecting the Assassination of Dr. M'Carthy, at Pisa.
                                                    PAGE 465
         [3019]   *L/C.* HC. 1 July, HL. 3 July 1862.

617   *Rome:* Papers respecting the French Occupation of Rome.
                                                    PAGE 479
         [3024]   *L/C.* HL. 4 July, HC. 7 July 1862.

618   Papers relating to the Treatment of Political Prisoners in Con-
      finement at Naples, and the Arrest of Mr. Bishop.   PAGE 493
         [3059]   *R–A.* (*HL. 7 July*), 4 Aug. 1862.

VOLUME LXIV (1862)

State Papers: Japan, Mexico, Morocco, Turkey

619   *Japan:* Correspondence respecting the Affairs in Japan.
      PAGE 1
      [2929]   *L/C.* HC. 20 Feb., HL. 21 Feb. 1862.

620   *Mexico:* Convention between Her Majesty the Queen of Spain,
      and the Emperor of the French, relative to Combined Opera-
      tions against Mexico.   PAGE 77
      [2907]   *L/C.* 6 Feb. 1862.

621   Despatches relating to British Claims on Mexico.   PAGE 85
      [3017]   *L/C.* 26 June 1862.

621 *a*   Correspondence relating to the Affairs of Mexico.   PAGE 101
      [2915]   *L/C.* 6 Feb. 1862.

621 *b*   do. (Part II) [Jan.–May 1862].   PAGE 263
      [2990]   *L/C.* 26 May 1862.

621 *c*   do. (Part III) [May, June 1862].   PAGE 405
      [3030]   *L/C.* 10 July 1862.

622   *Morocco:* Supplementary Convention between Her Majesty and
      the Emperor of Morocco, relative to a Loan to be raised in
      London by the Emperor; signed, in the English and Arabic
      Languages, at Tangier, January 18th, 1862.   PAGE 447
      [2937]   *L/C.* 4 Mar. 1862.

622 *a*   Convention between Her Majesty and the Emperor of Morocco,
      relative to a Loan to be raised in London by the Emperor;
      signed...at Tangier, October 24, 1861.   PAGE 453
      [2906]   *L/C.* 6 Feb. 1862.

622 *b*   Papers relating to the Loan raised by the Emperor of Morocco
      in London [1861–2].   PAGE 459
      [2916]   *L/C.* 6 Feb. 1862.

623   *Turkey:* Report on the Financial Condition of Turkey, by Mr.
      Foster and Lord Hobart, dated December 7th, 1861.   PAGE 475
      [2972]   *L/C.* HC. 28 Ap., HL. 2 May 1862.

SESSION 5 FEBRUARY TO 28 JULY 1863

VOLUME XXXVIII (1863)

Colonies, and Certain Places Abroad

VOLUME LXXI (1863)

Slave Trade

VOLUME LXXII (1863)

State Papers: North America

627 Despatch [13 Nov. 1862] respecting the Civil War in North America. PAGE 1

[3075]   *L/C.* 5 Feb. 1863.

627*a* Correspondence relating to the Civil War in the United States of North America [May 1862–Jan. 1863]. [*North America No. 1 (1863)*.] PAGE 7

[3107]   *L/C.* HC. 9 Mar., HL. 12 Mar. 1863.

627*b* Correspondence with Mr. Mason respecting the Blockade and Recognition of the Confederate States [Ap. 1862–Feb. 1863]. [*North America No. 2 (1863)*.] PAGE 65

[3108]   *L/C.* HC. 9 Mar., HL. 12 Mar. 1863.

627*c* Correspondence respecting the 'Alabama' [June 1862–Feb. 1863]. [*North America No. 3 (1863)*.] PAGE 85

[3109]   *L/C.* HC. 9 Mar., HL. 12 Mar. 1863.

627*d* Despatch from Her Majesty's Minister at Washington, dated 8th December 1862, enclosing Extracts of Papers relating to Foreign Affairs presented to Congress, December 1862. [*North America No. 4 (1863)*.] PAGE 137

[3119]   *L/C.* 19 Mar. 1863.

627*e* Correspondence respecting Instructions given to Naval Officers of the United States in regard to Neutral Vessels and Mails [Aug.–Dec. 1862]. [*North America No. 5 (1863)*.] PAGE 447

[3127]   *L/C.* HC. 13 Ap., HL. 14 Ap. 1863.

627*f* Correspondence with Mr. Adams respecting Neutral Rights and Duties [Ap.–May 1862]. [*North America No. 6 (1863)*.] PAGE 457

[3128]   *L/C.* HC. 13 Ap., HL. 14 Ap. 1863.

627*g* Correspondence respecting Despatch of Letters by Private Ships to Matamoros [16–18 Ap. 1863]. [*North America No. 7 (1863)*.] PAGE 467

[3144]   *L/C.* 24 Ap. 1863.

627*h* Correspondence with Mr. Adams respecting Confederate Agents in England [Feb.–Ap. 1863]. [*North America No. 8 (1863)*.] PAGE 473

[3146]   *L/C.* 27 Ap. 1863.

627*ij*   Correspondence with Mr. Adams respecting Enlistment of British Subjects in the Federal Army [Nov. 1862–Ap. 1863]. [*North America No. 9 (1863)*.]   PAGE 495

    [3147]   *L/C.* 27 Ap. 1863.

627*k*   Extract from a Despatch [10 Oct. 1862] to Mr. Stuart, Her Majesty's Chargé d'Affaires at Washington, respecting the Seizure of Mail Bags on board the 'Adela'. [*North America No. 10 (1863)*.]   PAGE 501

    [3149]   *L/C.* 28 Ap. 1863.

627*l*   Correspondence respecting Trade with Matamoros [Ap.–May 1863]. [*North America No. 11 (1863)*.]   PAGE 505

    [3183]   *L/C.* 25 June 1863.

627*m*   Correspondence respecting the Seizure of the British Schooner 'Will-o'-the-Wisp' by the United States Ship of War 'Montgomery', at Matamoros, June 3, 1863 [June 1862–June 1863]. [*North America No. 12 (1863)*.]   PAGE 513

    [3195]   *R–A. (HC. 16 June)*, HC. 2 July, HL. 3 July 1863.

627*n*   Memorial from certain Shipowners of Liverpool, suggesting an Alteration in the Foreign Enlistment Act. [*North America No. 13 (1863)*.]   PAGE 563

    [3200]   *R–A. (HC. 8 July)*, HC. 9 July, HL. 10 July 1863.

627*o*   Correspondence respecting Interference with Trade between New York and the Bahamas. [*North America No. 14 (1863)*.]   PAGE 569

    [3231]   *L/C.* 27 July 1863.

627*p*   *The Alabama:* Correspondence between the Commissioners of Customs and the Custom House Authorities at Liverpool, relating to the Building, Fitting out, and Sailing of the Vessel No. 290, since known as the Confederate Cruiser 'Alabama' [June–Sept. 1862].   PAGE 637

    125   *Pursuant to Order (HC. 20 Mar.)*, 23 Mar., O.T.B.P. 24 Mar. 1863.

627*q*   Letters or other Communications between the Collector of Customs at Liverpool and any Department of the Government in reference to the Detention of the Vessel 'Gibraltar' [Mar.–July 1863].   PAGE 653

    461   *Pursuant to Order (HC. 6 July)*, HC. 17 July, O.T.B.P. 20 July 1863.

627r   Number of Arms, etc., sent to British North America, from December 1861, and ordered in consequence of the Affair of the 'Trent'.   PAGE 663

   194   *R–A.* (*HC. 16 Ap.*), HC. 21 Ap., O.T.B.P. 22 Ap. 1863.

VOLUME LXXIII (1863)

State Papers: The Prince of Wales' Marriage, Belgium, etc.

628   Treaty between Her Majesty and the King of Denmark, for the Marriage of His Royal Highness the Prince of Wales with Her Royal Highness the Princess Alexandra, Daughter of Prince Christian of Denmark; signed at Copenhagen, January 15, 1863.
                                                                                        PAGE 1

   [3070]   *L/C.* 5 Feb. 1863.

629   *Belgium:* Treaty of Commerce and Navigation between Her Majesty and the King of the Belgians; signed at London, July 23, 1862.   PAGE 7

   [3071]   *L/C.* 5 Feb. 1863.

629a   Convention between Her Majesty and the King of the Belgians, relative to Joint Stock Companies; signed at London, November 13, 1862.   PAGE 21

   [3072]   *L/C.* 5 Feb. 1863.

630   *Belgrade:* Correspondence relating to the Bombardment of Belgrade, in June 1862.   PAGE 27

   [3126]   *L/C.* 27 Mar. 1863.

630a   Further Papers [May 1863].   PAGE 117

   [3163]   *L/C.* HC. 28 May, HL. 1 June 1863.

631   *Brazil:* Further Correspondence respecting the Plunder of the Wreck of the British Barque 'Prince of Wales', and the Ill-treatment of Officers of Her Majesty's Ship 'Forte' [June 1861–Feb. 1862].   PAGE 121

   [3087]   *L/C.* 19 Feb. 1863.

631a   do. [Jan. 1863].   PAGE 279

   [3094]   *L/C.* 26 Feb. 1863.

VOLUME LXXIV (1863)

State Papers: Holstein, etc.

VOLUME LXXV (1863)

State Papers: Naples, Paraguay, Poland, etc.

647 *Salvador:* Treaty of Friendship, Commerce and Navigation between Her Majesty and the Republic of Salvador; signed at Guatemala, October 24, 1862.   PAGE 375

 [3137]   *L/C.* 21 Ap. 1863.

648 *Turkey:* Order in Council and Correspondence respecting the Administration of Justice in the Ottoman Empire.   PAGE 387

 [3117]   *R–A. (HC. 27 Feb.)*, 16 Mar. 1863.

648*a* Return of Fines inflicted by Her Majesty's Consul and the Consular Court at Smyrna, from the Year 1856 to December 1862.   PAGE 497

 [3145]   *R–A. (HC. 23 Ap.)*, HC. 24 Ap. 1863.

648*b* Reports of Lord Hobart on Turkish Finances.   PAGE 503

 [3161]   *L/C.* HC. 28 May, HL. 1 June 1863.

HOUSE OF LORDS SESSIONAL PAPERS

VOLUME XXVII (1863)

State Correspondence, etc.

649 Correspondence relating to the Affairs of Rome. 1849.
                                                         PAGE 17
              L/C. HL. 27 Feb. 1863.

SESSION 4 FEBRUARY TO 29 JULY 1864

VOLUME LXII (1864)

State Papers: North America

650 Correspondence respecting the 'Alabama'. [*North America No. 1 (1864)*.]   PAGE 1

 [3241]   *L/C.* 4 Feb. 1864.

650*a* Correspondence respecting the Capture of the 'Saxon' by the United States Ship 'Vanderbilt'. [*North America No. 2 (1864)*.]
                                                        PAGE 61

 [3269]   *R–A. (HL. 16 Feb.)*, 25 Feb. 1864.

650*b* Correspondence respecting the 'Alabama'. [*North America No. 3 (1864)*.] PAGE 109

[3283] *L/C.* 4 Mar. 1864.

650*c* Communications between the Collector of Customs at Liverpool and Messrs. Klingender & Co., respecting Shipment of Guns on board the 'Gibraltar'. [*North America No. 4 (1864)*.] PAGE 131

[3284] *L/C.* 7 Mar. 1864.

650*d* Correspondence respecting Iron-clad Vessels building at Birkenhead. [*North America No. 5 (1864)*.] PAGE 137

[3285] *L/C.* 7 Mar. 1864.

650*e* Correspondence respecting the 'Tuscaloosa'. [*North America No. 6 (1864)*.] PAGE 173

[3291] *L/C.* 11 Mar. 1864.

650*f* Correspondence respecting the Enlistment of British Seamen at Queenstown, on board the United States Ship of War 'Kearsarge'. [*North America No. 7 (1864)*.] PAGE 209

[3298] *L/C.* 18 Mar. 1864.

650*g* Correspondence respecting Recruitment in Ireland for Military Service of the United States. [*North America No. 8 (1864)*.] PAGE 223

[3299] *L/C.* 18 Mar. 1864.

650*h* Papers relating to the Seizure of the United States Steamer 'Chesapeake'. [*North America No. 9 (1864)*.] PAGE 241

[3308] *R–A. (HC. 7 Mar.)*, 18 Mar. 1864.

650*ij* Despatch from Lord Lyons, referring to the alleged Report of the Secretary of the Navy of the so-styled Confederate States. [*North America No. 10 (1864)*.] PAGE 341

[3319] *R–A. (HC. 21 Ap.)*, HL. 22 Ap., HC. 25 Ap. 1864.

650*k* Return of Claims of British subjects against the United States Government from the Commencement of the Civil War to the 31st March 1864. [*North America No. 11 (1864)*.] PAGE 345

[3327] *L/C.* HC. 3 May, HL. 9 May 1864.

650*l* Further Correspondence respecting the Enlistment of British Seamen at Queenstown, on board the United States Ship of War 'Kearsarge'. [*North America No. 12 (1864)*.] PAGE 369

[3328] *L/C.* HC. 3 May, HL. 9 May 1864.

VOLUME LXIII (1864)

State Papers: Austria, Prussia, and Denmark, etc.

652a   Correspondence respecting the fitting-out, despatching to China, and ultimate withdrawal of the Anglo-Chinese Fleet, under the Command of Captain Sherard Osborn, and the Dismissal of Mr. Lay from the Chief Inspectorate of Customs. [*China No. 2 (1864)*.]   PAGE 57
　　　　[3271]   R–A. (*HC. 9 Feb.*), 25 Feb. 1864.

652b   Papers relating to the Affairs of China [*v. supra*, No. 632]. [*China No. 3 (1864)*.]   PAGE 103
　　　　[3295]   L/C. 14 Mar. 1864.

652c   Commercial Reports from Her Majesty's Consuls in China, for the year 1862. [*China No. 4 (1864)*.]   PAGE 311
　　　　[3302]   L/C. 18 Mar. 1864.

652d   Memorials, etc., on the Subject of opening up a Direct Commerce with the West of China, from the Port of Rangoon. [*China No. 5 (1864)*.]   PAGE 393
　　　　[3315]   R–A. (*HC. 17 Mar.*), 15 Ap. 1864.

652e   Extract of a Despatch from Sir F. Bruce, respecting Maintenance of Treaty Rights in China. [*China No. 6 (1864)*.]   PAGE 417
　　　　[3345]   L/C. 2 June 1864.

652f   Correspondence relative to Lieutenant Colonel Gordon's Position in the Chinese Service after the Fall of Soochow. [*China No. 7 (1864)*.]   PAGE 423
　　　　[3408]   R–A. (*HC. 1 July*), 25 July 1864.

652g   Copy of Prince Kung's Answer to Sir Frederick Bruce's Memorandum relative to the Affairs of China. [*China No. 8 (1864)*.]   PAGE 463
　　　　[3406]   R–A. (*HC. 26 July*), 28 July 1864.

653   Papers relating to the Seizure of the Chincha Islands by a Spanish Squadron.   PAGE 471
　　　　[3368]   R–A. (*HC. 9 June*), HC. 30 June, HL. 1 July 1864.

653a   Further Papers [May, June 1864].   PAGE 549
　　　　[3409]   R–A. (*HC. 19 July*), 25 July 1864.

654   Papers respecting the Settlement of Circassian Emigrants in Turkey, 1863–64.   PAGE 579
　　　　[3350]   R–A. (*HC. 6 June*), 7 June 1864.

654a   Map referred to at page 6 of the above Papers.   PAGE 593
　　　　[3350–I]   R–A. (*HC. 6 June*), 7 June 1864.

VOLUME LXIV (1864)

State Papers: Denmark and Germany (Nos. 1–4)

655 Correspondence respecting the Maintenance of the Integrity of the Danish Monarchy. [*Denmark and Germany No. 1 (1864)*.]

PAGE 1

[3257]   *L/C.* 9 Feb. 1864.

655a Correspondence respecting the Affairs of the Duchies of Holstein, Lauenburg, and Schleswig [Jan.–Sept. 1863]. [*Denmark and Germany No. 2 (1864)*.]   PAGE 7

[3267]   *L/C.* HC. 23 Feb., HL. 25 Feb. 1864.

655b do. [Sept.–Dec. 1863]. [*Denmark and Germany No. 3 (1864)*.]

PAGE 159

[3272]   *L/C.* 26 Feb. 1864.

655c do. [Dec. 1863–Jan. 1864]. [*Denmark and Germany No. 4 (1864)*.]

PAGE 411

[3276]   *L/C.* 1 Mar. 1864.

VOLUME LXV (1864)

State Papers: Denmark and Germany (Nos. 5–7), etc.

655d Correspondence respecting the Affairs of the Duchies of Holstein, Lauenburg, and Schleswig [Jan.–Mar. 1864]. [*Denmark and Germany No. 5 (1864)*.]   PAGE 1

[3300]   *L/C.* 18 Mar. 1864.

655e do. [Dec. 1863–Mar. 1864]. [*Denmark and Germany No. 6 (1864)*.]

PAGE 215

[3371]   *L/C.* 1 July 1864.

655f do. [28 June, 6 July 1864]. [*Denmark and Germany No. 7 (1864)*.]

PAGE 221

[3382]   *L/C.* 14 July 1864.

656 Correspondence respecting the Affairs of Denmark, 1850–53.

PAGE 229

[3301]   *L/C.* 18 Mar. 1864.

VOLUME LXVI (1864)

State Papers: France, Greece, Hudson's Bay, etc.

666   *Japan:* Correspondence respecting Affairs in Japan. [*Japan No. 1 (1864).*]   PAGE 175
       [3242]   *L/C.* 4 Feb. 1864.

666 *a*   do. [*Japan No. 2 (1864).*]   PAGE 297
       [3303]   *L/C.* 18 Mar. 1864.

667   *Persia:* Correspondence respecting the Construction of a Telegraph Line through Persia [1861–3].   PAGE 307
       [3306]   *R–A.* (*HC. 15 Feb.*), 18 Mar. 1864.

668   *Peru:* Correspondence between the British Officials in Peru and the Foreign Office, and of either of them, with the Peruvian Authorities, respecting Captain Wolfe Carvel.   PAGE 371
       413   *R–A.* (*HC. 10 May*), HC. 13 May, O.T.B.P. 20 June 1864.

668 *a*   Award made by the Senate of Hamburg, in the Case of Captain Melville White.   PAGE 457
       482   *R–A.* (*HC. 23 May*), HC. 10 June, O.T.B.P. 13 July 1864.

669   *Poland:* Correspondence relating to Poland [*v. supra*, No. 643 *h*].
                                             PAGE 575
       [3243]   *L/C.* 4 Feb. 1864.

669 *a*   Communication with the French Government respecting Poland.
                                             PAGE 585
       [3358]   *L/C.* 13 June 1864.

669 *b*   Papers relative to the arrest of the Rev. F. Anderson.   PAGE 595
       [3361]   *R–A.* (*HL. 6 June*), HL. 13 June, HC. 16 June 1864.

670   Correspondence respecting the Removal of Inhabitants of Polynesian Islands to Peru.   PAGE 607
       [3307]   *R–A.* (*HC. 15 Feb.*), HC. 18 Mar. 1864.

671   *Portugal:* Correspondence and Papers relating to the Claims of British Subjects on the Government of Portugal in respect of the Royal Union Mercantile Company.   PAGE 645
       551   *R–A.* (*HC. 25 July*), HC. 26 July, O.T.B.P. 27 July 1864.

672 *Prussia:* Convention between Her Majesty and the King of Prussia, for the mutual Surrender of Criminals. Signed at London, March 5, 1864. PAGE 799

[3314] *L/C.* 14 Ap. 1864.

673 Treaty and Convention for the Redemption of the Scheldt Toll, 1863. PAGE 805

[3245] *L/C.* 4 Feb. 1864.

674 *Slave Trade:* Class B. Correspondence with British Ministers and Agents in Foreign Countries, and with Foreign Ministers in England, relative to the Slave Trade [1 Jan.–31 Dec. 1863].

PAGE 947

[3339–I] *L/C.* HC. 20 May, HL. 31 May 1864.

675 Convention between the Governments of Great Britain and of Tunis, relative to the Holding of Real Property by British Subjects in Tunis; signed in the English and Arabic Languages, at Tunis, October 10, 1863. PAGE 1159

[3244] *L/C.* 4 Feb. 1864.

Session 7 February to 6 July 1865

Volume XXXVIII (1865)

China: Hong Kong: Ceylon, etc.

676 Report relative to the Foreign Customs Establishment in China. [*China No. 1 (1865)*.] PAGE 1

[3509] *L/C.* 29 May 1865.

676*a* Correspondence respecting direct Commerce with the West of China from Rangoon. [*China No. 2 (1865)*.]* PAGE 17

[3579] *R–A. (HC. 1 June)*, 6 July 1865.

* Further Papers were laid on this subject: 1864, LXII, 393; 1865, XL, 515; 1866, LII, 645; 1867, L, 749; 1867–8, LI, 653, 687, 757; 1868–9, XLVI, 281; 1873, LXI, 477.

VOLUME LVI (1865)

Slave Trade

677   Class B. Correspondence with the British Ministers and Agents
       in Foreign Countries, and with Foreign Ministers in England,
       relating to the Slave Trade [1 Jan.–31 Dec. 1864].   PAGE 193
       [3503–I]   L/C. 18 May 1865.

VOLUME LVII (1865)

State Papers: Abyssinia—Zollverein

678   Correspondence respecting the Attack on St. Albans, Vermont;
       and Naval Force on the North American Lakes, with Appendices.
       [North America No. 1 (1865).]   PAGE 1
       [3427]   L/C. 9 Feb. 1865.

678a   Papers respecting the Termination of the Reciprocity Treaty of
       5 June 1854, between Great Britain and the United States.
       [North America No. 2 (1865).]   PAGE 119
       [3470]   L/C. 23 Mar. 1865.

678b   Correspondence arising out of the Conflict between the 'Kear-
       sarge' and the 'Alabama'. [North America No. 3 (1865).]
                                                             PAGE 125
       [3511]   R–A. (HC. 19 May), 29 May 1865.

678c   Correspondence with the United States Government on the
       change of Form of Consular Exequaturs. [North America No. 4
       (1865).]   PAGE 143
       [3512]   R–A. (HC. 19 May), 29 May 1865.

678d   Correspondence respecting the Assassination of the late President
       of the United States. [North America No. 5 (1865).]   PAGE 155
       [3528]   L/C. 12 June 1865.

678e   Correspondence respecting the Cessation of Civil War in North
       America. [North America No. 6 (1865).]   PAGE 161
       [3538]   L/C. 19 June 1865.

678*f*   Correspondence respecting the Proclamation issued by the President of the United States on the 22d of May 1865. [*North America No. 7 (1865)*.]   PAGE 169

    [3539]   *L/C.* 19 June 1865.

678*g*   Correspondence with the United States Government respecting Compensation to the Widow of the late Mr. Gray, killed by Lieutenant Danenhower on board the 'Saxon'. [*North America No. 8 (1865)*.]   PAGE 175

    [3545]   *R–A.* (*HC. 20 June*), 27 June 1865.

678*h*   Further Correspondence respecting the Cessation of the Civil War in North America. [*North America No, 9 (1865)*.]   PAGE 183

    [3572]   *L/C.* 4 July 1865.

678*ij*   do. [May–July 1865]. [*North America No. 10 (1865)*.]   PAGE 191

    [3577]   *L/C.* 6 July 1865.

679   *Brazil and Rio de la Plata:* Correspondence respecting Hostilities in the River Plate, etc. (Part I).   PAGE 199

    [3463]   *R–A.* (*HC. 24 Feb.*), 13 Mar. 1865.

679*a*   do. (Part II) [Mar.–Ap. 1865].   PAGE 323

    [3514]   *R–A.* (*HC. 1 May*), HL. 29 May, HC. 30 May 1865.

679*b*   do. (Part IV) [Ap.–June 1865].   PAGE 359

    [3552]   *L/C.* 30 June 1865.

680   *China and Japan:* Order of Her Majesty the Queen in Council for the exercise of Jurisdiction in the Government of Her Majesty's Subjects in China and Japan, 9th March 1865.   PAGE 403

    [3497]   *L/C.* 11 May 1865.

681   *Denmark, etc.:* Correspondence respecting the Affairs of the Duchies of Holstein, Lauenberg, and Schleswig.   PAGE 449

    [3430]   *L/C.* 9 Feb. 1865.

681*a*   Correspondence respecting the Provisional Recognition of a Flag for the Duchies of Schleswig, Holstein, and Lauenberg.   PAGE 459

    [3469]   *L/C.* 20 Mar. 1865.

682   *France (Mr. Cobden):* Despatch [8 Ap. 1865] from M. Drouyn de Lhuys to the Prince de la Tour d'Auvergne.   PAGE 465

    [3486]   *L/C.* 28 Ap. 1865.

683   *Geneva, Convention of:* Accession of the British Government to the Convention, signed at Geneva, 22 August 1864, for the Amelioration of the Condition of the Wounded in Armies in the Field; signed at London, 18th February 1865, and acceptance thereof, signed at Berne, 3d March 1865.   PAGE 471

      [3479]   *L/C.* 6 Ap. 1865.

684   *Greece:* Correspondence relative to the Affairs of Greece.

                                                   PAGE 481

      [3432]   *L/C.* HC. 9 Feb., HL. 11 Feb. 1865.

685   Convention between Her Majesty and the Sultan for the Establishment of Telegraphic Communication between India and the Ottoman Territory; signed at Constantinople, 3d September 1864.   PAGE 487

      [3431]   *L/C.* 9 Feb. 1865.

686   *Ionian Islands:* Correspondence respecting Pensions to British Subjects formerly employed under the Ionian Government.

                                                   PAGE 497

      [3471]   *R–A. (HC. 17 Mar.),* 24 Mar. 1865.

686*a*   Act containing the Accession of the Sultan to the Treaty, concluded 29th March 1864, for the Union of the Ionian Islands to the Kingdom of Greece, and the Acceptance of that Accession; signed at Constantinople, 8th April 1865.   PAGE 531

      [3571]   *L/C.* 4 July 1865.

687   Correspondence respecting Affairs in Japan. [*Japan No. 1 (1865).*]   PAGE 543

      [3428]   *L/C.* 9 Feb. 1865.

687*a*   Despatch from Sir R. Alcock, respecting the Murder of Major Baldwin and Lieutenant Bird, at Kamakura, in Japan. [*Japan No. 2 (1865).*]   PAGE 707

      [3429]   *L/C.* 9 Feb. 1865.

687*b*   Further Papers [17–29 Dec. 1864]. [*Japan No. 3 (1865).*]   PAGE 741

      [3459]   *L/C.* 7 Mar. 1865.

688   *Spain:* Declaration of the British and Spanish Governments, for the abolition of the Practice of Firing on Merchant Vessels from British and Spanish Forts in the Straits of Gibraltar; signed at Madrid, 2d March 1865.   PAGE 759

      [3462]   *L/C.* HC. 10 Mar., HL. 13 Mar. 1865.

Session 1 February to 10 August 1866*

Volume XLIX (1866)

Colonies and British Possessions, etc.

696   Number of Chinese Pirate Vessels Captured, or Burnt, or otherwise Destroyed by Her Majesty's Vessels of War in the China Seas during the Command of Admiral King.   PAGE 179

    262   *Pursuant to Order (HC. 12 Ap.)*, HC. 10 May, O.T.B.P. 11 May 1866.

Volume LXXV (1866)

Slave Trade, State Papers, etc.

697   Class B. Correspondence with the British Ministers and Agents in Foreign Countries, and with Foreign Ministers in England, relating to the Slave Trade [1 Jan.–31 Dec. 1865].   PAGE 115

    [3635–I]   *L/C.* 22 Mar. 1866.

698   Further Correspondence respecting British Captives in Abyssinia.   PAGE 313

    [3748]   *R–A. (HC. 3 Aug.)*, 10 Aug. 1866.

699   Correspondence respecting the 'Shenandoah'.   PAGE 381

    [3581]   *L/C.* 6 Feb. 1866.

Volume LXXVI (1866)

State Papers: America (U.S.)—Prussia

700   *U.S.A.:* Correspondence respecting the Termination of the Reciprocity Treaty of the 5th June 1854, between the United States and Great Britain.   PAGE 1

    [3688]   *L/C.* 25 June 1866.

701   *Austria:* Treaty of Commerce between Her Majesty and the Emperor of Austria, with the final Protocol.   PAGE 21

    [3588]   *L/C.* 6 Feb. 1866.

---

* The Earl of Clarendon became Secretary of State for Foreign Affairs on 3 November 1865, *v. supra*, p. 162.

702   *Brazil, etc.:* Papers respecting the renewal of Diplomatic Relations with Brazil [1863–5].   PAGE 31
     [3585]   *L/C.* 6 Feb. 1866.

702 *a*   Correspondence respecting Hostilities in the River Plate.
                                                   PAGE 65
     [3630]   *R–A.* (*HC. 2 Mar.*), HC. 20 Mar., HL. 23 Mar. 1866.

703   *Chile:* Correspondence respecting the War between Chile and Spain [1865–6].   PAGE 95
     [3663]   *L/C.* 28 May 1866.

704   Return of Treaties now in Force between Great Britain and Foreign States, relative to Commerce, Navigation, Reciprocity, etc. [1809–65].   PAGE 335
     [3693]   *L/C.* HL. 25 June, HC. 26 June 1866.

705   *France:* Correspondence respecting the proposed Assembly of a Conference at Paris (1866).   PAGE 341
     [3684]   *L/C.* 18 June 1866.

705 *a*   Correspondence respecting the Extradition Treaty with France [1865–6].   PAGE 371
     [3725]   *L/C.* HC. 30 July, HL. 31 July 1866.

706   *Italy:* Correspondence respecting the Suppression of Ecclesiastical Corporations in Italy.   PAGE 411
     [3741]   *R–A.* (*HC. 31 July*), 7 Aug. 1866.

707   *Japan:* Correspondence respecting Affairs in Japan, 1865–66.
                                                PAGE 427
     [3615]   *L/C.* 26 Feb. 1866.

708   *Persia:* Convention between Her Majesty and the Shah of Persia, relative to Telegraphic Communication between Europe and India.   PAGE 521
     [3687]   *L/C.* 25 June 1866.

709   *Portugal:* Correspondence with Her Majesty's Minister at Lisbon respecting the opening of the Douro Wine Trade [1865–6].
                                                PAGE 529
     [3584]   *L/C.* 6 Feb. 1866.

710   *Prussia:* Treaty of Navigation between Her Majesty and the King of Prussia; signed at Gastein, 16th August 1865.
                                                PAGE 541
     [3614]   *L/C.* 26 Feb. 1866.

THE BLUE-BOOK POLICY OF DERBY AND STANLEY*

1866–7

THE last Derby Ministry was hardly in office long enough to formulate a new Blue-Book policy, even had they desired to do so. The demands for papers enforced by the Commons on the Cabinet do not seem to differ much from previous ones. Abyssinia (Nos. 735, 735 a and b) excited some interest; as did Russia (Nos. 729 and 729 a). The Government had to explain an incident with Spain (No. 731). In so far as the public gave a definite lead it was over East Europe. Information was extracted as to the treatment of Christians in Turkey (No. 732 a), and over the Cretan Insurrection (No. 739 b). There was one technical paper laid on Address over China (No. 738).

* Edward Henry, Lord Stanley became Secretary of State for Foreign Affairs on 6 July 1866.

Session 5 February to 21 August 1867

Volume LXXIII (1867)

Slave Trade, State Papers

711   Class B. Correspondence with the British Ministers and Agents in Foreign Countries, and with Foreign Ministers in England, relating to the Slave Trade [1 Jan.–31 Dec. 1866].   PAGE 121
     [3816–I]   *L/C.* 26 Mar. 1867.

712   *Abyssinia:* Further Correspondence respecting the British Captives in Abyssinia [1865–7].   PAGE 381
     [3918]   *R–A. (HC. 8 July)*, 1 Aug. 1867.

Volume LXXIV (1867)

State Papers: America—Russia

713   Correspondence respecting British and American Claims arising out of the late Civil War in the United States. [*North America No. 1 (1867)*.]   PAGE 1
     [3937]   *L/C.* 16 Aug. 1867.

714   *Cape Spartel:* Convention relative to the Establishment and Maintenance of a Lighthouse at Cape Spartel (signed, in the French and Arabic Languages, at Tangiers, 31st May 1865).   PAGE 49
     [3800]   *L/C.* HC. 12 Mar., HL. 19 Mar. 1867.

715   *Colombia:* Treaty of Friendship, Commerce and Navigation, between Her Majesty and the United States of Colombia.   PAGE 57
     [3756]   *L/C.* 7 Feb. 1867.

716   *Corfu, Zante, and Cephalonia:* Despatches from Her Majesty's Consuls in Corfu, Zante, and Cephalonia, containing Information on the State of those Islands since the withdrawal of British Protection, and their Annexation to the Kingdom of Greece.   PAGE 71
     [3827]   *L/C.* 12 Ap. 1867.

VOLUME LXXV (1867)

State Papers: Servia—Turkey

SESSION 19 NOVEMBER 1867 TO 31 JULY 1868

VOLUME XL (1867–8)

Finance, etc.

VOLUME LXIV (1867–8)

Slave Trade, etc.

VOLUME LXXII (1867–8)

State Papers: Abyssinia

VOLUME LXXIII (1867–8)

State Papers: America—Spain

738   *China:* Memorials addressed by Chambers of Commerce in China to the British Minister at Peking, on the subject of the Revision of the Treaty of Tien-Tsing.   PAGE 37

    [3996]   *R–A. (HC. 24 Feb.),* 13 Mar. 1868.

739   *Crete:* Correspondence respecting the Disturbances in Crete, 1867.   PAGE 81

    [3965]   *L/C.* 2 Dec. 1867.

739*a*   Further Correspondence [Nov. 1867–Mar. 1868].   PAGE 397

    [3965–II]   *L/C.* 21 May 1868.

739*b*   Reports by Consul General Longworth respecting the Island of Crete, 1858.   PAGE 503

    [3965–I]   *R–A. (HC. 19 Mar.),* 24 Mar. 1868.

740   *Danube:* Convention for the guarantee of a Loan to complete the Works at the Sulina Mouth, and Branches of the Danube; signed at Galetz, 30th April 1868.   PAGE 513

    [4050]   *L/C.* 3 July 1868.

741   *Egypt:* Papers respecting Judicial Reforms in Egypt [1867].
    PAGE 523

    [4040]   *L/C.* 18 June 1868.

742   *France:* Convention between Her Majesty and the Emperor of the French, relative to Fisheries in the Seas between Great Britain and France, signed at Paris, 11th November 1867.
    PAGE 533

    [3974]   *L/C.* 20 Feb. 1868.

743   *Italy:* Declaration exchanged between the British and Italian Governments relative to Joint Stock Companies, signed at Florence, 26th November 1867.   PAGE 553

    [3973]   *L/C.* 20 Feb. 1868.

744   *Mexico:* Papers relating to the withdrawal of the British Mission from Mexico, 1867–1868.   PAGE 557

    [3989]   *L/C.* HC. 6 Mar., HL. 9 Mar. 1868.

745   *North German Confederation and Spain:* Despatch enclosing Copy of a Treaty of Commerce and Navigation between the North German Confederation and Spain, signed at Madrid, 30th March 1868.   PAGE 579

    [4023]   *L/C.* 15 May 1868.

THE BLUE-BOOK POLICY OF THE FIRST GLADSTONE ADMINISTRATION*

1868–74

THE interest of this period from the point of view of Foreign Office Blue Books naturally centres on the years 1870–1, when foreign affairs pressed themselves on the attention of the Cabinet. In 1869 and the early weeks of 1870, the papers laid roused little attention even in Parliament itself. The 'Tornado' correspondence (Nos. 763, 763 a and 789) indeed raised a light wind of controversy, but its most important effect came later, when in July 1870 Gladstone re-stated the Rule of the House that 'public despatches, documents and papers relating to public affairs which were read and quoted by Ministers' must be placed on the table.† He was insisting at the time on his right to withhold a paper which was a memorandum of a conversation 'within the precincts of the House'. But there were more important occasions when papers were denied. The plea that communications were of a 'confidential character' was frequently used. There were complaints in the Lords in 1873 when a document, which had been excluded from the voluminous Blue Books on the Alabama question because it was 'confidential', was published in the United States,‡ and the paper was subsequently laid. But normally the argument was accepted. It was not disputed in June 1870 when it was used in answer to a request for dispatches referring to the unsuitability of the Greek constitution to the Greek nation,§ or a month later in relation to papers dealing with Franco-Prussian frontier negotiations since 1866;‖ or again in 1873 in discussion of Boundaries in Central Asia. A more general principle was asserted in relation to papers

---

* George, Earl of Clarendon was appointed Secretary of State for Foreign Affairs on 9 December 1868. He died on 27 June 1870, and George, Earl Granville was appointed on 6 July 1870.
† *Hans. Deb.* 3rd Ser. ccIII, 1115–21.
‡ *Hans. Deb.* 3rd Ser. ccxI, 990.
§ *Hans. Deb.* 3rd Ser. ccI, 1768, 9 June 1870.
‖ *Hans. Deb.* 3rd Ser. ccIII, 1094–5, 28 July 1870.

on the Roman question. A member had moved for 'all Despatches from...Rome since the 1st day of August 1870'. Gladstone said, in reply, that the motion was in a form which it was impossible to accept. 'It has been the custom of the House to leave to the Government a discretion as to those despatches which it may be advisable to lay before Parliament, and as to those other despatches, or portions of them, which it may be advisable to withhold.'* On this principle in 1873 papers relating to the Diplomatic relations with the Vatican were denied altogether.† In the case of the Disarmament proposals at the beginning of 1870 it was stated that much of the correspondence was among Clarendon's private letters, a statement which is borne out by the collection now in the Public Record Office.‡

On the whole, while Blue Books were plentiful, great consideration was given to the susceptibilities of foreign powers. As regards Austria-Hungary, it is true, Gladstone destroyed the effect of this courtesy by an accident in 1870. He referred in the House to Austrian sympathies for France at the outset of the Franco-Prussian war, though the dispatches on which his information was based had been excluded from the Blue Book. The need for consulting foreign powers in connection with the papers on this subject was given in explanation when Disraeli complained that the Blue Book was slow in coming. 'It was absolutely necessary', said Gladstone, 'in conformity with usage and obvious motives of policy, that we should give opportunities of communication with our chief representatives abroad.'§ The reason was probably the true one, for the Greek Brigandage papers (the Lord Muncaster case), where such consultation was not needed, were laid in large quantities and remarkable speed, some of the documents at the time of presentation being only twenty hours old‖ (Nos. 783–783*s*). When the papers on the Franco-

---

* *Hans. Deb.* 3rd Ser. CCIV, 649–50, 21 February 1871.
† *Hans. Deb.* 3rd Ser. CCXIV, 447–8, 14 February 1873.
‡ *Hans. Deb.* 3rd Ser. CCIII, 1408–9, 2 August 1870. Cp. Clarendon Papers, F.O. 361/1.
§ *Hans. Deb.* 3rd Ser. CCIII, 883–5, 25 July 1870.
‖ *Hans. Deb.* 3rd Ser. CC, 1730–1.

Prussian War were laid (Nos. 782–782*b*, 803–803*g*), little complaint was made against them, and in fact they fulfilled reasonably well Granville's promise that they would contain 'all the information which will enable you to form a judgment on the conduct of Her Majesty's Government'.* There were in fact, of course, omissions. Private correspondence was used freely to supplement dispatches, as is shown by Lord Newton's *Life of Lord Lyons*, and the dispatches themselves were frequently published in extract. For an example of the latter reference can be made to H. Temperley, 'Lord Acton on the Origins of the War of 1870', *Cambridge Historical Journal* [1926], pp. 73–4. This records the omissions made in the famous dispatch from Loftus of 13 July 1870; one of them conceals the fact that Bismarck referred to Napoleon III and his Cabinet as 'a band of Robbers'. The Belgian negotiations were much less fully represented. The texts of the treaties with France and Prussia were laid, but no correspondence, and Gladstone's statement in the Commons describing the attitude of Austria-Hungary and Russia to the Treaties as 'generally favourable' was definitely misleading. Curiously, although these treaties were much criticised, no complaints were made of lack of papers; and the later experience of the Treaty of Washington, where papers were plentiful, proved that laying Blue Books was no safeguard. The most interesting proposal made on this occasion was that treaties ought to be laid before they were ratified, a view which Gladstone successfully rebutted.†

The criticisms of the Black Sea Conference papers (Nos. 808–808*c*) were by far the most serious. On this occasion, indeed, the Government met disaster on two sides, for though the documents were cut severely to please foreign powers—particularly Austria-Hungary—their mutilation failed of its purpose in that direction and was the subject of serious protest in the Commons. Unfortunately for the Government the Index prefaced to the papers had been compiled before the cuts were made. Dispatches 'five lines long' had almost as much space in the Index. 'There are several places...'

---

* *Hans. Deb.* 3rd Ser. cciii, 317–18, 15 July 1870.
† *Hans. Deb.* 3rd Ser. ccxiv, 448–59.

as Sir Charles Dilke pointed out, 'where the Foreign Office index-maker has behaved in this tantalizing way....I do not know whether this index to Parliamentary Papers is intended to contain a précis even of passages which have not been printed; but, at all events, it is so here...it is certainly a convenient course for those who are not in the secrets of the Administration.'* The inferences drawn from these cuts were not wholly fair to the Foreign Office; for Granville's first selection had been substantially reduced after consultation with the Austro-Hungarian ambassador. Apponyi himself reported that he had 'eliminated some which seem to me compromising' and acknowledged the truth of Granville's comment that he had 'made generous use of the right of exclusion'. 'I must do him the justice', he wrote, 'to say that he agreed with the best grace in the world to the numerous suppressions for which I asked'.† In fact Granville gained little by this, for Beust instructed Apponyi to protest vigorously against the publication of one document (*No.* 87 in No. 808) which had been allowed to pass. It must be noted, however, that on one important point Dilke's criticism was justified. Apponyi, favourable though he was to Granville, commented regretfully on the contrast between his vigorous condemnation of Gorčakov's circular in private and the mildness of the British official reply, falling back on the explanation that Granville's own views had been modified in the Cabinet. This reflection and other documents in the Anglo-Austrian correspondence showing Austro-Hungarian anxiety that Britain should take a stronger line, give some substance to Dilke's comments on an 'extract' of three and a half lines included in the Blue Book (*No.* 101 in No. 808). This 'ridiculous abortion', in which Count Beust disclaimed any desire to prevent a peaceful settlement or to encourage the Porte to resistance, does in fact give a misleading impression of the course of Anglo-Austrian negotiations.

The concentration of attention on the Treaty of 1856, and

* *Hans. Deb.* 3rd Ser. ccv, 899, 906–7.
† W.S.A. viii/82. Rapports d'Angleterre, ff. 394–402. Apponyi to Beust, No. 33 A–B. Secret. 27 April 1871.

on our obligation to Belgium, combined with the policy of the Government in defence to produce the one important paper of the period which was printed by the order of either House. This was the new edition of the return on Treaties of Guarantee (Nos. 813, 813 a) which was the result of a motion in the Lords made by Salisbury with spirited vigour on 6 March 1871.* It elicited a defence from Granville at the time,† but provided the basis for a further motion for an Address in the Commons a year later‡ and a full statement by Gladstone resulted.§ Apart from this the Blue Books, with few exceptions, were laid by command, and, in one case where this was not so, it was the Government that had suggested the procedure because of the mass of printing then occupying the time of the Foreign Office press (No. 785). Among the exceptions to the general rule are some of the papers relating to the Treaty of Washington. Two of these (Nos. 822 and 822 a) were returned to Addresses in the Commons, and although the speed with which they were laid suggests that they were already in print, the demand for them was in fact evidence of Parliamentary criticism. Three reports on trade matters were also the result of an Order or an Address (Nos. 792–4), but these fall outside the ordinary classes of papers, and two of them were Reports of Select Committees, a category in which printing by the House was the rule. Another example of the same kind is supplied by the Reports of the Select Committees on the Diplomatic and Consular Services (Nos. 768, 791, 791 a, 816). In these cases there was also another reason for the form in which printing took place, for technical papers and returns were generally the result of an Address and ordered to be printed by the House (cp. Nos. 771, 772 d, 843). Papers relating to trade or to personal questions were also frequently the result of an Address at this period (e.g. Nos. 837, 858 c, 859). But generally it must be recognised that the formalising of procedure by this time meant that the pressure of Parliamentary opinion was no longer, to so great an extent

* *Hans. Deb.* 3rd Ser. cciv, 1360–8, 6 March 1871.
† *Hans. Deb.* 3rd Ser. cciv, 1368–75.
‡ *Hans. Deb.* 3rd Ser. ccx, 1151–65.
§ *Hans. Deb.* 3rd Ser. ccx, 1176–83, 12 April 1872.

as before, expressed in Addresses for Papers. The Blue Books issued in this period were on the whole full, and the policy—largely that of Gladstone himself—compares favourably with that of preceding administrations. One distinction can perhaps be drawn. The idea of influencing public opinion by opportune publication was less evident as a factor in Gladstone's policy than in that of Russell.

Session 10 December 1868 to 11 August 1869

Volume LVI (1868–9)

Slave Trade, etc.

Volume LXIII (1868–9)

State Papers: Abyssinia—America

VOLUME LXIV (1868–9)

State Papers: Belgium—Zollverein

754   Convention between Her Majesty and the King of the Belgians for the Establishment of a System of Post Office Money Orders between Great Britain and Belgium. Signed at London, 31 May 1869.   PAGE 1

    [4170]   *L/C.* 24 June 1869.

755   Correspondence respecting the Relations between Great Britain and China. [*China No. 1 (1869)*.]   PAGE 9

    [4097]   *L/C.* 16 Feb. 1869.

755*a*   Correspondence respecting the Attack on British Protestant Missionaries at Yang Chow Foo, August 1868. [*China No. 2 (1869)*.]   PAGE 19

    [4097–I]   *L/C.* 16 Feb. 1869.

755*b*   Correspondence respecting Missionary Disturbances at Chefoo and Taiwan (Formosa). [*China No. 3 (1869)*.]   PAGE 103

    [4097–II]   *L/C.* 13 May 1869.

755*c*   Correspondence respecting the Engagement of Her Majesty's Ship 'Algerine' with Piratical Junks off Namoa Harbour. [*China No. 4 (1869)*.]   PAGE 161

    [4097–III]   *L/C.* 13 May 1869.

755*d*   Correspondence respecting the Suppression of Piracy in the River Han. [*China No. 5 (1869)*.]   PAGE 169

    [4097–IV]   *L/C.* 13 May 1869.

755*e*   Correspondence respecting Outrage on British Merchants at Bauer, in Formosa. [*China No. 6 (1869)*.]   PAGE 179

    [4097–V]   *L/C.* 13 May 1869.

755*f*   Correspondence respecting Attack on Boats of Her Majesty's Ship 'Cockchafer' by Villagers near Swatow. [*China No. 7 (1869)*.]   PAGE 193

    [4097–VI]   *L/C.* 13 May 1869.

755*g*   Correspondence with Sir Rutherford Alcock respecting Missionaries at Hankow, and State of Affairs at various Ports in China. [*China No. 8 (1869)*.]   PAGE 231

    [4097–VII]   *L/C.* 13 May 1869.

755*h*   Papers respecting the Proceedings of Her Majesty's Ship 'Janus' at Sharp Peak Island, near Foo Chow Foo. [*China No. 9 (1869)*.]
                                                              PAGE 239
     [4097–VIII]   L/C. 13 May 1869.

755*ij*   Further Correspondence respecting the Attack on British Protestant Missionaries at Yang Chow Foo, August 1868. [*China No. 10 (1869)*.]   PAGE 247
     [4097–IX]   L/C. 13 May 1869.

755*k*   Abstract of Trade and Customs Revenue Statistics from 1864 to 1868, published by the Imperial Maritime Customs. [*China No. 11 (1869)*.]   PAGE 269
     [4097–X]   L/C. 5 July 1869.

755*l*   Correspondence with the Chamber of Commerce at Shanghai respecting the Revision of the Treaty of Tien-Tsin. [*China No. 12 (1869)*.]   PAGE 285
     [4097–XI]   L/C. 23 July 1869.

756   *China and Japan:* Reports of Journeys in China and Japan performed by Mr. Alabaster, Mr. Oxenham, Mr. Markham, and Dr. Willis, of Her Majesty's Consular Service in those Countries.
                                                              PAGE 297
     [4187]   L/C. HL. 20 July, HC. 22 July 1869.

757   *Denmark:* Declaration for the exemption of British Subjects in Denmark and Danish Subjects in Great Britain from Forced Loans and Compulsory Military Service. Signed at Copenhagen, 14 June 1869.   PAGE 341
     [4173]   L/C. HL. 29 June, HC. 30 June 1869.

758   *Mecklenburg-Schwerin:* Accession of Mecklenburg-Schwerin to the Treaty of Navigation between Great Britain and Prussia. Signed at Berlin, 9 January 1869.   PAGE 345
     [4099]   L/C. 16 Feb. 1869.

759   Accession of Mecklenburg-Schwerin, Mecklenburg-Strelitz, Lauenberg, and Lubeck to the Treaty of Commerce between Great Britain and the Zollverein. Signed at Berlin, 9 January 1869.   PAGE 349
     [4100]   L/C. 16 Feb. 1869.

760   Papers relative to the Complaints made against Mr. Grenville Murray as Her Majesty's Consul General at Odessa, and to his Dismissal from Her Majesty's Service, 1858–69.   PAGE 353
     [4163]   R–A. (*HC. 16 Mar.*), HC. 14 June 1869.

761   Declaration renouncing the uses in time of War of Explosive
      Projectiles under 400 grammes weight. Signed at St. Petersburg,
      29 November/11 December 1868.   PAGE 659

      [4154]   *L/C.* 7 June 1869.

762   *Sandwich Islands:* Declaration cancelling part of Article VII of
      the Treaty of 10 July 1851, between Great Britain and the
      Sandwich Islands, and continuing the rest of the Treaty for
      Seven years fixed duration. Signed at Paris, 29 June 1869.
                                                       PAGE 665

      [4176]   *L/C.* HC. 5 July, HL. 6 July 1869.

763   *Spain:* Correspondence respecting the Seizure of 'The Tornado'
      off Madeira, by the Spanish Frigate 'Gerona'. [*Tornado No. 1
      (1869).*]   PAGE 669

      [4126]   *R–A. (HC. 19 Mar.),* 12 Ap. 1869.

763*a* Further Papers. [*Tornado No. 2 (1869).*]   PAGE 721

      [4126–I]   *L/C.* 13 May 1869.

764   Convention between Her Majesty and the Shah of Persia for
      extending and securing Telegraphic Communication between
      Europe and Asia. Signed in English and Persian at Tehran,
      2 April 1868.   PAGE 727

      [4101]   *L/C.* 16 Feb. 1869.

765   *Turkey:* Protocol relative to the Admission of British Subjects in
      Turkey to the right of holding Real Property. Signed at
      Constantinople, 28 July 1868.   PAGE 733

      [4145]   *L/C.* 31 May 1869.

766   *Turkey and Greece:* Correspondence respecting the Rupture of
      Diplomatic Relations between Turkey and Greece, 1868–9.
                                                       PAGE 743

      [4116]   *L/C.* 2 Mar. 1869.

767   *Zollverein:* Declaration for the Admission, Duty Free, into Great
      Britain and the Zollverein of Patterns and Samples imported by
      Commercial Travellers. Signed at Berlin, 1 April 1869.
                                                       PAGE 975

      [4128]   *L/C.* HC. 13 Ap., HL. 15 Ap. 1869.

SESSION 8 FEBRUARY TO 10 AUGUST 1870

VOLUME VII (1870)

Conventual and Monastic Institutions, etc.,
Diplomatic and Consular Services

VOLUME XLIV (1870)

Navy Estimates: Navy, Coast Guard, etc.

VOLUME L (1870)

Colonies and British Possessions

VOLUME LVI (1870)

House, Elections, Miscellaneous

VOLUME LXI (1870)

Trade, Slave Trade

VOLUME LXVI (1870)

Diplomatic Service, etc.

VOLUME LXIX (1870)

State Papers: America—Egypt

VOLUME LXX (1870)

State Papers: France—Venezuela

783*m* Further Correspondence [May 1870]. [*Greece No. 13 (1870)*.]
PAGE 381
    [C. 128]   *L/C.* 30 May 1870.

783*n* do. [May 1870]. [*Greece No. 14 (1870)*.]   PAGE 393
    [C. 133]   *L/C.* HC. 9 June, HL. 13 June 1870.

783*o* do. [May, June 1870]. [*Greece No. 15 (1870)*.]   PAGE 431
    [C. 135]   *L/C.* 16 June 1870.

783*p* do. [June 1870]. [*Greece No. 16 (1870)*.]   PAGE 465
    [C. 136]   *L/C.* 21 June 1870.

783*q* do. [Translations of papers in Nos. 1–16]. [*Greece No. 17 (1870)*.]
PAGE 487
    [C. 157]   *L/C.* 24 June 1870.

783*r* do. [June 1870]. [*Greece No. 18 (1870)*.]   PAGE 529
    [C. 158]   *L/C.* 1 July 1870.

783*s* do. [June 1870]. [*Greece No. 19 (1870)*.]   PAGE 541
    [C. 169]   *L/C.* 28 July 1870.

784 Correspondence respecting Affairs in Japan. [*Japan No. 3 (1870)*.]   PAGE 557
    [C. 129]   *L/C.* 31 May 1870.

785 *Netherlands, Belgium and Luxemburg:* Treaty relative to the Nether-lands. Signed at London, 15th November 1831; Treaties relative to the Netherlands and Belgium. Signed at London, 19th April 1839; and Treaty relative to the Grand Duchy of Luxemburg. Signed at London, 11th May 1867.   PAGE 661
    407   HC. O.T.B. reprinted, 2 Aug., HL. O.T.B.P. 4 Aug. 1870.

786 Correspondence respecting the Transfer of the Persian Mission to the Foreign Office.   PAGE 709
    [C. 105]   *L/C.* HC. 17 May, HL. 19 May 1870.

787 *Spain:* Correspondence respecting the Captures of Messrs. John and John Antonio Bonnell by Spanish Brigands, near Gibraltar.
PAGE 721
    [C. 166]   *R–A. (HC. 20 June)*, 1 July 1870.

788 Correspondence respecting the capture of the Gibraltar Schooner 'Garibaldi' by a Spanish Revenue Cruiser, 1868–69. PAGE 789
    [C. 81]   *R–A. (HC. 14 Mar.)*, HC. 11 Ap., HL. 28 Ap. 1870.

SESSION 9 FEBRUARY TO 21 AUGUST 1871

VOLUME VII (1871)

Admiralty, Board of, etc.

VOLUME XII (1871)

Slave Trade (East Coast of Africa)

VOLUME LI (1871)

East India

794   *Trade of Persian Gulf:* Report by Colonel Pelly to the Indian
Government....   **PAGE 407**

     456   *R–A.* (*HC. 10 Aug.*), HC. 11 Aug., O.T.B.P.
          12 Aug. 1871.

VOLUME LXII (1871)

Trade, Slave Trade

795   Class A. West Coast of Africa: Correspondence respecting the
Slave Trade and other Matters [1 Jan.–31 Dec. 1870].
                           PAGE 589

   [C. 339]   *L/C.* 15 May 1871.

795*a*   Class B. East Coast of Africa: Correspondence respecting the
Slave Trade and other Matters [1 Jan.–31 Dec. 1870].
                           PAGE 709

   [C. 340]   *L/C.* 15 May 1871.

795*b*   Class C. Correspondence respecting Slavery and the Slave
Trade in Foreign Countries, and other Matters [1 Jan.–
31 Dec. 1870].   **PAGE 785**

   [C. 341]   *L/C.* 15 May 1871.

795*c*   Recent Correspondence respecting the Slave Trade [East Coast
of Africa].   **PAGE 921**

   [C. 385]   *L/C.* 22 June 1871.

VOLUME LXX (1871)

State Papers

796   Correspondence respecting the appointment of a Joint High
Commission to consider the various Questions affecting the
Relations between Great Britain and the United States of
America. [*North America No. 1* (*1871*).]   **PAGE 1**

   [C. 262]   *L/C.* 23 Feb. 1871.

796*a* Despatch from Her Majesty's High Commissioners, with Copy annexed, of the Treaty signed at Washington, May 8th, 1871. [*North America No. 2 (1871)*.]   PAGE 9
  [C. 344]   L/C. 23 May 1871.

796*b* Instructions to Her Majesty's High Commissioners, and Protocols of Conferences held at Washington, between February 27th and May 6th, 1871. [*North America No. 3 (1871)*.]   PAGE 25
  [C. 346]   L/C. HC. 2 June, HL. 5 June 1871.

796*c* Treaty between Her Majesty and the United States of America, signed at Washington, May 8th, 1871.   PAGE 45
  [C. 386]   L/C. 27 June 1871.

796*d* Convention between Her Majesty and the United States of America supplementary to the Convention of May 13th, 1870, respecting Naturalization, signed at Washington, February 23rd, 1871.   PAGE 59
  [C. 345]   L/C. 5 June 1871.

797 *Austro-Prussian War:* Statement of the Expenditure incurred by Prussia in the last Austro-Prussian War, and of the Amount of Money received as Compensation from the Allied States.
                                              PAGE 65
  [C. 309]   R–A. (*HC. 7 Mar.*), HC. 3 Ap., HL. 21 Ap. 1871.

797*a* Note from the German Ambassador, relating to the Expenditure incurred by Prussia in the last Austro-Prussian War.   PAGE 71
  [C. 337]   L/C. 5 May 1871.

798 *Belgium:* Treaty between Her Majesty and the Emperor of the French relative to the Independence and Neutrality of Belgium, signed at London, August 11th, 1870.*   PAGE 75
  [C. 240]   L/C. 9 Feb. 1871.

798*a* Treaty between Her Majesty and the King of Prussia relative to the Independence and Neutrality of Belgium, signed at London, August 9th, 1870.*   PAGE 81
  [C. 241]   L/C. 9 Feb. 1871.

799 Circular of the Chinese Government, communicated by the French Chargé d'Affaires, relative to Missionaries residing in China, etc. [*China No. 3 (1871)*.]   PAGE 87
  [C. 366]   L/C. 12 June 1871.

  * The texts of these two Treaties were published in the *London Gazette* on 2 September 1870. Cp. *infra*, p. 276, note.

Volume LXXI (1871)

State Papers

VOLUME LXXII (1871)

State Papers

HOUSE OF LORDS SESSIONAL PAPERS

VOLUME XIV (1871)

Miscellaneous Subjects

Session 6 February to 10 August 1872

Volume VII (1872)

Accounts, Public, etc., Diplomatic and Consular Services

Volume IX (1872)

Elementary Schools, etc., Euphrates Valley Railway

Volume XLV (1872)

East India

Volume LIV (1872)

Trade, Slave Trade

818*a*   Class B. East Coast of Africa: Correspondence with Her Majesty's Consul at Zanzibar, and Report from Naval Officers on the Station.   PAGE 765

   [C. 657]   *L/C.* HL. 8 Aug., HC. 9 Aug. 1872.

818*b*   Return of Particulars of Vessels Captured for being engaged in the Slave Trade; also Name of the Capturing Ship, Amount of Bounty Awarded, etc., from the 1st July 1869 to the 31st December 1870.   PAGE 867

   174   *Pursuant to Order (HC. 25 Mar.),* HC. 25 Ap., O.T.B.P. 26 Ap.; *Pursuant to Order (HL. 29 Ap.),* HL. 29 Ap. 1872.

VOLUME LX (1872)

Consular Establishments

819   Reports relative to British Consular Establishments, 1858 and 1871. Part I. Austria, Belgium, Denmark, France, Germany, Greece, Italy.   PAGE 1

   [C. 497]   *L/C.* HC. 29 Feb. 1872.

819*a*   Further Reports. Part II. Netherlands, Portugal, Russia, Spain, Sweden and Norway, Switzerland.   PAGE 317

   [C. 501]   *L/C.* HC. 5 Ap. 1872.

819*b*   do. Part III. Ottoman Dominions.   PAGE 579

   [C. 530]   *L/C.* HC. 23 Ap. 1872.

VOLUME LXI (1872)

Consular Establishments, etc.

819*c*   Reports relative to British Consular Establishments, 1858–1871. Part IV. Non-European Countries.   PAGE 1

   [C. 544]   *L/C.* HC. 10 May 1872.

819*d*   Further Reports. Part V.   PAGE 285

   [C. 551]   *L/C.* HC. 4 June 1872.

819*e*   do. Part VI.   PAGE 351

   [C. 661]   *L/C.* HL. 9 Aug., HC. 10 Aug. 1872.

VOLUME LXII (1872)

Consular Services (Foreign Countries), etc.

VOLUME LXIX (1872)

State Papers: America (Treaty of Washington)

* Vol. VII only is in the bound sets of Parliamentary Papers. A note on the title-page states 'The other six Volumes of the Appendix are too bulky for distribution. Copies have been placed in the Library of each House for reference'. A supplementary MS. note in the House of Commons volume in the British Museum refers to a reprint in *U.S. House Documents 42–2*, vols XIV and XVI.

VOLUME LXX (1872)

State Papers

828 Correspondence on the Non-payment of Dividends on the Ecuador Loan.   PAGE 221

    [C. 658]   R–A. (HC. 18 July), 9 Aug. 1872.

829 Treaties with Foreign States for the Extradition of Criminals.

                                              PAGE 235

    [C. 660]   L/C. 9 Aug. 1872.

830 Correspondence respecting the Treaty of Commerce between Great Britain and France of 1860 [v. supra, No. 570 a]. [France. Commercial No. 1 (1872).]   PAGE 257

    [C. 499]   L/C. 25 Mar. 1872.

830a Correspondence respecting the Immigration of Communist Prisoners from French Ports to England.   PAGE 447

    [C. 565]   L/C. 13 June 1872.

830b Correspondence respecting Passports in France.   PAGE 481

    [C. 529]   L/C. 22 Ap. 1872.

831 Treaty between Her Majesty and the Emperor of Germany for the Mutual Surrender of Fugitive Criminals, signed at London, May 14th, 1872.   PAGE 505

    [C. 564]   L/C. 13 June 1872.

831a Order in Council, dated 25th June 1872, for carrying into effect the above Treaty.   PAGE 515

    [C. 568]   Pursuant to Act, 27 June 1872.

832 Convention [Post Office Money Orders]...between Great Britain and Italy, signed at London, March 4th, 1872.

                                            PAGE 523

    [C. 547]   L/C. 3 June 1872.

833 Despatches addressed by Dr. Livingstone, Her Majesty's Consul, Inner Africa, to Her Majesty's Secretary of State for Foreign Affairs in 1870, 1871 and 1872.   PAGE 529

    [C. 598]   L/C. 5 Aug. 1872.

834 Netherlands: Convention between Her Majesty and the King of the Netherlands, for the transfer to Great Britain of the Dutch Possessions on the Coast of Guinea, signed at the Hague, February 25th, 1871.   PAGE 557

    [C. 474]   L/C. HC. 19 Feb., HL. 20 Feb. 1872.

835   Convention between Her Majesty and the King of the Netherlands, relative to the Emigration of Labourers from India to the Dutch Colony of Surinam, signed at the Hague, September 8th, 1870.   PAGE 565

    [C. 473]   L/C. HC. 19 Feb., HL. 20 Feb. 1872.

836   Convention between Her Majesty and the King of the Netherlands for the Settlement of their Mutual Relations in the Island of Sumatra, signed at the Hague, November 2nd, 1871.   PAGE 577

    [C. 475]   L/C. HC. 19 Feb., HL. 20 Feb. 1872.

837   *Portugal:* Correspondence respecting Commercial Negotiations with Portugal. [*Portugal No. 1 (1872)*.]   PAGE 583

    [C. 634]   *R–A.* (*HC. 10 June*), HL. 8 Aug., HC. 9 Aug. 1872.

837 *a*   Convention between Her Majesty and the King of Portugal, additional to the Treaty signed at Lisbon, July 3rd, 1842, for suspension of the Traffic in Slaves, signed at London, July 18th, 1871.   PAGE 651

    [C. 470]   L/C. HL. 16 Feb., HC. 19 Feb. 1872.

838   Papers (with a Map) relating to recent proceedings at Salangore, consequent upon the seizure by Pirates of a Junk, owned by Chinese Merchants of Penang: and the Murder of the Passengers and Crew.   PAGE 661

    [C. 466]   L/C. 6 Feb. 1872.

839   Correspondence between the British and Spanish Governments respecting the International Society, 1872.   PAGE 715

    [C. 502]   L/C. 11 Ap. 1872.

840   Correspondence respecting the Assault on Mr. Henry Diedrich Jencken, at Lorea in Spain.   PAGE 723

    [C. 593]   *R–A.* (*HC. 6 June*), HC. 12 July, HL. 15 July 1872.

841   Return of Student Interpreters in China, Japan and Siam, 1847–1872.   PAGE 747

    [C. 532]   L/C. HC. 25 Ap. 1872.

842   Correspondence relative to the Cession by the Netherlands Government of the Dutch Settlements in the West Coast of Africa.   PAGE 753

    [C. 670]   L/C. 6 Feb. 1872.

Session 6 February to 5 August 1873

Volume LIII (1873)

House, Elections, Miscellaneous

Volume LXI (1873)

Trade, Slave Trade

Volume LXXIV (1873)

State Papers: America (United States of)

845*b* 2. Papers relating to the Proceedings òf the Tribunal of Arbitration at Geneva. Part I. Protocols, Correspondence, etc. [*North America No. 1 (1873).*] PAGE 9

   [C. 688] *L/C.* 6 Feb. 1873.

845*c* do. Part II. Award of the Tribunal, and the Reasons of Sir Alexander Cockburn for dissenting from the Award. [*North America No. 2 (1873).*] PAGE 419

   [C. 689] *L/C.* 6 Feb. 1873.

846 3. *North West American Water Boundary:* (A) Case of the Government of Her Britannic Majesty submitted to the Arbitration and Award of His Majesty the Emperor of Germany, in accordance with Article XXXIV of the Treaty [of Washington, 8 May 1871]. [*North America No. 3 (1873).*] PAGE 681

   [C. 690] *L/C.* HC. 6 Feb., HL. 7 Feb. 1873.

846*a* (B) Memorial on the Canal de Haro as the Boundary Line of the United States of America, presented in the name of the American Government to His Majesty William I, German Emperor and King of Prussia, as Arbitrator, by the American Plenipotentiary, George Bancroft. [*North America No. 4 (1873).*] PAGE 727

   [C. 691] *L/C.* HC. 6 Feb., HL. 7 Feb. 1873.

846*b* (C) Second and definitive Statement on behalf of the Government of Her Britannic Majesty submitted to His Majesty the Emperor of Germany. [*North America No. 5 (1873).*] PAGE 765

   [C. 692] *L/C.* HC. 6 Feb., HL. 7 Feb. 1873.

846*c* (D) Reply of the United States to the Case of the Government of Her Britannic Majesty. [*North America No. 6 (1873).*] PAGE 821

   [C. 693] *L/C.* HC. 6 Feb., HL. 7 Feb. 1873.

846*d* (E) Maps annexed to the Case of the Government of Her Britannic Majesty. [*North America No. 7 (1873).*] PAGE 869

   [C. 694] *L/C.* HC. 6 Feb., HL. 7 Feb. 1873.

846*e* (F) Maps annexed to the Memorial and Reply of the United States Government. [*North America No. 8 (1873).*] PAGE 881

   [C. 695] *L/C.* HC. 6 Feb., HL. 7 Feb. 1873.

846*f* (G) Correspondence respecting the Award of the Emperor of Germany in the matter of the Boundary Line between Great Britain and the United States. [*North America No. 9 (1873).*] PAGE 911

   [C. 696] *L/C.* HC. 6 Feb., HL. 7 Feb. 1873.

VOLUME LXXV (1873)

State Papers

THE EASTERN QUESTION PAPERS OF THE DISRAELI ADMINISTRATION*

1874–80

THE main interest of the period 1874–80 as regards Blue Books centres in the Eastern crisis. On other subjects there is little to distinguish this period from its predecessor. Most, though not all, of the papers were laid by command, and there were complaints from time to time both of delay and of denial. The need for considering the attitude of foreign powers was still given as a reason for delaying or withholding papers, the most interesting occasion—other than those connected with the Eastern crisis—being at the time of the War scare, when Russell moved in the Lords for correspondence relating to the peace of Europe.†

As regards the Eastern crisis, however, this explanation does not cover the whole ground, and in particular it cannot be put forward to excuse the glaring omissions in the 1876 papers. The Blue Books on the crisis started in this year. They were peculiarly full. Even Granville, seeking for criticism, felt some apparent hesitation in making it, and it was probably a result of their size that the worst deficiencies were little realised at the time. Perhaps, too, the Foreign Office compiler was too skilful; there were no mistakes in the Index, such as those which betrayed the omissions in Granville's papers on the Black Sea negotiations (*supra*, p. 219). The credit for the skill and certainly the main responsibility for the omissions lay with the Permanent Under-Secretary, Tenterden.‡ His private papers, now in the Public Record Office, contain

---

* Edward Stanley, Earl of Derby was appointed Secretary of State for Foreign Affairs on 21 February 1874; Robert Cecil, Marquis of Salisbury on 1 April 1878.

† *Hans. Deb.* 3rd Ser. ccxxiv, 1091. Cp. also in May 1875, on the Ultramontane negotiations between Germany and Belgium, *ibid.* ccxxiii, 1948–9, and in July 1875 on the Rumanian question, *ibid.* ccxxv, 23–4. Some papers were laid on both these subjects (Nos. 881, 895 *e*).

‡ Cp. H. Temperley, 'The Bulgarian and other Atrocities, 1875-8, in the light of historical criticism', *Proceedings of the British Academy*, xvii (Milford). App. I. 'Excisions and Omissions in Blue Books dealing with 1875–6', p. 31.

several indications of this fact. Even Disraeli wrote to him about the contents of the Blue Books, and it was he who corresponded with the English ambassadors who were consulted about them. This delegation to a permanent official was, indeed, probably inevitable, in view of the bulk of the papers. At the time of the 1853 crisis, when Blue Books, though considerable, were not nearly as voluminous, it was said that their selection 'forms a very heavy item in his [the Secretary of State's] labours'.* 'Turkey No. 1 of 1877' was 757 pages in length (No. 940), occupying a whole volume of the bound set; and in all there were twenty-eight Turkey papers in that year. The careful comparison which Dr Temperley has made of the Blue Books covering the period 1875–6 with the original documents in the Public Record Office makes it clear that the Government was open to very serious charges. Not only was the Government saved directly from criticism by the omission of Odo Russell's protests against the British refusal of the Berlin Memorandum, but consular reports from Turkey were printed in extract form with damaging evidence carefully deleted. Some Turkish atrocities were thus deliberately concealed, such as the massacre of refugees returning from Popovo, while others were minimised. Dr Temperley's article on 'The Bulgarian and other Atrocities' gives the most glaring examples, such as the omissions from Consul Dupuis's dispatch of 19 May 1876.† Another dispatch from the same source was published with a paragraph missing. The paragraph ends: 'According to other accounts the whole of the country is being laid waste by Bashi-Bazouks and the troops under his [Hafons Pasha's] orders.'‡ The reports of Consul Holmes were treated in the same way. In the first Blue Book of 1876 on the Eastern crisis, his criticisms of the instructions given to him at the time of the consular intervention were omitted.§ In May 1876, he wrote in one dispatch: 'All I can say is that during the whole of this business I have remarked that the sole object of the Porte

---

* F.O. 83/207. Letter of 4 July 1853.   † H. Temperley, *op. cit.* p. 31.
‡ F.O. 78/2458. Dupuis to Elliot, No. 16 of 12 May 1876. Cp. *A. & P.* [1876], LXXXIV [C. 1531], 457–8, *No.* 289 [*v. infra*, No. 917 *a*].
§ Cp. H. Temperley, *op. cit.* p. 29.

apparently seems to be to remove every functionary who exhibits any capacity or truthfulness and to replace them by those who are utterly devoid of such qualities, and I declare that it is hopeless to expect that any of the promises of the Government can be carried out under such circumstances.'* Later in the month he despaired of the situation. 'I see', he wrote, 'that the disturbances, which I told your Excellency I expected in Bulgaria, if the actual state of affairs were prolonged, have seriously commenced. This greatly aggravates the situation here and I fear that it will now require a most decisive European intervention to restore order, if it be still possible.'† Both these passages were omitted in the Blue Book. In some cases, it is true, Elliot was to blame, since he delayed transmission of some reports and failed to send others altogether.‡ But the second weeding out by Tenterden immensely increased the falsity of the picture.

While Derby must be assumed to be at least cognisant of these omissions, there is little indication of the knowledge of Disraeli. There is, in fact, clearer evidence of his irritation with the Foreign Office for not calling his attention to dispatches which betrayed the facts, than of his complicity in their concealment. He wrote to Derby on 14 July 1876: 'I must again complain of the management of your office, and request your personal attention to it.'§ Careful analyses both of the Parliamentary Papers and the confidential correspondence were made by Tenterden from time to time, and although Disraeli's impatience with 'Tenterdenism' has been exaggerated, he certainly complained that he had been misled about the Bulgarian atrocities. Moreover, his letter to Tenterden of 24 January 1877, proposing the inclusion in the next Blue Book of two dispatches on Anglo-Russian negotia-

---

* F.O. 78/2537. Holmes to Elliot, Affairs of the Herzegovina, No. 15, 12 May 1876. Cp. *A. & P.* [1876], LXXXIV [C. 1531], 464–5, *No.* 297 [*v. infra,* No. 917 *a*].

† F.O. 78/2537. Holmes to Elliot, Affairs of the Herzegovina, No. 17, 25 May 1876. Cp. *A. & P.* [1876], LXXXIV [C. 1531], 504–5, *No.* 373 [*v. infra,* No. 917 *a*].

‡ H. Temperley, *op. cit.* pp. 31–2. For the alleged responsibility of Consul-General Francis, *v. ibid.* pp. 32–6.

§ Cp. Buckle, *Life of Disraeli*, VI, 44–5.

tions omitted in the previous year, suggests that by that date at least he thought that concealment had been carried too far: 'the reserve respecting our sayings and doings in the matter has only led to misrepresentation and misconception. ...All this would have disposed of the charge of our changing our policy.'*

The omission for which he was then proposing a remedy was in line with a large number of others throughout the papers on the crisis. At every stage there were confidential negotiations with Russia and Austria-Hungary and Germany, which were excluded. Sometimes Parliament suspected that papers were missing. Granville complained in the Lords, in February 1877, that the recent Blue Book contained no reports of Salisbury's conversations with Bismarck, Mac-Mahon and Decazes, but, unusually mindful of his own practice, he put into Derby's mouth the excuse that they were confidential.† He objected more vigorously to the scantiness of the paper relating to the London Protocol. There were only nine pages of this, and even then some of the space was occupied with translations, whereas 1200 pages had been presented earlier in the year.‡ Austria-Hungary was still particularly sensitive about publication. 'I learn from his own people', Buchanan wrote of Andrássy, 'that as he generally speaks with great frankness, there is nothing that annoys him so much, in their communications with him, as a reference to an observation, which he may have made to them previously.'§ The Anglo-Austrian negotiations, therefore, of May–December 1877 were all excluded, as the result of a direct representation from the Austro-Hungarian Ambassador, Beust. According to him, Derby agreed to their suppression unwillingly, and he thought probably after 'pression salutaire' from Beaconsfield.‖ The contemporary communications to Russia were published in part. Derby's dispatch of 6 May

* F.O. 363/1. Cited by H. Temperley, *op. cit.* p. 31, note 2.
† *Hans. Deb.* 3rd Ser. ccxxxii, 252–4, 13 February 1877.
‡ *Hans. Deb.* 3rd Ser. ccxxxiii, 1180–1, 16 April 1877.
§ F.O. 78/3203. Buchanan to Tenterden, 19 April 1877.
‖ W.S.A. viii/170. Angleterre I. Geheim. Entente entre l'Autriche-Hongrie et l'Angleterre dans la question orientale. 1877–8.

1877, and the Russian reply, appeared in June 1877 (No. 936); and his subsequent communication of 13 December was laid in the following January with correspondence arising from it (No. 962). But the intervening memorandum to Count Schuvalov of 17 July was not published at all*—not even in February 1878, when other papers on the negotiations of that period were issued (No. 962 o).

The crisis at the beginning of 1878 had its effect on publication, in that after the first Turkey Blue Book of that year (No. 962) there came a long series of short papers laid at intervals of a few days only from the end of January to the middle of March. When there was no need to consider the attitude of foreign powers, remarkable speed was shown in production. The Salisbury circular, drafted as we now know on the night of 29–30 March,† was laid before both Houses in print on 1 April, the day of its dispatch (No. 962 s), and circulated to Members on the following morning. There were, however, certain gaps. In the correspondence relating to the proposal for a conference (No. 962 r) there was, as was remarked in the Commons at the time,‡ a whole month's interval (between 7 February and 7 March). This complaint was comparatively easy to answer, and so was the contemporary request for papers showing the attitude of other powers. The serious gap of the pre-Congress period came a little later, when Salisbury opened the negotiations with Russia, Austria-Hungary and Turkey, which led to the Salisbury-Schuvalov Memoranda, the Anglo-Austrian Convention of 6 June, and the Cyprus Convention of 4 June. Here Salisbury took elaborate precautions to preserve secrecy.§ Curiously enough, Parliamentary publicity was in the three cases directly proportionate to the care taken in concealment. The negotiations with Turkey—so secret that they were conducted wholly by private correspondence—were covered by the famous dispatch of 30 [24] May, published with the Treaty (No. 963), and a slight paper of supplementary correspondence was

* F.O. 65/986.   † Cp. *Cecil*, II, 226.
‡ *Hans. Deb.* 3rd Ser. ccxxxix, 288–9, 1 April 1878.
§ Cp. L. Penson, 'The Principles and Methods of Lord Salisbury's Foreign Policy,' *Camb. Hist. Journ.* [1935], vol. v, 89, note 17.

added later (No. 963 a). The correspondence with Austria-Hungary—the only one of the three to be recorded by the normal procedure in official dispatches—was never subjected to the test of Parliamentary criticism, the documents being preserved separately as secret in both countries.* In the case of Russia similar secrecy might have been preserved, had it not been for the betrayal to the *Globe*. Even after this un-authorised publication, however, the documents embodying the Salisbury-Schuvalov arrangement were not laid before Parliament. Only two of the three memoranda of 30–31 May were published in the *Globe*. Salisbury failed to obtain the consent of Russia to the laying of all three before Parliament, and was forced to accept the position since the terms of the third had stipulated that it should not be published without Russian consent even if the other two documents were dis-closed.† In consequence the two Salisbury-Schuvalov memoranda were printed in the *Annual Register* for the year 1878 from the *Globe* text, and the third remained unknown until the archives were opened.

The papers relating to the Congress itself (Nos. 975–975 h) were naturally formal in character. Except in so far as it is reflected in the Protocols, no reference exists to Salisbury's Straits' policy, while the conversations which both Beaconsfield and Salisbury held with Waddington about Tunis were looked upon as too informal to need recording in the archives. It was due only to the persistence of Waddington that papers existed which Granville published in 1881,‡ and Salisbury took great care that they should be as innocuous as possible, having apparently in mind the danger that they might ultimately be laid before Parliament. It may conveniently

---

* On the British side all reference to these negotiations was excluded from the ordinary volumes of Confidential Print (from which the selection was normally made for Blue Books) and the papers were laid before the Cabinet in a separate and secret form. On the Austro-Hungarian side the originals were filed separately and secretly, as they still are in the bundle cited *supra*, p. 254, note.

† These papers and the correspondence regarding their publication are in F.O. 65/1022 and F.O. 65/1005 respectively.

‡ A. & P. [1881], xcix [C. 2886], 501–7; [v. *infra*, No. 1061]. Cp. D.D.F. 1ère sér. ii, 361–7, Nos. 330–2; pp. 369–74, Nos. 334–7; pp. 377–9, No. 342; Newton, *Life of Lord Lyons* [1913], ii, 154–6.

be remarked here, in relation to the Congress papers, that just after the Treaty had been laid the Government presented a return showing the normal procedure in the laying of treaties (No. 960). Out of the long list of political treaties (those of commerce were excluded) varying in date from 1839 to 1878, there were only four instances in which the texts were presented to Parliament before ratifications were complete. Two of these four were the Anglo-Turkish Convention of 4 June and the Treaty of Berlin of 13 July 1878.

Salisbury's method throughout the later stages of the Eastern question was to publish freely, if he published at all, and to use private letters to supplement dispatches, restricting to the former those transactions which he was unwilling to see included in a Blue Book. Thus the papers referring to the Asiatic reforms are voluminous in 1878–9 (Nos. 998–998 b), as are also those relating to the settlement of the European provinces; and while both need supplementing on some points by private correspondence (i.e. in particular that with Layard) they represent on the whole a fair as well as a full selection from the papers in the official archives. The difficulties of secrecy may indeed well have impressed themselves on an administration whose hands were forced on different occasions by the *Daily News*, the *Daily Telegraph* and *The Times*, and which was put into a position of ignomiy and embarrassment by the *Globe*.

Most of the Blue Books of this period—even on so controversial a subject as the Eastern crisis—were laid by command. It is, however, interesting to note that certain of those which were the result of Addresses were outside the category of personal, commercial and financial subjects. (With regard to such topics as these, Addresses remained the rule long after the procedure had become unusual in other matters.) These exceptions bear witness to the zeal of the Commons in obtaining information about the treatment of the subjects of Turkey (Nos. 937, 943, 945, and 945 a), and on other questions bearing upon the situation in the Near East (Nos. 958 and 958 a, 974, 975 ij). The failure to deliver Consul Blunt's report on the 'Russian Invasion of Roumelia' (No. 972) is significant.

Session 5 March to 7 August 1874

Volume LXII (1874)

Trade, Slave Trade

VOLUME LXVIII (1874)

Commercial Reports

VOLUME LXXV (1874)

State Papers: America (United States of)

VOLUME LXXVI (1874)

State Papers

868*b* Correspondence respecting Horse Breeding Establishments in France. [*France No. 1 (1874)*.] PAGE 131

    [C. 1008]   *L/C.* 7 July 1873.

869 Declaration exchanged between the British and German Governments relative to Joint Stock Companies, signed at London, 27th March 1874. [*Germany No. 1 (1874)*.] PAGE 139

    [C. 942]   *L/C.* 30 Mar. 1874.

870 Treaty between Her Majesty and the King of the Netherlands for the mutual surrender of Criminals, signed at the Hague, 19th June 1874. [*Netherlands No. 1 (1874)*.] PAGE 145

    [C. 1061]   *L/C.* HL. 6 Aug., HC. 7 Aug. 1874.

871 Treaty between Her Majesty and the Emperor of Russia, for the Marriage of His Royal Highness the Duke of Edinburgh with Her Imperial Highness the Grand Duchess Marie Alexandrowna of Russia, signed at St. Petersburg, 22nd January 1874. [*Russia No. 1 (1874)*.] PAGE 155

    [C. 901]   *L/C.* 19 Mar. 1874.

872 Correspondence respecting Central Asia. [*Russia No. 2 (1874)*.] PAGE 169

    [C. 919]   *L/C.* 19 Mar. 1874.

873 Decree annulling the Agreement of 28th December 1872, by which the Peninsula and Bay of Samana were leased to an American Company. [*Santo Domingo No. 1 (1874)*.] PAGE 183

    [C. 993]   *L/C.* 1 June 1874.

874 Correspondence respecting the 'Deerhound'. [*Spain No. 1 (1874)*.] PAGE 189

    [C. 906]   *L/C.* 19 Mar. 1874.

874*a* Correspondence respecting the Proceedings of Her Majesty's Ships of War on the South-east Coast of Spain. [*Spain No. 2 (1874)*.] PAGE 225

    [C. 918]   *L/C.* 19 Mar. 1874.

874*b* Correspondence respecting the Capture of the 'Virginius'. [*Spain No. 3 (1874)*.] PAGE 299

    [C. 991]   *L/C.* 22 May 1874.

874*c* Further Correspondence [May–Aug. 1874]. [*Spain No. 4 (1874)*.] PAGE 391

    [C. 1063]   *L/C.* HL. 6 Aug., HC. 7 Aug. 1874.

875   Treaty between Her Majesty and the King of Sweden and
      Norway for the mutual surrender of Fugitive Criminals, signed
      at Stockholm, 26th June 1873. [*Sweden No. 1 (1874)*.]   PAGE 397
      [C. 900]   *L/C.* 19 Mar. 1874.

876   Correspondence respecting Turkish Proceedings in the neigh-
      bourhood of Aden. [*Turkey No. 1 (1874)*.]   PAGE 405
      [C. 920]   *L/C.* 19 Mar. 1874.

876a Correspondence on the Ottoman Loans of 1858 and 1862.
      [*Turkey No. 2 (1874)*.]   PAGE 449
      [C. 1077]   *R–A. (HC. 16 July)*, HL. 6 Aug., HC. 7 Aug.
                          1874.

SESSION 5 FEBRUARY TO 13 AUGUST 1875

VOLUME LX (1875)

Education, etc., Miscellaneous

877   Return showing alterations in the Consular Service since
      1 January 1872, with a Statement of Consular Posts Established,
      Increased, Reduced, Abolished, etc. [*Consular No. 3 (1875)*.]
                                                               PAGE 631
      [C. 1287]   *R–A. (HC. 27 May)*, 11 Aug. 1875.

VOLUME LXXI (1875)

Trade, Slave Trade

878   Correspondence with British Representatives and Agents Abroad,
      and Reports from Naval Officers, relative to the East African
      Slave Trade. [*Slave Trade No. 1 (1875)*.]   PAGE 759
      [C. 1168]   *L/C.* 18 Mar. 1875.

878a Correspondence respecting Slavery in Cuba and Puerto Rico,
      and the State of the Slave Population and Chinese Coolies in
      those Islands. [*Slave Trade No. 2 (1875)*.]   PAGE 905
      [C. 1215]   *R–A. (HC. 15 Ap.)*, HL. 13 May, HC. 21 May
                          1875.

VOLUME LXXXII (1875)

State Papers

VOLUME LXXXIII (1875)

State Papers

890   Papers relating to the Meeting and Proceedings of the Diplomatic Conference at Paris, for making Provision, by means of a Convention, for effecting the objects of the International Metric Commission.   PAGE 13

  [C. 1331]   L/C. 9 Aug. 1875.

891   Correspondence with Her Majesty's Legation at Lima relative to the Imprisonment of British Subjects. [*Peru No. 1 (1875)*.]
                 PAGE 61

  [C. 1360]   R–A. (*HC. 19 July*), 11 Aug. 1875.

892   Correspondence on the Claims of Her Majesty's Government with respect to Delagoa Bay. [*Portugal No. 1 (1875)*.]   PAGE 137

  [C. 1361]   L/C. 11 Aug. 1875.

893   Correspondence respecting the Recognition of Prince Alfonso as King of Spain. [*Spain No. 2 (1875)*.]   PAGE 409

  [C. 1235]   L/C. HC. 4 June, HL. 8 June 1875.

893 *a*   Further Correspondence respecting the Capture of the 'Virginius'. [*Spain No. 1 (1875)*.]   PAGE 419

  [C. 1133]   L/C. 12 Feb. 1875.

894   Treaty between Her Majesty and the Swiss Confederation for the mutual Surrender of Fugitive Criminals, signed at Berne, 31st March, 1874. [*Switzerland No. 1 (1875)*.]   PAGE 427

  [C. 1160]   L/C. 22 Feb. 1875.

895   *Turkey:* Consular Courts: Returns of all Cases tried since 1856, etc. [*Consular No. 5 (1875)*.]   PAGE 439

  [C. 1368]   R–A. (*HC. 9 Aug.*), 13 Aug. 1875.

895 *a*   Further Correspondence respecting the Ottoman Loan of 1862 [June, Aug. 1866]. [*Turkey No. 1 (1875)*.]   PAGE 459

  [C. 1127]   L/C. 5 Feb. 1875.

895 *b*   Further Correspondence [Dec. 1874, Jan. 1875]. [*Turkey No. 2 (1875)*.]   PAGE 465

  [C. 1163]   L/C. 2 Mar. 1875.

895 *c*   Further Correspondence respecting the Ottoman Loans of 1858 and 1862 [Feb.–Ap. 1875]. [*Turkey No. 3 (1875)*.]   PAGE 471

  [C. 1210]   R–A. (*HC. 12 Ap.*), 3 June 1875.

895 *d*   do. [Ap.–July 1875]. [*Turkey No. 6 (1875)*.]   PAGE 489

  [C. 1288]   R–A. (*HC. 22 July*), 13 Aug. 1875.

Session 8 February to 15 August 1876

Volume XXVIII (1876)

Elections (Boston), Fugitive Slaves

Volume LII (1876)

Colonies and British Possessions

Volume LIV (1876)

Colonies and British Possessions

VOLUME LXX (1876)

Trade, Slave Trade, etc.

899 Correspondence respecting the Reception of Fugitive Slaves on Board Her Majesty's Ships. [*Slave Trade No. 1 (1876)*.]
PAGE 257
[C. 1413] *L/C.* 15 Feb. 1876.

899*a* Circulars respecting Slaves in Foreign Countries, addressed to British Military and Naval Officers. [*Slave Trade No. 2 (1876)*.]
PAGE 311
[C. 1480] *R–A. (HL. 13 Mar.)*, 18 May 1876.

899*b* Instructions respecting Reception of Fugitive Slaves on Board Her Majesty's Ships. [*Slave Trade No. 5 (1876)*.] PAGE 323
[C. 1593] *L/C.* 11 Aug. 1876.

899*c* Correspondence with British Representatives and Agents Abroad, and Reports from Naval Officers, relating to the Slave Trade. [*Slave Trade No. 4 (1876)*.] PAGE 327
[C. 1588] *L/C.* 8 Aug. 1876.

899*d* Despatches with respect to the Practice of the Slave Trade by the Subjects of the Native Princes of India. PAGE 703
[C. 1546] *L/C.* HL. 4 July, HC. 26 July 1876.

899*e* Communications from Dr. Kirk respecting the Suppression of the Land Slave Traffic in the Dominions of the Sultan of Zanzibar. [*Slave Trade No. 3 (1876)*.] PAGE 719
[C. 1521] *L/C.* HC. 22 June, HL. 27 June 1876.

VOLUME LXXXII (1876)

State Papers

900 Correspondence respecting Extradition. [*North America No. 1 (1876)*.] PAGE 1
[C. 1482] *L/C.* 29 May 1876.

900*a* Further Correspondence [May–July 1876]. [*North America No. 2 (1876)*.] PAGE 125
[C. 1526] *L/C.* 4 July 1876.

900 *b*   Correspondence respecting the Extradition of Bennet G. Burley.
[*North America No. 3 (1876)*.]   PAGE 153
   [C. 1528]   *R–A. (HC. 5 July)*, 14 July 1876.

900 *c*   Correspondence respecting the Extradition of Richard Baker
Caldwell. [*North America No. 4 (1876)*.]   PAGE 189
   [C. 1529]   *R–A. (HC. 5 July)*, 14 July 1876.

900 *d*   Cases of Extradition of Prisoners under Treaty between Great
Britain and the United States. [*North America No. 9 (1876)*.]
                                                        PAGE 199
   [C. 1557]   *R–A. (HC. 23 May)*, HL. 3 Aug., HC. 4 Aug.
                        1876.

900 *e*   Further Return. [*North America No. 10 (1876)*.]   PAGE 207
   [C. 1621]   *L/C.* 15 Aug. 1876.

900 *f*   Correspondence respecting the Non-admission of Fish and Fish
Oils, the produce of British Columbia, into the United States,
Free of Duty, under the Treaty of Washington, 8th May 1871.
[*North America No. 5 (1876)*.]   PAGE 285
   [C. 1548]   *L/C.* 24 July 1876.

900 *g*   Correspondence respecting the imposition of Duty by the United
States Authorities on Tin Cans containing Fish from Canada.
[*North America No. 7 (1876)*.]   PAGE 301
   [C. 1550]   *L/C.* 24 July 1876.

900 *h*   Correspondence respecting the Navigation of the United States
Canals by Canadian Vessels. [*North America No. 6 (1876)*.]
                                                        PAGE 323
   [C. 1549]   *L/C.* 24 July 1876.

900 *ij* Further Correspondence respecting the Determination of the
Boundary between Canada and the United States. [*North
America No. 8 (1876)*.]   PAGE 357
   [C. 1552]   *L/C.* 28 July 1876.

901   Treaty between Her Majesty and the King of the Belgians for
the Mutual Surrender of Fugitive Criminals. Signed at Brussels,
20th May 1876. [*Belgium No. 2 (1876)*.]   PAGE 371
   [C. 1553]   *L/C.* 28 July 1876.

901 *a*   Convention between Her Majesty and the King of the Belgians,
regulating the Communications by Post between the British and
Belgian Dominions. Signed at London, 17th February 1876.
[*Belgium No. 1 (1876)*.]   PAGE 383
   [C. 1423]   *L/C.* 3 Ap. 1876.

VOLUME LXXXIII (1876)

State Papers

905c Memoranda by Lord Tenterden and Mr. F. S. Reilly, relative to the Suez Canal Shares. [*Egypt No. 5 (1876)*.]   PAGE 383
      [C. 1415]   L/C. 17 Feb. 1876.

905d Concessions, Conventions, and Statutes of the Suez Canal Company, with the Sultan's Firman. [*Egypt No. 6 (1876)*.]
                                                                       PAGE 433
      [C. 1416]   L/C. 17 Feb. 1876.

906   Declaration recording the Adhesion of British India to the General Postal Union of 9th October 1874. Signed at Berne, 1st July 1876. [*Misc. No. 8 (1876)*.]   PAGE 485
      [C. 1554]   L/C. 28 July 1876.

907   Agreement between the Governments of Great Britain and Greece relative to Merchant Seamen Deserters. Signed at Athens, August 7/19, 1875. [*Greece No. 1 (1876)*.]   PAGE 489
      [C. 1414]   L/C. 15 Feb. 1876.

908   Treaty between Her Majesty and the President of the Republic of Hayti for the Mutual Surrender of Fugitive Criminals. Signed at Port-au-Prince, 7th December 1874. [*Hayti No. 1 (1876)*.]
                                                                       PAGE 495
      [C. 1385]   L/C. 8 Feb. 1876.

909   Treaty between Her Majesty and the Republic of Honduras for the Mutual Surrender of Criminals. Signed at Guatemala, 6th January 1874. [*Honduras No. 1 (1876)*.]   PAGE 505
      [C. 1386]   L/C. 8 Feb. 1876.

909a Correspondence with Señor Gutierrez on the subject of the Report of the Select Committee of the House of Commons on Foreign Loans. [*Honduras No. 2 (1876)*.]   PAGE 515
      [C. 1417]   L/C. 21 Feb. 1876.

910   Declaration prolonging the Duration of the Treaty of Commerce and Navigation between Her Majesty and the King of Italy of the 6th of August 1863. Signed at Rome, 22nd May 1876. [*Commercial No. 7 (1876)*.]   PAGE 571
      [C. 1483]   L/C. 1 June 1876.

911   Correspondence respecting the Treaty between Japan and Corea. [*Japan No. 1 (1876)*.]   PAGE 575
      [C. 1530]   L/C. 24 July 1876.

VOLUME LXXXIV (1876)

State Papers

SESSION 8 FEBRUARY TO 14 AUGUST 1877

VOLUME LXXVIII (1877)

Trade; Slave Trade

VOLUME LXXXVIII (1877)

State Papers

926   Declaration recording the Adhesion of Ceylon, the Straits
       Settlements, Labuan, Trinidad, British Guiana, Bermuda,
       Jamaica, Mauritius and its Dependencies, and Hong Kong to
       the General Postal Union of 9th October 1874, signed at Berne,
       23rd February 1877. [*Misc. No. 1 (1877)*.]   PAGE 499
           [C. 1666]   L/C. HC. 5 Ap., HL. 13 Ap. 1877.

927   Declaration prolonging the Duration of the Treaty of Commerce
       and Navigation between Great Britain and Italy, dated 6th
       August 1863; signed at Rome, 10th April 1877. [*Commercial
       No. 9 (1877)*.]   PAGE 505
           [C. 1736]   L/C. 26 Ap. 1877.

928   Declaration between Great Britain and Italy, relative to the
       Disposal of the Estates of Deceased Seamen of the Two Nations,
       signed at London, 17th April 1877. [*Commercial No. 8 (1877)*.]
                                                              PAGE 509
           [C. 1735]   L/C. 23 Ap. 1877.

929   Correspondence respecting the Introduction into, and Employ-
       ment in this Country of Italian Children. [*Italy No. 1 (1877)*.]
                                                              PAGE 515
           [C. 1764]   L/C. 14 June 1877.

930   Correspondence respecting Mr. C. G. H. Shorting's Complaints
       against the Italian Government and their Agents. [*Italy No. 2
       (1877)*.]   PAGE 523
           [C. 1773]   R–A. (HC. 30 Ap.), 29 June 1877.

931   Correspondence respecting the Complaints of the Holders of
       Peruvian Bonds as to the Disposal of the Guano and Nitrate of
       Soda Deposits. [*Peru No. 2 (1877)*.]   PAGE 597
           [C. 1835]   L/C. 14 Aug. 1877.

932   Correspondence relating to the Engagement between Her
       Majesty's Ships 'Shah' and 'Amethyst' and the 'Huascar'.
       [*Peru No. 1 (1877)*.]   PAGE 613
           [C. 1833]   L/C. 10 Aug. 1877.

933   *Poland:* Despatch from Earl Russell to Lord Napier bearing date
       17th June 1863, respecting the Insurrection in Poland in that
       Year [*v. supra*, No. 643].   PAGE 643
           168   HC. O.T.B. reprinted 19 Ap. 1877.

VOLUME LXXXIX (1877)

State Papers

934 Declaration for regulating provisionally the Commercial Relations between Great Britain and Roumania. Signed at London, 30th November 1876. [*Commercial No. 3 (1877)*.] PAGE 1
  [C. 1644] *L/C.* 8 Feb. 1877.

934*a* Correspondence respecting Commercial Negotiations between Great Britain and Roumania. [*Commercial No. 11 (1877)*.]
              PAGE 5
  [C. 1765] *L/C.* 5 June 1877.

934*b* Protocol prolonging for Nine Months the Duration of the Declaration...of 30th November 1876. Signed at Bucharest 30th April/12th May 1877. [*Commercial No. 12 (1877)*.]
              PAGE 59
  [C. 1767] *L/C.* 8 June 1877.

935 Correspondence respecting the Treatment of the Members of the United Greek Church in Russia. [*Russia No. 1 (1877)*.]
              PAGE 63
  [C. 1715] *R–A. (HC. 5 Mar.*), HC. 6 Ap., HL. 13 Ap. 1877.

935*a* Despatch of Prince Gortchakoff to the Russian Representatives Abroad respecting Relations between Russia and Rome [*v. supra,* No. 729]. PAGE 105
  169 HC. O.T.B. reprinted 19 Ap. 1877.

936 Correspondence respecting the War between Russia and Turkey. [*Russia No. 2 (1877)*.] PAGE 133
  [C. 1770] *L/C.* 21 June 1877.

937 Correspondence respecting the Condition and Treatment of the Jews in Servia and Roumania, 1875–76. [*Principalities No. 1 (1877)*.] PAGE 141
  [C. 1742] *R–A. (HC. 15 Feb.*), HC. 10 May, HL. 14 May 1877.

938 Translation of the New Spanish Tariff, dated 17th July 1877, with an Explanatory Report by Sir J. Walsham, Bart., Her Majesty's Chargé d'Affaires at Madrid. [*Commercial No. 19 (1877)*.] PAGE 513
  [C. 1836] *L/C.* 14 Aug. 1877.

VOLUME XC (1877)

State Papers: Turkey

VOLUME XCI (1877)

State Papers: Turkey

* This is the Blue Book which contains Baring's report on the Bulgarian atrocities of 1 September 1876 (pp. 142–96), which was sent to the Foreign Office as an enclosure in Sir H. Elliot's dispatch of 5 September, together with the reports of Schulyer and Chakis Bey and the 'Report presented to...the Porte by the extraordinary tribunal at Philippopolis...'. All these documents were, in fact, published on 19 September 1876 as a supplement to the *London Gazette*. Publication in this form was frequently used in relation to papers of immediate public interest if Parliament was not sitting at the time.

VOLUME XCII (1877)

State Papers

942c Despatches [14–29 Mar. 1877] from Mr. Consul Holmes respecting Reports of Outrages in the North of Bosnia. [*Turkey No. 11 (1877)*.]   PAGE 543
   [C. 1717]   *L/C.* HC. 10 Ap., HL. 13 Ap. 1877.

942d Further Despatch respecting the State of Affairs in Bosnia [18 May 1877]. [*Turkey No. 20 (1877)*.]   PAGE 551
   [C. 1768]   *L/C.* HC. 15 June, HL. 18 June 1877.

942e do. [6 June 1877]. [*Turkey No. 21 (1877)*.]   PAGE 561
   [C. 1771]   *L/C.* 26 June 1877.

942f do. [22 June 1877]. [*Turkey No. 22 (1877)*.]   PAGE 571
   [C. 1799]   *L/C.* 10 July 1877.

943   Return stating the Names and Posts of all British Consuls and Vice-Consuls in Bulgaria and the Balkan Districts of Turkey, 1870–76. [*Turkey No. 7 (1877)*.]   PAGE 577
   [C. 1664]   *R–A. (HC. 28 Feb.)*, 27 Mar. 1877.

943a Return of the Sentences Pronounced and Executed upon Persons concerned in the Bulgarian Rising, and in the Suppression of the same. [*Turkey No. 13 (1877)*.]   PAGE 581
   [C. 1721]   *L/C.* 23 Ap. 1877.

943b Further Return. [*Turkey No. 14 (1877)*.]   PAGE 589
   [C. 1737]   *L/C.* HC. 27 Ap., HL. 3 May 1877.

944   Correspondence respecting the Removal from Her Majesty's Navy of Captain Hobart, and his subsequent Reinstatement. [*Turkey No. 10 (1877)*.]   PAGE 595
   [C. 1716]   *R–A. (HC. 20 Feb.)*, HC. 9 Ap., HL. 13 Ap. 1877.

945   Reports by Her Majesty's Diplomatic and Consular Agents in Turkey, respecting the Condition of the Christian Subjects of the Porte, 1868–75. [*Turkey No. 16 (1877)*.]   PAGE 617
   [C. 1739]   *R–A. (HC. 5 Mar.)*, 4 May 1877.

945a Instructions addressed to Her Majesty's Embassy at Constantinople, respecting Financial and Administrative Reform, and the Protection of Christians in Turkey, 1856–75. [*Turkey No. 17 (1877)*.]   PAGE 769
   [C. 1740]   *R–A. (HC. 9 Feb.)*, 7 May 1877.

945 *b*   Correspondence respecting the Ottoman Loans. [*Turkey No. 19 (1877).*]   PAGE 921

    [C. 1744]   *R–A. (HC. 22 Mar.),* HC. 31 May, HL. 4 June 1877.

945 *c*   Warrant of Her Majesty's Secretary of State for Foreign Affairs for the Seizure of the 'Hamadieh', under 'The Foreign Enlistment Act, 1870'. [*Turkey No. 27 (1877).*]   PAGE 993

    [C. 1831]   L/C. 10 Aug. 1877.

946   Treaties relating to the Ottoman Empire, 1841, 1856 and 1871 [*v. supra,* Nos. 293, 509, 808 *c*]. [*Turkey No. 4 (1877).*]   PAGE 997

    [C. 1658]   L/C. HC. 15 Feb., HL. 16 Feb. 1877.

SESSION 17 JANUARY TO 16 AUGUST 1878

VOLUME XLIX (1878)

Navy Estimates, Navy, etc.

947   Telegraphic Orders sent to Vice-Admiral Hornby, in reference to the Movements of the Mediterranean Fleet, and Vice-Admiral Hornby's Replies thereto.   PAGE 597

    [C. 1933]   L/C. 29 Jan. 1878.

VOLUME LXVII (1878)

Shipping; Slave Trade

948   Treaty of Friendship, Commerce, and for the Suppression of the Slave Trade, between Her Majesty and the King of Dahomey, signed at Whydah, 12th May 1877. [*Africa No. 1 (1878).*]
                                          PAGE 419

    [C. 1902]   L/C. 17 Jan. 1878.

948 *a*   Convention between the British and Egyptian Governments for the Suppression of the Slave Trade, signed at Alexandria, 4th August 1877. [*Egypt No. 1 (1878).*]   PAGE 485

    [C. 1900]   L/C. 17 Jan. 1878.

VOLUME LXXVI (1878)

Commercial Reports, Miscellaneous

VOLUME LXXX (1878)

State Papers

953   Declaration prolonging the Duration of the Treaty of Commerce
      between Great Britain and Austria, dated 5th December 1876;
      signed at Buda-Pest, 26th November 1877. [*Austria-Hungary
      No. 1 (1878).*]   PAGE 663

      [C. 1904]   *L/C.* 17 Jan. 1878.

954   Declaration between the British and Belgian Governments
      extending the Extradition Treaty, of 20th May 1876, to certain
      additional Crimes, signed at London, 23rd July 1877. [*Belgium
      No. 1 (1878).*]   PAGE 667

      [C. 1899]   *L/C.* 17 Jan. 1878.

955   Declaration recording the Accession of the German Empire to
      the Cape Spartel (Morocco) International Lighthouse Conven-
      tion of 31st May 1865, signed at Tangier, 4th March 1878.
      [*Commercial No. 8 (1878).*]   PAGE 673

      [C. 1991]   *L/C.* 8 Ap. 1878.

956   Treaty between Her Majesty and the French Republic for the
      Mutual Surrender of Fugitive Criminals, signed at Paris,
      14th August 1876. [*France No. 1 (1878).*]   PAGE 679

      [C. 2008]   *L/C.* 23 May 1878.

957   Declaration recording the adhesion of Canada to the General
      Postal Union of 9th October 1874, signed at Berne, 28th May
      1878. [*Misc. No. 1 (1878).*]   PAGE 691

      [C. 2050]   *L/C.* 25 June 1878.

958   Papers relating to the Establishment of the Kingdom of Greece,
      1826–32 (Translations) [*v. supra*, Nos. 158, 159, 171, 173]. [*Greece
      No. 1 (1878).*]   PAGE 695

      [C. 1974]   *R–A. (HC. 20 Mar.)*, HC. 7 May, HL.
                             14 May 1878.

958a Map of Greece.   PAGE 749

      [C. 1974–I]   *R–A. (HC. 20 Mar.)*, HC. 7 May, HL.
                             14 May 1878.

959   Declaration for prolonging the Duration of the Treaty of
      Commerce and Navigation between Her Majesty and the King
      of Italy of the 6th August 1863 till 31st March 1878, signed at
      Rome, 17th December 1877. [*Italy No. 1 (1878).*]   PAGE 751

      [C. 1903]   *L/C.* 17 Jan. 1878.

959a Declaration for prolonging the Duration of the above-mentioned
      Treaty until the 31st December 1878, signed at Rome, 5th March
      1878. [*Commercial No. 5 (1878)*.]   PAGE 755
      [C. 1972]   *L/C.* 25 Mar. 1878.

960   Return of Political Treaties concluded between Great Britain
      and Foreign Powers, 1839–78. [*Misc. No. 2 (1878)*.] PAGE 759
      [C. 2106]   *L/C.* HC. 1 Aug., HL. 2 Aug. 1878.

961   Convention prolonging the Duration of the Extradition Treaty
      between Great Britain and Switzerland of 31st March 1874, for
      Six Months from 22nd June 1878, signed at Berne, 19th June
      1878. [*Switzerland No. 1 (1878)*.]   PAGE 767
      [C. 2082]   *L/C.* 22 July 1878.

VOLUME LXXXI (1878)

State Papers

962   Further Correspondence [June–Dec. 1877] respecting the Affairs
      of Turkey. [*Turkey No. 1 (1878)*.]   PAGE 1
      [C. 1905]   *L/C.* 17 Jan. 1878.

962a Further Correspondence [Dec. 1877–Jan. 1878] (Overtures for
      Peace). [*Turkey No. 2 (1878)*.]   PAGE 607
      [C. 1906]   *L/C.* 17 Jan. 1878.

962b Further Correspondence [Dec. 1877–Jan. 1878] respecting the
      Affairs of Turkey. [*Turkey No. 3 (1878)*.]   PAGE 627
      [C. 1923]   *L/C.* 28 Jan. 1878.

962c do. [29 Jan.]. [*Turkey No. 4 (1878)*.]   PAGE 649
      [C. 1924]   *L/C.* HC. 30 Jan., HL. 31 Jan. 1878.

962d do. [25–31 Jan.]. [*Turkey No. 5 (1878)*.]   PAGE 653
      [C. 1925]   *L/C.* 31 Jan. 1878.

962e do. [27 Jan.–1 Feb.]. [*Turkey No. 6 (1878)*.]   PAGE 661
      [C. 1926]   *L/C.* 1 Feb. 1878.

962f do. [31 Jan.–6 Feb.]. [*Turkey No. 7 (1878)*.]   PAGE 667
      [C. 1927]   *L/C.* 7 Feb. 1878.

VOLUME LXXXII (1878)

State Papers

VOLUME LXXXIII (1878)

State Papers

* This paper is not in the volume.

Session 5 December 1878 to 15 August 1879

Volume LVI (1878-9)

East India

Volume LXVI (1878-9)

Trade; Slave Trade

VOLUME LXXIII (1878–9)

Commercial Reports, Miscellaneous

VOLUME LXXVII (1878–9)

State Papers

980*b* Despatches from the Governor General of India in Council to the Secretary of State in 1867, with Minutes enclosed, on Central Asia and Quetta; and Reply. PAGE 109

    73 *R–A.* (*HC. 20 Feb.*), HC. 24 Feb. 1878.

981 Agreement between Great Britain and Belgium for facilitating the application of a Word Tariff for Telegraphic Correspondence exchanged by way of Belgium between Great Britain and Germany. Signed at London, 31st December 1878. [*Commercial No. 5 (1879).*] PAGE 167

    [C. 2230] *L/C.* 1 Ap. 1879.

982 Declaration by the Sultan of Borneo extending the Provisions of Clause VIII of the Treaty with Great Britain of May 1847 to the Case of Wrecked Vessels belonging to the States in Amity with Great Britain. [*Commercial No. 27 (1878).*] PAGE 171

    [C. 2181] *L/C.* 5 Dec. 1878.

983 Correspondence respecting the Denunciation of the Treaties of Commerce between Great Britain and France. [*Commercial No. 2 (1879).*] PAGE 175

    [C. 2208] *L/C.* 13 Feb. 1879.

983*a* Correspondence respecting the Prolongation of the Commercial Treaties between Great Britain and France and the existing French Conventional Tariff. [*Commercial No. 15 (1879).*]

    PAGE 191

    [C. 2322] *L/C.* 26 May 1879.

983*b* Further Correspondence [Aug. 1879]. [*Commercial No. 28 (1879).*]

    PAGE 205

    [C. 2431] *L/C.* 13 Aug. 1879.

983*c* Declaration between the British and French Governments for regulating the Mode of dealing with the Proceeds of Vessels wrecked upon the Coasts of the two States. Signed at London, 16th June 1879. [*Commercial No. 18 (1879).*] PAGE 211

    [C. 2329] *L/C.* 19 June 1879.

984 Treaty between Her Majesty and the German Emperor, King of Prussia, for the Marriage of H.R.H. the Duke of Connaught with H.R.H. the Princess Louise Margaret of Prussia. Signed at Berlin, 26th February 1879. [*Germany No. 1 (1879).*]

    PAGE 217

    [C. 2225] *L/C.* 13 Mar. 1879.

VOLUME LXXVIII (1878–9)

State Papers: Egypt

VOLUME LXXIX (1878–9)

State Papers: Turkey

VOLUME LXXX (1878–9)

State Papers: Turkey

VOLUME LXXXI (1878–9)

State Papers: Turkey

THE BLUE-BOOK POLICY OF GRANVILLE

1880–5*

THE mass of papers presented during Granville's third period at the Foreign Office is overwhelmingly great; for while at its opening the interest in European and Asiatic Turkey had scarcely begun to abate, from 1882 onwards the Egyptian crisis involved extensive publication. In each of the sessions 1882, 1883, and 1884 papers on Egypt occupy two volumes of the bound set, and there are two more for the session 1884–5. Apart from these, there are several other series of special interest, in particular those including papers on Tunis and on other African problems. Most of the African Blue Books were issued under the aegis of the Colonial Office, and are indeed far fuller on the colonial than on the diplomatic side. But they cannot be excluded from this survey, since they contain some Foreign Office dispatches of considerable importance, and the negotiations which they embody formed an influential factor in Anglo-German relations.†

In all these categories of papers, despite their fullness, there are notable omissions. The second Blue Book on Asiatic reforms, for example, (No. 1033g), omits Granville's dispatch to Goschen of 10 June 1880, whose tenor caused so much disturbance to the Queen.‡ This dispatch was of particular importance because it expressed both the attitude of the Government to the Cyprus Convention and the new policy in relation to Armenian reforms. Moreover, many of the reports of the consuls and other officials in Asia Minor, such as those of Wilson and Baker, were published in extract only, while the use of extract form permitted the omission of the supporting representations of Goschen, the new Ambassador

* George, Earl Granville was appointed Secretary of State for Foreign Affairs on 23 April 1880.

† Cp. W. O. Aydelotte, 'The First German Colony', *Camb. Hist. Journ.* [1937], vol. v, no. 3, 291–313.

‡ F.O. 78/3074. Granville to Goschen No. 71 of 10 June 1880. For the Queen's attitude *v. Letters*, 2nd ser. iii, 111–13. Cp. also L. Penson, 'The Principles and Methods of Lord Salisbury's Foreign Policy', *Camb. Hist. Journ.* [1935], vol. v, no. 1, 97, note 54.

at Constantinople.* Thus their insistence on the need for special powers in pressing for reform was concealed, as well as the pronouncement of the Government that such special powers, based on the Cyprus Convention, were withdrawn.

The Tunis papers of 1881 provided the first of the two important instances in which Gladstone and Granville defended their attitude by the presentation of the dispatches of Salisbury—the second case being in 1884 with reference to Egypt (*v. infra*, pp. 299–301). In the treatment of the Tunis question the Liberal administration was genuinely hampered by the previous commitments of the Conservatives, and partly influenced by premature publication in the Press. Gladstone explained his position in the Commons on 16 May 1881 thus: 'It is right I should say that when the Papers are produced, the most important portions of the Correspondence that we shall lay before the House, as far as they involve the proceedings of this country, are portions which belong not to the time of the present, but to the time of the previous Administration.'† The first Blue Book on Tunis (No. 1061), therefore, contained Waddington's communication of 26 July 1878, and Salisbury's dispatch to Lyons of 7 August, which embodied his reply.‡ With these were printed Salisbury's dispatch to Wood, then Consul-General in Tunis, also of 7 August, which, though verbally consistent with the dispatch to Lyons, was hardly so in spirit. The only document of the Granville period was one of 17 June 1880, recording a conversation with the French Ambassador in which reference was made to these earlier assurances. All were printed in full, and Granville's dispatch of 1880 even drew attention to the difference between Salisbury's unofficial and his official language. Papers of 1881 were laid simultaneously or within a few days (Nos. 1061 a–1061 e) and were fairly full, although some documents were printed in extract only. The presenta-

---

* E.g. Wilson's report enclosed in Goschen's dispatch No. 70 of 22 June 1880. F.O. 78/3088; published in extract in No. 1033 g. The part included is purely descriptive; the part omitted emphasised the need for action by the consuls in pressing for reform. Cp. L. Penson, *op. cit.* p. 97, note 57.

† *Hans. Deb.* 3rd Ser. CCLXI, 574.

‡ Cp. *D.D.F.* 1ère Sér. II, 361–3, No. 330; pp. 366–7, No. 332; pp. 369–74, Nos. 334–7; pp. 377–9, No. 342.

tion in the same session of the correspondence relating to the Firman of 1871 (No. 1061 g) showed that British policy in the previous Liberal administration had been concerned with the maintenance of the Porte's claim to suzerainty, but the scantiness of the papers hid the fact that the Firman marked the triumph of the British Consul, Wood, in his long struggle with his French colleague. The circumstances of Wood's withdrawal in 1879 would have completed the story, but these never appeared in a Blue Book, and indeed became known in full only when the German and French documents of the period were published in recent years.*

The presentation of the Egyptian papers of 1882 was hampered by the attitude of France. The first substantial Blue Book of that year was laid on 27 March, and the second on 1 June (Nos. 1092 b, 1092 d). Ten days before the first of these dates, the *Directeur politique* called to see the British ambassador, Lyons, 'to say that, for his part, Monsieur de Freycinet would much rather no Blue Book on Egyptian matters should appear at the moment'.† He acknowledged, indeed, that this was entirely a matter for the British Government and he 'would *not* be willing that any objection on his part should be assigned by Her Majesty's Government as a reason for delaying the presentation of a Blue Book on Egypt'. If the papers were laid he wished particularly for the exclusion of the French communication of 13 September 1881, condemning the dispatch of a Turkish general or of Turkish troops to take part in the suppression of the military insurrection.‡ Granville, on reading the letter in which these requests were given, wrote a minute '*Festina lente* G.', and as a measure of concession the first Blue Book stopped short at

---

* Cp. especially *D.D.F.* 1ère Sér. II, 413, No. 369. There is a reference, however, to the German representations about Wood in F.O. 64/931, Russell to Salisbury, No. 12, Confidential, of 6 Jan. 1879. Cp. also Newton, *Life of Lord Lyons*, II, 164.

† F.O. 78/3503. Lyons to Tenterden, 19 March 1882.

‡ The text is in F.O. 146/2337 (Embassy Archives). It was sent to Lyons as an enclosure in Granville's dispatch No. 952 A, Most Confidential, of 30 September 1881, F.O. 27/2486. Granville gives here a long account of the interview with M. d'Aunay at Walmer of which a short report is printed in *D.D.F* 1ère Sér. IV, 140, No. 150. Granville's dispatch is given with some omissions in *A. & P.* [1882], LXXXII [C. 3161], 36–7 [v. infra, No. 1092 b].

October 1881 and the second in the following February—despite the desire of Parliament for information. At the end of May Granville, indeed, passed off a request for further papers with jesting,* but a few days later promised that they should be presented 'to a very late date' as soon as the necessary communication with the French had taken place.†
The March Blue Book did not contain the French communication of 13 September, for whose omission M. de Freycinet had asked, and Granville's dispatches of 21 and 30 September describing the Anglo-French negotiations were cut in several places. The Blue Book distributed in June (No. 1092 *d*)‡ was, however, less reticent. It dealt, in the main, with the Gambetta period, extending only to the first ten days of negotiations with M. de Freycinet. Lyons, indeed, warned Tenterden that it was desirable that the papers of the Gambetta period should be published quickly and fully, and explained that his reason was that he expected Gambetta to ask for the production of any that did not appear in the Blue or Yellow Books.§ This second collection is fairly full on the negotiations leading to the Dual Note of 8 January, and does not conceal the opposition of M. de Freycinet to intervention by the Porte. Moreover, in revising the papers of still more recent date, Granville specifically ruled that the French attitude on this point should not be concealed,‖ although as a concession to the French he decided to omit the proposal to substitute Halim for Tewfik,¶ saying that Lyons should make 'a favour of it'. Granville ruled also that papers relating to action on the organic law should be omitted, since the action had by then been suspended. 'It will certainly not do to show a difference of opinion on it.'** The result of this exchange of views was that M. de Freycinet said that he 'would not object

* *Hans. Deb.* 3rd Ser. CCLXIX, 1242–3, 22 May 1882.
† *Hans. Deb.* 3rd Ser. CCLXIX, 1772, 1 June 1882.
‡ The date of presentation was 1 June. But the Blue Book must have been laid in dummy since it was at that date only in proof stage and the final decision as to its contents had not yet been reached. F.O. 78/3503.
§ F.O. 78/3503, Lyons to Tenterden, 4 June 1882.
‖ F.O. 78/3503, Marginal notes by Granville on minute by Tenterden, dated 3 June 1882.
¶ Cp. *D.D.F.* 1ere Sér. IV, 290–1, Nos. 299–300.
** F.O. 78/3503. Tenterden to Lyons, 3 June 1882.

in principle to the publication of Egyptian papers up to a recent date, if it were done with great discretion'. He asked, however, for the omission of Lyons' dispatch No. 503, Very Confidential, of 29 May, describing a conversation on the subject of Turkish intervention, and not only was this record omitted from the Blue Book, but the conversation was also concealed in the long dispatch from Granville to Dufferin of 11 July 1882 (laid as a separate paper on 20 July) which recounted the whole course of the negotiations (No. 1092 *ij*). Probably this dispatch was written with an eye to publication, for it was laid without omissions or alterations.* But while Granville did something to meet the views of the French, M. de Freycinet's attitude to publication was not wholly hidden from Parliament, for Sir Charles Dilke said in the Commons on 12 June that 'the French Government has given its consent, not indeed to the publication of everything, but to enough to enable us to put our case before the House'.†
Some criticisms were made in Parliament on the score of omissions. A request for a telegram from Malet 'as to the desirability of Turkish co-operation' was refused in the Commons because publication would not be 'in the interests of the Public Service'.‡ This was at the end of June. A few days later, when the next series of papers had been laid (No. 1092 *g*) attention was called to the lack of dispatches from Constantinople during the months December 1881 to May 1882. The existence of two such dispatches was acknowledged in reply, but it was stated that they could not be laid because they were highly confidential.§ The reports of the Conference which met at Constantinople on 23 June were also regarded as secret, the responsibility for secrecy being attributed in Parliament to 'the desire of the Powers', but the instructions to Dufferin were presented in the meagre paper bearing the name of the Conference (No. 1092 *l*).

---

* This was certainly the case with Granville's earlier dispatch to Malet of 4 November 1881, which was presented in full as a separate paper on 7 February 1882 (No. 1092).

† *Hans. Deb.* 3rd Ser. CCLXX, 822.

‡ *Hans. Deb.* 3rd Ser. CCLXXI, 769, 29 June 1882.

§ *Hans. Deb.* 3rd Ser. CCLXXI, 1600–1, 6 July 1882.

It was in a debate in the Lords on 24 July 1882 that the question of the responsibility of the Conservative Government for British policy in Egypt first came into dispute. The debate opened with an explanation by Granville of his policy in recent events.* It included a speech by Salisbury, calling attention to certain points in Granville's recently presented dispatch to Dufferin of 11 July (No. 1092 *ij*) and in particular to the implication 'that the idea of co-operating with France [in Egypt] originated at the Congress of Berlin'.† According to Salisbury's contention the source of this policy of co-operation must be traced farther back, since, as he said, it 'took an efficient and emphatic form at the time that Mr. Goschen and M. Joubert went out to Egypt', i.e. in 1876. 'Nothing', said Salisbury, 'was done at Berlin to increase, much less to diminish, that co-operation. No kind of obligation or engagement was entered into then, or at any time during the term of office of the late Government, which has imposed upon this country the duty of co-operating with France a moment further than the interests of this country would dictate.' This contest in responsibility did not end with the debate of July 1882. It was raised in an acute form nearly two years later, through a statement made by Gladstone in the Commons, and it resulted in the laying of an extract from a dispatch of 1879 (No. 1147 *k*). On 3 April 1884, reference was made in the House to Gladstone's letter to the Workmen's Peace Association replying to a protest against the war in the Soudan; in the course of this letter he had stated that 'the covenants under which this Country has been acting in Egypt were not made by the present Government'.‡ A few days later the question was raised again in a slightly different form, and, in the discussion arising from it, Bourke, the late

* *Hans. Deb.* 3rd Ser. CCLXXII, 1484–94. The speech was in the form of a motion for an address for papers, an early example of the use of this form by a Minister of the Crown [*v. infra*, No. 1092 *m*].

† *Hans. Deb.* 3rd Ser. CCLXXII, 1498. Cp. Granville's statement in his dispatch (*A. & P.* [1882], LXXXII [C. 3258], 442 [*v. infra*, No. 1092 *ij*]). The reference is to 'despatches exchanged between Lord Salisbury and M. Waddington, after the Congress of Berlin in July and August 1878'. The policy is described as having been 'subsequently put into operation' and Granville added that it 'was in full operation' before he entered office.

‡ *Hans. Deb.* 3rd Ser. CCLXXXVI, 1521–2.

Under-Secretary, said that the late Government had no objection whatever to the production of the documents to which reference had been intended.* Accordingly, when an Egyptian Blue Book was presented on 24 April (No. 1147k), an extract was included from Salisbury's secret and separate dispatch to Malet of 19 September 1879, describing a conversation with Waddington at Dieppe.† The extract omitted paragraphs 2–7 which detailed the course of the conversation, but it included almost in full the series of seven points on which Salisbury and Waddington had 'agreed', as a result. The third of these was that the 'native government' was to be 'earnestly supported'. A dispatch from Lyons to Granville of 25 February 1881 was printed with this document in 1884, and also two dispatches from Granville to Malet of 3 and 7 March, referring to the decision of England and France to 'sustain the authority of the Khedive'. When this Blue Book appeared Salisbury complained in the Lords that his dispatch had been printed in a misleading form, and an amended extract was accordingly laid as a separate paper on 1 May (No. 1148a). The document, it is true, was even then only an extract, but it contained part of the preliminary account of the conversation, and in Salisbury's interpretation a substantial difference existed between the two versions. The first might be taken to imply a general promise to support the Khedive; the fuller text (and still more the original—though even this was far from clear) was at least open to the interpretation that the earnest support was to be given to the system by which the Khedive's ministry would no longer contain European ministers but would be wholly native.‡

By May 1884, it is true, it would be hard to blame the

---

* *Hans. Deb.* 3rd Ser. CCLXXXVI, 1800.

† The original draft of this document in Salisbury's own hand, as well as the final text, is in F.O. 78/2940. Reference to the discussion at Dieppe is made in Cecil, *Salisbury*, II, 358, 363–4. Cp. also *D.D.F.*, Ière Sér. II, 571–2, No. 470.

‡ Cp. *Hans. Deb.* 3rd Ser. CCLXXXVII, 1015–16. Granville's explanation of the way in which the extract was made is substantially borne out by the record of its preparation in the archives. He himself wrote to Waddington explaining the reason for publication, and asking whether he objected. He added, as an afterthought, 'probably with omissions of the second, third, fourth, fifth and sixth and seventh paragraphs'. F.O. 78/3740. Granville to Waddington, 16 April 1884.

Liberal Government for any expedient useful in defending their policy in Egypt. Though the worst disaster of the year was yet to come, from the Parliamentary standpoint the vote of censure in the Lords on 12 February was sufficiently damaging, and it was from their own Blue Books that the case against them was built up.*

If the publication of dispatches in the Egyptian Blue Books brought disputes in Parliament and discussions with France, the colonial papers of 1884–5 brought difficulties with Germany. In this case, these difficulties were, however, to a large extent the reflection of the general irritation which the colonial question caused on both sides. On this subject Bismarck published White Books himself, the first to be laid before the Reichstag,† and while his publication was to some extent a reply to English practice, the appearance of the White Books in turn stimulated publication here. Thus the paper presented on 20 February 1885, describing Meade's conversations at Berlin (No. 1152), was the result of the appearance of the German White Book on *German Interests in the South Seas* presented on 4 February. There were, nevertheless, vigorous attacks on the English Parliamentary Papers in the German Press, and Bismarck found it hard to forgive the appearance in a Blue Book of a dispatch of 24 January 1885, recording a confidential conversation between himself and Malet.‡ Actually, considerable discretion had been shown. The original dispatch§ had been divided into two, and one part—in which Bismarck had expressed his strong disapproval of Münster—had been marked 'secret' and was withheld from publication. The section which was published, however, contained a reference to Bismarck's instructions to Münster of 5 May 1884, explaining his attitude on colonial questions. These were the instructions which Münster failed

---

* Cp. *Hans. Deb.* 3rd Ser. CCLXXXIV, 567–658, especially Salisbury's speech, pp. 567–80.

† Cp. J. Sass, *Die deutschen Weissbücher zur auswärtigen Politik, 1870–1914* [Berlin and Leipzig, 1928]; cp. W. O. Aydelotte, *Bismarck and British Colonial Policy* [1937], App. II, which analyses both the German White Books and the English Blue Books.

‡ *A. & P.* [1884–5], LIV [C. 4273], 389–90.

§ F.O. 64/1076. Malet to Granville, No. 45, Secret, of 24 January 1885.

to communicate to Granville, and which were described by Sir Eyre Crowe in 1907 as 'the famous bogey document'.* Bismarck's disapproval, moreover, was not limited to particular dispatches. He alleged that publication had frequently taken place of confidential communications on which he had not been consulted;† and his irritation undoubtedly threatened to increase estrangement between the two countries. When the Conservatives returned to power in the summer of 1885, Malet advised the Foreign Office to be particularly careful in its selection of documents for publication, lest the Chancellor should 'feel that he can trust this Government as little as he did the last'.‡

* Gooch and Temperley, *British Documents on the Origin of the War*, III, 422. Sir Eyre Crowe was wrong in saying that this document was published in the White Book. The text is in *G.P.* IV, 50–2.

† Cp. Fitzmaurice, *Life of Granville*, II, 427–9.

‡ Malet to Pauncefote, 31 October 1885. F.O. 78/3863.

SESSION 1. 5 FEBRUARY TO 24 MARCH 1880

SESSION 2. 29 APRIL TO 7 SEPTEMBER 1880

VOLUME LIII (1880)

East India

VOLUME LIX (1880)

Law and Crime; Police; Prisons

VOLUME LXIX (1880)

Trade, Slave Trade, etc.

VOLUME LXXV (1880)

Commercial Reports

VOLUME LXXVIII (1880)

State Papers

VOLUME LXXIX (1880)

State Papers

1029   Agreement between the British and Spanish Governments
        respecting Telegraphic Messages between Gibraltar and Spain.
        (Signed at London, 20th March 1880.) [*Commercial No. 16
        (1880)*.]   PAGE 561
             [C. 2540]   L/C. HC. 5 May, HL. 20 May 1880.

1030   Convention prolonging the Duration of the Extradition Treaty
        between Great Britain and Switzerland, of the 31st March 1874,
        for Twelve Months, from the 22nd December 1879. (Signed at
        Berne, 8th December 1879.) [*Switzerland No. 1 (1880)*.]
                                                           PAGE 565
             [C. 2467]   L/C. 5 Feb. 1880.

                    VOLUME LXXX (1880)

                 State Papers: Turkey

1031   Correspondence respecting the Commission sent by the Porte
        to inquire into the Condition of the Vilayet of Aleppo. [*Turkey
        No. 1 (1880)*.]   PAGE 1
             [C. 2468]   L/C. 5 Feb. 1880.

1031 a Further Correspondence respecting the European Commissions
        appointed for the Demarcation of Frontiers under the Treaty
        of Berlin [*v. supra*, No. 999 a]. [*Turkey No. 2 (1880)*.]   PAGE 147
             [C. 2471]   L/C. HL. 20 Feb., HC. 23 Feb. 1880.

1031 b Correspondence respecting the Condition of the Populations in
        Asia Minor and Syria. [*Turkey No. 4 (1880)*.]   PAGE 647
             [C. 2537]   L/C. 20 May 1880.

                    VOLUME LXXXI (1880)

                 State Papers: Turkey

1032   Correspondence respecting the Condition of the Mussulman,
        Greek and Jewish Populations in Eastern Roumelia. [*Turkey
        No. 5 (1880)*.]   PAGE 1
             [C. 2552]   L/C. 20 May 1880.

1032a   Correspondence respecting the Arrest of Dr. Koelle by the
        Turkish Police. [*Turkey No. 6 (1880)*.]   PAGE 323
             [C. 2553]   L/C. 20 May 1880.

VOLUME LXXXII (1880)

State Papers: Turkey

HOUSE OF LORDS SESSIONAL PAPERS

VOLUME XIX (1880)

Foreign Countries. State Correspondence, Treaties, etc.

SESSION 6 JANUARY TO 27 AUGUST 1881

VOLUME LXX (1881)

East India

VOLUME XCI (1881)

Commercial Reports

VOLUME XCVIII (1881)

State Papers

VOLUME XCIX (1881)

State Papers

1047*b*   Declaration for prolonging the Duration of the Treaty of
         Commerce and Navigation between Her Majesty and the King
         of Italy, of 6th August 1863, till 31st December 1881. Signed
         at Rome, 11th December 1880. [*Commercial No. 4 (1881)*.]
                                                          PAGE 75
              [C. 2750]   L/C. 6 Jan. 1881.

1048   Treaty between Her Majesty and the King of the Netherlands,
         Grand Duke of Luxemburg, for the Mutual Surrender of
         Fugitive Criminals. Signed at Luxemburg, 24th November
         1880. [*Luxemburg No. 1 (1881)*.]   PAGE 79
              [C. 2803]   L/C. 7 Mar. 1881.

1049   Convention between Great Britain, Germany, Austria-Hungary,
         Belgium, Denmark, Spain, The United States, The French
         Republic, Italy, Morocco, The Netherlands, Portugal, and
         Sweden and Norway, for the Settlement of the Right of Pro-
         tection in Morocco. Signed at Madrid, 3rd July 1880. [*Morocco
         No. 1 (1881)*.]   PAGE 89
              [C. 3053]   L/C. 23 Aug. 1881.

1050   Papers relating to the Arbitration of the Emperor of Austria in
         the Differences between the Government of Her Britannic
         Majesty and of the Republic of Nicaragua respecting the Inter-
         pretation of certain Articles of the Treaty of Managua. Signed
         on the 28th January 1860. [*Nicaragua No. 1 (1881)*.] PAGE 101
              [C. 3057]   L/C. 27 Aug. 1881.

1050*a*   Further Papers. [*Nicaragua No. 2 (1881)*.]   PAGE 135
              [C. 3058]   L/C. 27 Aug. 1881.

1051   Correspondence respecting the Condition of the Nestorian
         Community in the District of Oroomiah. [*Persia No. 1 (1881)*.]
                                                          PAGE 253
              [C. 2884]   L/C. 13 May 1881.

1052   Agreement between the Governments of Great Britain and
         Portugal for increasing the Limits of Weight and the Dimensions
         of Packets of Patterns of Merchandise exchanged through the
         Post between the two Countries. Signed at London, 23rd
         October 1880. [*Commercial No. 2 (1881)*.]   PAGE 267
              [C. 2745]   L/C. 6 Jan. 1881.

1052*a*   Correspondence respecting the Results of the Treaty of Com-
         merce between Her Majesty and the King of Portugal and the
         Algarves. Signed at Lisbon, 26th December 1878. [*Commercial
         No. 34 (1881)*.]   PAGE 271
              [C. 3035]   L/C. 23 Aug. 1881.

VOLUME C (1881)

State Papers

SESSION 7 FEBRUARY TO 2 DECEMBER 1882

VOLUME XLVIII (1882)

East India

VOLUME LXV (1882)

Trade, Slave Trade

VOLUME LXXII (1882)

Commercial Reports

VOLUME LXXX (1882)

State Papers

1066*d*   Further Correspondence [May, Dec. 1882]. [*United States No. 5 (1882).*]   PAGE 85

  [C. 3446]   L/C. 2 Dec. 1882.

1067   Agreement between the British and Austro-Hungarian Governments for the Mutual Relief of Distressed Seamen, signed at London, 26th November 1880. [*Commercial No. 14 (1882).*]
                                                          PAGE 103

  [C. 3189]   L/C. HC. 27 Ap., HL. 28 Ap. 1882.

1068   Correspondence respecting the Affairs in Central Asia. [*Central Asia No. 1 (1882).*]   PAGE 107

  [C. 3136]   L/C. 13 Mar. 1882.

1069   Despatch from Her Majesty's Chargé d'Affaires at St. Petersburgh, enclosing Copy of a Treaty between Russia and China. Signed at St. Petersburgh, 12th February 1881, with Documents relating thereto. [*China No. 1 (1882).*]   PAGE 123

  [C. 3134]   L/C. 2 Mar. 1882.

1069*a*   Correspondence respecting the Agreement between the Ministers Plenipotentiary of the Governments of Great Britain and China, signed at Cheefoo, 13th September 1876 [*v. supra,* No. 1014]. [*China No. 3 (1882).*]   PAGE 147

  [C. 3395]   L/C. 17 Aug. 1882.

1070   Additional Act to the Public Act of 2nd November 1865 relative to the Navigation of the Mouths of the Danube, signed at Galatz, 28th May 1881. [*Danube No. 1 (1882).*]   PAGE 249

  [C. 3253]   L/C. 4 July 1882.

1070*a*   Correspondence respecting the Execution of the Provisions of the Treaty of Berlin with regard to the Navigation of the Danube. [*Danube No. 2 (1882).*]   PAGE 259

  [C. 3392]   L/C. 17 Aug. 1882.

1071   Additional Articles, dated 16th of January/27th of February 1882, to the Money Order Convention between the...United Kingdom, and...Denmark, dated 22nd of April/16th of May 1871.   PAGE 291

  [C. 3222]   L/C. HC. 17 Ap., HL. 20 Ap. 1882.

VOLUME LXXXI (1882)

State Papers

1075   *Treaty of Commerce*, etc.: Declaration between the British and
        Italian Governments prolonging till the 31st May 1882 the
        Treaty of Commerce and Navigation between Great Britain
        and Italy of 6th August 1863. Signed at Rome, 29th November
        1881. [*Commercial No. 2 (1882)*.]   PAGE 1

   [C. 3102]   L/C. 7 Feb. 1882.

1075a   Declaration for prolonging the Duration of the Treaty of Com-
        merce and Navigation...of 6th August 1863, till the 30th June
        1883. Signed at Rome, 31st May 1882. [*Commercial No. 20
        (1882)*.]   PAGE 5

   [C. 3233]   L/C. 8 June 1882.

1075b   Additional Articles...relative to the Exchange of Money Orders
        between the United Kingdom of Great Britain and Ireland and
        the Kingdom of Italy, 1881.   PAGE 9

   [C. 3140]   L/C. 16 Feb. 1882.

1076   Convention between the General Post Office of the United
        Kingdom and the Post Office of the Empire of Japan for an
        Exchange of Money Orders, dated the 10th May/25th July
        1881.   PAGE 17

   [C. 3116]   L/C. 7 Feb. 1882.

1077   Treaty of Friendship, Commerce and Navigation, between Her
        Majesty and the Prince of Montenegro. Signed at Cettinjé,
        21st January 1882. [*Commercial No. 18 (1882)*.]   PAGE 27

   [C. 3231]   L/C. 8 June 1882.

1078   Regulations respecting the Mode of Payment, etc., of the
        Agrarian Tax and the Gate Tax. [*Morocco No. 1 (1882)*.]
                                                              PAGE 39

   [C. 3163]   L/C. 30 Mar. 1882.

1078a   Correspondence respecting Libellous Statements concerning
        Her Majesty's Minister in Morocco. [*Morocco No. 2 (1882)*.]
                                                              PAGE 51

   [C. 3164]   L/C. 30 Mar. 1882.

1079   Papers relating to the Affairs of Sulu and Borneo, and to the Grant of a Charter of Incorporation to the 'British North Borneo Company'. Part II. Correspondence respecting the Claims of Holland. [*Netherlands No. 1 (1882).*]   PAGE 59
         [C. 3109]   *L/C.* 7 Feb. 1882.

1080   Correspondence between Her Majesty's Government and the Governments of Peru and Chili relative to the Claims of Peruvian Bondholders. [*Peru No. 1 (1882).*]   PAGE 121
         [C. 3448]   *L/C.* 2 Dec. 1882.

1081   Correspondence respecting Mr. John Dixon's claim against the Portuguese Government. [*Commercial No. 31 (1882).*]
                                                                        PAGE 157
         [C. 3303]   *L/C.* 11 Aug. 1882.

1081 *a* Convention between Her Majesty and the King of Portugal, Supplementary to the Treaty of Commerce and Navigation of 3rd July 1842 [*v. supra*, No. 297 *a*]. Signed at Lisbon, 22nd May 1882. [*Commercial No. 28 (1882).*]   PAGE 177
         [C. 3255]   *L/C.* 6 July 1882.

1081 *b* Treaty of Friendship and Commerce between the South African Republic, now the Transvaal State, and His Majesty the King of Portugal, with Protocol annexed. Signed at Lisbon, 11th December 1875. [*Portugal No. 1 (1882).*]   PAGE 181
         [C. 3410]   *L/C.* HC. 23 Nov., HL. 24 Nov. 1882.

1082   Correspondence respecting the Treatment of Jews in Russia. [*Russia No. 1 (1882).*]   PAGE 205
         [C. 3132]   *L/C.* 9 Feb. 1882.

1082 *a* Further Correspondence [Jan.–May 1882]. [*Russia No. 2 (1882).*]   PAGE 235
         [C. 3250]   *L/C.* 29 June 1882.

1083   Treaty between Her Majesty and the Republic of Salvador for the Mutual Surrender of Fugitive Criminals. Signed at Paris, 23rd June 1881. [*Salvador No. 1 (1882).*]   PAGE 279
         [C. 3445]   *L/C.* 2 Dec. 1882.

1084   Correspondence respecting Commercial Relations between Spain and Great Britain. [*Commercial No. 38 (1882).*] PAGE 289
         [C. 3346]   *L/C.* 17 Aug. 1882.

VOLUME LXXXII (1882)

State Papers: Egypt

1092*a*   Despatch [10 Jan. 1882] from Her Majesty's Agent and Consul
General at Cairo, forwarding a Copy of the Note presented to
the Khedive by the English and French Agents. [*Egypt No. 2
(1882)*.]   PAGE 5

  [C. 3106]   *L/C.* 7 Feb. 1882.

1092*b*   Correspondence respecting the Affairs of Egypt [9 Sept.–4 Nov.
1881]. [*Egypt No. 3 (1882)*.]   PAGE 9

  [C. 3161]   *L/C.* 27 Mar. 1882.

1092*c*   Return showing the Number of Foreigners in the Service of the
Egyptian Government. [*Egypt No. 4 (1882)*.]   PAGE 89

  [C. 3188]   *L/C.* HC. 4 Ap., HL. 21 Ap. 1882.

1092*d*   Correspondence respecting the Affairs of Egypt [5 Nov. 1881–
6 Feb. 1882]. [*Egypt No. 5 (1882)*.]   PAGE 97

  [C. 3230]   *L/C.* 1 June 1882.

1092*e*   Despatch [18 May 1882] from Sir E. Malet forwarding a List
of Europeans in the Service of the Egyptian Government.
[*Egypt No. 6 (1882)*.]   PAGE 189

  [C. 3237]   *L/C.* 15 June 1882.

1092*f*   Further Correspondence respecting the Affairs of Egypt [6 Feb.–
16 May 1882]. [*Egypt No. 7 (1882)*.]   PAGE 213

  [C. 3249]   *L/C.* 22 June 1882.

1092*g*   do. [11–31 May 1882]. [*Egypt No. 8 (1882)*.]   PAGE 367

  [C. 3251]   *L/C.* 3 July 1882.

1092*h*   Extract from a Despatch [16 Jan. 1882] addressed to Viscount
Lyons respecting the Affairs of Egypt. [*Egypt No. 9 (1882)*.]

                                                      PAGE 435
  [C. 3257]   *L/C.* 14 July 1882.

1092*ij* Despatch from Earl Granville to the Earl of Dufferin [11 July
1882] respecting the Affairs of Egypt. [*Egypt No. 10 (1882)*.]

                                                      PAGE 439
  [C. 3258]   *L/C.* 20 July 1882.

1092*k*   Correspondence respecting the Affairs of Egypt [May, June
1882]. [*Egypt No. 11 (1882)*.]   PAGE 455

  [C. 3295]   *L/C.* 21 July 1882.

VOLUME LXXXIII (1882)

State Papers: Egypt

Session 15 February to 25 August 1883

Volume XLVI (1883)

Colonies and British Possessions

Volume XLVII (1883)

Colonies and British Possessions

Volume XLVIII (1883)

Colonies and British Possessions

1097a Correspondence respecting the Territory on the West Coast of
Africa lying between 5° 12′ and 8° of South Latitude, 1847–77.
[*Africa No. 2 (1883)*.]   PAGE 103

    [C. 3531]   *L/C.* HC. 30 Mar., HL. 3 Ap. 1883.

VOLUME LXIV (1883)

Trade, etc.

1098 *Suez Canal:* Return showing what Proportion of the Trade of
the United Kingdom with the East goes through the Suez Canal,
and what round the Cape; the Proportion of such Trade
through the Canal to the whole Foreign Trade of the United
Kingdom, etc.   PAGE 773

    41   *Pursuant to Order (HC. 1 Dec. 1882),* HC. 19 Feb.,
    O.T.B.P. 27 Feb. 1883.

1098a Copy of Heads of Agreement between the Representatives of
Her Majesty's Government and the President of the Suez Canal
Company.   PAGE 805

    249   *Pursuant to Order (HC. 11 July),* HC. 11 July 1883.

VOLUME LXVI (1883)

Trade; Slave Trade

1099 Correspondence with British Representatives and Agents
Abroad, and Reports from Naval Officers and the Treasury
relative to the Slave Trade, 1882–83. [*Slave Trade No. 1 (1883)*.]
PAGE 285

    [C. 3547]   *L/C.* 10 Ap. 1883.

1099a Declaration between Great Britain and Turkey amending the
Convention of the 25th January 1880, between Her Majesty
and the Sultan for the Suppression of the Slave Trade. Signed
at Constantinople, 3rd March 1883. [*Slave Trade No. 2 (1883)*.]
PAGE 511

    [C. 3590]   *L/C.* HC. 21 May, HL. 24 May 1883.

1099b Reports on the State of the Slave Trade and Slavery in
Morocco. [*Slave Trade No. 4 (1883)*.]   PAGE 535

    [C. 3700]   *L/C.* 2 Aug. 1883.

1099*c*   Convention between Her Majesty and the Sultan of Mohilla
for the Suppression of Slavery and the Slave Trade. Signed
at Doani, 24th October 1882. [*Slave Trade No. 5 (1883)*.]

PAGE 545

[C. 3702]   *L/C.* 3 Aug. 1883.

1099*d*   Convention between Her Majesty and the Sultan of Johanna
for the Suppression of Slavery and the Slave Trade. Signed
at Bambao, 10th October 1882. [*Slave Trade No. 6 (1883)*.]

PAGE 551

[C. 3727]   *L/C.* 3 Aug. 1883.

VOLUME LXXV (1883)

Commercial Reports, etc.

1100   *China:* Despatch from Her Majesty's Chargé d'Affaires at
Peking, forwarding a Report by Mr. A. Hosie, Student Inter-
preter in the China Consular Service, of a Journey through the
Provinces of Kueichow and Yünnan. [*China No. 1 (1883)*.]

PAGE 161

[C. 3457]   *L/C.* 15 Feb. 1883.

1100*a*   Correspondence respecting a Statement in the 'Kölnische
Zeitung' as to the Negotiations with China in 1860. [*China
No. 3 (1883)*.]   PAGE 199

[C. 3469]   *L/C.* 19 Feb. 1883.

1101   Agreement between the Governments of Great Britain and
Siam for regulating the Traffic in Spirituous Liquors; signed at
London, 6th April 1883. [*Siam No. 1 (1883)*.]   PAGE 307

[C. 3549]   *L/C.* 12 Ap. 1883.

1102   *Treaties of Commerce and Navigation:* List of Treaties of Commerce
and Navigation between Great Britain and Foreign Powers,
containing Most Favoured Nation Clauses, stating the Period
when Terminable, and showing whether they apply to the
British Colonies. [*Commercial No. 30 (1883)*.]   PAGE 899

[C. 3735]   *L/C.* 23 Aug. 1883.

VOLUME LXXXII (1883)

State Papers

1103   Declaration additional to the Articles signed on the 26/28th
September 1871, as additional Articles to the Convention of the
31st of May 1869, for the Exchange of Money Orders between
the United Kingdom...and the Kingdom of Belgium.   PAGE 1
   [C. 3480]   L/C. 15 Feb. 1883.

1104   Correspondence relating to Article XXXVIII of the Treaty
of Berlin (Balkan Railways). [*Commercial No. 33 (1883)*.]
                                                              PAGE 5
   [C. 3782]   L/C. 23 Aug. 1883.

1105   Despatches from Her Majesty's Ambassador at St. Petersburgh,
forwarding Translations of the published Reports of Mr. Lessar's
Journeys in Central Asia. [*Central Asia No. 1 (1883)*.]
                                                             PAGE 57
   [C. 3586]   L/C. 4 May 1883.

1106   Despatch [5 Jan. 1883] from Her Majesty's Chargé d'Affaires
in Chile, forwarding a Convention for the Settlement of the
Claims of British Subjects. Signed at Santiago on the 4th
January 1883. [*Chile No. 1 (1883)*.]   PAGE 81
   [C. 3546]   L/C. 10 Ap. 1883.

1106a   Convention between Great Britain and the Republic of Chile,
for the Settlement of the Claims of British Subjects. Signed at
Santiago, 4th January 1883. [*Chile No. 2 (1883)*.]   PAGE 87
   [C. 3699]   L/C. 31 July 1883.

1107   Correspondence respecting the Navigation of the Danube.
[*Danube No. 1 (1883)*.]   PAGE 95
   [C. 3525]   L/C. 15 Mar. 1883.

1107a   Protocols of Conferences held in London respecting the Navigation of the Danube. [*Danube No. 2 (1883)*.]   PAGE 161
   [C. 3526]   L/C. 15 Mar. 1883.

1107b   Despatch [14 Mar.] to Her Majesty's Representatives Abroad
respecting the Navigation of the Danube, and the Conferences
relating thereto, held in London, 1883. [*Danube No. 3 (1883)*.]
                                                            PAGE 245
   [C. 3527]   L/C. 15 Mar. 1883.

VOLUME LXXXIII (1883)

State Papers: Egypt

VOLUME LXXXIV (1883)

State Papers: Egypt

SESSION 5 FEBRUARY TO 14 AUGUST 1884

VOLUME LV (1884)

Colonies and British Possessions

VOLUME LVI (1884)

Colonies and British Possessions

VOLUME LXXV (1884)

Trade, Slave Trade, etc.

VOLUME LXXXIII (1884)

Commercial Reports

1127   Correspondence respecting the Claims of the Rustchuk and Varna Railway Company under Article X of the Treaty of Berlin. [*Commercial No. 13 (1884)*.]   PAGE 505

       [C. 3931]   R–A. (*HL. 26 Feb.*), 28 Mar. 1884.

VOLUME LXXXVII (1884)

State Papers

1128   Correspondence relating to the Mission of Vice Admiral Sir W. Hewett to King John of Abyssinia, and Treaty between Great Britain, Egypt, and Abyssinia. Signed at Adowa, 3rd June 1884. [*Abyssinia No. 1 (1884)*.]   PAGE 1

       [C. 4103]   L/C. 22 July 1884.

1129   Correspondence with the United States...respecting the Sentence passed upon the Convict O'Donnell. [*United States No. 2 (1884)*.]   PAGE 11

       [C. 3835]   L/C. HC. 5 Feb., HL. 7 Feb. 1884.

1129a   Correspondence respecting the Termination of the Fishery Articles of the Treaty of Washington of the 8th May 1871. [*United States No. 3 (1884)*.]   PAGE 15

       [C. 3848]   L/C. HC. 5 Feb., HL. 7 Feb. 1884.

1129b   Further Correspondence respecting the Clayton-Bulwer Treaty, and the Projected Panama Canal. [*United States No. 1 (1884)*.]   PAGE 21

       [C. 3834]   L/C. HC. 5 Feb., HL. 7 Feb. 1884.

1130   Agreement between the Governments of Great Britain and the Argentine Republic for Increasing the Limits of Weight and the Dimensions of Packets of Patterns of Merchandise exchanged through the Post. Signed at Buenos Ayres, 10th June 1884. [*Commercial No. 32 (1884)*.]   PAGE 31

       [C. 4101]   L/C. 24 July 1884.

1131   Further Correspondence relating to Article XXXVIII of the Treaty of Berlin (Balkan Railways). [*Commercial No. 16 (1884)*.]
PAGE 35
        [C. 3961]   L/C. HC. 7 Ap., HL. 21 Ap. 1884.

1132   Correspondence respecting the Affairs of Asia [*v. supra*, No. 1039*c*]. [*Central Asia No. 1 (1884)*.]   PAGE 57
        [C. 3930]   L/C. 1 Ap. 1884.

1133   Correspondence respecting the Co-operation of Neutral Powers for the Protection of their Subjects in China in case of necessity. [*China No. 3 (1884)*.]   PAGE 185
        [C. 3846]   L/C. HC. 5 Feb., HL. 7 Feb. 1884.

1134   Treaty of Friendship and Commerce between Her Majesty and His Majesty the King of Corea. Signed at Hanyang, 26th November 1883. [*Corea No. 2 (1884)*.]   PAGE 203
        [C. 4044]   L/C. 20 June 1884.

1135   Direct Exchange of Money Orders with Iceland. Additional Articles, dated the 14th/31st of December 1883, to the Money Order Convention between the...United Kingdom, and... Denmark, dated the 22nd April/16th May 1871.   PAGE 219
        [C. 3956]   L/C. 24 Mar. 1884.

1136   International Convention for the Protection of Industrial Property. Signed at Paris, 20th March 1883. Acceded to by Her Majesty's Government, 17th March 1884. [*Commercial No. 28 (1884)*.]   PAGE 225
        [C. 4043]   L/C. 20 June 1884.

1137   Papers respecting the Renewal of Diplomatic Relations with Mexico. [*Mexico No. 1 (1884)*.]   PAGE 239
        [C. 4176]   L/C. 12 Aug. 1884.

1138   Correspondence respecting the Wreck of the 'Nisero', and the Detention of her Crew by the Rajah of Tenom. [*Netherlands No. 1 (1884)*.]   PAGE 255
        [C. 4024]   L/C. 23 May 1884.

1138*a* Further Correspondence [5–31 May 1884]. [*Netherlands No. 2 (1884)*.]   PAGE 361
        [C. 4041]   L/C. 9 June 1884.

1138*b* do. [1 May–19 July 1884]. [*Netherlands No. 3 (1884)*.]
PAGE 387
        [C. 4102]   L/C. 21 July 1884.

1138c do. [19–31 July 1884]. [*Netherlands No. 4 (1884)*.]   PAGE 465
       [C. 4108]   L/C. 1 Aug. 1884.

1139   Convention between Her Majesty, the German Emperor, King
       of Prussia, the King of the Belgians, the King of Denmark, the
       President of the French Republic, and the King of the Nether-
       lands, for Regulating the Police of the North Sea Fisheries.
       Signed at the Hague, 6th May 1882. [*Commercial No. 11 (1884)*.]
                                                              PAGE 487
       [C. 3928]   L/C. 27 Mar. 1884.

1140   Further Correspondence respecting Mr. John Dixon's Claim
       against the Guimaràes Railway Company. [*Commercial No. 24
       (1884)*.]   PAGE 505
       [C. 4021]   R–A. (*HC. 13 Mar.*), 20 May 1884.

1141   Treaty between Her Majesty and His Majesty the King of Siam
       for the Prevention of Crime in the Territories of Chiengmai,
       Lakon, Lampoonchi, and for the Promotion of Commerce
       between British Burmah and the Territories aforesaid. Signed
       at Bangkok, 3rd September 1883. [*Siam No. 1 (1884)*.]
                                                              PAGE 549
       [C. 4049]   L/C. 30 June 1884.

1142   Protocol of Agreement and Declaration between the Govern-
       ments of Great Britain and Spain respecting the Commercial
       Relations of the two Countries. [*Commercial No. 5 (1884)*.]
                                                              PAGE 557
       [C. 3847]   L/C. HC. 5 Feb., HL. 7 Feb. 1884.

1142a Correspondence respecting the Commercial Relations between
       Great Britain and Spain. [*Commercial No. 6 (1884)*.]   PAGE 563
       [C. 3880]   L/C. 14 Feb. 1884.

1142b Memorial from the Association of Chambers of Commerce
       on the Subject of the Commercial Negotiations with Spain.
       [*Commercial No. 18 (1884)*.]   PAGE 573
       [C. 3963]   R–A. (*HC. 27 Mar.*), HC. 8 Ap., HL.
                            21 Ap. 1884.

1142c Despatch to Her Majesty's Chargé d'Affaires at Madrid on the
       Subject of the Protocol of 1st December 1883, respecting the
       Commercial Relations of Great Britain and Spain. [*Commercial
       No. 23 (1884)*.]   PAGE 581
       [C. 4004]   L/C. 13 May 1884.

VOLUME LXXXVIII (1884)

State Papers: Egypt

Volume LXXXIX (1884)

State Papers: Egypt

Note. A paper with the title 'Correspondence respecting the condition of the Populations in the Asiatic Provinces of the Ottoman Empire' was laid before both Houses on 11 August 1884 as *Turkey No. 1 (1884)*. The Index to the House of Commons series of Accounts and Papers gives it the command number [C. 4133]. No copy, however, exists in the bound set of either House, and there is a record in Vol. xxviii (1884) of the *House of Lords Sessional Papers* to the effect that it was 'not printed'.

Session 23 October 1884 to 14 August 1885

Volume LIII (1884–5)

Colonies and British Possessions

Volume LIV (1884–5)

Colonies and British Possessions

VOLUME LV (1884–5)

Colonies and British Possessions

VOLUME LVI (1884–5)

Colonies and British Possessions

1157   Further Correspondence respecting the Settlement at Angra Pequeña, on the South West Coast of Africa [*v. supra*, No. 1125].

PAGE 1

    [C. 4262]   *L/C.* 6 Dec. 1884.

1157*a*   Despatch from the Earl of Derby to Her Majesty's High Commissioner in South Africa, relative to the Establishment of a German Protectorate at Angra Pequeña, and along the neighbouring Coast.

PAGE 89

    [C. 4265]   *L/C.* 6 Dec. 1884.

VOLUME LXIX (1884–5)

Shipping

1158   Despatch from the British Directors of the Suez Canal Company, enclosing Revised Regulations for the Navigation of the Suez Canal. [*Commercial No. 28 (1885)*.]

PAGE 535

    [C. 4591]   *L/C.* HC. 12 Aug., HL. 13 Aug. 1885.

VOLUME LXXI (1884–5)

Trade, etc.

1159   Correspondence respecting the negotiation of a Treaty Regulating Trade between the British West India Colonies and the United States. [*Commercial No. 4 (1885)*.]

PAGE 75

    [C. 4340]   *L/C.* 20 Mar. 1885.

* A paper entitled 'Further Correspondence respecting the Affairs of Central Asia' was laid in the House of Lords on 13 August 1885 and in the Commons on the 14th, as *Central Asia No. 6 (1885)*. In the Index to the House of Commons Papers it is given a command number [C. 4593], but it was not included in the bound set of either House.

* There is no entry in *L.J.* for the laying of this paper, but the paper is included in Vol. xxviii of the *House of Lords Sessional Papers* for the year 1884–5, and is indexed as having been laid in August 1885, with no day of the month indicated.

VOLUME LXXXVIII (1884–5)

State Papers: Egypt

Volume LXXXIX (1884–5)

State Papers: Egypt

HOUSE OF LORDS SESSIONAL PAPERS

VOLUME XII (1884–5)

THE GREEK AND BULGARIAN
BLUE BOOKS, 1886*

THE spectacular events which marked the Bulgarian crisis at every stage of its development, and their intimate connection with the old political controversies over the Treaty of Berlin, combined with the uncertainty of party circumstances to produce the very full Blue Books of 1886. One was laid in February, at the time of Salisbury's fall, and the other in June, when the brief Liberal period was nearly ended. Both dealt with very recent events—when the February Blue Book was issued the last documents were little more than a month old. Both appeared in close proximity to a general election. In 1886, however, Ireland and not the Near East was the centre of party politics. Gladstone was wholly preoccupied with the Irish question; at the Foreign Office, Rosebery was taking the first steps towards his great task of subordinating party to general interests; Salisbury's Bulgarian policy had changed. Thus it is the date of presentation alone which betrays the fact that the two great Blue Books on Bulgaria were sponsored by different parties.

But if internal dissension did not materially affect the contents of the Blue Books relations with the Great Powers did. The attitudes of France, Russia, Austria-Hungary, and Germany were all reflected in the selection of the documents and in the omissions that were made from them. The old fear of Russian predominance is carefully concealed, although it influenced Salisbury as much now in favour of the union of the two Bulgarias as it had once influenced him against it. Nor were the suspicions of Austria-Hungary's unwillingness to restrain Servia from invading Macedonia allowed to appear. Again, by the curtailment of documents, Salisbury avoided all mention of Bismarck's original sponsorship of the proposal

* Lord Salisbury became Prime Minister and Secretary of State for Foreign Affairs on 24 June 1885; Mr Gladstone succeeded him as Prime Minister and Lord Rosebery as Secretary of State for Foreign Affairs on 6 February 1886; on 3 August of the same year Lord Iddesleigh became Secretary of State for Foreign Affairs in the second administration of Lord Salisbury.

to send ships to the Piraeus for the restraint of Greece, and lessened the evidence of M. de Freycinet's unreadiness to risk a Greek conflict.* These omissions made Salisbury's task of explaining his policy difficult. He tried to meet this difficulty by his long dispatch to Sir William White in November 1885, which was published in full, but even so the true reasons for his action are not fully represented, and the line which he took appears less intelligible than in fact it was.†

If in the Bulgarian Blue Books the identity of policy between the Conservatives and the Liberals is implied, it is specifically stated in those relating to Greece. On the day of Gladstone's accession to power he, at this date the only Minister who had kissed hands, wrote a letter to M. Gennadius explaining that continuity was to be maintained. This indeed does not appear in the Blue Book, but on the appointment of Lord Rosebery a more official statement was made. In both cases emphasis was laid on the recognition by the Government of the commitments incurred by their predecessors, and on their intention to maintain a similar policy. Thus, as Rosebery said, 'a bridge of honour' was provided for Greece 'as it could be no discredit to her to yield to the advice of so old and approved a friend' as Gladstone (No. 1197b, Rosebery to Rumbold, 8 February 1886). This statement appears in the third Greek Blue Book laid in this Session, a collection of correspondence going back to December 1885. The fourth was laid on the same day, 24 June, and together they carried the course of negotiations down to 8 June. The earlier papers were laid on 10 May. They are comparatively meagre, for the first one (No. 1197) gave merely the texts of the collective notes to Greece of 26 April, 6 and 8 May, and of the Greek reply of 6 May, while the other (No. 1197a) consists wholly of a circular dispatch—also of 6 May—summarising British policy since the beginning of the Bulgarian crisis and repudiating the view that there had been any hostility towards Greece. The policy of the two

* For details of these omissions cp. L. Penson, 'The Principles and Methods of Lord Salisbury's Foreign Policy', *Camb. Hist. Journ.* [1935], vol. v, no. 1, 91–2.

† Salisbury to White, No. 403 A of 2 November 1885. *A. & P.* [1886], LXXV [C. 4612], 221–3 [*v. infra*, No. 1198].

Governments is treated in this dispatch as equally unworthy of criticism, and the debates in Lords and Commons were correspondingly dull.

One Blue Book of the period of Rosebery's tenure of the Foreign Office requires special mention; for although it lies outside the Greek and Bulgarian spheres its subject is to some extent connected with them, and it has a special importance of its own. This is the 'Correspondence respecting the Port of Batoum' laid on 19 August 1886 (No. 1189). It contains three documents, two of which were printed in full. In the third, Rosebery's dispatch of 3 July, only one passage is omitted, although it is marked as an 'extract'. The omitted passage refers to the damage to the validity of the Treaty of Berlin involved in the Russian action, and the same view was reiterated in different terms in the dispatch of 13 July which was given without excision. It is clear indeed that the dispatch of 13 July was written with a view to publication, as M. de Giers himself realised, and as a proclamation of general principles rather than as an attempt to alter Russian policy. Its closing paragraph, drafted with great care, said that it 'must be for the other Powers to judge how far they can acquiesce in this breach of an international engagement'; and it is significant that, as Baron de Staal commented at the time, the foreign Press was at pains to assert that the matter was one which concerned 'almost exclusively the interests of England'.*

* A. Meyendorff, *Correspondance Diplomatique du Baron de Staal* [1929], I, 301.

Session 1. 12 January to 25 June 1886
Session 2. 5 August to 25 September 1886

Volume XLI (1886)

Navy, etc.

Volume XLVI (1886)

Colonies and British Possessions

Volume XLVII (1886)

Colonies and British Possessions

1181b   General Act of the Conference of Berlin. Signed, 26 February
         1885 [v. supra, No. 1154b]. [Africa No. 3 (1886).]   PAGE 97
         [C. 4739]   L/C. 10 June 1886.

1181c   Supplementary Arrangement between England and Germany,
         relative to their respective Spheres of Action in the Gulf of
         Guinea. [Africa No. 4 (1886).]   PAGE 123
         [C. 4858]   L/C. HC. 7 Sept., HL. 9 Sept. 1886.

VOLUME LXVII (1886)

Trade; Slave Trade

1182   Correspondence with the British Representatives and Agents
         Abroad, and Reports from Naval Officers and the Treasury,
         relative to the Slave Trade, 1885. [Slave Trade No. 1 (1886).]
                                                                PAGE 515
         [C. 4776]   L/C. 24 June 1886.

VOLUME LXXIII (1886)

State Papers

1183   Declaration for prolonging the Duration of the Telegraphic
         Convention between Great Britain and Belgium of the 19th
         March 1880, till the 2nd January 1889. Signed at Brussels,
         26th June 1886. [Commercial No. 25 (1886).]   PAGE 1
         [C. 4854]   L/C. 19 Aug. 1886.

1184   Correspondence respecting the French Treaty with Annam,
         and Negotiations between France and China. [China No. 1
         (1886).]   PAGE 5
         [C. 4655]   L/C. HC. 8 Ap., HL. 9 Ap. 1886.

1184a   Agreement between the Governments of Great Britain and
         China for the Settlement of the Yünnan Case, Official Inter-
         course, and Trade between the Two Countries. Signed in the
         English and Chinese Languages, at Chefoo, 13th September
         1876; with an additional Article thereto, for regulating the
         Traffic in Opium. Signed at London, 18th July 1885. [China
         No. 3 (1886).]   PAGE 67
         [C. 4735]   L/C. 25 May 1886.

1184*b*   Despatch from Her Majesty's Minister in China, transmitting a Convention between Her Majesty and His Majesty the Emperor of China relating to Burmah. Signed at Peking, 24th July 1886. [*China No. 5 (1886)*.]   PAGE 77
    [C. 4861]   *L/C*. 25 Sept. 1886.

1185   Treaty between Her Majesty and the Republic of the Equator for the Mutual Surrender of Fugitive Criminals. Signed at Quito, 20th September 1880. [*Equator No. 1 (1886)*.]   PAGE 81
    [C. 4786]   *L/C*. 24 June 1886.

1185*a*   Treaty of Friendship, Commerce and Navigation between Her Majesty and the Republic of the Equator. Signed at Quito, 18th October 1880. [*Commercial No. 22 (1886)*.]   PAGE 93
    [C. 4785]   *L/C*. 24 June 1886.

1186   Convention respecting copyright between Her Majesty and His Majesty the German Emperor. Signed at London, 2nd June 1886. [*Commercial No. 24 (1886)*.]   PAGE 107
    [C. 4853]   *L/C*. 19 Aug. 1886.

1187   Declaration for prolonging the Duration of the Copyright Convention, between Her Majesty and the King of Italy, of the 30th November 1860, till the 31st December 1886. Signed at London, 28th December 1885. [*Italy No. 1 (1886)*.]   PAGE 113
    [C. 4605]   *L/C*. 21 Jan. 1886.

1187*a*   Declaration recording the Accession of Italy to the Convention concluded between the Governments of Great Britain and Egypt, on the 4th August 1877, for the Suppression of the Slave Trade. Signed at Cairo, 21st December 1885. [*Italy No. 2 (1886)*.]   PAGE 117
    [C. 4607]   *L/C*. 21 Jan. 1886.

1187*b*   Convention concluded between the Governments of Great Britain and Italy for the Exchange of Postal Parcels. Signed at Rome, 26th July 1886. [*Commercial No. 27 (1886)*.]
                                      PAGE 121
    [C. 4860]   *L/C*. 25 Sept. 1886.

1188   Treaty of Friendship, Commerce and Navigation between Her Majesty and the Republic of Paraguay. Signed at Assumption, 16th October 1884. [*Commercial No. 13 (1886)*.]   PAGE 141
    [C. 4764]   *L/C*. HC. 21 June, HL. 22 June 1886.

1189   Correspondence respecting the Port of Batoum. [*Russia No. 1 (1886)*.]   PAGE 153
    [C. 4857]   *L/C*: 19 Aug. 1886.

VOLUME LXXV (1886)

State Papers: Turkey

THE BLUE-BOOK POLICY OF SALISBURY*

1887–92

A SURVEY of the Blue Books of Salisbury's third period at the Foreign Office reveals in the first place the careful reticence of his policy towards the Great Powers. The period which opened with the Mediterranean Agreements, which contained more than one moment of Anglo-German *rapprochement*, and the actual conclusion of the Zanzibar-Heligoland Treaty; a period, moreover, which saw the turning point in the movement of Salisbury's interests from the Near East to Africa and the Pacific, could hardly fail to produce Blue Books of interest. But they show little of all these things. Egypt and the Near East provide the largest bulk in the papers and the greatest interest as well—in 1887 and 1888 there is in each case a volume in the bound set given wholly to Egypt, and the interest is continuous throughout. But this profusion, while it portrays in greater or less detail the many points of specific negotiation between England and the Powers, leaves out of account the records of more nebulous and less conclusive intercourse. The famous letter from Bismarck of 22 November 1887, and Salisbury's reply of the 30th, were alike excluded from the Foreign Office archives† from which the Blue-Book selections were made. And the papers concerning the *Accord à Trois* were rigidly shielded from publicity, so that there should be no danger of betrayal or subsequent publication.‡ The Anglo-German Treaty of 1 July 1890 was, indeed, laid before Parliament, but it was accompanied by very few papers, and none that were of importance except Salisbury's dispatch to Malet of 14 June

---

* Lord Salisbury became Secretary of State for Foreign Affairs on 14 January 1887, in succession to Lord Iddesleigh who held that office in the first six months of Lord Salisbury's second administration and then died. A fuller account of Lord Salisbury's Blue-Book policy is given *infra*, pp. 421–5.

† Cp. *Cecil*, IV, 72–7.

‡ Cp. *Gooch and Temperley*, VIII, 1–18. The Bulgarian Blue Books laid in January 1887 (Nos. 1220 and 1220a) and in June 1888 (No. 1246) throw indirectly some light on the situation.

(No. 1276), which was clearly written for publication.* The Heligoland Treaty has in one respect a peculiar position, since the cession of territory was regarded as making a special discussion in Parliament desirable, and the debates thus caused were more vigorous than debates on foreign policy normally were during this period. But even so the full character of the 1890 settlement was not revealed, and for the history of its negotiation we are largely dependent on German sources,† except for the additional material provided by Lady Gwendolen Cecil's extracts from her father's private correspondence.‡ There is, however, some valuable local material relating to Zanzibar (Nos. 1231, 1231a, 1251) which should be studied in this connection.

The numerous other negotiations affecting African problems varied in the fullness of their treatment, and there was sometimes not even a covering dispatch. Texts were laid of the Anglo-French agreements of 1887 and 1888 respecting the New Hebrides (No. 1239); of the declaration of 1888 which abrogated that of 1847 with reference to the islands in the neighbourhood of Tahiti (No. 1239a); and of the West African agreement of 10 August 1889 (No. 1275). In the last of these cases there was a covering dispatch. The Anglo-French declaration of 5 August 1890, which resulted from the bargaining with France consequent upon the German Treaty, was laid within a few days of signature (No. 1287). In 1891 Anglo-Italian protocols of March and April marked out spheres of influence in East Africa (No. 1320), while on 11 June an Anglo-Portuguese Treaty brought to an end the prolonged negotiations which seemed at one time likely to destroy British zeal for the defence of Portuguese colonies (No. 1324). In the case of this Anglo-Portuguese Treaty correspondence was laid separately (Nos. 1308–1308b). But of the constant flow of dispatches and telegrams which this negotiation involved the Blue Books give little indication.

* The draft is in F.O. 64/1233. It is in Salisbury's own hand.
† Cp. *G.P.* viii, chap. li, *passim*.
‡ *v. Cecil*, iv, 277–316, *passim*. The account in the *Cambridge History of British Foreign Policy*, vol. iii, summarises the information known before these sources were available.

Session 27 January to 16 September 1887

Volume LVIII (1887)

Colonies and British Possessions

Volume LIX (1887)

Colonies and British Possessions

Volume LXI (1887)

Colonies and British Possessions

1203   Further Correspondence respecting the Claims of British Subjects in the German Protectorate, on the South West Coast of Africa.   PAGE 1

     [C. 5180]   *L/C.* HC. 23 Aug., HL. 25 Aug. 1887.

Volume LXIII (1887)

East India

1204   Correspondence respecting the Affairs of Central Asia. [*Central Asia No. 1 (1887)*.]   PAGE 581

     [C. 5114]   *L/C.* 15 Aug. 1887.

1204a   Further Correspondence. [*Central Asia No. 2 (1887)*.]

                                               PAGE 601

     [C. 5235]   *L/C.* HC. 10 Sept., HL. 12 Sept. 1887.

Volume LXXVIII (1887)

Trade, etc.

1205   Correspondence relative to the Slave Trade, 1886. [*Slave Trade No. 1 (1887)*.]   PAGE 313

     [C. 5111]   *L/C.* 12 Aug. 1887.

Volume LXXXI (1887)

Commercial Reports

1206   Return of National Treatment Clauses in existing Treaties of Navigation between Great Britain and Foreign Powers. [*Commercial No. 13 (1887)*.]   PAGE 181

     [C. 5108]   *R–A.* (*HC. 10 June*), 28 July 1887.

VOLUME XCI (1887)

State Papers

1207 Declaration between the Governments of Great Britain and Austria-Hungary for the Admission, Duty Free, of Patterns and Samples, Imported by Commercial Travellers. Signed at London, 15th February 1887. [*Commercial No. 5 (1887)*.]

PAGE 1

    [C. 4939]   *L/C.* 22 Feb. 1887.

1208 Translation of a Report of the Committee upon a Bill, presented to the Belgian Chamber of Representatives, proposing to establish Import Duties on Horses, Cattle, and Meat, 1886. PAGE 5

    [C. 5021]   *L/C.* 24 Mar. 1887.

1208a Declaration between the British and Belgian Governments, for Amending Article I of the Extradition Treaty of 20th May 1876. Signed at London, 21st April 1887. [*Belgium No. 1 (1887)*.]

PAGE 79

    [C. 5045]   *L/C.* 20 May 1887.

1208b Additional Article to the Postal Convention of the 17th February 1876, between Great Britain and Belgium. Signed at London, 8th January 1887. [*Commercial No. 4 (1887)*.]   PAGE 83

    [C. 4922]   *L/C.* 27 Jan. 1887.

1209 Correspondence respecting the Temporary Occupation of Port Hamilton by Her Majesty's Government. [*China No. 1 (1887)*.]

PAGE 87

    [C. 4991]   *L/C.* 10 Mar. 1887.

1209a Despatch from Her Majesty's Minister at Pekin, forwarding a Report by Mr. H. E. Fulford, Student-Interpreter in the China Consular Service, of a Journey to Manchuria. [*China No. 2 (1887)*.]   PAGE 135

    [C. 5048]   *L/C.* HC. 22 June, HL. 23 June 1887.

1209b Convention between Her Majesty and His Majesty the Emperor of China, relative to Burmah and Tibet. Signed at Pekin, 24th July 1886. [*China No. 3 (1887)*.]   PAGE 157

    [C. 5164]   *L/C.* 30 Aug. 1887.

1210 Correspondence respecting the proposed International Exhibition at Paris in 1889. [*France No. 1 (1887)*.]   PAGE 161

    [C. 5049]   *L/C.* 8 July 1887.

VOLUME XCII (1887)

State Papers: Egypt

SESSION 9 FEBRUARY TO 24 DECEMBER 1888

VOLUME LXVIII (1888)

Navy, etc.

VOLUME LXXIII (1888)

Colonies and British Possessions

VOLUME LXXIV (1888)

Colonies and British Possessions

VOLUME LXXVII (1888)

East India

1232   Further Correspondence respecting the Affairs of Central Asia.
[*Central Asia No. 1 (1888)*.]   PAGE 729
   [C. 5254]   *L/C.* 9 Feb. 1888.

1232 *a*   do. [*Central Asia No. 2 (1888)*.]   PAGE 757
   [C. 5518]   *L/C.* 11 Aug. 1888.

VOLUME XCIII (1888)

Trade, etc.

1233   Correspondence relative to the Slave Trade, 1887. [*Slave Trade
No. 1 (1888)*.]   PAGE 283
   [C. 5428]   *L/C.* 25 June 1888.

VOLUME XCVIII (1888)

Commercial Reports, etc.

1234   Report by Mr. F. S. A. Bourne of a Journey in South Western
China. [*China No. 1 (1888)*.]   PAGE 121
   [C. 5371]   *L/C.* 18 June 1888.

1235   Return of Treaties of Commerce in force between the United
Kingdom and Foreign Powers which preclude preferential
fiscal treatment of British Goods in the Colonies and De-
pendencies of the British Crown. [*Commercial No. 8 (1888)*.]
                                                                 PAGE 247
   [C. 5369]   *R–A.* (*HC. 27 Ap.*), 11 June 1888.

1236   Further Return of National Treatment Clauses in existing
Treaties of Navigation between Great Britain and Foreign
Powers [*v. supra*, No. 1206]. [*Commercial No. 9 (1888)*.]
                                                                 PAGE 511
   [C. 5427]   *L/C.* HC. 19 June, HL. 25 June 1888.

VOLUME CIX (1888)

State Papers

VOLUME CX (1888)

State Papers: Egypt

SESSION 21 FEBRUARY TO 30 AUGUST 1889

VOLUME LVI (1889)

Colonies and British Possessions

VOLUME LXXII (1889)

Trade, etc.

VOLUME LXXXVI (1889)

State Papers

Volume LXXXVII (1889)

State Papers

SESSION 11 FEBRUARY TO 18 AUGUST 1890

VOLUME XLIX (1890)

Colonies and British Possessions

1271   Articles of Capitulation of Heligoland in 1807.   PAGE 499
     309   *R–A.* (*HC. 8 July*), HC. 16 July, O.T.B.P. 17 July 1890.

1271a   Return of the Orders in Council of the 7th day of January 1864 and the 29th day of February 1868 as to the Government of Heligoland.   PAGE 503
     308   *R–A.* (*HC. 7 July*), HC. 16 July, O.T.B.P. 17 July 1890.

1272   Correspondence respecting Sir L. Simmon's Special Mission to the Vatican relative to the Religious Question in the Island of Malta. [*Miscellaneous No. 1 (1890).*]   PAGE 515
     [C. 5975]   *L/C.* 8 May 1890.

VOLUME L (1890)

Colonies and British Possessions

1273   General Act of the Brussels Conference, 1889–90, with annexed Declaration. [*Africa No. 7 (1890).*]   PAGE 1
     [C. 6048]   *L/C.* HC. 6 Aug., HL. 7 Aug. 1890.

1274   Protocols and General Act of the Slave Trade Conference, held at Brussels, 1889–90, with annexed Declaration. [*Africa No. 8 (1890).*]   PAGE 41
     [C. 6049]   *L/C.* HC. 6 Aug., HL. 7 Aug. 1890.

1274a   Translations of Protocols and General Act of the Slave Trade Conference, held at Brussels, 1889–90, with annexed Declaration. [*Africa No. 8A (1890).*]   PAGE 657
     [C. 6049–I]   *L/C.* HC. 6 Aug., HL. 7 Aug. 1890.

VOLUME LI (1890)

Colonies and British Possessions

VOLUME LXXXI (1890)

State Papers

1281 *a*   Agreement between the Governments of Great Britain, Belgium, and France, respecting Telegraphic Correspondence....Signed at London, 4th December 1889. [*Commercial No. 2 (1890)*.]
PAGE 7

   [C. 5899]   *L/C.* 11 Feb. 1890.

1282   Correspondence respecting a Provisional Commercial Agreement with Bulgaria. [*Commercial No. 7 (1890)*.]   PAGE 11

   [C. 5913]   *L/C.* HC. 24 Feb., HL. 25 Feb. 1890.

1283   Treaty between Great Britain and the Republic of Columbia for the mutual surrender of Fugitive Criminals. Signed at Bogota, 27th October 1888. [*Columbia No. 1 (1890)*.]   PAGE 21

   [C. 5902]   *L/C.* 11 Feb. 1890.

1284   Declaration between the Government of the United Kingdom...and the Government of the French Republic, with reference to the Disposal of the Proceeds of Wrecks on their respective Coasts. Signed at Paris, 23rd October 1889. [*Commercial No. 5 (1890)*.]   PAGE 31

   [C. 5909]   *L/C.* 18 Feb. 1890.

1285   Correspondence respecting the Newfoundland Fisheries, 1884–90. [*France No. 1 (1890)*.]   PAGE 37

   [C. 6044]   *L/C.* 26 June 1890.

1286   International Convention for the Protection of Submarine Telegraph Cables, signed at Paris, 14th March 1884, with a List of British Colonies which have acceded thereto under the Additional Article. [*Commercial No. 6 (1890)*.]   PAGE 487

   [C. 5910]   *L/C.* 17 Feb. 1890.

1287   Declarations exchanged between the Government of Her Britannic Majesty and the Government of the French Republic with respect to Territories in Africa. Signed at London, 5th August 1890. [*Africa No. 9 (1890)*.]   PAGE 511

   [C. 6130]   *L/C.* 11 Aug. 1890.

1288   Convention between Her Majesty and the President of the French Republic for the exchange of Uninsured Postal Parcels between France and the Island of Malta. Signed at London, 1st July 1889. [*Commercial No. 1 (1890)*.]   PAGE 515

   [C. 5898]   *L/C.* 11 Feb. 1890.

1289   German Law of 1st June 1870, respecting Nationality. [*Germany No. 1 (1890)*.]   PAGE 523

   [C. 6047]   *L/C.* 22 July 1890.

1295   Amended Agreement between the Post Office of the United
        Kingdom...and the Department of Communications of the
        Empire of Japan for an Exchange of Money Orders, dated the
        21st March and 20th May 1890.   PAGE 781
            [C. 6128]   L/C. HC. 6 Aug., HL. 7 Aug. 1890.

1295a   Agreement between the Governments of Great Britain and
        Japan for increasing the Limits of Weight and the Dimensions
        of Packets of Patterns of Merchandize exchanged through the
        Post....Signed at London, 31st October 1887. [*Commercial
        No. 3 (1890)*.]   PAGE 791
            [C. 5900]   L/C. 11 Feb. 1890.

1296   Convention between the United Kingdom...and the Kingdom
        of Norway for the Exchange of Post Office Money Orders,
        dated 12th and 17th October 1889.   PAGE 795
            [C. 5923]   L/C. 11 Feb. 1890.

1296a   Agreement between the Post Office of the United Kingdom...
        and the Post Office of Roumania, dated 5th and 9th June 1890.
                                                         PAGE 811
            [C. 6162]   L/C. 11 Aug. 1890.

1297   Correspondence respecting the Seizure of the British Schooner
        'Araunah' off Copper Island by the Russian Authorities.
        [*Russia No. 1 (1890)*.]   PAGE 825
            [C. 6041]   R–A. (*HC. 13 May*), HC. 2 June, HL.
                             5 June 1890.

1298   Further Correspondence respecting the Affairs of Samoa [*v. supra*,
        No. 1264]. [*Samoa No. 1 (1890)*.]   PAGE 855
            [C. 5907]   L/C. 11 Feb. 1890.

1298a   Final Act of the Conference on the Affairs of Samoa. Signed at
        Berlin, 14th June 1889. [*Samoa No. 2 (1890)*.] PAGE 955
            [C. 5911]   L/C. HC. 24 Ap., HL. 25 Ap. 1890.

1299   Provisional Commercial Agreement between the Governments
        of Great Britain and Servia. Signed at Belgrade, 2nd February
        (14) 1890. [*Commercial No. 11 (1890)*.]   PAGE 967
            [C. 5917]   L/C. 13 Mar. 1890.

1300   Accession of the Dutch Colonies of Curaçao and Surinam to
        the International Union for the Protection of Industrial
        Property. [*Switzerland No. 1 (1890)*.]   PAGE 971
            [C. 5971]   L/C. 28 Mar. 1890.

1301   Arrangement between the British and French Governments
extending to Tunis the Provisions of the Extradition Treaty
between Great Britain and France of 14th August 1876. Signed
at Paris, 31st December 1889. [*Tunis No. 1 (1890)*.]   PAGE 975
[C. 5976]   *L/C.* 16 May 1890.

VOLUME LXXXII (1890)

State Papers: Turkey; United States

1302   Correspondence respecting the Condition of the Populations in
Asiatic Turkey and the Trial of Moussa Bey. [*Turkey No. 1
(1890)*.]   PAGE 1
[C. 5912]   *L/C.* 11 Feb. 1890.

1302*a* Further Correspondence respecting the Affairs of Crete [*v. supra*,
No. 1267]. [*Turkey No. 2 (1890)*.]   PAGE 135
[C. 5967]   *L/C.* 13 Mar. 1890.

1303   Extradition Convention between Her Majesty and the United
States of America, Supplementary to the Xth Article of the
Treaty between the same High Contracting Parties of 9th
August 1842. Signed at Washington, 12th July 1889. [*United
States No. 1 (1890)*.]   PAGE 353
[C. 5972]   *L/C.* HC. 14 Ap., HL. 17 Ap. 1890.

1304   Correspondence respecting the Behring Sea Seal Fisheries,
1886–90. [*United States No. 2 (1890)*.]   PAGE 359
[C. 6131]   *L/C.* 11 Aug. 1890.

VOLUME LXXXIII (1890)

State Papers: United States; Egypt

1305   Summary of the Protocols and Final Act of the International
Marine Conference held at Washington, October to December
1889. [*Commercial No. 18 (1890)*.]   PAGE 1
[C. 6050]   *L/C.* HC. 9 Aug., HL. 11 Aug. 1890.

1305*a* Correspondence respecting the International Marine Conference held at Washington, 1888–89. [*Commercial No. 19
(1890)*.]   PAGE 53
[C. 6132]   *L/C.* 14 Aug. 1890.

Session 25 November 1890 to 5 August 1891

Volume LVII (1890–1)

Colonial and British Possessions

VOLUME LXXXIII (1890–1)

Commercial Reports, etc.

VOLUME XCVI (1890–1)

State Papers

1315   Additional Article to the Agreement between Great Britain and China of 13th September 1876, signed at Peking, 31st March 1890. [*China No. 1 (1890–1)*.]   PAGE 147
   [C. 6216]   *L/C.* 29 Jan. 1891.

1315*a*   Convention between Great Britain and China relating to Sikkim and Tibet, signed at Calcutta, 17th March 1890. [*Commercial No. 2 (1890–1)*.]   PAGE 151
   [C. 6208]   *L/C.* 25 Nov. 1890.

1315*b*   Correspondence respecting Anti-Foreign Riots in China. [*China No. 3 (1891)*.]   PAGE 155
   [C. 6431]   *L/C.* 28 July 1891.

1316   Despatch from the Earl of Lytton respecting the Re-organization of the French 'Conseil Supérieur des Colonies'. [*France No. 1 (1891)*.]   PAGE 193
   [C. 6251]   *L/C.* HC. 25 Feb., HL. 26 Feb. 1891.

1317   Further Correspondence respecting the Newfoundland Fisheries (1890–91). [*France No. 2 (1891)*.]   PAGE 203
   [C. 6256]   *L/C.* 16 Mar. 1891.

1318   Despatch to Her Majesty's Ambassador at Paris enclosing a Copy of a New Postal Convention between Her Majesty and the President of the French Republic. Signed at London, 30th August 1890. [*Commercial No. 8 (1891)*.]   PAGE 309
   [C. 6257]   *L/C.* 17 Mar. 1891.

1318*a*   Convention between Her Majesty and the President of the French Republic respecting Postal Communications. Signed at London, 30th August 1890. [*Commercial No. 10 (1891)*.]   PAGE 319
   [C. 6315]   *L/C.* HC. 13 Ap., HL. 14 Ap. 1891.

1318*b*   Convention between Her Majesty and the President of the French Republic for the Exchange of Uninsured Postal Parcels between France and the Island of Cyprus. Signed at Paris, 8th May 1890. [*Commercial No. 3 (1890–1)*.]   PAGE 329
   [C. 6210]   *L/C.* 25 Nov. 1890.

1318*c*   Declaration between the Government of the United Kingdom...and the Government of the French Republic with reference to the disposal of the Proceeds of Wrecks on their respective Coasts. Signed at Paris, 23rd October 1889. [*Commercial No. 26 (1891)*.]   PAGE 337
   [C. 6513]   *L/C.* 4 Aug. 1891.

VOLUME XCVII (1890–1)

State Papers

SESSION 1. 9 FEBRUARY TO 28 JUNE 1892
SESSION 2. 4 AUGUST TO 18 AUGUST 1892

VOLUME LVI (1892)

Colonies and British Possessions

VOLUME LXXIV (1892)

Trade, etc.

VOLUME XCV (1892)

State Papers

1351   Convention between Great Britain and the Netherlands defining
Boundaries in Borneo, signed at London, 20th June 1891.
Ratifications exchanged at London, 11th May 1892. [*Treaty
Series No. 11 (1892)*.]   PAGE 721

    [C. 6553]   *L/C.* HC. 26 May, HL. 27 May 1892.

1352   Agreements between the British and Persian Governments
prolonging existing Conventions between Her Majesty and the
Shah of Persia relative to Telegraphic Communication between
Europe and India. Signed at Tehran, 7th January 1892.
[*Treaty Series No. 6 (1892)*.]   PAGE 727

    [C. 6631]   *L/C.* 24 Mar. 1892.

1353   Convention between Great Britain and Roumania relative to
Trade Marks. Signed at Bucharest, 4th May 1892. Ratifica-
tions exchanged at Bucharest, 3rd June 1892. [*Treaty Series
No. 12 (1892)*.]   PAGE 731

    [C. 6700]   *L/C.* 16 June 1892.

1354   Treaty between Her Majesty and Her Majesty the Queen
Regent of Spain in the Name of His Majesty the King of Spain
for the Suppression of the African Slave Trade. Signed at
Brussels, 2nd July 1890. Ratifications exchanged at Brussels,
2nd December 1890. [*Treaty Series No. 3 (1892)*.]   PAGE 735

    [C. 6592]   *L/C.* 24 Mar. 1892.

1355   Arrangement between Great Britain, Spain, France, Switzerland, and Tunis for the Prevention of False Indications of
Origin on Goods. Signed at Madrid, 14th April 1891. Ratifications exchanged at Madrid, 15th June 1892. [*Treaty Series
No. 13 (1892)*.]   PAGE 741

    [C. 6818]   *L/C.* HC. 11 Aug., HL. 15 Aug. 1892.

1356   Agreement between Great Britain and Tonga relative to the
Trial of British Subjects by the Tonga Courts. Signed at
Nukualofa, 2nd June 1891. [*Treaty Series No. 5 (1892)*.]
                                                                     PAGE 747

    [C. 6594]   *L/C.* 24 Mar. 1892.

VOLUME XCVI (1892)

State Papers

THE BLUE-BOOK POLICY OF
ROSEBERY AND KIMBERLEY*

1892-5

THE second short administration, in which Rosebery
either conducted or profoundly influenced foreign
affairs, lasted from August 1892 to June 1895. Half-
way through the period Kimberley followed Rosebery at the
Foreign Office, when the latter succeeded to the Premiership.

The period is an important one in foreign affairs. The
development of the Franco-Russian entente, coinciding as it
did with the Anglo-French crisis over Siam, drove England
nearer to the Triple Alliance. Hence Rosebery entered upon
the important negotiations of 1893-4 for the renewal of the
Mediterranean Agreements. The conflict with Germany as well
as with France over the Congo Treaty wore down Rosebery's
patience and was a powerful factor in preventing the realisation of this project. Close upon the heels of the Congo
controversy came the Armenian massacres—the revenge of
Turkey-in-Asia for Liberal policy in the 'eighties—while in
point of date only a few weeks separated the climax of this
tragedy from the crisis in the Far East, where the Sino-
Japanese War brought problems for the Powers. Armenia
and Shimonoseki belong indeed partly to the next period,
and the fact that no papers upon them were laid under
Rosebery and Kimberley is therefore easily understood.

The treatment of the other subjects varied. The Blue Books
of this time contain in the first place—as did those of the
preceding Salisbury administration—a large number of
African agreements. England and France delimited their
boundaries on the Gold Coast (No. 1373 b) and on the East
in Somaliland (No. 1408), and again on the West Coast, North
and East of Sierra Leone (No. 1427); England and Germany

* Lord Rosebery became Secretary of State for Foreign Affairs on 18 August
1892 in Mr Gladstone's fourth administration; he succeeded Mr Gladstone as
Prime Minister on 4 March 1894, and Lord Kimberley became Secretary of
State for Foreign Affairs on the 11th.

defined their positions in East and West Africa in July and November 1893 (Nos. 1374*a*, *b*); England and Portugal delimited spheres of influence in the Zambesi (No. 1384), while with Italy a Protocol of May 1894 settled spheres of influence in East Africa (No. 1411). All these agreements were laid without correspondence and so was the similar agreement with the Netherlands respecting New Guinea signed on 16 May 1895 (No. 1432*a*)*. But other colonial questions were given fuller publicity. A Blue Book of some 250 pages (No. 1390) carried the history of the difficulties over Samoa from the point at which they were left by the preceding paper of 1890 (No. 1298). The most controversial questions were, however, those concerned with Siam and the Congo. On the former the Blue Books opened with the texts of the agreements of 31 July and 25 November 1893, laid—with their covering dispatches and accompanying letters—on 11 December (No. 1392). The flood of controversy had not, however, begun at that time, and the paper by which the fullness of publication must be judged is the bulky book of correspondence laid on 14 August 1894 (No. 1417).

The treatment of the Siamese question is far fuller than that of the Congo. The papers here are scanty and bear evidence of the atmosphere of tension in which they were produced. The text of the Agreement was laid on 21 May 1894—nine days after its signature (No. 1404). The covering dispatch of 23 May appeared a few days later (No. 1399); records of the German protest followed on 11 June (No. 1404*a*), and in August came the Declaration of the withdrawal of Article III (No. 1404*b*). The date—11 June—on which the Anglo-German correspondence was laid was deliberately chosen. German consent to publication was given on that day † and it was decided to lay the papers at once 'as in view of the ill-humour of the Germans it may be prudent to commit them to the comparatively harmless attitude they have taken'. The early date avoided the record

---

* This agreement was laid before Parliament by the Salisbury administration.

† F.O. 64/1335. Malet to Kimberley, Tel. No. 10 Africa of 11 June 1894, D. 12.26, R. 12.30 p.m. Cp. also *G.P.* VIII, 450.

of the more acute phase of the crisis, for it was on the 11th that a further German protest was made, as a result of which Rosebery told the Austro-Hungarian ambassador on the 13th that he might have to recover a 'free hand'.* A second Blue Book was promised and was in fact laid on 23 August, but its contents are uncertain as it was never printed.† The result was that while the persistence of German pressure was betrayed—contrary to Rosebery's wishes—in the wording of the Declaration withdrawing Article III (No. 1404 b), the documents leading to this Declaration never appeared. Equal secrecy attended the French negotiations. No papers on this subject were printed at the time, and the first record relating to them appeared in 1899, when the Blue Book on Fashoda included in its Appendix Kimberley's dispatch to Dufferin of 14 August 1894 which discussed the French objections at some length (No. 1552).

The contemporary Anglo-Austro-Hungarian and Anglo-Italian negotiations are not represented in the Blue Books. This is natural enough, and for two reasons. They never reached any specific result, and their object was the renewal of the entente of 1887, which had always been regarded as peculiarly secret. Rosebery, indeed, was not as meticulous as Salisbury in avoiding any reference to these negotiations in official dispatches, but, even at this stage, such reference is rare, and no hint of them appeared in public. Rosebery himself had taken the precaution, on his accession to power, of refusing to read the text of the *Accord à Trois*, although he knew of its existence, and while he had all Salisbury's realisation of the transforming effect of publicity, he had an additional motive for secrecy since press rumours in 1888–91 had led to severe Liberal criticism in the Commons.‡ Although Rosebery's whole policy is obscure without an understanding of these secret *pourparlers*, the student of published documents

* Cp. Temperley and Penson, *Foundations of British Foreign Policy*, 491–2.
† *v. infra*, p. 566, *App. I.*
‡ Cp. *Hans. Deb.* 3rd Ser. CCCXXII, 152–3, Question in House of Commons 10 February, p. 377, do. 14 February; pp. 557–8, do. 16 February; pp. 1172–95, Address in answer to Queen's Speech, 22 February 1888; also CCCXXXVIII, 850–1, Question in House of Commons, 19 July 1889; CCCLIII, 1464–6, do. 2 June 1891.

has to rely on the echoes of the negotiations in the *Grosse Politik*, and the extracts made by historians from the Vienna archives.* Rosebery, like Salisbury, sacrificed much of the intelligibility of his policy when he conformed to conventions of secrecy in this respect.

The reticence of the Blue Books on these important if rather nebulous aspects of Government policy adds a special importance to the replies to Parliamentary questions. Indeed it may be said generally that, as the nineteenth century advanced, questions in Parliament grew steadily in significance. They were constantly used as a method of eliciting statements on foreign relations. In the time of the Rosebery administration, Sir Edward Grey was serving his first apprenticeship in Foreign Affairs as Under-Secretary of State, and by this period the duty of preparing answers—once the task of the Permanent Under-Secretary—largely devolved on the holder of the Parliamentary Secretaryship. There is ample evidence in the archives of the care with which answers were drafted and—in important matters—revised by the Secretary of State himself. Sir Edward Grey describes the procedure in the time of Lord Kimberley: 'As draft answers...were presented to him he would read each, consider it rapidly but thoroughly, and initial the draft either as it stood or with amendment in firm, distinct handwriting.'† It is doubtful, however, whether Sir Edward Grey's recollection is accurate when he states that on one of the most important of the declarations which were made in answer to Parliamentary questions at this period the usual procedure was broken. This is in connection with his reply on 28 March 1895 to a question on French penetration to the Nile Valley.‡ It is true indeed that a draft reply on this subject has not been preserved, but there is plenty of evidence that the famous declaration which Sir Edward Grey made then was fully in accord with the tenour of Foreign Office correspondence and minutes on the subject. Indeed in a conversation with the

* Cp. Temperley and Penson, *Foundations of British Foreign Policy*, 470–93.
† Grey, *Twenty-Five Years 1892–1916* [1925], I, 18.
‡ *Hans. Deb.* 4th Ser. XXXII, 404–7.

French minister on the day of the speech Kimberley referred to the disquiet caused by 'rumours of a French expedition towards the basin of the Nile' and said that 'it was probable that they would be referred to in the House of Commons to-night'.* The declaration was published in the Fashoda Blue Book (No. 1552) with the dispatch from Kimberley to Dufferin to which reference has already been made. At the same time an extract was laid from a conversation between Lord Kimberley and Baron de Courcel on 1 April in which the declaration was defended and explained.†

* F.O. 27/3229. Kimberley to Dufferin, No. 111 of 28 March 1895. Cp. Temperley and Penson, *Foundations of British Foreign Policy*, 501–4.

† F.O. 27/3229. Kimberley to Dufferin, No. 112 A of 1 April 1895. *A. & P.* [1899], cxii [C. 9054], 884.

Session 31 January 1893 to 5 March 1894

Volume LIV (1893–4)

Navy, etc.

Volume LXII (1893–4)

Colonies and British Possessions

VOLUME LXXXV (1893–4)

Trade, etc.

VOLUME LXXXIX (1893–4)

Commercial, General Interests, etc.

VOLUME CIX (1893–4)

State Papers

1370   Procès-verbal recording the Deposit of the Ratifications of the International Sanitary Convention. Signed at Venice, 30th January 1892; Rome, 18th November 1893. [*Treaty Series No. 1 (1894)*.]   PAGE 1

    [C. 7250]   *L/C.* HC. 9 Jan., HL. 12 Jan. 1894.

1370*a*   International Sanitary Convention. Signed at Venice, 30th January 1892. Ratifications deposited at Rome. [*Treaty Series No. 8 (1893)*.]   PAGE 9

    [C. 6966]   *L/C.* HC. 13 Ap., HL. 18 Ap. 1893.

1371   Correspondence respecting the Extradition of Jabez Spencer Balfour. [*Argentine Republic No. 1 (1893)*.]   PAGE 43

    [C. 7034]   *L/C.* 25 July 1893.

1371*a*   Treaty between Great Britain and the Argentine Republic for the Mutual Extradition of Fugitive Criminals. Signed at Buenos Ayres, 22nd May 1889. Ratifications exchanged at Buenos Ayres, 15th December 1893. [*Treaty Series No. 2 (1894)*.]   PAGE 61

    [C. 7260]   *L/C.* HL. 8 Feb., HC. 12 Feb. 1894.

1372   Convention between Great Britain and Ecuador relative to Trade Marks. Signed at Quito, 26th August 1892. Ratifications exchanged at Quito, 3rd February 1893. [*Treaty Series No. 6 (1893)*.]   PAGE 73

    [C. 6917]   *L/C.* HC. 22 Mar., HL. 23 Mar. 1893.

1372*a*   Convention between Great Britain and Ecuador relative to Trade Marks. Signed at Quito, 26th August 1892, with a List of British Colonies which have acceded thereto under Article II. [*Treaty Series No. 3 (1894)*.]   PAGE 77

    [C. 7261]   *L/C.* 20 Feb. 1894.

1373   Agreement between Great Britain and France for the Establishment of an Express Delivery Service. Signed at Paris, 27th February 1893. [*Treaty Series No. 5 (1893)*.]   PAGE 81

    [C. 6916]   *L/C.* HC. 22 Mar., HL. 23 Mar. 1893.

1373a Despatch from the Marquess of Dufferin and Ava forwarding the Agreement, signed on the 6th February 1893, relative to Trade between Canada and France. [*Commercial No. 7 (1893)*.]

PAGE 85

[C. 6968]   *L/C.* 18 Ap. 1893.

1373b Arrangement between Great Britain and France fixing the Boundary between the British and French Possessions on the Gold Coast. Signed at Paris, 12th July 1893. [*Treaty Series No. 13 (1893)*.]   PAGE 93

[C. 7108]   *L/C.* HL. 31 Aug., HC. 1 Sept. 1893.

1373c Protocols and Agreement between Great Britain and France respecting Territories in the region of the Upper Mekong. Signed at Paris, 31st July and 25th November 1893. [*Treaty Series No. 18 (1893)*.]   PAGE 101

[C. 7232]   *L/C.* 19 Dec. 1893.

1374 Agreement between Great Britain and Germany respecting the Rio del Rey on the West Coast of Africa. Signed at Berlin, 14th April 1893. [*Treaty Series No. 9 (1893)*.]   PAGE 105

[C. 7026]   *L/C.* 16 June 1893.

1374a Agreement between Great Britain and Germany respecting the Boundaries in East Africa. Signed at Berlin, 25th July 1893. [*Treaty Series No. 14 (1893)*.]   PAGE 111

[C. 7203]   *L/C.* HC. 2 Nov., HL. 9 Nov. 1893.

1374b Agreement between Great Britain and Germany respecting Boundaries in Africa. Signed at Berlin, 15th November 1893. [*Treaty Series No. 17 (1893)*.]   PAGE 125

[C. 7230]   *L/C.* HC. 11 Dec., HL. 12 Dec. 1893.

1374c Agreement supplementary to the Convention for the exchange of uninsured Postal Parcels concluded on the 7th and 13th December 1885 between the General Post Office of the United Kingdom...and the Imperial German Post Office.   PAGE 133

[C. 7278]   *L/C.* 15 Feb. 1894.

1375 Despatch from Her Majesty's Chargé d'Affaires at Berlin enclosing Translation of the Oath taken by Duke Alfred of Saxe-Cobourg-Gotha upon his Accession to the Ducal Throne. [*Germany No. 1 (1894)*.]   PAGE 139

[C. 7251]   *L/C.* HC. 9 Jan., HL. 12 Jan. 1894.

1384   Agreement between Great Britain and Portugal relative to Spheres of Influence North of the Zambesi. [*Treaty Series No. 10 (1893)*.]   PAGE 307

    [C. 7032]   *L/C.* 26 June 1893.

1385   Convention between Great Britain and Roumania relative to Trade Marks. Signed at Bucharest, 4th May 1892, with a List of British Colonies which have acceded thereto under Article II. [*Treaty Series No. 11 (1893)*.]   PAGE 313

    [C. 7033]   *L/C.* HL. 10 July, HC. 12 July 1893.

1386   Treaty between Great Britain and Roumania for the Marriage of Her Royal Highness Princess Marie of Great Britain and Ireland with His Royal Highness the Prince Ferdinand of Roumania. Signed at Bucharest, 15th December 1892. Ratifications exchanged at Bucharest, 27th December 1892. [*Treaty Series No. 1 (1893)*.]   PAGE 317

    [C. 6846]   *L/C.* HL. 2 Feb., HC. 3 Feb. 1893.

1387   Commercial Convention between Great Britain and Roumania. Signed at Bucharest, 13th August 1892. Ratifications exchanged at Bucharest, 31st January 1893. [*Treaty Series No. 4 (1893)*.]   PAGE 323

    [C. 6852]   *L/C.* 27 Feb. 1893.

1387*a*   Convention between Great Britain and Roumania relative to Trade Marks. Signed at Bucharest, 4th May 1892, with a List of British Colonies which have acceded thereto under Article II. [*Treaty Series No. 11 (1893) (Amended)*.]   PAGE 329

    [C. 7205]   *L/C.* HC. 2 Nov., HL. 9 Nov. 1893.

1388   Correspondence respecting an Agreement for the Protection of Russian Sealing Interests in the North Pacific Ocean during the Year 1893. [*Russia No. 1 (1893)*.]   PAGE 333

    [C. 6952]   *L/C.* 1 June 1893.

1388*a*   Correspondence respecting the Seizures of British Sealing Vessels by Russian Cruizers in the North Pacific Ocean. [*Russia No. 2 (1893)*.]   PAGE 365

    [C. 7028]   *L/C.* 19 June 1893.

1388*b*   Despatch from Sir R. Morier enclosing the Reply of the Russian Government in regard to the Seizures of British Sealing Vessels by Russian Cruizers in the North Pacific Ocean. [*Russia No. 3 (1893)*.]   PAGE 489

    [C. 7029]   *L/C.* 19 June 1893.

1389   Agreement between the General Post Office of the United Kingdom...and the Postal Administration of Salvador for the exchange of Postal Parcels.   PAGE 505
    [C. 6934]   L/C. 7 Mar. 1893.

1390   Further Correspondence respecting the Affairs of Samoa [v. supra, No. 1298]. [Samoa No. 1 (1893).]   PAGE 525
    [C. 6973]   L/C. HC. 11 May, HL. 12 May 1893.

1391   Exchange of Notes prolonging to 1st July 1893 the Provisional Commercial Agreement of 14th February 1890 between Great Britain and Servia. Belgrade, January 1893. [Treaty Series No. 2 (1893).]   PAGE 781
    [C. 6850]   L/C. 10 Feb. 1893.

1391a   Provisional Agreement between Great Britain and Servia respecting Commercial Relations. Signed at Belgrade, 4th July 1893. [Treaty Series No. 12 (1893).]   PAGE 785
    [C. 7102]   L/C. 3 Aug. 1893.

1391b   Treaty of Commerce between Great Britain and Servia. Signed at Belgrade, June 28/July 10 1893. Ratifications exchanged at Belgrade, October 4/16 1893. [Treaty Series No. 15 (1893).]
                        PAGE 789
    [C. 7204]   L/C. HC. 6 Nov., HL. 9 Nov. 1893.

1392   Despatches from Her Majesty's Ambassador at Paris relative to the Agreement between Great Britain and France for constituting a Neutral State between their Possessions in Indo-China. [Siam No. 1 (1893).]   PAGE 797
    [C. 7231]   L/C. HC. 11 Dec., HL. 12 Dec. 1893.

1393   Correspondence respecting the Imprisonment of a British Seaman at Bilbao. [Spain No. 1 (1893).]   PAGE 803
    [C. 6971]   L/C. 4 May 1893.

1393a   Despatch from Sir Henry Drummond Wolff forwarding the Commercial Agreement between Great Britain and Spain. Signed at Madrid, 18th July 1893. [Commercial No. 15 (1893).]
                        PAGE 813
    [C. 7162]   L/C. HC. 21 Sept., HL. 22 Sept. 1893.

1394   Agreement supplementary to the Convention concluded on the 16th March 1886–13th April 1886, between the Post Office of the United Kingdom...and the Post Office of Sweden concerning the exchange of Postal Parcels. [Signed at London, 19 December 1893, and at Stockholm, 17 November 1893.]   PAGE 819
    [C. 7277]   L/C. 15 Feb. 1894.

1396e   Argument presented on the part of the Government of Her
        Britannic Majesty to the Tribunal of Arbitration constituted
        under Article I of the Treaty of Washington....[*United States
        No. 4 (1893)*.]   PAGE 759
        [C. 6921]   *L/C.* HC. 30 Mar., HL. 18 Ap. 1893.

VOLUME CXI (1893-4)

State Papers: United States, Egypt

1396f   The Case of the United States before the Tribunal of Arbitra-
        tion, convened at Paris under the provisions of the Treaty
        between the United States of America and Great Britain, con-
        cluded 29th February 1892; including the Reports of the Behring
        Sea Commission. [*United States No. 6 (1893)*.]   PAGE 1
        [C. 6949]   *L/C.* HC. 30 Mar., HL. 18 Ap. 1893.

1396g   The Counter Case of the United States before the Tribunal of
        Arbitration, convened at Paris under the provisions of the
        Treaty between the United States of America and Great
        Britain, concluded 29th February 1892. [*United States No. 7
        (1893)*.]   PAGE 459
        [C. 6950]   *L/C.* HC. 30 Mar., HL. 18 Ap. 1893.

1396h   Argument of the United States before the Tribunal of Arbitra-
        tion, convened at Paris under the provisions of the Treaty
        between the United States of America and Great Britain,
        concluded 29th February 1892. [*United States No. 8 (1893)*.]
                                                             PAGE 621
        [C. 6951]   *L/C.* HC. 30 Mar., HL. 18 Ap. 1893.

1396ij Papers relating to the Proceedings of the Tribunal of Arbitra-
        tion, constituted under Article I of the Treaty concluded at
        Washington on the 29th February 1892, between Her Britannic
        Majesty and the United States of America. [*United States No. 11
        (1893)*.]   PAGE 955
        [C. 7161]   *L/C.* HC. 21 Sept., HL. 22 Sept. 1893.

1396k   Award of the Tribunal of Arbitration, constituted under
        Article I of the Treaty concluded at Washington on the 29th
        February 1892, between Her Britannic Majesty and the United
        States of America. [*United States No. 10 (1893)*.]   PAGE 1065
        [C. 7107]   *L/C.* HC. 23 Aug., HL. 24 Aug. 1893.

SESSION 12 MARCH TO 25 AUGUST 1894

VOLUME LVII (1894)

Colonies and British Possessions

1399   Papers relating to the Agreement between Great Britain and
        His Majesty the King of the Belgians, Sovereign of the In-
        dependent State of the Congo. Signed at Brussels, 12 May
        1894. [*Africa No. 4 (1894).*]*   PAGE 701
            [C. 7360]   L/C. HC. 24 May, HL. 28 May 1894.

1400   Report by Commissioner Johnston of the First Three Years'
        Administration of the Eastern Portion of British Central Africa,
        dated 31st March 1894. [*Africa No. 6 (1894).*]   PAGE 741
            [C. 7504]   L/C. 23 Aug. 1894.

VOLUME XC (1894)

Commercial and General Interests

1401   Further Report on the Improvements made in the Navigation
        of the Danube, 1878–93, with Plan. [*Commercial No. 6 (1894).*]
                                                            PAGE 199
            [C. 7502]   L/C. 21 Aug. 1894.

VOLUME XCVI (1894)

State Papers

1402   Convention respecting Liquor Traffic in the North Sea. Signed
        at the Hague, 16th November 1887. [*Treaty Series No. 13
        (1894).*]   PAGE 1
            [C. 7354]   L/C. 7 May 1894.

1403   Convention between Great Britain and Austria-Hungary for
        the Establishment of International Copyright. Signed at
        Vienna, 24th April 1893. Ratifications exchanged at Vienna,
        14th April 1894. [*Treaty Series No. 12 (1894).*]   PAGE 13
            [C. 7353]   L/C. HC. 2 May, HL. 4 May 1894.

* A paper entitled 'Correspondence relating to the Independent State of the
Congo' was laid by command on 23 August under the short title *Africa No. 7 (1894)*
and numbered [C. 7505]. But it was not printed by either House. Cp. *infra*, p. 566,
App. I.

1404   *Belgium: Congo Independent State:* Agreement between Great
Britain and His Majesty King Leopold II, Sovereign of the
Independent State of the Congo, relating to the Spheres of
Influence of Great Britain and the Independent State of the
Congo in East and Central Africa. Signed at Brussels, 12th May
1894. [*Treaty Series No. 15 (1894).*]   PAGE 23

    [C. 7358]   *L/C.* HC. 21 May, HL. 28 May 1894.

1404*a*   Further Papers relating to the Agreement between Great
Britain and His Majesty the King of the Belgians, Sovereign
of the Independent State of the Congo. Signed at Brussels,
12th May 1894. [*Africa No. 5 (1894).*]   PAGE 31

    [C. 7390]   *L/C.* 11 June 1894.

1404*b*   Declaration as to withdrawal of Article III of the Agreement
of 12th May 1894, between Great Britain and His Majesty
King Leopold II, Sovereign of the Independent State of the
Congo, relating to the Spheres of Influence of Great Britain
and the Independent State of the Congo in East and Central
Africa. Signed at Brussels, 22nd June 1894. [*Treaty Series
No. 20 (1894).*]   PAGE 43

    [C. 7549]   *L/C.* HC. 24 Aug., HL. 25 Aug. 1894.

1405   Agreement concerning the exchange of Postal Parcels between
the Post Office of the United Kingdom...and the Administration
of the Belgian State Railways.   PAGE 47

    [C. 7317]   *L/C.* 15 Mar. 1894.

1406   Convention between Great Britain and Chile for the Settlement
of Claims arising out of the Civil War of 1891. Signed at
Santiago, 26th September 1893. Ratifications exchanged at
Santiago, 24th April 1894. [*Treaty Series No. 18 (1894).*]
        PAGE 73

    [C. 7391]   *L/C.* 18 June 1894.

1407   Convention between Great Britain and China relative to
Sikkim and Tibet. Signed at Calcutta, 17th March 1890, with
Regulations appended thereto, signed at Darjeeling, 5th
December 1893. [*Treaty Series No. 11 (1894).*]   PAGE 81

    [C. 7312]   *L/C.* 17 Ap. 1894.

1407*a*   Convention between Great Britain and China, giving effect to
Article III of the Convention of 24th July 1886, relative to
Burmah and Tibet. Signed at London, 1st March 1894.
Ratifications exchanged at London, 23rd August 1894. [*Treaty
Series No. 19 (1894).*]   PAGE 89

    [C. 7547]   *L/C.* 23 Aug. 1894.

1408 Agreement between the Governments of Great Britain and France with regard to the Somali Coast, February 1888. [*France No. 1 (1894)*.] PAGE 103

  [C. 7389] *L/C.* 7 June 1894.

1409 Correspondence respecting the recent Assassination of the President of the French Republic. [*France No. 2 (1894)*.] PAGE 109

  [C. 7394] *L/C.* HC. 15 Aug., HL. 16 Aug. 1894.

1410 Treaty of Commerce and Navigation between Germany and Russia. Signed at Berlin, 29th January (10th February) 1894. [*Commercial No. 4 (1894)*.] PAGE 119

  [C. 7359] *L/C.* HC. 25 May, HL. 28 May 1894.

1410*a* Convention between Great Britain and Germany establishing a Customs Union between the Gold Coast Colony, east of the Volta, and Togoland. Signed at Berlin, 24th February 1894. [*Treaty Series No. 16 (1894)*.] PAGE 145

  [C. 7387] *L/C.* HC. 25 May, HL. 28 May 1894.

1410*b* International Sanitary Convention. Signed at Dresden, 15th April 1893, and Protocol recording the Accession of Great Britain, 13th and 15th July 1893. Ratifications deposited at Berlin, 1st February 1894. [*Treaty Series No. 4 (1894)*.] PAGE 153

  [C. 7304] *L/C.* 15 Mar. 1894.

1411 Protocol between Great Britain and Italy respecting the Demarcation of their respective Spheres of Influence in Eastern Africa. Signed at Rome, 5th May 1894. [*Treaty Series No. 17 (1894)*.] PAGE 181

  [C. 7388] *L/C.* 31 May 1894.

1412 Correspondence respecting the revision of the Treaty Arrangements between Great Britain and Japan. [*Japan No. 1 (1894)*.] PAGE 185

  [C. 7548] *L/C.* 23 Aug. 1894.

1413 Treaty between Great Britain and Liberia for the Mutual Surrender of Fugitive Criminals. Signed at London, 16th December 1892. Ratifications exchanged at London, 31st January 1894. [*Treaty Series No. 6 (1894)*.] PAGE 337

  [C. 7306] *L/C.* HC. 20 Mar., HL. 26 Mar. 1894.

1414   Treaty of Friendship, Commerce and Navigation between
          Great Britain and Muskat. Signed at Muskat, 19th March
          1891, with a List of British Colonies which have acceded thereto
          under Article XXI. [*Treaty Series No. 5 (1894)*.]   PAGE 345
               [C. 7305]   L/C. 15 Mar. 1894.

1415   Agreement between Great Britain and Portugal for the In-
          surance of Postal Parcels. Signed at Lisbon, 10th March 1894.
          [*Treaty Series No. 9 (1894)*.]   PAGE 355
               [C. 7310]   L/C. 13 Ap. 1894.

1415a   Treaty between Great Britain and Portugal for the Mutual
          Surrender of Fugitive Criminals. Signed at Lisbon, 17th
          October 1892. Ratifications exchanged at Lisbon, 13th
          November 1893. [*Treaty Series No. 7 (1894)*.]   PAGE 363
               [C. 7307]   L/C. HC. 19 Mar., HL. 26 Mar. 1894.

1416   Convention between Great Britain and Roumania respecting
          false indications of origin on Goods. Signed at Bucharest,
          20th March and 1st April 1893. Ratifications exchanged at
          Bucharest, 1st and 13th March 1894. [*Treaty Series No. 8 (1894)*.]
                                                                 PAGE 377
               [C. 7309]   L/C. HC. 11 Ap., HL. 12 Ap. 1894.

1416a   Treaty between Great Britain and Roumania for the Mutual
          Surrender of Fugitive Criminals. Signed at Bucharest, 9th and
          12th March 1893. Ratifications exchanged at Bucharest,
          1st and 13th March 1894. [*Treaty Series No. 14 (1894)*.]
                                                                 PAGE 383
               [C. 7357]   L/C. HC. 21 May, HL. 28 May 1894.

1417   Correspondence respecting the Affairs of Siam. [*Siam No. 1
          (1894)*.]   PAGE 399
               [C. 7395]   L/C. HL. 13 Aug., HC. 14 Aug. 1894.

1418   Convention between Great Britain and the United States,
          supplementary to the Convention respecting Boundaries of
          22nd July 1892. (Alaska and Passamaquoddy Bay.) Signed at
          Washington, 3rd February 1894. Ratifications exchanged at
          Washington, 28th March 1894. [*Treaty Series No. 10 (1894)*.]
                                                                 PAGE 641
               [C. 7311]   L/C. 17 Ap. 1894.

1419   Report on the Finances, Administration and Condition of
          Egypt, and the Progress of Reforms. [*Egypt No. 1 (1894)*.]
                                                                 PAGE 645
               [C. 7308]   L/C. 9 Ap. 1894.

SALISBURY—THE LAST PHASE*

1895–1900

SALISBURY's final period at the Foreign Office, June 1895–November 1900, was of first importance from the standpoint of British relations with the continental powers. From one aspect it may be said to have extended from Salisbury's *pourparlers* of 1895, as yet only half understood, on the subject of the future of Turkey, to the eve of the final stage of those Anglo-German negotiations whose failure determined the line of British foreign policy in the pre-war era. From another it ran from the Jameson raid nearly to the close of the second Boer War. From yet another its main characteristic is Anglo-French colonial discord, announced to all the world at Fashoda, and affecting by its reverberations the whole tenour of the Franco-Russian alliance. How much or how little of all this can we glean from the Blue Books?

In the first place, the Turkish question, in all its phases, continues to be well documented. Asiatic reform, imbued once again with urgency by the Armenian tragedy, was the subject of several substantial Blue Books in 1895 and 1896. Some indeed, both in 1895 (No. 1440) and 1896 (No. 1458*b*), went back over the period of the preceding administration, but the others tell in detail the story of the joint efforts of Britain, France, and Russia, to compel Turkey to reform. This flood of information continued in full force to 1897, although in that year the papers on the Cretan question were even more voluminous. On both Armenia and Crete the Parliamentary Papers provide an invaluable account of local events, negotiations with Turkey and Greece, and the actions of the Powers. But there is one subject which was treated throughout with reticence. All references of a general or

* Lord Salisbury became Prime Minister and Secretary of State for Foreign Affairs on 29 June 1895; he was succeeded as regards the Foreign Office by Lord Lansdowne on 12 November 1900. Lord Salisbury resigned the office of Prime Minister on 10 July 1902.

speculative kind to the relations with the members of the Triple or the Dual Alliance were carefully excluded. The warning to Turkey, for example, with which Salisbury opened his administration lost some of its point by the omission of his references to the attitude of the Central Powers who were, he said, not 'likely to thwart the policy of Great Britain in this matter'. Similarly the full text reveals, as the published version does not, the danger to Turkey of an Anglo-Russian *rapprochement*. 'France acted entirely with Russia, and...the sole hold upon existence which the Ottoman Empire retained was the fact that Russia and Great Britain were not wholly agreed. If, by the movement of events, the policy of those Powers and public opinion in the two countries should coincide, the Ottoman Empire must disappear.'* The omissions indeed worked in two ways; for if the possibility of an Anglo-Russian *rapprochement* was concealed, so also were the contemporary conversations between Salisbury and the Austro-Hungarian ambassador. There is no hint in the Blue Books of Count Deym's expression of anxiety in October 1895, nor do they reveal Salisbury's reassurance that 'there was no fear of any movement of public opinion in this country which would result in the withdrawal of English naval forces from the Mediterranean'.† And they are as silent under Salisbury as they had been under his predecessors on the subject of the negotiations for a possible renewal of the Mediterranean Agreements, traces of which are to be found in the archives for the years 1895, 1896 and 1897.‡ The principle followed throughout this period is that while the details of action at Constantinople are given in full, the tentative movements which Salisbury made towards Russia on the one hand and Austria-Hungary on the other are omitted. The traditional view that Salisbury's policy in 1895 was a reversal of his earlier attitude receives no contradiction from the Blue Books. It is true that the archives are themselves defective, but

---

* F.O. 78/4606. Salisbury to Currie, No. 275 of 10 July 1895. Cp. *A. & P.* [1896], xcv [C. 7923], 222 [*v. infra*, No. 1457].

† F.O. 7/1224. Salisbury to Monson, No. 98 of 18 October 1895.

‡ Cp. *Gooch and Temperley*, VIII, 13, No. 2; IX (I), 775–6, App. II; Temperley and Penson, *Foundations of British Foreign Policy*, 495–9.

there is enough material in them to show that there was no sudden break in policy, but a gradual development. It was not until the end of 1897 that his change in attitude was completed.

As a cause of Blue-Book publication the colonial question in these years vied with that of the Near East. Salisbury's last period saw the completion of his long series of African boundary agreements. In Anglo-French relations there were still two regions of outstanding importance, the Niger and the Nile valleys. The former was the subject of the Anglo-French Convention of 14 June 1898 (No. 1489) and the completing Declaration of 21 March 1899 (No. 1538). The Convention was laid on 17 June, with a covering dispatch, but ratifications were not exchanged until after the Declaration had been concluded.* In the case of the Nile the danger and excitement of Fashoda necessitated the laying of correspondence (Nos. 1552, 1552a), and the Declaration on this subject was presented six days after it was signed (No. 1557). It is true that the correspondence was not extensive and had important omissions,† although the earlier British warnings to France were given in full.‡ The publication of Sir Edward Grey's statement in the Commons on 28 March 1895 was a reminder to the House as well as to France that the policy pursued by Britain at Fashoda had no peculiarly Conservative colouring, while the note to M. Hanotaux of 10 December 1897 emphasised the continuity of policy. But on more current matters care was taken to avoid hurting the susceptibilities of France. References to Count Muraviev's visit to Paris were omitted, although Monson's Secret and Most Confidential telegram of 25 October 1898 had reported his belief in its importance.§ The Blue Book omitted also two other telegrams from him, sent on 28 and 30 September, in which he recorded conversations with M. Delcassé at the height of the crisis. According to the earlier telegram, the French Foreign

---

* Cp. *Gooch and Temperley*, I, 158, Ed. Note.

† For these omissions cp. the full texts published in *Gooch and Temperley*, I, 158–93, *passim.*

‡ Cp. *supra*, p. 406.

§ *v. Gooch and Temperley*, I, 182, No. 215.

Minister had asked: 'You surely would not break with us over Fashoda?'—a question to which Monson replied with an unmistakable warning; the second telegram reported that he had again intimated the unlikelihood of a retreat by Britain.* A comparison of the Blue Books with the original documents suggests that Salisbury by his reticence on points such as these aimed at constructing a 'bridge of honour' for France, and the papers give in consequence little impression of the tensity of feeling which existed on both sides at the time.

With Germany there were two arrangements of first importance during this period—the convention relating to the Portuguese Colonies and the agreement relating to China, commonly, if inaccurately, called the Yangtse Agreement (Nos. 1563 c, 1585).† The former finds no reflection in the Blue Books. Both the agreement with Germany and the subsequent Declaration with Portugal remained strictly secret.‡ The concealment of the Anglo-Portuguese Declaration was indeed unfortunate for Salisbury, for the misconceptions that arose in consequence gave to this aspect of his policy—in any case rather difficult to defend—a reputation in Germany far worse than it deserved. Its erroneous association with the visit of the King of Portugal to Windsor in the spring of 1899—an antedating by six months—and the consequent obscuring of its connection with the events in South Africa both worked against Salisbury's reputation; while the full text in fact reveals that no obligation was created other than those already binding under the ancient treaties. The presentation in 1899 of a new edition of the Treaties of Guarantee gave the relevant extracts from these in full (No. 1530).

On the Chinese question in all its aspects several papers were laid (Nos. 1500, 1501, 1501 a, 1514, 1535–1535 d). On the whole they gave a fairly full record of events, although,

---

* v. Gooch and Temperley, I, 171–2, Nos. 198, 200. Salisbury's interesting threat of publication if the situation continued is also omitted. Ibid. p. 171, No. 197.

† Cp. infra, pp. 458–9.

‡ The texts of the Anglo-German Conventions of 30 August 1898 are printed in Gooch and Temperley, I, 71–5, Nos. 90–2; that of the Anglo-Portuguese Declaration of 14 October 1899, ibid. 93–4, No. 118. Cp. also Temperley and Penson, Foundations of British Foreign Policy, 514–16.

as is shown by the relevant chapters of Gooch and Temperley, *British Documents on the Origins of the War*, vols. I and II, there were substantial omissions. The most important of these omissions, however, are of the type normal in Blue Books of the period. The movements of Britain towards either the Dual or the Triple Alliance were consistently concealed. Thus Salisbury's overture to Russia of 1898 was omitted,* and so were the nearly contemporary *pourparlers* with Germany.† On the latter, indeed, the archives themselves contain little, since their unofficial character led to their being recorded almost wholly in the private papers of Chamberlain.‡ From the point of view of the public this was an unsatisfactory system. For if the negotiations had succeeded, the full extent of the private *pourparlers* could hardly have been revealed, and the references in the official correspondence must necessarily have been misleading.

* *v. Gooch and Temperley*, I, 5–18, Nos. 5–24.
† *v. ibid.* I, 42–4, Nos. 62–4.
‡ Cp. J. L. Garvin, *Life of Joseph Chamberlain* [1934], III, 259–60, 263–6, 271–2, 273–5, 276–7.

426

VOLUME CIX (1895)

State Papers

1428a   Agreement between the British and German Post Offices, concerning the exchange of Parcels by Parcel Post.   PAGE 61
[C. 7612]   L/C. 5 Feb. 1895.

1429   Declaration between Great Britain and Greece respecting Trade
Marks, Industrial Designs and Patterns. Signed at Athens,
27th July 1894. [*Treaty Series No. 21 (1894)*.]   PAGE 83
[C. 7586]   L/C. 5 Feb. 1895.

1430   Withdrawal of Guatemala from the Industrial Property Convention of 30th March 1883. [*Treaty Series No. 26 (1894)*.]
                                                     PAGE 87
[C. 7591]   L/C. 5 Feb. 1895.

1431   Treaty of Commerce and Navigation between Great Britain
and Japan. Signed at London, 16th July 1894. Ratifications
exchanged at Tôkiô, 25th August 1894. [*Treaty Series No. 23
(1894)*.]   PAGE 91
[C. 7588]   L/C. 5 Feb. 1895.

1431a   Notes exchanged between Great Britain and Japan extending
for six months the term for the Conclusion of a Convention,
supplementary to the Treaty of 16th July 1894. Tôkiô, 20th
December 1894. [*Treaty Series No. 3 (1895)*.]   PAGE 107
[C. 7598]   L/C. 22 Feb. 1895.

1431b   Despatch from Her Majesty's Minister at Tôkiô, forwarding a
copy of the Treaty of Peace concluded between China and
Japan, 17th April 1895. [*Japan No. 1 (1895)*.]   PAGE 111
[C. 7714]   L/C. HL. 24 June, HC. 25 June 1895.

1432   Convention between Great Britain and the Netherlands, submitting to Arbitration the Claims arising out of the Arrest of
the Captain of the 'Costa Rica Packet' of Sydney. Signed at
the Hague, 16th May 1895. Ratifications exchanged at the
Hague, 20th July 1895. [*Treaty Series No. 11 (1895)*.] PAGE 119
[C. 7832]   L/C. HC. 16 Aug., HL. 19 Aug. 1895.

1432a   Convention between Great Britain and the Netherlands defining
the Boundaries between the British and Netherland Possession
in the Island of New Guinea. Signed at the Hague, 16th May
1895. Ratifications exchanged at the Hague, 20th July 1895.
[*Treaty Series No. 12 (1895)*.]   PAGE 127
[C. 7834]   L/C. HL. 19 Aug., HC. 20 Aug. 1895.

1432 *b*   Additional Articles to the Convention of the 7th and 14th October 1871, between the General Post Office of the United Kingdom...and the General Post Office of the Kingdom of the Netherlands for an exchange of Post Office Money Orders.

PAGE 131

[C. 7870]   *L/C.* HC. 27 Aug., HL. 30 Aug. 1895.

1433   Accession of Lichtenstein to the International Sanitary Convention, signed at Dresden, 15th April 1893. 20th September 1894. [*Treaty Series No. 24 (1894).*]   PAGE 135

[C. 7589]   *L/C.* 5 Feb. 1895.

1434   Accession of the Orange Free State to the General Act of the Brussels Conference of 2nd July 1890. 3rd August 1894. [*Treaty Series No. 1 (1895).*]   PAGE 139

[C. 7594]   *L/C.* 5 Feb. 1895.

1435   Commercial Convention between Great Britain and Roumania. Signed at Bucharest, 13th August 1892. Ratifications exchanged at Bucharest, 31st January 1893; with a List of British Colonies which have acceded thereto under Article IV. [*Treaty Series No. 22 (1894).*]   PAGE 143

[C. 7587]   *L/C.* 5 Feb. 1895.

1435 *a*   Convention between Great Britain and Roumania respecting false Indications of Origin on Goods. Signed at Bucharest, 20th March/1st April 1893. Ratifications exchanged at Bucharest, 1st/13th March 1894. [*Treaty Series No. 7 (1895).*]

PAGE 151

[C. 7642]   *L/C.* 1 Ap. 1895.

1436   *Russia: Pamirs:* Agreement between the Governments of Great Britain and Russia with regard to the spheres of influence of the two Countries in the region of the Pamirs. London, 11th March 1895. [*Treaty Series No. 8 (1895).*]   PAGE 159

[C. 7643]   *L/C.* 5 Ap. 1895.

1437   Correspondence respecting the agreement with Russia relative to the Seal Fishery in the North Pacific. [*Russia No. 1 (1895).*]

PAGE 163

[C. 7713]   *L/C.* 21 June 1895.

1438   Accession of Servia to the International Sanitary Convention, signed at Dresden, 15th April 1893. 16th July 1894. [*Treaty Series No. 2 (1895).*]   PAGE 223

[C. 7595]   *L/C.* 7 Feb. 1895.

1438*a* Treaty of Commerce between Great Britain and Servia. Signed at Belgrade, 28th June/10th July 1893. Ratifications exchanged at Belgrade, 4th/16th October 1893; with a List of British Colonies and Foreign Possessions which have acceded thereto under Article VI. [*Treaty Series No. 10 (1895)*.]

PAGE 227

[C. 7831] . L/C. 15 Aug. 1895.

1439 Accession of Siam to the Convention, signed at Geneva, 22nd August 1864, for the Amelioration of the condition of the wounded in Armies in the Field, 29th June 1895. [*Treaty Series No. 13 (1895)*.] PAGE 235

[C. 7835] L/C. HC. 29 Aug., HL. 30 Aug. 1895.

1440 Correspondence relating to the Asiatic Provinces of Turkey, Events at Sassoon, and Commission of Inquiry at Moush. Part I. [*Turkey No. 1 (1895) (Part I)*.] PAGE 239

[C. 7894] L/C. HL. 4 Sept., HC. 5 Sept. 1895.

1440*a* Do. Commission of Inquiry at Moush: Procès-verbaux and separate Depositions. Part II. [*Turkey No. 1 (1895) (Part II)*.]

PAGE 465

[C. 7894–I] L/C. HL. 4 Sept., HC. 5 Sept. 1895.

1441 Correspondence respecting Claims for Compensation on Account of British Vessels seized in Behring Sea by United States Cruisers. [*United States No. 1 (1895)*.] PAGE 847

[C. 7836] L/C. HC. 3 Sept., HL. 4 Sept. 1895.

1442 Report on the Finances, Administration, and Condition of Egypt, and the Progress of Reforms. [*Egypt No. 1 (1895)*.]

PAGE 895

[C. 7644] L/C. HL. 4 Ap., HC. 5 Ap. 1895.

1442*a* Agreement between the British and Egyptian Post Offices concerning the Exchange of Parcels by Parcel Post. PAGE 929

[C. 7844] L/C. 15 Aug. 1895.

1442*b* Reports by Mr. Villiers Stuart, respecting the progress of re-organisation in Egypt, since the British Occupation in 1882. [*Egypt No. 2 (1895)*.] PAGE 941

[C. 7712] L/C. HC. 31 May, HL. 17 June 1895.

Session 11 February to 14 August 1896

Volume LIV (1896)

Navy, etc.

Volume LVIII (1896)

Colonies and British Possessions

Volume LIX (1896)

Colonies and British Possessions

VOLUME LXI (1896)

East India

VOLUME XCV (1896)

State Papers

1450*a*   Despatch from Her Majesty's Ambassador at Paris inclosing the Draft Law submitted to the French Chamber of Deputies for the Approval of the Treaties between France and China. Signed at Peking on the 20th June 1895. [*France No. 1 (1896)*.]
PAGE 23

  [C. 7975]   L/C. HC. 6 Mar., HL. 9 Mar. 1896.

1450*b*   Convention between Great Britain and France amending Articles VII and IX of the Extradition Treaty of the 14th August 1876. Signed at Paris, 13th February 1896. Ratifications exchanged at Paris, 19th February 1896. [*Treaty Series No. 4 (1896)*.]   PAGE 41

  [C. 7973]   L/C. 5 Mar. 1896.

1451   Supplementary Convention between Great Britain and Japan respecting the Duties to be charged on British Goods imported into Japan. Signed at Tôkiô, 16th July 1895. Ratifications exchanged at Tôkiô, 21st November 1895. [*Treaty Series No. 2 (1896)*.]   PAGE 45

  [C. 7931]   L/C. 27 Feb. 1896.

1452   Convention and Protocol between Great Britain and Nicaragua, for the Settlement of certain Claims arising out of the Disturbances in the Mosquito Reserve in 1894. Signed at London, 1st November 1895. Ratifications exchanged at London, 30th June 1896. [*Treaty Series No. 11 (1896)*.]   PAGE 53

  [C. 8103]   L/C. HC. 10 July, HL. 14 July 1896.

1453   Accession of Norway to the International Union for the protection of Literary and Artistic Works, 13th April 1896. [*Treaty Series No. 8 (1896)*.]   PAGE 61

  [C. 8017]   L/C. 4 May 1896.

1454   *Portugal: Boundaries of the Zambesi:* Agreement between Great Britain and Portugal prolonging the 'Modus Vivendi' of 1893 respecting the Boundaries of their respective spheres of influence to the North of the Zambesi. London, 20th January 1896. [*Treaty Series No. 3 (1896)*.]   PAGE 65

  [C. 7971]   L/C. 28 Feb. 1896.

1454*a*   Notes exchanged between Great Britain and Portugal respecting the Boundary between the British Protectorate of Tongaland and the neighbouring Portuguese Possessions. Lisbon, 24th September and 5th October 1895. [*Treaty Series No. 7 (1896)*.]
PAGE 69

  [C. 8014]   L/C. HC. 14 Ap., HL. 21 Ap. 1896.

Volume XCVI (1896)

State Papers: Turkey

VOLUME XCVII (1896)

State Papers

1461   Correspondence respecting the Question of the Boundary of British Guiana. [*United States No. 1 (1896)*.]   PAGE 911

   [C. 7926]   *L/C.* 11 Feb. 1896.

1462   Convention between Great Britain and the United States for submission to Arbitration of British Claims in connection with the Behring Sea Seal Fishery. Signed at Washington, 8th February 1896. Ratifications exchanged in London, 3rd June 1896. [*Treaty Series No. 10 (1896)*.]   PAGE 947

   [C. 8101]   *L/C.* 9 June 1896.

1462a   Correspondence between the Governments of Great Britain and the United States with respect to Proposals for Arbitration. [*United States No. 2 (1896)*.]   PAGE 955

   [C. 8105]   *L/C.* 17 July 1896.

1463   Report on the Finances, Administration, and Condition of Egypt, and the Progress of Reforms. [*Egypt No. 1 (1896)*.]   PAGE 989

   [C. 7978]   *L/C.* 12 Mar. 1896.

1463a   Statement of the Revenue and Expenditure of Egypt, and Tabular Statements of the various Egyptian Loans and the Charges for their Service. [*Egypt No. 2 (1896)*.]   PAGE 1039

   [C. 8102]   *L/C.* 22 June 1896.

1463b   Convention between Great Britain and Egypt for the Suppression of Slavery and the Slave Trade. Signed at Cairo, 21st November 1895. [*Treaty Series No. 16 (1895)*.]   PAGE 1047

   [C. 7929]   *L/C.* 27 Feb. 1896.

1463c   Convention between Great Britain and Egypt for the Suppression of Slavery and the Slave Trade. Signed at Cairo, 21st November 1895 (with Annexes and Egyptian Decrees). [*Treaty Series No. 6 (1896)*.]   PAGE 1057

   [C. 8011]   *L/C.* 16 Mar. 1896.

Session 19 January to 6 August 1897

Volume LXII (1897)

Colonies and British Possessions

Volume LXXXVIII (1897)

Commercial and General Interests, etc.

1469   Report from Her Majesty's Ambassador at Paris respecting
Nationality and Naturalization in the French Colonies. [*Misc.
No. 1 (1897)*.]   PAGE 363
[C. 8425]   *L/C.* 14 May 1897.

Volume CI (1897)

State Papers

1470   General Index to Treaty Series, 1892–96. [*Treaty Series No. 2
(1897)*.]   PAGE 1
[C. 8336]   *L/C.* 25 Mar. 1897.

1471   Parcel Post Agreement with Detailed Regulations between
Great Britain and Austria-Hungary.   PAGE 71
[C. 8483]   *L/C.* 13 May 1897.

1472   Convention between Great Britain and Belgium amending the
Extradition Treaty of 20th May 1876. Signed at London,
27th August 1896. Ratifications exchanged at London,
30th September 1896. [*Treaty Series No. 16 (1896)*.]   PAGE 93
[C. 8285]   *L/C.* 19 Jan. 1897.

1473   Parcel Post Convention with Detailed Regulations between
Great Britain and Chile. Signed at Santiago, 2nd June 1896.
[*Treaty Series No. 13 (1896)*.]   PAGE 97
[C. 8281]   *L/C.* 19 Jan. 1897.

1474   Convention between Great Britain and Columbia referring to
Arbitration certain questions connected with the Antioquia
Railway. Signed at London, 31st July 1896. Ratifications
exchanged at London, 11th November 1896. [*Treaty Series
No. 15 (1896)*.]   PAGE 121
[C. 8284]   *L/C.* 19 Jan. 1897.

1475   Protocol between Great Britain, Germany, and Spain explanatory of Article IV of the Protocol of 7th March 1885, respecting
the importation of Fire-arms, munitions of War, and Alcohol
into the Sulu Archipelago. Signed at Madrid, 30th March
1897. [*Treaty Series No. 4 (1897)*.]   PAGE 129
[C. 8431]   *L/C.* HC. 17 June, HL. 18 June 1897.

1483*a*   Correspondence respecting the Disturbances at Constantinople
        in August 1896. [*Turkey No. 1 (1897)*.]   PAGE 301
           [C. 8303]   *L/C.* 19 Jan. 1897.

1483*b*   Further Correspondence respecting the Asiatic Provinces of
        Turkey and events in Constantinople. [*Turkey No. 3 (1897)*.]
                                                           PAGE 359
           [C. 8305]   *L/C.* HC. 22 Jan., HL. 28 Jan. 1897.

1483*c*   do. [*Turkey No. 7 (1897)*.]   PAGE 481
           [C. 8395]   *L/C.* 30 Mar. 1897.

VOLUME CII (1897)

State Papers

1484   Notes addressed by the Representatives of Great Britain,
        Austria-Hungary, France, Germany, Italy, and Russia to the
        Turkish and Greek Governments in regard to Crete. [*Turkey
        No. 4 (1897)*.]   PAGE 1
           [C. 8333]   *L/C.* 8 Mar. 1897.

1484*a*   Replies of the Turkish and Greek Governments to the Notes
        addressed to them on 2nd March 1897 by the Representatives
        of Great Britain, Austria-Hungary, France, Germany, Italy, and
        Russia in regard to Crete. [*Turkey No. 5 (1897)*.]   PAGE 7
           [C. 8334]   *L/C.* 11 Mar. 1897.

1484*b*   Reply of the Turkish Government to the Note Presented on
        5th March 1897 by the Representatives of Great Britain,
        Austria-Hungary, France, Germany, Italy, and Russia in regard
        to Crete. [*Turkey No. 6 (1897)*.]   PAGE 15
           [C. 8335]   *L/C.* HC. 16 Mar., HL. 18 Mar. 1897.

1484*c*   Further Correspondence respecting the Affairs of Crete. [*Turkey
        No. 8 (1897)*.]   PAGE 19
           [C. 8398]   *L/C.* HC. 12 Ap., HL. 3 May 1897.

1484*d*   Reports on the Situation in Crete. [*Turkey No. 9 (1897)*.]
                                                           PAGE 153
           [C. 8429]   *L/C.* 28 May 1897.

1484e Further Correspondence respecting the Affairs of Crete. [*Turkey No. 10 (1897)*.]   PAGE 205

    [C. 8437]   *L/C.* 8 July 1897.

1485 Despatch from Her Majesty's Ambassador at Washington, forwarding a Copy of the Treaty of General Arbitration between Great Britain and the United States. Signed at Washington, 11th January 1897. [*United States No. 1 (1897)*.]   PAGE 429

    [C. 8331]   *R–A. (HC. 3 Feb.)*, 15 Feb. 1897.

1485a Report by Professor D'Arcy Thompson on his Mission to Behring Sea in 1896. Dated 4th March 1897. [*United States No. 3 (1897)*.]   PAGE 437

    [C. 8426]   *L/C.* HC. 18 May, HL. 20 May 1897.

1485b Correspondence with the Government of the United States respecting the Communication to other Governments of the Rules of the Treaty of Washington of May 1871. [*United States No. 2 (1897)*.]   PAGE 481

    [C. 8393]   *R–A. (HC. 12 Mar.)*, 29 Mar. 1897.

1486 Treaty between Great Britain and the United States of Venezuela respecting the Settlement of the Boundary between the Colony of British Guiana and the United States of Venezuela. Signed at Washington, 2nd February 1897. Ratifications exchanged at Washington, 14th June 1897. [*Treaty Series No. 5 (1897)*.]   PAGE 495

    [C. 8439]   *L/C.* HC. 20 July, HL. 22 July 1897.

1487 Report on the Finances, Administration, and Condition of Egypt, and the Progress of Reforms. [*Egypt No. 2 (1897)*.]
                                    PAGE 505

    [C. 8332]   *L/C.* 16 Feb. 1897.

1487a Correspondence respecting the Law-suit brought against the Egyptian Government in regard to the Appropriation of Money from the General Reserve Fund to the Expenses of the Dongola Expedition. [*Egypt No. 1 (1897)*.]   PAGE 539

    [C. 8306]   *L/C.* HC. 22 Jan., HL. 28 Jan. 1897.

1487b Reports on the Province of Dongola. [*Egypt No. 3 (1897)*.]
                                    PAGE 587

    [C. 8427]   *L/C.* 14 May 1897.

1487c Memorials from the Egyptian Exiles in Ceylon. [*Egypt No. 4 (1897)*.]   PAGE 607

    [C. 8436]   *L/C.* HC. 7 July, HL. 8 July 1897.

SESSION 8 FEBRUARY TO 12 AUGUST 1898

VOLUME LVI (1898)

Navy Estimates

VOLUME LX (1898)

Colonies and British Possessions

* This paper was laid in recess and circulated as [C. 8440] of 1897.

VOLUME CV (1898)

State Papers

1500   Correspondence respecting the Affairs of China. [*China No. 1*
        (1898).]   PAGE 53
        [C. 8814]   *L/C.* 21 Ap. 1898.

1501   Agreement between Great Britain and China modifying the
        Convention of 1st March 1894, relative to Burmah and Thibet,
        with Map. Signed at Peking, 4th February 1897. Ratifications
        exchanged at Peking, 5th June 1897. [*Treaty Series No. 7
        (1897)*.]   PAGE 129
        [C. 8654]   *L/C.* 8 Feb. 1898.

1501 a Despatch from Her Majesty's Minister at Peking forwarding
        copies of the Notes exchanged with the Chinese Government
        respecting the non-alienation of the Yang-Tsze Region. [*China
        No. 2 (1898)*.]   PAGE 139
        [C. 8940]   *L/C.* 25 July 1898.

1502   Treaty between Great Britain and Ethiopia. Signed by the
        Emperor Menelik II and by Her Majesty's Envoy at Adis
        Abbaba, 14th May 1897. Ratified by the Queen, 28th July
        1897. [*Treaty Series No. 2 (1898)*.]   PAGE 143
        [C. 8715]   *L/C.* 8 Feb. 1898.

1503   Convention between Great Britain and France for the exchange
        of Postal Parcels between India and France. Signed at Paris,
        1st December 1897. Ratifications exchanged at Paris, 8th
        January 1898. [*Treaty Series No. 1 (1898)*.]   PAGE 155
        [C. 8704]   *L/C.* 8 Feb. 1898.

1503 a Convention between Great Britain and France for the exchange
        of Postal Parcels between Australia and France. Signed at
        Paris, 1st December 1897. Ratifications exchanged at Paris,
        25th January 1898. [*Treaty Series No. 3 (1898)*.]   PAGE 165
        [C. 8717]   *L/C.* 24 Feb. 1898.

1503 b Agreement between the United Kingdom and France respect-
        ing the express delivery of Parcels. Signed at Paris, 13th April
        1898. [*Treaty Series No. 7 (1898)*.]   PAGE 175
        [C. 8852]   *L/C.* 17 May 1898.

1503 c Additional Act modifying the International Copyright Con-
        vention of 9th September 1886. Signed at Paris, 4th May
        1896. Ratifications deposited at Paris, 9th September 1897.
        [*Treaty Series No. 14 (1897)*.]   PAGE 179
        [C. 8681]   *L/C.* 8 Feb. 1898.

1504　Convention between Great Britain and France relative to Tunis. Signed at Paris, 18th September 1897. Ratifications exchanged at Paris, 15th October 1897. [*Treaty Series No. 11 (1897)*.]
PAGE 193

　　　[C. 8678]　　　*L/C.* 8 Feb. 1898.

1505　Correspondence relating to the Finances of Greece. [*Greece No. 2 (1898)*.]　　　PAGE 197

　　　[C. 8818]　　　*L/C.* 6 May 1898.

1505a　Further Correspondence. [*Greece No. 3 (1898)*.]　　　PAGE 287

　　　[C. 8849]　　　*L/C.* 6 May 1898.

1505b　Despatch from Her Majesty's Minister at Athens, enclosing the Greek Law of Control. [*Greece No. 1 (1898)*.]　　　PAGE 299

　　　[C. 8778]　　　*L/C.* HL. 31 Mar., HC. 1 Ap. 1898.

1505c　Convention between the United Kingdom, France, Greece, and Russia, to facilitate the conclusion of a Loan by the Greek Government. Signed at Paris, 29th March 1898. Ratifications deposited at Paris, 18th May 1898. [*Treaty Series No. 9 (1898)*.]
PAGE 327

　　　[C. 8856]　　　*L/C.* 23 June 1898.

1506　Accession of Hayti to the Additional Act and Declaration, signed at Paris, 4th May 1896, modifying the International Copyright Convention of 9th September 1886. 17th January 1898. [*Treaty Series No. 6 (1898)*.]　　　PAGE 339

　　　[C. 8813]　　　*L/C.* HC. 18 Ap., HL. 21 Ap. 1898.

1507　Agreement for the Express Delivery of Parcels exchanged between the United Kingdom...and Holland.　　　PAGE 343

　　　[C. 8672]　　　*L/C.* 8 Feb. 1898.

1508　Agreement between the General Post Office of the United Kingdom...and the Postal Administration of the State of Honduras, in the Greater Republic of Central America for the Exchange of Postal Parcels.　　　PAGE 347

　　　[C. 8670]　　　*L/C.* 8 Feb. 1898.

1508a　Accession of the Republics of Honduras and Nicaragua to the Convention, signed at Geneva, 22nd August 1864, for the amelioration of the condition of the Wounded in Armies in the Field. [*Treaty Series No. 10 (1898)*.]　　　PAGE 363

　　　[C. 8939]　　　*L/C.* 25 July 1898.

1509   Protocol between Great Britain and Japan respecting Patents, Trade Marks, and Designs. Signed at London, 20th October 1897. [*Treaty Series No. 12 (1897)*.]   PAGE 367

    [C. 8679]   *L/C.* 8 Feb. 1898.

1510   Treaty and Additional Article between Great Britain and Mexico, respecting the Boundary between Mexico and British Honduras (with Map). Signed at Mexico, 8th July 1893, and 7th April 1897. Ratifications exchanged at Mexico, 21st July 1897. [*Treaty Series No. 6 (1897)*.]   PAGE 371

    [C. 8653]   *L/C.* 8 Feb. 1898.

1511   Correspondence relating to the Accession of the Orange Free State to the Postal Union Convention, signed at Vienna, 4th July 1891.   PAGE 381

    [C. 8833]   *L/C.* 22 Ap. 1898.

1511*a*   Accession of the Orange Free State to the Red Cross Convention, signed at Geneva, 22nd August 1864. 28th September 1897. [*Treaty Series No. 13 (1897)*.]   PAGE 385

    [C. 8680]   *L/C.* 8 Feb. 1898.

1512   Agreement between the United Kingdom and Portugal, modifying the Postal Money Order Agreement of 17th January 1883. Signed at Lisbon, 3rd February 1898. [*Treaty Series No. 5 (1898)*.]   PAGE 389

    [C. 8779]   *L/C.* HC. 4 Ap., HL. 5 Ap. 1898.

1513   Accession of Roumania to the International Sanitary Convention, signed at Dresden, 15th April 1893. 3rd April 1897. [*Treaty Series No. 10 (1897)*.]   PAGE 397

    [C. 8666]   *L/C.* 8 Feb. 1898.

1514   Despatch from Her Majesty's Ambassador at St. Petersburg, enclosing an Agreement concluded between the Chinese Government and the Russo-Chinese Bank for the Construction of the Manchurian Railway. [*Russia No. 1 (1898)*.]   PAGE 403

    [C. 8777]   *L/C.* HL. 31 Mar., HC. 1 Ap. 1898.

1515   Accession of Servia and the Dominican Republic to Protocol III of the Madrid Conference respecting the Endowment of the International Office. [*Treaty Series No. 15 (1897)*.]   PAGE 413

    [C. 8682]   *L/C.* 8 Feb. 1898.

VOLUME CVI (1898)

State Papers: Turkey

VOLUME CVII (1898)

State Papers: Turkey, Egypt

SESSION 1. 7 FEBRUARY TO 9 AUGUST 1899
SESSION 2. 17 OCTOBER TO 27 OCTOBER 1899

VOLUME LXIII (1899)

Colonies and British Possessions

VOLUME CIX (1899)

State Papers

1532c   Exchange of Notes establishing a Provisional Modus Vivendi
         between the United Kingdom and Belgium pending the con-
         clusion of a Treaty of Commerce and Navigation between the
         two Countries, 27th July 1898. [*Treaty Series No. 11 (1898)*.]
                                                                PAGE 199
            [C. 9050]   L/C. 7 Feb. 1899.

1532d   Exchange of Notes extending [the above] to Cyprus..., 25th
         November 1898. [*Treaty Series No. 2 (1899)*.]   PAGE 203
            [C. 9127]   L/C. HL. 16 Feb., HC. 17 Feb. 1899.

1532e   Exchange of Notes extending [do.] to Ceylon and Lagos...,
         5th January 1899. [*Treaty Series No. 4 (1899)*.]   PAGE 207
            [C. 9129]   L/C. HC. 22 Feb., HL. 23 Feb. 1899.

1532f   Exchange of Notes extending [do.] to Queensland..., 6th
         February 1899. [*Treaty Series No. 7 (1899)*.]   PAGE 211
            [C. 9234]   L/C. HC. 19 Ap., HL. 20 Ap. 1899.

1532g   Convention between the United Kingdom and Belgium relative
         to the Remittance of Money Orders by Telegraph between
         the two countries. Signed at London, 15th September 1899.
         Ratifications exchanged at London, 29th September 1899.
         [*Treaty Series No. 17 (1899)*.]   PAGE 215
            [C. 9505]   L/C. 17 Oct. 1899.

1533   Treaty between Great Britain and Bolivia for the Mutual
         Surrender of Fugitive Criminals. Signed at Lima, 22nd
         February 1892. Ratifications exchanged at Lima, 7th March
         1898. [*Treaty Series No. 10 (1899)*.]   PAGE 223
            [C. 9239]   L/C. 1 May 1899.

1534   Treaty between the United Kingdom and Chile for the Mutual
         Surrender of Fugitive Criminals. Signed at Santiago, 26th
         January 1897. Ratifications exchanged at Santiago, 14th April
         1898. [*Treaty Series No. 12 (1898)*.]   PAGE 237
            [C. 9051]   L/C. 7 Feb. 1899.

1535   Correspondence respecting the Affairs of China. [*China No. 1
         (1899)*.]   PAGE 251
            [C. 9131]   L/C. 13 Mar. 1899.

1535a   Convention between the United Kingdom and China respecting
         Wei-Hai-Wei. Signed at Peking, 1st July 1898. Ratifications
         exchanged at London, 5th October 1898. [*Treaty Series No. 14
         (1898)*.]   PAGE 635
            [C. 9081]   L/C. 7 Feb. 1899.

1535*b*   Convention between the United Kingdom and China respecting
an Extension of Hong Kong Territory, with a Map. Signed at
Peking, 9th June 1898. Ratifications exchanged at London,
6th August 1898. [*Treaty Series No. 16 (1898)*.]   PAGE 639
      [C. 9087]   *L/C.* 7 Feb. 1899.

1535*c*   Correspondence between Her Majesty's Government and the
Russian Government, with regard to their respective Railway
interests in China. [*China No. 2 (1899)*.]   PAGE 645
      [C. 9329]   *L/C.* 5 June 1899.

1535*d*   Despatch from Her Majesty's Minister at Peking, forwarding
a Report by the Acting British Consul at Ssŭmao on the trade
of Yunnan. [*China No. 3 (1898)*.]   PAGE 745
      [C. 9083]   *L/C.* 7 Feb. 1899.

1536   Further Correspondence with the French Government respecting Madagascar. [*France No. 1 (1899)*.]   PAGE 759
      [C. 9091]   *L/C.* 7 Feb. 1899.

1537   Agreement respecting the admission of Parcels to be delivered
free of all charges into the Parcel Post Exchange between Great
Britain and France.   PAGE 823
      [C. 9118]   *L/C.* 7 Feb. 1899.

1537*a*   Additional Convention to the Convention of 1st December 1897
between the United Kingdom and France for the Exchange of
Postal Parcels between Australia and France. Signed at Paris,
24th December 1898. Ratifications exchanged at Paris,
1st February 1899. [*Treaty Series No. 6 (1899)*.]   PAGE 829
      [C. 9132]   *L/C.* HC. 15 Mar., HL. 16 Mar. 1899.

1537*b*   Return of Exports from Great Britain and France to Tunis
during the years 1880, 1885, 1890, 1895, and 1897. [*Tunis No. 1
(1899)*.]   PAGE 833
      [C. 9425]   *R–A.* (*HC. 17 July*), HC. 4 Aug., HL.
                           7 Aug. 1899.

1538   *West Niger Convention:* Convention between the United Kingdom
and France for the Delimitation of their respective Possessions
to the West of the Niger, and of their respective Possessions and
Spheres of Influence to the East of that river. Signed at Paris,
14th June 1898, with a declaration completing the same.
Signed at London, 21st March 1899. Ratifications exchanged
at Paris, 13th June 1899. [*Treaty Series No. 15 (1899)*.]
                                                      PAGE 837
      [C. 9334]   *L/C.* 21 July 1899.

VOLUME CX (1899)

State Papers

1539   Additional Articles to the Money Order Convention of the 10th–18th of January 1871, between the General Post Office of the United Kingdom...and the General Post Office of North Germany.   PAGE 1

      [C. 9180]   *L/C.* 17 Feb. 1899.

1540   Agreement concerning the Exchange of Postal Parcels concluded between the Post Office of the United Kingdom and the Postal Administration of Guatemala.   PAGE 5

      [C. 9149]   *L/C.* 7 Feb. 1899.

1540*a*   Convention between the United Kingdom and Guatemala relative to Trade Marks, signed at Guatemala, July 20, 1898. Ratifications exchanged at Guatemala, July 28, 1899. [*Treaty Series No. 16 (1899)*.]   PAGE 25

      [C. 9504]   *L/C.* 17 Oct. 1899.

1541   Treaty between the United Kingdom and the Netherlands for the Mutual Surrender of Fugitive Criminals, signed at London, September 26, 1898. Ratifications exchanged at London, December 14, 1898. [*Treaty Series No. 1 (1899)*.]   PAGE 29

      [C. 9089]   *L/C.* 7 Feb. 1899.

1541*a*   Additional Articles to the Money Order Convention of the 7th–14th of October 1871, between the General Post Office of the United Kingdom...and the General Post Office of the Netherlands.   PAGE 47

      [C. 9532]   *L/C.* 17 Oct. 1899.

1541*b*   Convention between the United Kingdom and the Netherlands providing that Submarine Cables connecting the two Countries shall be their joint property, signed at The Hague, April 5, 1898. Ratifications exchanged at The Hague, December 13, 1898. [*Treaty Series No. 9 (1899)*.]   PAGE 51

      [C. 9238]   *L/C.* 1 May 1899.

1542   Accession of Japan to the Industrial Property Convention of March 20, 1883. [*Treaty Series No. 12 (1899)*.]   PAGE 63

      [C. 9327]   *L/C.* 2 June 1899.

1542*a*   Accession of Japan to the International Union for the Protection
of Literary and Artistic Works, July 15, 1899. [*Treaty Series
No. 13 (1899)*.]   PAGE 67

   [C. 9328]   L/C. HC. 6 June, HL. 8 June 1899.

1543   Withdrawal of Montenegro from the International Union for
the Protection of Literary and Artistic Works. [*Treaty Series
No. 14 (1899)*.]   PAGE 71

   [C. 9330]   L/C. HC. 9 June, HL. 12 June 1899.

1544   Agreement for the Express Delivery of Parcels exchanged
between the United Kingdom...and Portugal (including
Madeira and the Azores).   PAGE 75

   [C. 9310]   L/C. 16 May 1899.

1545   Exchange of Notes between Great Britain and Portugal relative
to the Delimitation of the Frontier between the British and
Portuguese Possessions in Amatongaland. [*Treaty Series No. 3
(1899)*.]   PAGE 81

   [C. 9128]   L/C. 20 Feb. 1899.

1546   Correspondence respecting the proposal of His Majesty the
Emperor of Russia for a Conference on Armaments. [*Russia
No. 1 (1899)*.]   PAGE 85

   [C. 9090]   L/C. 7 Feb. 1899.

1546*a*   Correspondence respecting the Peace Conference held at The
Hague in 1899. [*Misc. No. 1 (1899)*.]   PAGE 93

   [C. 9534]   L/C. HL. 26 Oct., HC. 27 Oct. 1899.

1547   Exchange of Notes between the United Kingdom and Russia
with regard to their respective Railway Interests in China.
[*Treaty Series No. 11 (1899)*.]   PAGE 455

   [C. 9241]   L/C. HC. 5 May, HL. 8 May 1899.

1548   Correspondence respecting the Affairs of Samoa, Report of the
Joint Commission. [*Samoa No. 1 (1899)*.]   PAGE 461

   [C. 9506]   L/C. 17 Oct. 1899.

1549   Further Correspondence respecting the Affairs of Crete.
[*Turkey No. 5 (1898)*.]   PAGE 489

   [C. 9084]   L/C. 7 Feb. 1899.

VOLUME CXI (1899)

State Papers

1551*c*   The case of the United States of Venezuela before the Tribunal of Arbitration to convene at Paris, under the Provisions of the Treaty between the United States of Venezuela and Her Britannic Majesty, signed at Washington, February 2nd, 1897. Vol. I. [*Venezuela No. 4 (1899)*.]   PAGE 585
  [C. 9499]   *L/C.* 17 Oct. 1899.

1551*d*   The Counter-case of the United States of Venezuela before the Tribunal of Arbitration to convene at Paris under the Provisions of the Treaty of Washington, February 2nd, 1897. Vol. I. [*Venezuela No. 5 (1899)*.]   PAGE 825
  [C. 9500]   *L/C.* 17 Oct. 1899.

VOLUME CXII (1899)

State Papers

1551*e*   The printed argument on behalf of the United States of Venezuela before the Tribunal of Arbitration. [*Venezuela No. 6 (1899)*.]   PAGE 1
  [C. 9501]   *L/C.* 17 Oct. 1899.

1551*f*   Award of the Tribunal of Arbitration constituted under Article I of the Treaty of Arbitration, signed at Washington, 2nd February 1897, between Great Britain and the United States of Venezuela. [*Venezuela No. 7 (1899)*.]   PAGE 855
  [C. 9533]   *L/C.* 19 Oct. 1899.

1552   Correspondence with the French Government respecting the Valley of the Upper Nile. [*Egypt No. 2 (1898)*.]   PAGE 863
  [C. 9054]   *L/C.* 7 Feb. 1899.

1552*a*   Further Correspondence. [*Egypt No. 3 (1898)*.]   PAGE 889
  [C. 9055]   *L/C.* 7 Feb. 1899.

1553   Papers relating to the Contract for the Atbara Bridge. [*Egypt No. 6 (1899)*.]   PAGE 905
  [C. 9424]   *L/C.* 4 Aug. 1899.

1554   Despatches from Her Majesty's Agent and Consul-General in Egypt respecting the conduct of the British and Egyptian Troops after the Battle of Omdurman. [*Egypt No. 1 (1899)*.]   PAGE 919
  [C. 9133]   *L/C.* HC. 21 Mar., HL. 23 Mar. 1899.

THE BLUE-BOOK POLICY OF
LORD LANSDOWNE*

1900–5

THE papers laid before Parliament during the period of Lord Lansdowne's tenure of the Foreign Secretaryship follow closely the lines laid down by his predecessors. In general they are most full when the interest of the Great Powers was least engaged, although the strength of public excitement counteracted this tendency on some occasions, as in the case of the North Sea incident. They continue to be most voluminous on questions relating to the affairs of China and Turkey, where commercial interests were involved and a mass of detailed evidence was available. The Chinese question was naturally prominent in the last year of Salisbury's period at the Foreign Office, for the Boxer disturbances were at their height, and requests for papers were frequently made in the Commons. There was, however, little complaint of their contents, and on the whole there is considerable justification for the claim made by the Under-Secretary of State (Mr Brodrick) on 2 August 1900, when he said that there were 'ample materials for those who read between the lines' in the Blue Book laid in the previous March (No. 1563).† The Chinese papers of 1900 stretch to over 600 pages, and those of 1901 are even more voluminous. It is significant, however, that while the material relating to the Boxer revolt is full, there is comparatively little contemporary publication on either the Anglo-German Agreement of 16 October 1900 (No. 1563c)‡ or the Russo-Chinese Agreement as to Manchuria (No. 1582). The papers on the Anglo-German Agreement successfully conceal the difficulties with Germany about the wording of the text and

* Lord Lansdowne became Secretary of State for Foreign Affairs on 12 November 1900. Lord Salisbury remained Prime Minister until 10 July 1902, when he was succeeded by Mr A. J. Balfour.
† *Hans. Deb.* 4th Ser. LXXXVII, 488–9. Cp. *Gooch and Temperley*, II, 11 *et seq.*
‡ The Agreement was concluded before Lord Salisbury left the Foreign Office (cp. *supra*, p. 424), but the papers were laid by Lord Lansdowne.

the attitude of Russia to the conclusion of the treaty. The Blue Book is in fact very meagre, and contains none of the 'hundred other documents' to which Lord Cranborne referred in March 1901 as pledging the German Government 'to maintain the integrity of China'.* Sir Charles Dilke complained that there had been delay in producing some of the Chinese papers of this year, and in particular one (No. 1581) which was not issued until after the Foreign Office vote. 'He could not but think that it was kept back on purpose, as the latest despatch upon the matter contained in it was dated the 1st May, and the latest important despatches early in April.' It was laid, however, on 17 August, and the complaint was clearly not taken very seriously. Lord Cranborne replied with an apology, and the now well-known explanation: 'Blue-books take a long time to prepare and delays are unavoidable owing to the necessity of communication with other Powers as to the publication of documents in which they are committed.'† Some of the most important correspondence on Chinese affairs did not appear until 1904, when papers were published relating to the Russian occupation of Manchuria and Newchwang (No. 1646d). Even these, however, were carefully selected; and the difficulties with Germany over the interpretation of the Anglo-German Agreement were still concealed.‡

The 'Correspondence respecting the Evacuation of Shanghae' (No. 1599a) was much curtailed in order to meet the wishes of Germany and to avoid arousing public feeling.§ Count Metternich asked on 26 November 1902 that 'we should avoid the publication of any papers likely to create ill-feeling between our two countries'. Lord Lansdowne said that he 'had revised the proofs with this object', asking only for a pledge that the documents and passages omitted should not be made public in Germany.‖ The result of this revision was that several documents which it had been intended

---

* *Hans. Deb.* 4th Ser. xcii, 182–3, 23 March 1901.
† *Hans. Deb.* 4th Ser. cx, 707, 736, 3 July 1902.
‡ On this subject cp. *Gooch and Temperley*, ii, 22–31.
§ *v. Gooch and Temperley*, ii, 138, Ed. Note.
‖ *v. ibid.* ii, 149–50, No. 166.

to include were omitted altogether, and others were published in extract form. By this means Lord Lansdowne concealed his dissatisfaction with the action of Germany in negotiating direct with China on points connected with the evacuation, and avoided direct indication of Anglo-German friction. On the other hand he refused to omit a passage which contained the statement that 'the British Government did not consider themselves bound by the German arrangement with China', since this was 'an important declaration as to the manner in which we regarded the German arrangement about China'.*

With reference to Turkey the main subject covered in the Blue Books was that of Macedonian reform (Nos. 1633–1633 b, 1655–1655 b, 1692 a, b). These papers contain a mass of information covering the years 1901–5, and, although here also there were omissions obviously designed to conceal differences among the Powers, these omissions were not so striking as those in the papers relating to the evacuation of Shanghae, and they compare favourably on the whole with earlier Turkish Blue Books.†

The selection of documents for publication in the 'Correspondence relating to the North Sea Incident' (No. 1687 a) was clearly made with great care. Some important dispatches were omitted altogether. Among these may be mentioned Sir Charles Hardinge's dispatches of 31 October 1904‡ and 7 November 1904.§ The former, which gained the special approval of King Edward VII, contained a full account of the ambassador's audience with the Tsar on 29 October; the latter gave a valuable analysis of Russian opinion and policy, and, as King Edward said, raised 'serious reflections for certain eventualities'. Both these documents are, indeed, of a kind that is rarely found in Blue Books. Again, all papers referring to the attitude of France during this crisis were omitted.‖ Many other dispatches and telegrams

---

* v. Gooch and Temperley, II, 145–6, No. 160; 147, No. 163; 148–52, Nos. 165–8. For the passage which Lansdowne refused to omit v. A. & P. [1902], cxxx [Cd. 1369], 369–70.

† On this subject cf. Gooch and Temperley, v, 49–99, chapters xxxi, xxxii.

‡ This dispatch is printed in full in Gooch and Temperley, iv, 25–8, No. 24.

§ v. Gooch and Temperley, iv, 33–5, No. 26.

‖ Cp. ibid. iv, 8–9, No. 9; 22, No. 21; 36, No. 27.

were published in extract form, or were subjected to alteration before publication, again clearly with the object of avoiding any excitement of public feeling.* It is perhaps significant that the Blue Book was laid during recess, and that there were no debates upon it.

Among other points of interest in connection with the papers of this period, mention may be made of two. The two great treaties—that with Japan of 30 January 1902 (No. 1605), and that with France of 8 April 1904 (No. 1648)— were laid before Parliament before ratification, in the former case twelve days, and in the latter only four days after signature; but they were accompanied only by covering dispatches evidently written for the purpose. The Japanese Treaty was published in full. The French Treaty on the other hand contained secret clauses. It is significant that no reference to these secret articles appeared in the original draft of the covering dispatch. By this time the practice of laying treaties without correspondence was well established, and no comment was made in Parliament. Moreover, the covering dispatches, particularly in the case of the Anglo-French Treaty, gave a useful description of the negotiations. The second point which may be included here is the reiteration by Mr Balfour, after he assumed the Premiership, of the principle which governed the publication of papers. Mr Gibson Bowles had asked whether papers would be laid on the question of the Declaration of Paris of 1856 and the discussions with Russia as to the Status of the Volunteer Fleet. Mr Balfour said: 'I am very reluctant to lay Papers on the Table. Of course, if questions of practical importance leading to grave national issues were at stake, the House of Commons would rightly insist on being made fully acquainted with all that occurred; but I do not think it would be desirable that I should promise at this moment to lay Papers on this subject before the House.'† On the previous day, in answer to a question on the same topic, Mr Balfour had

---

* Cp. the passages indicated, *Gooch and Temperley*, IV, 28–30, No. 25; enclosures 2 and 3 to this dispatch were omitted altogether.
† *Hans. Deb.* 4th Ser. CXXXVIII, 1224, 26 July 1904.

stated: 'This question does touch on what I must, at all events at present, regard as forbidden ground. It does raise a controversy which I think will be better settled if the House will, for the moment at all events, content itself with what I have said.'*

Among the papers included in the list given here for this period is one whose relevance is indirect (No. 1643). The development of the Committee of Imperial Defence was however of such importance at a later date that the sole reference to it in Parliamentary Papers of this period is worthy of note. The Treasury minute, dated 4 May 1904, gives some useful information on the origin of the Committee, and was productive of considerable discussion in Parliament.†

It would be difficult to say that Lord Lansdowne was more generous in the publication of papers than Lord Salisbury. He did not go out of his way to seek publicity for his foreign policy, and had, indeed, no connection with the Press. Upon occasion he used Parliamentary debate for important definitions of policy, as on 5 May 1903 when he made his declaration on British policy in the Persian Gulf.‡ The concealment from the public of the secret articles of the Anglo-French Treaty was, indeed, a new departure. There were precedents for withholding a secret agreement from Parliament—e.g. the Anglo-German Convention of 1898; but there was no recent precedent for partial publication of an agreement, while secret articles remained unacknowledged. Sir Edward Grey, in November 1911, justified this unusual action 'because they were not articles which commit this House to serious obligations,' an argument certainly open to dispute.§

* *Hans. Deb.* 4th Ser. cxxxviii, 1063-4, 25 July 1904.
† *Hans. Deb.* 4th Ser. cxxxix, 605-46, 2 August 1904. Cp. Mr Balfour's speech on 5 March 1903, *ibid.* cxviii, 1578-86, and the subsequent debate pp. 1586-1649, when Mr Balfour moved 'That, in the opinion of this House, the growing needs of the Empire require the establishment of the Committee of Defence on a permanent footing'. Cp. also Mr Balfour's statement on 11 May 1905, *ibid.* cxlvi, 62-84.
‡ *Hans. Deb.* 4th Ser. cxxi, 1348. Cp. *Gooch and Temperley,* iv, 371, No. 321.
§ *v. infra,* p. 498.

SESSION 1. 30 JANUARY TO 8 AUGUST 1900
SESSION 2. 3 DECEMBER TO 15 DECEMBER 1900

VOLUME LVI (1900)

Colonies and British Possessions

VOLUME CV (1900)

State Papers

1568   Declaration between the United Kingdom and the Grand
       Duchy of Luxemburg respecting the Reciprocal Protection of
       Trade Marks; signed at Luxemburg; January 25, 1900.
       [*Treaty Series No. 4 (1900)*.]   PAGE 817

       [Cd. 31]   *L/C.* 13 Feb. 1900.

1569   Agreement relating to the Telegraph Service between Great
       Britain and Roumania.   PAGE 821

       [Cd. 377]   *L/C.* 6 Dec. 1900.

1570   Procès verbal recording the Accession of the Russian Empire
       to the Cape Spartel International Lighthouse Convention of
       May 31, 1865; signed at Tangier, May 31, 1899. [*Treaty
       Series No. 5 (1900)*.]   PAGE 825

       [Cd. 32]   *L/C.* 5 Mar. 1900.

1571   Despatch to Her Majesty's Chargé d'Affaires at Berlin,
       enclosing Copies of the Convention and Declaration between
       Great Britain and Germany of November 14th, 1899, for the
       Settlement of Samoan and other Questions. [*Germany No. 1
       (1899)*.]   PAGE 829

       [Cd. 7]   *L/C.* 30 Jan. 1900.

1571*a* Convention and Declaration between the United Kingdom and
       Germany for the Settlement of the Samoan and other Questions;
       signed at London, November 14, 1899, ratifications exchanged
       at London and Berlin, February 16th 1900. [*Treaty Series No. 7
       (1900)*.]   PAGE 835

       [Cd. 38]   *L/C.* 22 Mar. 1900.

1571*b* Convention between the United Kingdom, Germany, and the
       United States of America for the Adjustment of Questions
       relating to Samoa; signed at Washington, December 2nd,
       1899, ratifications exchanged at London, Berlin, and Washing-
       ton, February 16, 1900. [*Treaty Series No. 8 (1900)*.] PAGE 843

       [Cd. 39]   *L/C.* 22 Mar. 1900.

1571*c* Convention between the United Kingdom, Germany, and the
       United States of America relating to the Settlement of certain
       Claims in Samoa by Arbitration; signed at Washington,
       November 7th, 1899, ratifications exchanged at Washington,
       March 7, 1900. [*Treaty Series No. 10 (1900)*.]   PAGE 849

       [Cd. 98]   *L/C.* 10 May 1900.

1574d Correspondence respecting the Seizure of the British Vessels "Springbok" and "Peterhoff" by United States' Cruisers in 1863. [*Misc. No. 1 (1900)*.]   PAGE 913

[Cd. 34]   *L/C.* 12 Mar. 1900.

1575 Accession of the Republic of Uruguay to the Convention; signed at Geneva, August 22nd, 1864, for the Amelioration of the Condition of Wounded in Armies in the Field. [*Treaty Series No. 12 (1900)*.]   PAGE 987

[Cd. 102]   *L/C.* HL. 5 July, HC. 6 July 1900.

1575a Convention between the United Kingdom and Uruguay renewing the Treaty of Friendship, Commerce, and Navigation of November 13, 1885; signed at Monte Video, July 15, 1899, ratifications exchanged at Monte Video, June 9, 1900. [*Treaty Series No. 15 (1900)*.]   PAGE 991

[Cd. 255]   *L/C.* 24 July 1900.

1576 Reports by Her Majesty's Agent and Consul-General on the Finances, Administration, and Condition of Egypt and the Soudan in 1899. [*Egypt No. 1 (1900)*.]   PAGE 995

[Cd. 95]   *L/C.* 9 Ap. 1900.

1576a Agreement concerning the Exchange of Postal Parcels concluded between the Post Office of the United Kingdom...and the Postal Administration of Egypt.   PAGE 1063

[Cd. 24]   *L/C.* 30 Jan. 1900.

SESSION 23 JANUARY TO 17 AUGUST 1901

VOLUME XLII (1901)

Navy Estimates

1577 Return showing the Fleets of Great Britain, France, Russia, Germany, Italy, United States of America, and Japan....

PAGE 111

112   *Pursuant to Order (HC. 12 Dec. 1900), HC. 29 Mar. 1901.*

VOLUME XLVIII (1901)

Colonies and British Possessions

VOLUME XCI (1901)

State Papers

1584   Agreement additional to the Convention between the United
        Kingdom and France of December 8th, 1882, relative to the
        Exchange of Telegraph Money Orders between the two Coun-
        tries; signed at Paris, October 10, 1900 (ratifications exchanged
        at Paris, March 16th, 1901). [*Treaty Series No. 4 (1901)*.]
                                                        PAGE 783
        [Cd. 440]   *L/C.* HC. 18 Ap., HL. 22 Ap. 1901.

1584*a* Convention between the United Kingdom and France referring
        to Arbitration the Settlement of Differences in connection with
        the Waïma and Serjeant Malamine incidents; signed at Paris,
        April 3rd, 1901 (ratifications exchanged at Paris, July 17, 1901).
        [*Treaty Series No. 6 (1901)*.]   PAGE 789
        [Cd. 673]   *L/C.* 2 Aug. 1901.

1585   *Anglo-German Agreement:* Agreement between the United King-
        dom and Germany relative to China, October 16, 1900.
        [*Treaty Series No. 1 (1901)*.]   PAGE 795
        [Cd. 432]   *L/C.* 14 Feb. 1901.

1586   Convention between the United Kingdom and Japan for the
        Protection of the Estates of Deceased Persons; signed at Tôkiô,
        April 26, 1900, ratifications exchanged at Tôkiô, October 25,
        1900. [*Treaty Series No. 2 (1901)*.]   PAGE 799
        [Cd. 433]   *L/C.* 14 Feb. 1901.

1587   Agreement between the British and Norwegian Post Offices
        concerning the Exchange of Parcels by Parcel Post. PAGE 803
        [Cd. 482]   *L/C.* HC. 15 Feb., HL. 19 Feb. 1901.

1588   Accession of the Kingdom of Sweden to the Venice Sanitary
        Convention of March 19, 1897, and to the Declaration addi-
        tional thereto of January 24, 1900. [*Treaty Series No. 3 (1901)*.]
                                                        PAGE 823
        [Cd. 437]   *L/C.* 25 Feb. 1901.

1588*a* Additional Articles to the Convention of the 7th–12th of
        September 1881 relative to the Exchange of Money Orders
        between the United Kingdom and the Kingdom of Sweden,
        dated the 1st–8th of September 1900.   PAGE 827
        [Cd. 498]   *L/C.* 5 Mar. 1901.

1589   Further Correspondence respecting the Affairs of Crete.
        [*Turkey No. 1 (1901)*.]   PAGE 833
        [Cd. 592]   *L/C.* HC. 22 May, HL. 10 June 1901.

SESSION 16 JANUARY TO 18 DECEMBER 1902

VOLUME LX (1902)

Navy, etc.

VOLUME LXIX (1902)

Colonies and British Possessions

VOLUME LXX (1902)

East India

VOLUME CXXX (1902)

State Papers

1598   Treaty between the United Kingdom and the United States of
        Brazil relative to the Boundary between Brazil and British
        Guiana; signed at London, November 6, 1901. Ratifications
        exchanged at Rio de Janeiro, January 28, 1902. [*Treaty Series
        No. 4 (1902)*.]   PAGE 53
        [Cd. 916]   *L/C.* 11 Mar. 1902.

1599   Correspondence respecting the Affairs of China [*v. supra*, No.
        1580 *b*]. [*China No. 1 (1902)*.]   PAGE 61
        [Cd. 1005]   *L/C.* 17 Mar. 1902.

1599 *a* Correspondence respecting the Evacuation of Shanghae.
        [*China No. 3 (1902)*.]   PAGE 353
        [Cd. 1369]   *L/C.* 2 Dec. 1902.

1599 *b* Despatch from His Majesty's Special Commissioner inclosing
        the Treaty between Great Britain and China; signed at
        Shanghae, September 5, 1902. [*China No. 2 (1902)*.]
                                                            PAGE 375
        [Cd. 1079]   *L/C.* HC. 20 Oct., HL. 3 Nov. 1902.

1600   Convention between the United Kingdom and Denmark for
        the Exchange of Press Telegrams at Reduced Rates; signed at
        Copenhagen, August 15, 1901. [*Treaty Series No. 7 (1901)*.]
                                                            PAGE 389
        [Cd. 795]   *L/C.* 16 Jan. 1902.

1601   Treaties between the United Kingdom and Ethiopia and be-
        tween the United Kingdom, Italy and Ethiopia, relative to the
        Frontiers between the Soudan, Ethiopia, and Eritrea; signed
        at Adis Ababa, May 15, 1902. Ratifications delivered at
        Adis Ababa, October 28, 1902; with a Map. [*Treaty Series
        No. 16 (1902)*.]   PAGE 397
        [Cd. 1370]   *L/C.* 8 Dec. 1902.

1602   Agreement additional to the Postal Convention between the
        United Kingdom and France of August 30th, 1890; signed at
        Paris, December 11, 1901. Ratifications exchanged at Paris,
        January 17, 1902. [*Treaty Series No. 1 (1902)*.]   PAGE 405
        [Cd. 912]   *L/C.* HC. 21 Feb., HL. 24 Feb. 1902.

1602 *a* Convention regulating the Telephone Service between Great
        Britain and France; signed at Paris, July 29, 1902. [*Treaty
        Series No. 12 (1902)*.]   PAGE 409
        [Cd. 1077]   *L/C.* 16 Oct. 1902.

1602b Awards given by Baron Lambermont in the cases of the Waïma
Incident and of the 'Serjeant Malamine', Brussels, July 15,
1902. [*France No. 1 (1902)*.]   PAGE 417
[Cd. 1076]   L/C. HC. 4 Aug., HL. 5 Aug. 1902.

1602c Agreement between the United Kingdom and France respecting
Commercial Relations between France and Zanzibar; signed
at London, June 27, 1901. Ratifications exchanged at London,
February 22, 1902. [*Treaty Series No. 10 (1902)*.]   PAGE 431
[Cd. 1014]   L/C. HC. 22 Ap., HL. 24 Ap. 1902.

1603 *Germany:* Agreement between the United Kingdom and
Germany relative to the Boundary of the British and German
Spheres of Interest between Lakes Nyassa and Tanganyika;
signed at Berlin, February 23, 1901. [*Treaty Series No. 8 (1902)*.]
                                                      PAGE 435
[Cd. 1009]   L/C. HC. 7 Ap., HL. 14 Ap. 1902.

1604 International Convention with respect to the laws and customs
of war by land; signed at the Hague, July 29, 1899 (with an
Appendix containing Certificates of Exchange of such Ratifications of Powers parties to the Convention as had been
deposited at the Hague down to July 15, 1901). [*Treaty Series
No. 11 (1901)*.]   PAGE 443
[Cd. 800]   L/C. 16 Jan. 1902.

1604a International Convention for adapting to maritime warfare the
principles of the Geneva Convention of August 22, 1864; signed
at the Hague, July 29, 1899 (with an Appendix containing
Certificates of Exchange of such Ratifications of Powers parties
to the Convention as had been deposited at the Hague down to
July 15, 1901). [*Treaty Series No. 10 (1901)*.]   PAGE 485
[Cd. 799]   L/C. 16 Jan. 1902.

1604b International Convention for the Pacific Settlement of International Disputes; signed at the Hague, July 29, 1899 (with an
Appendix containing Certificates of Exchange of such Ratifications of Powers parties to the Convention as had been deposited
at the Hague down to July 15, 1901). [*Treaty Series No. 9
(1901)*.]   PAGE 517
[Cd. 798]   L/C. 16 Jan. 1902.

1605 Despatch to His Majesty's Minister at Tôkiô forwarding
Agreement between Great Britain and Japan, of January 30,
1902. [*Japan No. 1 (1902)*.]   PAGE 569
[Cd. 911]   L/C. HC. 11 Feb., HL. 13 Feb. 1902.

1605 *a* *China and Corea:* Agreement between the United Kingdom and Japan relative to China and Corea; signed at London, January 30, 1902. [*Treaty Series No. 3 (1902)*.]   PAGE 575

[Cd. 914]   *L/C.* 3 Mar. 1902.

1606 Agreement for the Exchange of Money Orders between the United Kingdom and the Republic of Liberia.   PAGE 579

[Cd. 1122]   *L/C.* HC. 27 May, HL. 2 June 1902.

1607 Agreement for the Exchange of Press Telegrams, dated 24th January–1st February, 1902, between the General Post Office of the United Kingdom and the General Post Office in Norway.
PAGE 595

[Cd. 1061]   *L/C.* HC. 9 Ap., HL. 14 Ap. 1902.

1608 Convention between the United Kingdom and Persia extending the System of Telegraphic Communication between Europe and India through Persia; signed at Tehran, August 16, 1901. Ratifications exchanged at Tehran, January 13, 1902. [*Treaty Series No. 5 (1902)*.]   PAGE 601

[Cd. 1004]   *L/C.* 11 Mar. 1902.

1609 Decision given by His Majesty Oscar II, King of Sweden and Norway, as Arbitrator under the Convention signed at Washington, November 7, 1899, between the German Empire, the United Kingdom and the United States of America, relating to the Settlement of certain Claims on account of military operations conducted in Samoa in the year 1899, given at Stockholm, the 14th October 1902. [*Samoa No. 1 (1902)*.]
PAGE 607

[Cd. 1083]   *L/C.* HC. 17 Nov., HL. 18 Nov. 1902.

1610 Treaty between the United Kingdom and Servia for the Mutual Surrender of Fugitive Criminals; signed at Belgrade, November 6–November 23, 1900. Ratifications exchanged at Belgrade, March 13–February 28, 1901. [*Treaty Series No. 8 (1901)*.]
PAGE 613

[Cd. 797]   *L/C.* 16 Jan. 1902.

1611 Agreement for the Exchange of Press Telegrams by night at reduced rates between the United Kingdom and Sweden.
PAGE 627

[Cd. 1373]   *L/C.* 17 Dec. 1902.

SESSION 17 FEBRUARY TO 14 AUGUST 1903

VOLUME XL (1903)

Navy, etc.

VOLUME XLV (1903)

Colonies and British Possessions

1625*a* Despatch from His Majesty's Minister at Pekin, forwarding a Report by Mr. W. J. Clennell, His Majesty's Consul at Kiu-Kiang, respecting the Province of Kiangsi. [*China No. 1 (1903).*]
PAGE 69

[Cd. 1402] *L/C.* 20 Feb. 1903.

1626 Convention between the United Kingdom and Denmark for regulating the Fisheries outside Territorial Waters in the ocean surrounding the Faröe Islands and Iceland; signed at London, June 24, 1901. Ratifications exchanged at London, May 28, 1902. [*Treaty Series No. 5 (1903).*] PAGE 115

[Cd. 1530] *L/C.* HC. 21 Ap., HL. 27 Ap. 1903.

1626*a* Accession of Denmark to the International Convention of September 9, 1886, establishing an International Union for the protection of Literary and Artistic Works, and also to the Additional Act and Declaration; signed at Paris, May 4, 1896–July 1, 1903. [*Treaty Series No. 11 (1903).*] PAGE 135

[Cd. 1633] *L/C.* 17 July 1903.

1627 Convention between the United Kingdom and France for the Exchange of insured and uninsured Parcels between France and the British Colony of Gibraltar; signed at Paris, October 22, 1902. Ratifications exchanged at Paris, December 10, 1902. [*Treaty Series No. 2 (1903).*] PAGE 139

[Cd. 1392] *L/C.* 17 Feb. 1903.

1628 Accession of the Republic of Guatemala to the Convention signed at Geneva, August 22, 1864, for the Amelioration of the Condition of the Wounded in Armies in the Field, March 24, 1903. [*Treaty Series No. 6 (1903).*] PAGE 151

[Cd. 1533] *L/C.* HC. 1 May, HL. 4 May 1903.

1629 Accession of the Empire of Corea to the Convention signed at Geneva, August 22, 1864...January 8th 1903. [*Treaty Series No. 3 (1903).*] PAGE 155

[Cd. 1404] *L/C.* HC. 25 Feb., HL. 26 Feb. 1903.

1630 Convention between the United Kingdom and the Netherlands regulating the allowances to Witnesses in Fishery cases; signed at the Hague, April 26, 1902. Ratifications exchanged at the Hague, May 22, 1903. [*Treaty Series No. 9 (1903).*] PAGE 159

[Cd. 1627] *L/C.* HC. 1 July, HL. 2 July 1903.

1630*a* Parcel Post Agreement, with Detailed Regulations, between Great Britain and the Netherlands.   PAGE 165

    [Cd. 1591]   *L/C.* HC. 12 May, HL. 11 June 1903.

1631   Commercial Convention between the United Kingdom and Persia. Signed at Tehran, February 9, 1903. Ratifications exchanged at Tehran, May 27, 1903. [*Treaty Series No. 10 (1903)*.]   PAGE 193

    [Cd. 1629]   *L/C.* 9 July 1903.

1632   Despatch from His Majesty's Consul-General at Odessa, forwarding a Report on the Riots at Kishiniev. [*Russia No. 1 (1903)*.]   PAGE 255

    [Cd. 1721]   *L/C.* 11 Aug. 1903.

1633   Correspondence respecting the Affairs of South-Eastern Europe. [*Turkey No. 1 (1903)*.]   PAGE 261

    [Cd. 1403]   *L/C.* 20 Feb. 1903.

1633*a* Further Correspondence [17–27 Feb., 1903]. (Reforms in the Administration of the Vilayets of Salonica, Monastir and Kossovo.) [*Turkey No. 2 (1903)*.]   PAGE 575

    [Cd. 1467]   *L/C.* HC. 4 Mar., HL. 5 Mar. 1903.

1633*b* Further Correspondence [Dec. 1902–Mar. 1903]. [*Turkey No. 3 (1903)*.]   PAGE 583

    [Cd. 1532]   *L/C.* HC. 29 Ap., HL. 30 Ap. 1903.

1634   Convention signed at Washington, January 24, 1903, for the Adjustment of the boundary between the Dominion of Canada and the territory of Alaska. [*United States No. 1 (1903)*.]
                                        PAGE 687

    [Cd. 1400]   *L/C.* 17 Feb. 1903.

1634*a* Convention between the United Kingdom and the United States of America for the adjustment of the Boundary between the Dominion of Canada and the territory of Alaska; signed at Washington, January 24, 1903. Ratifications exchanged at Washington, March 3, 1903. [*Treaty Series No. 4 (1903)*.]
                                        PAGE 693

    [Cd. 1472]   *L/C.* HC. 31 Mar., HL. 27 Ap. 1903.

SESSION 2 FEBRUARY TO 15 AUGUST 1904

VOLUME LIII (1904)

Navy, etc.

VOLUME LXII (1904)

Colonies and British Possessions

VOLUME LXVII (1904)

East India

VOLUME LXXIX (1904)

Miscellaneous

VOLUME CX (1904)

State Papers

1646*f* Treaty between the United Kingdom and China, respecting
Commercial Relations, etc., signed at Shanghae, September 5,
1902. Ratifications exchanged at Pekin, July 28, 1903. [*Treaty
Series No. 17 (1903)*.]   PAGE 269
   [Cd. 1834]   *L/C.* 2 Feb. 1904.

1647   Agreement between the Post Office of the United Kingdom and
the Post Office of Denmark for the Exchange of Postal Parcels.
Dated 14 September/22 August 1903.   PAGE 287
   [Cd. 1887]   *L/C.* 2 Feb. 1904.

1648   *Anglo-French Agreements:* Despatch to His Majesty's Ambassador
at Paris forwarding Agreements between Great Britain and
France, of April 8, 1904. [*France No. 1 (1904)*.]   PAGE 313
   [Cd. 1952]   *L/C.* HC. 12 Ap., HL. 19 Ap. 1904.

1648*a* Notes exchanged between the Marquis of Lansdowne and the
French Ambassador on signature of the Convention and Declara-
tion of April 8, 1904. [*France No. 2 (1904)*.]   PAGE 343
   [Cd. 2095]   *L/C.* HC. 31 May, HL. 7 June 1904.

1649   Agreement between the United Kingdom and France, providing for the Settlement by Arbitration of certain classes of
questions which may arise between the two Governments.
(Signed at London, October 14, 1903.) [*Treaty Series No. 18
(1903)*.]   PAGE 351
   [Cd. 1837]   *L/C.* 2 Feb. 1904.

1649*a* Convention between the United Kingdom and France, re-
specting Commercial Relations between France and Jamaica.
Signed at London, August 8, 1902. Ratifications exchanged at
London, August 12, 1903. [*Treaty Series No. 12 (1903)*.]
                                                      PAGE 355
   [Cd. 1771]   *L/C.* 2 Feb. 1904.

1650   Accession of Germany to the Industrial Property Convention
of March 20, 1883, etc., May 1, 1903. [*Treaty Series No. 14
(1903)*.]   PAGE 359
   [Cd. 1774]   *L/C.* 2 Feb. 1904.

1651   Agreement between the United Kingdom and Italy, providing
for the Settlement by Arbitration of certain classes of questions
which may arise between the two Governments. Signed at
Rome, February 1st, 1904. [*Treaty Series No. 3 (1904)*.]
                                                      PAGE 363
   [Cd. 1937]   *L/C.* 16 Feb. 1904.

VOLUME CXI (1904)

State Papers

SESSION 14 FEBRUARY TO 11 AUGUST 1905

VOLUME XLVIII (1905)

Navy, etc.

Volume LV (1905)

Colonies and British Possessions

1662   Memorandum on the State of the African Protectorates administered under the Foreign Office. [*Africa No. 3 (1905)*.]
                                                                    PAGE 1
         [Cd. 2408]   *L/C.* 30 Mar. 1905.

Volume LVI (1905)

Colonies and British Possessions

1663   Report by Mr. A. E. Butter on the Survey of the proposed new Frontier between British East Africa and Abyssinia (with a map). [*Africa No. 13 (1904)*.]   PAGE 233
         [Cd. 2312]   *L/C.* 14 Feb. 1905.

1664   Further Correspondence respecting the administration of the Independent State of the Congo. [*Africa No. 1 (1905)*.]
                                                                    PAGE 437
         [Cd. 2333]   *L/C.* 14 Feb. 1905.

1665   Award of His Majesty the King of Italy respecting the Western Boundary of the Barotse Kingdom (with a map). [*Africa No. 5 (1905)*.]   PAGE 541
         [Cd. 2584]   *L/C.* HC. 19 July, HL. 20 July 1905.

1666   Correspondence respecting Slavery in the Islands of Zanzibar and Pemba. [*Africa No. 14 (1904)*.]   PAGE 551
         [Cd. 2330]   *L/C.* 14 Feb. 1905.

Volume LVIII (1905)

East India

1667   Further Papers relating to Tibet, No. III.   PAGE 433
         [Cd. 2370]   *L/C.* 14 Feb. 1905.

VOLUME LXXXV (1905)

Commercial and General Interests, etc.

1668   *German Tariff:* Statement showing:

 (1) The New German General Customs Tariff.

 (2) The modifications made in that Tariff by each of the New German Treaties with Russia, Switzerland, Italy, Roumania, Belgium, Austria-Hungary, and Servia.

 (3) The New German 'Conventional' Tariff resulting from all these modifications; with Comparisons with the existing German Rates of Duty on Imports from the United Kingdom.   PAGE 499

 [Cd. 2414]   *L/C.* HC. 3 Mar., HL. 9 Mar. 1905.

1669   Report on the Condition and Prospects of British Trade in Oman, Bahrein, and Arab Ports in the Persian Gulf, by H. W. Maclean, Special Commissioner of the Commercial Intelligence Committee of the Board of Trade.   PAGE 731

 [Cd. 2281]   *L/C.* 14 Feb. 1905.

VOLUME CIII (1905)

State Papers

1670   Convention between the United Kingdom and Austria-Hungary, providing for the Settlement by Arbitration of certain classes of Questions which may arise between the respective Governments. Signed at London, January 11, 1905. Ratifications exchanged at London, May 17, 1905. [*Treaty Series No. 14 (1905)*.]   PAGE 1

 [Cd. 2529]   *L/C.* HC. 1 June, HL. 2 June 1905.

1671   Convention between the United Kingdom and China, respecting the Employment of Chinese Labour in British Colonies and Protectorates. Signed at London, May 13, 1904. [*Treaty Series No. 7 (1904)*.]   PAGE 7

 [Cd. 2246]   *L/C.* 14 Feb. 1905.

1671*a*   Report by Consul-General Hosie on the Province of Ssuch'uan. (With two Maps.) [*China No. 5 (1904)*.]   PAGE 15

 [Cd. 2247]   *L/C.* 14 Feb. 1905.

1671*b* Report by Mr. A. Hosie, His Majesty's Consul-General at Chengtu, on a journey to the Eastern Frontier of Thibet. (With a Map.) [*China No. 1 (1905)*.] PAGE 123

[Cd. 2586] *L/C*. HC. 2 Aug., HL. 3 Aug. 1905.

1672 Accession of Cuba to the Industrial Property Convention, 1883, etc., November 17, 1904. [*Treaty Series No. 12 (1904)*.] PAGE 215

[Cd. 2314] *L/C*. 14 Feb. 1905.

1672*a* Accession of Cuba to arrangements respecting False Indications of Origin on Goods and the International Registration of Trade Marks (Industrial Property Union), January 1, 1905. [*Treaty Series No. 1 (1905)*.] PAGE 219

[Cd. 2345] *L/C*. 14 Feb. 1905.

1672*b* Treaty between the United Kingdom and Cuba for the Mutual Surrender of Fugitive Criminals. Signed at Havana, October 3, 1904. Ratifications exchanged at Havana, January 10, 1905. [*Treaty Series No. 15 (1905)*.] PAGE 223

[Cd. 2530] *L/C*. HC. 1 June, HL. 2 June 1905.

1673 Agreements between the United Kingdom and France, referring to Arbitration the question of the Grant of the French Flag to Muscat Dhows. Signed at London, October 13, 1904, and January 13, 1905. Ratifications of Agreement of October 13, 1904, exchanged at London, January 18, 1905. [*Treaty Series No. 3 (1905)*.] PAGE 235

[Cd. 2380] *L/C*. 20 Feb. 1905.

1674 Convention between the United Kingdom and France, respecting Newfoundland, and West and Central Africa. Signed at London, April 8, 1904. Ratifications exchanged at London, December 8th, 1904. [*Treaty Series No. 5 (1905)*.] PAGE 241

[Cd. 2383] *L/C*. HC. 28 Feb., HL. 2 Mar. 1905.

1675 Convention between the United Kingdom and France, respecting Commercial Relations between France and the British Protectorates of East Africa, Central Africa, and Uganda. Signed at London, February 23, 1903. Ratifications exchanged at London, March 27, 1905. [*Treaty Series No. 10 (1905)*.] PAGE 255

[Cd. 2486] *L/C*. HC. 19 Ap., HL. 8 May 1905.

1675*a* Convention between the United Kingdom and France, respecting Commercial Relations between France and India. Signed at London, February 19, 1903. Ratifications exchanged at London, March 27, 1905. [*Treaty Series No. 9 (1905)*.]
PAGE 259

[Cd. 2485] *L/C.* HC. 19 Ap., HL. 8 May 1905.

1676 Declaration between the United Kingdom and France, respecting Egypt and Morocco. Signed at London, April 8, 1904. [*Treaty Series No. 6 (1905)*.] PAGE 265

[Cd. 2384] *L/C.* HC. 28 Feb., HL. 2 Mar. 1905.

1676*a* Declaration between the United Kingdom and France, concerning Siam, Madagascar, and the New Hebrides. Signed at London, April 8, 1904. [*Treaty Series No. 7 (1905)*.] PAGE 285

[Cd. 2385] *L/C.* HC. 28 Feb., HL. 2 Mar. 1905.

1677 Convention between the United Kingdom and France, respecting Commercial Relations between France and the Seychelles Islands. Signed at London, April 16, 1902. Ratifications exchanged at London, March 27, 1905. [*Treaty Series No. 11 (1905)*.] PAGE 289

[Cd. 2487] *L/C.* HC. 19 Ap., HL. 8 May 1905.

1678 Convention between the United Kingdom and France, respecting Commercial Relations between France and Ceylon. Signed at London, February 19, 1903. Ratifications exchanged at London, March 27, 1905. [*Treaty Series No. 12 (1905)*.]
PAGE 293

[Cd. 2488] *L/C.* HC. 19 Ap., HL. 8 May 1905.

1679 Agreement between the United Kingdom and Germany, providing for the Settlement by Arbitration of certain classes of questions which may arise between the two Governments. Signed at London, July 12, 1904. [*Treaty Series No. 6 (1904)*.]
PAGE 297

[Cd. 2245] *L/C.* 14 Feb. 1905.

1680 Award of the Arbitration Tribunal appointed to pronounce on certain questions as to the Interpretation of Treaties with Japan, with regard to Leases held in perpetuity. [*Japan No. 1 (1905)*.] PAGE 301

[Cd. 2583] *L/C.* HC. 19 July, HL. 20 July 1905.

1681   Convention between the United Kingdom and Japan respecting
        the Commercial Relations between Japan and India. Signed
        at Tôkiô, August 29, 1904. Ratifications exchanged at Tôkiô,
        March 15, 1905. [*Treaty Series No. 13 (1905)*.]   PAGE 315

        [Cd. 2489]   *L/C.* HC. 2 May, HL. 8 May 1905.

1682   Convention between the United Kingdom and Mexico re-
        specting Postal Rates upon Letters passing between New
        Zealand and Mexico. Signed at Mexico, February 1st, 1904.
        Ratifications exchanged at Mexico, January 12, 1905. [*Treaty
        Series No. 4 (1905)*.]   PAGE 319

        [Cd. 2381]   *L/C.* 21 Feb. 1905.

1682 *a* Agreement for the Exchange of Post Office Money Orders
        between the United Kingdom and Mexico.   PAGE 323

        [Cd. 2388]   *L/C.* 14 Feb. 1905.

1683   Additional Articles to the Convention of 7th–14th October
        1871 for the Exchange of Post Office Money Orders between
        the United Kingdom and the Netherlands.   PAGE 341

        [Cd. 2387]   *L/C.* 14 Feb. 1905.

1683 *a* Convention between the United Kingdom and the Netherlands
        providing for the Settlement by Arbitration of certain classes
        of Questions which may arise between the two Governments.
        Signed at London, February 15, 1905. Ratifications exchanged
        at London, July 12, 1905. [*Treaty Series No. 19 (1905)*.]
                                                       PAGE 345

        [Cd. 2585]   *L/C.* HL. 21 July, HC. 24 July 1905.

1684   Industrial Property Convention. Accession of New Zealand
        to the Additional Act of December 14, 1900, and Accession
        of Ceylon to the Convention of 1883, as modified by the
        Additional Act of December 14, 1900. [*Treaty Series No. 17
        (1905)*.]   PAGE 349

        [Cd. 2533]   *L/C.* HC. 23 June, HL. 26 June 1905.

1685   Agreement between the United Kingdom and Norway re-
        specting Telegraphic Communications between the two Coun-
        tries. Signed at Stockholm, February 2nd, 1905. [*Treaty Series
        No. 8 (1905)*.]   PAGE 353

        [Cd. 2405]   *L/C.* HC. 10 Mar., HL. 13 Mar. 1905.

1690 *a*   Convention between the United Kingdom and Sweden and Norway, providing for the Settlement by Arbitration of certain classes of questions which may arise between the respective Governments. Signed at London, August 11th, 1904. Ratifications exchanged at London, November 9, 1904. [*Treaty Series No. 8 (1904)*.]   PAGE 521

   [Cd. 2309]   *L/C.*   14 Feb. 1905.

1690 *b*   Accession of Sweden to the International Copyright Convention. September 9, 1886, and Declaration of May 4, 1896. August 1, 1904. [*Treaty Series No. 11 (1904)*.]   PAGE 525

   [Cd. 2313]   *L/C.*   14 Feb. 1905.

1690 *c*   Treaty between Great Britain and Sweden and Norway for the Marriage of Her Royal Highness Princess Margaret of Great Britain and Ireland with His Royal Highness Prince Gustavus Adolphus of Sweden and of Norway. Signed at Stockholm, May 20, 1905. Ratifications exchanged at Stockholm, June 14, 1905. [*Treaty Series No. 18 (1905)*.]   PAGE 529

   [Cd. 2582]   *L/C.*   27 June 1905.

1691   Agreement between the United Kingdom and Switzerland providing for the Settlement by Arbitration of certain classes of questions which may arise between the two Governments. Signed at London, November 16, 1904. [*Treaty Series No. 9 (1904)*.]   PAGE 535

   [Cd. 2310]   *L/C.*   14 Feb. 1905.

1691 *a*   Convention between the United Kingdom and Switzerland, supplementing Article XVIII of the Treaty of Extradition of November 26, 1880. Signed at London, June 29, 1904. Ratifications exchanged at London, March 29, 1905. [*Treaty Series No. 16 (1905)*.]   PAGE 539

   [Cd. 2532]   *L/C.*   HC. 20 June, HL. 26 June 1905.

1692   Ottoman Public Debt. Decree September 1 (14), 1903, as an Annex to the Decree of 28 Mouharrem 1299 (December 8 (20), 1881). [*Turkey No. 1 (1905)*.]   PAGE 543

   [Cd. 2407]   *L/C.*   HC. 23 Mar., HL. 24 Mar. 1905.

1692 *a*   Further Correspondence respecting the Affairs of South-Eastern Europe. [*Turkey No. 4 (1904)*.]   PAGE 555

   [Cd. 2249]   *L/C.*   14 Feb. 1905.

1692 *b*   do. [Aug. 1904–Jan. 1905]. [*Turkey No. 2 (1905)*.]   PAGE 793

   [Cd. 2490]   *L/C.*   HC. 3 May, HL. 8 May 1905.

1692 c   Correspondence respecting the Asiatic Provinces of Turkey.
         [*Turkey No. 3 (1904)*.]   PAGE 929

         [Cd. 2248]   *L/C.* 14 Feb. 1905.

1693   Agreement between the Post Office of the United Kingdom
         and the Post Office Department of the United States of America
         for the direct exchange of Parcels by Post.   PAGE 1021

         [Cd. 2512]   *L/C.* HC. 4 May, HL. 8 May 1905.

1694   Correspondence respecting the International Conference on
         the 'White Slave Traffic', held at Paris, July 1902. [*Misc.
         No. 3 (1905)*.]   PAGE 1027

         [Cd. 2667]   *L/C.* 10 Aug. 1905.

1695   Reports by His Majesty's Agent and Consul-General on the
         Finances, Administration, and Condition of Egypt and the
         Soudan in 1904. [*Egypt No. 1 (1905)*.]   PAGE 1087

         [Cd. 2409]   *L/C.* HC. 17 Ap., HL. 8 May 1905.

THE BLUE-BOOK POLICY OF
SIR EDWARD GREY*

1905–14

THE first nine years of the Foreign Secretaryship of Sir Edward Grey were very prolific in Parliamentary Papers relating to the affairs of his department, but we look among them in vain for the records of those numerous unfinished transactions which make up the major part of British foreign policy in his time. As has already been indicated, the exclusion of unfinished negotiations from Blue Books was a principle long since accepted by all parties in the House.

In the first place, there are numerous texts of treaties. Many, as in previous years, deal with purely technical questions—more, indeed, than before, since the number of commercial and social matters dealt with by international regulation was steadily increasing, and the period opened with a series of arbitration agreements. There were moreover many treaties which dealt with colonial boundaries. There is no new observation to make on these: they follow the example set in the time of Salisbury. Among the treaties of wider significance, however, some require special mention. The publication of the Anglo-Japanese Alliance of 12 August 1905 was delayed until the end of September, because Lord Lansdowne ruled that it would be better to wait until the Treaty of Portsmouth had been signed,† and then further because Count Hayashi asked that publication should be deferred until after ratification.‡ In September Parliament was in recess; hence the official date on which the paper was laid was 19 February 1906, and it fell nominally within the period of the Liberal administration (No. 1717). A covering dispatch was published with it, in accordance with what had

---

* Sir Edward Grey became Secretary of State for Foreign Affairs on 11 December 1905 and held office until 11 December 1916.
† v. *Gooch and Temperley*, IV, 171, No. 161.
‡ v. *ibid.* IV, 180, No. 174.

by now become common form.* In this case, however, the covering dispatch contains certain features of interest, as there was some discussion as to its wording. As a result the statement that there were no secret articles was omitted, in case 'on future occasions absence of such a statement may give rise to comment'. A paragraph was also omitted at the suggestion of Mr Balfour. This was to the effect that 'The geographical limits within which such co-operation may take place and the nature of that co-operation are questions that must be for the decision of the Contracting Parties themselves'. Then Lord Lansdowne himself, who on second thoughts had already deleted a reference to the 'chronic misgovernment' of Corea, decided that he would also omit the words, in the same connection, 'and the danger arising from its weakness'.† The dispatch, thus amended, was communicated to Russia and France before it was published.

The form given to the paper laid in connection with the renewal of the Anglo-Japanese Alliance was thus no concern of the Liberal administration, and their responsibility for it was purely nominal. But they presented their own treaties in much the same way. The Anglo-Spanish Notes "respecting the maintenance of the territorial 'Status Quo' in the Mediterranean and the East Atlantic Ocean" were laid in June 1907 without even an explanatory dispatch (No. 1766), as was also the declaration relative to the Independence of Norway (No. 1779); and the dispatches accompanying the text of the Declarations relating to the maintenance of the *Status Quo* in the North Sea were wholly formal (No. 1785). Again the Anglo-Russian Convention of 31 August 1907 (No. 1804) was accompanied by the most formal of covering dispatches from Sir A. Nicolson. Attached to the text also, however, was the dispatch from Sir Edward Grey to Sir A. Nicolson authorising signature. This was of great importance, since it contained a statement that the Russian Government had 'explicitly stated that they do not deny the special interests of Great Britain in the Persian Gulf'.

---

* v. Gooch and Temperley, IV, 173–4, Ed. Note, and 174–5, No. 166.
† v. ibid. IV, 174, No. 166, note 3, and 175, No. 168.

The Agadir crisis of the summer of 1911 had two interesting effects as far as publication was concerned. In the first place, public interest in the settlement of the dispute resulted in the laying of three papers giving the texts of speeches made by Herr von Bethmann Hollweg in the Reichstag on 9 and 10 November and 5 December 1911, and by Herr von Kiderlen-Waechter before the Budget Commission of the Reichstag on 17 November (Nos. 1898–1898b). Accounts of these speeches had already appeared in the Press, and the statements made by Herr von Kiderlen-Waechter had caused some annoyance here, since, unlike those of the Chancellor, they were unconciliatory in tone. Herr von Kiderlen-Waechter recapitulated the course of Anglo-German conversations from the time of Mr Lloyd George's speech of 21 July, thereby, as Sir Eyre Crowe commented, making 'a breach of the well-established diplomatic rule that communications exchanged with foreign governments shall not be published without the latter's consent'.* Sir Edward Grey, at the opening of his speech in the House on 27 November 1911, when he moved 'that the foreign policy of His Majesty's Government be now considered', said that he 'would gladly have waited before saying anything here on the Morocco question until the conclusion of the discussion in the French and German Parliaments as to the negotiations for a settlement between their two countries....But so much has been said in Germany already, especially by the recent disclosures of the German Foreign Secretary, that...I feel bound to make a somewhat full statement to the House.'† The result was that, while none of the dispatches recording Sir Edward Grey's conversations with the German Ambassador was laid before the House, a full analysis of the most important of them was given in his speech, and the text of Herr von Kiderlen-Waechter's account of the same negotiations was presented to Parliament a fortnight later.

In the course of this important speech Sir Edward Grey

* *v. Gooch and Temperley*, VII, 699, No. 697, *min.*
† *v. ibid.* VII, 725–6, No. 721. Cp. *Hans. Deb.* 5th Ser., House of Commons, XXXII, 43–65.

referred to the second publication which resulted from the crisis. On 8 November 1911 *Le Matin* published the secret Franco-Spanish Treaty of 3 October 1904. This was of some interest in England, owing to its bearing on the crisis, and it was finally laid before Parliament with other texts relating to Morocco at the end of 1911 (No. 1927).* A series of other revelations followed. On the 10th *Le Figaro* published the Franco-Spanish negotiations of 1902. On the 11th *Le Temps* completed the list with the Franco-Spanish Treaty of 1 September 1905, and a summary of the secret Articles of the Anglo-French Declaration of 8 April 1904.† The last of these disclosures immediately determined Sir Edward Grey to ask French consent for the publication of these articles. He consulted Lord Lansdowne on this point, and finally the text was presented to the Commons on 24 November (No. 1892). In the course of his speech on the 27th Sir Edward Grey said: 'We have laid before the House the secret Articles of the Agreement with France of 1904. There are no other secret engagements. The late Government made that Agreement in 1904....In my opinion they were entirely justified in keeping those Articles secret, because they were not Articles which commit this House to serious obligations.‡ I saw a comment made the other day, when these Articles were published, that if a Government would keep little things secret, *a fortiori*, they would keep big things secret. That is absolutely untrue. There may be reasons why a Government should make secret arrangements of that kind...if they are subsidiary to matters of great importance. But that is the very reason why the British Government should not make secret engagements which commit Parliament to obligations of war....For ourselves we have not made a single secret article of any kind since we came into office.'§ Ten days later Mr Asquith replied to a question in the House as to the existence of other secret engagements, saying that there were 'no secret engagements with France other than those that

* Cp. *Hans. Deb.* 5th Ser., House of Commons, xxxii, 6–7, 1556–7.
† *v. Gooch and Temperley*, vii, 676–7, No. 675.   ‡ *v. supra*, p. 462.
§ *v. Gooch and Temperley*, vii, 731–2, No. 721. *Hans. Deb.* 5th Ser., House of Commons, xxxii, 57–8.

have now been published, and there are no secret engagements with any foreign Government that entail upon us any obligation to render military or naval assistance to any other Power. They are none of them of recent date.'*

The question of the degree to which foreign policy should be conducted in secret was much discussed in all its implications at this time. Mr Dillon complained on the occasion of Sir Edward Grey's motion of 27 November that the 'House was summoned for this discussion to-day without any Papers whatsoever.... We ought to have had a Blue Book containing the diplomatic history of the Morrocan question',† and he contrasted the existing practice of the Foreign Office unfavourably with that of twenty-five years before. When the debate was renewed on 14 December, other speakers also referred to the absence of Papers.‡

There is, however, a more important criticism which could have been made, although this was not realised at the time. The Blue Book published on 13 December 1911 (No. 1898 a) prints the first sentence of the dispatch from Sir E. Goschen to Sir Edward Grey, which enclosed the text of Herr von Bethmann Hollweg's speech. The whole of the rest of the dispatch was omitted. But, as this first sentence is not described as an 'extract', the reader must (and was undoubtedly intended to) suppose that the whole of the dispatch was given. The omitted part (*v. Gooch and Temperley*, VII, 757, No. 738 and *note* (1)) refers to 'the points which had formed the basis of the [German] Conservative and Nationalist attacks on England, namely the prejudiced and provocative attitude of Great Britain towards Germany throughout the Morocco negotiations, the mistrust with which His Majesty's Government had received the German explanations', etc. There can be little doubt that these passages were omitted

---

* *Hans. Deb.* 5th Ser., House of Commons, XXXII, 1400, 6 December 1911. Cp. Mr Asquith's earlier statement of 27 November, *Gooch and Temperley*, VII, 725, No. 720; *Hans. Deb.* 5th Ser., House of Commons, XXXII, 106–7.

† *Hans. Deb.* 5th Ser., House of Commons, XXXII, 80.

‡ The main subject of discussion on this date was, however, the question of Persia—on which in fact a fairly continuous series of Blue Books appeared (Nos. 1802, 1842, 1842 a, 1872, 1902, 1929–1929 d, 1946, 1965–1965 a).

in order not further to inflame public opinion on both sides of the North Sea. But the failure in the Blue Book to note this omission by describing the dispatch as an extract was misleading to the public. The case is one which is happily rare in the history of nineteenth-century Blue Books. *

In certain directions Sir Edward Grey was more liberal than any of his immediate predecessors in publishing Blue Books, particularly in connection with humanitarian questions. He inherited the Congo problem and Blue Books on this subject had already appeared, but in the years 1911–13 he gave to the public unusually ample information on the conditions of labour and the treatment of natives in Central Africa (Nos. 1875, 1910, 1910a, 1938). There was a public agitation about the conditions of the natives in Portuguese West Africa, where virtual slavery was suspected, and here again during the years 1912–13 Sir Edward Grey anticipated the public desire for information (Nos. 1910b, 1910c). A still more extreme example of this policy is seen in the question of what came to be known as the 'Putumayo Atrocities'. Reports having been circulated as to the treatment of native tribes in the interior of Peru, Sir Roger Casement was sent to carry out an investigation. His report pictured horrible scenes of cruelty, and remonstrances were accordingly addressed to the Government of Peru. As these proved ineffectual, the whole story was set out in Blue Books and given to the world in 1912 (Nos. 1908, 1908a, 1914, 1936, 1939). The aim was clearly to appeal to British public opinion, in the hope that thus pressure might be brought to bear where official action had proved useless. Public opinion was severely shocked and some improvement followed. It will be seen, therefore, that Sir Edward Grey acted with vigour in humanitarian matters, and took a line that was not only courageous, but in some respects represented a departure from official routine. This fact would suggest that, in a less disturbed period, he would have been more generous in publication than he actually was able to be in time of crisis.

* Instances of some rather dubious practices in Blue-Book publications in 1871 may be found *supra*, pp. 218–19.

The debate of 27 November, 14 December 1911, to which reference has already been made, led Sir Edward Grey to state the fundamental principles which governed the laying of papers. In referring to the Moroccan crisis he said: 'I dealt very fully with the Moroccan question the other day. Nothing that I said has been challenged, and nothing has been contradicted. It is therefore unnecessary, as far as my statement of the other day is concerned, that I should lay Papers to support what is unchallenged. The history of what passed is there to be read by everybody who wishes to know it; it is on the Records of the House, and can be seen by everybody who wishes to read it.' And then he added a further argument. Referring to the recent speech by the German Chancellor he quoted his wish that there should be a 'clean slate on which there should be fair writing. If I published a great many Papers dealing with those controversial matters of the last two months, is it not possible that we would be taken as beginning to cover the slate with writing relating to past events instead of beginning afresh?'* He gave explanations also of the absence of any papers on the Turkish question. 'It is quite true that there has been no publication of Papers since the new regime came into power. If we had published Papers about events in Macedonia and Albania at the beginning of the new regime we should have been told that we were not giving the new regime a chance. To publish them at the present moment, while war is going on between Turkey and Italy, would undoubtedly be taken as reflecting upon one of the belligerents. I do not for a moment wish to withhold information from the House, but I cannot publish Papers at the present moment without it being supposed that they were published for a purpose....There is really no object in publishing Papers unless the state of things is such as to demand and require interference, and unless you must interfere. If we and other great Powers of Europe are not going to intervene in Turkish internal affairs, then the publication of Papers may be a provocation, and will be absolutely useless....There is one thing more for comment in

* *Hans. Deb.* 5th Ser., House of Commons, xxxii, 2608–9, 14 December 1911.

the interesting speech of the hon. Member for South Donegal (Mr Swift MacNeill), and that is the subject of secrecy. This is an age of inventions, and perhaps some day something will be invented by which it is possible to publish Papers in the House of Commons which shall not be known elsewhere. I can assure the House that the motive for secrecy in ninety-nine cases out of a hundred is not to withhold information from the House, but is the difficulty of giving information to the House without giving it to the world at large; and the knowledge we give to the world at large may cause difficulties abroad which are unnecessary....And also in a great many cases we are dealing with matters in which we are only one party, and matters which may have been communicated confidentially to us by other Governments, and...were we to embark on a procedure of as much publicity as the hon. Member for South Donegal desires I think we should soon land ourselves in this position, that other Governments would cease to have negotiations with us, and we should have very little to communicate.'*

These principles represent fairly enough the practice of these pre-war years under Sir Edward Grey, and throw light indeed upon the whole character of publication in the half-century before the war. In conjunction with the principle which excluded from publication unfinished negotiations, they reduced diplomatic correspondence, as distinct from the texts of treaties and engagements, to comparatively small dimensions. Fullness of publication comparable with that of the mid-nineteenth century can be found only in the Blue Books relating to the Turkish question in the earlier part of Sir Edward Grey's period and to the affairs of Persia in the middle years. There is then some justification for the statement that diplomacy had become more secret. On the other hand, the secrecy can easily be exaggerated. Explanations in the Commons—of which the most important have been quoted—were unusually full and frank. The texts of treaties were published with greater rapidity than in previous years; and there is ample evidence that on the two great negotiations

* *Hans. Deb.* 5th Ser., House of Commons, xxxii, 2610–11, 2613.

with Germany that marked the last two years of peace—those concerning the Portuguese colonies in Africa and the Bagdad Railway—publication was intended by Sir Edward Grey, and was prevented only by the outbreak of war. The correspondence on the former of these topics proves conclusively how strongly he deprecated the making of agreements which were not to be published.* The fact is that the circumstances of these years militated against Parliamentary publication. In the great issues of the period, the negotiations all fell into one of two categories: they were either concerned with crises in which Britain was only one of the Great Powers involved, and then not the most closely; or else they represented movements which were never completed. In this period, then, we have the culmination of the development of Blue-Book history. Parliamentary Papers were viewed, and, indeed, had to be viewed, primarily as explanations of action to the world at large. Great Britain was far more closely linked than before with European Powers to whom publication was a strange phenomenon; and the measure of British reticence was also the measure of British influence on the affairs of Europe. In such circumstances Blue Books, although essential for the more formal records of foreign affairs, must be a disappointing source for the student of British policy. Sir Edward Grey felt something of this himself. He welcomed Herr von Kiderlen-Waechter's speech in November 1911, as it enabled him to state the British case in public. 'It [the speech] has freed my hands or rather my mouth considerably.' † This minute, which is penned with evident satisfaction, provides a key to his real sentiments.

* Cp. *Gooch and Temperley*, x (ii), 511, No. 328; 561, No. 364.
† Minute by Sir Edward Grey of about 22 November 1911. *Gooch and Temperley*, vii, 700, No. 697, *min.*

Session 13 February to 21 December 1906

Volume LXX (1906)

Navy, etc.

1696　Return showing the Fleets of Great Britain, France, Russia, Germany, Italy, United States of America, and Japan, on the 31st day of March 1906....　　　　　　　　　PAGE 89

　　129　　*Pursuant to Order (HC. 20 Mar.)*, HC. 24 Ap. 1906.

Volume LXXIX (1906)

Colonies and British Possessions

1697　Correspondence respecting the Report of the Commission of Enquiry into the Administration of the Independent State of the Congo. [*Africa No. 1 (1906)*.]　　　　　PAGE 1

　　[Cd. 3002]　　*L/C.* 15 June 1906.

Volume CXXXVI (1906)

State Papers

1698　Agreements between the Argentine Republic and the Republic of Chile, signed on May 28, 1902, July 10, 1902, and January 9, 1903. [*Misc. No. 4 (1905)*.]　　　　　　PAGE 1

　　[Cd. 2739]　　*R–A. (HC. 8 Aug. 1905)*, 19 Feb. 1906.

1699　Agreement between the Post Office of the United Kingdom and the Royal Imperial Austrian Postal Administration concerning the Exchange of Money Orders.　　　　　PAGE 11

　　[Cd. 2913]　　*L/C.* HC. 9 Ap., HL. 30 Ap. 1906.

1700　Despatch from His Majesty's Minister at Brussels transmitting Convention respecting Liquors in Africa, signed at Brussels, November 3, 1906. [*Africa No. 2 (1906)*.]　　　　PAGE 19

　　[Cd. 3264]　　*L/C.* 12 Feb. 1907.

1700*a*   Agreement between the United Kingdom and Belgium respecting Travellers' Samples. Signed at Brussels, November 10, 1906. [*Treaty Series No. 18 (1906)*.]   PAGE 27
   [Cd. 3261]   L/C. 3 Dec. 1906.

1701   Despatch from His Majesty's Agent and Consul-General at Sofia, transmitting the Commercial Convention between the United Kingdom and Bulgaria. Signed [at Sofia], December 9, 1905. [*Commercial No. 1 (1906)*.]   PAGE 31
   [Cd. 2763]   L/C. 19 Feb. 1906.

1702   Agreement between the United Kingdom and Chile for the Exchange of Money Orders. Signed at London, July 30, 1906. [*Treaty Series No. 10 (1906)*.]   PAGE 69
   [Cd. 3090]   L/C. 23 Oct. 1906.

1703   Convention between the United Kingdom and China, respecting the Junction of the Chinese and Burmese Telegraph Lines, being a revision of the Convention of September 6, 1894 (Treaty Series, No. 9, 1895). Signed in English and Chinese·Texts at Pekin, May 23, 1905. [*Treaty Series No. 22 (1905)*.]   PAGE 89
   [Cd. 2687]   L/C. 19 Feb. 1906.

1703*a*   Report by Mr. Walter J. Clennell, His Majesty's Consul at Kiukiang, on a journey in the interior of Kiangsi. (With a Map.) [*China No. 2 (1905)*.]   PAGE 95
   [Cd. 2762]   L/C. 19 Feb. 1906.

1703*b*   Convention between the United Kingdom and China, respecting Tibet. Signed at Peking, April 27, 1906. (To which is annexed the Convention between the United Kingdom and Tibet. Signed at Lhassa, September 7, 1904.) Ratifications exchanged at London, July 23, 1906. [*Treaty Series No. 9 (1906)*.]   PAGE 119
   [Cd. 3088]   L/C. 1 Aug. 1906.

1703*c*   Correspondence relating to the Decree issued by the Chinese Government on May 9, 1906, respecting Chinese Imperial Maritime Customs. [*China No. 1 (1906)*.]   PAGE 127
   [Cd. 3089]   L/C. 23 Oct. 1906.

1703*d*   Further Correspondence. [*China No. 2 (1906)*.]   PAGE 133
   [Cd. 3263]   L/C. 13 Dec. 1906.

1710*a* Agreement between the United Kingdom and France, relative to the Arbitral Tribunal contemplated by Article III of the Convention of April 8, 1904, respecting Newfoundland. Signed at London, April 7, 1905. [*Treaty Series No. 27 (1905)*.]
PAGE 209

[Cd. 2758] *L/C.* 19 Feb. 1906.

1710*b* Agreement additional to the Money Order Convention of December 8, 1882, between the United Kingdom and France. Signed at Paris, April 20, 1904. Ratifications exchanged at Paris, January 10, 1906. [*Treaty Series No. 1 (1906)*.]
PAGE 213

[Cd. 2814] *L/C.* 19 Feb. 1906.

1710*c* Convention between the United Kingdom and France, respecting Telegraphic Communication between Mauritius and Reunion. Signed at Paris, December 6, 1905. Ratifications exchanged at Paris, January 10, 1906. [*Treaty Series No. 2 (1906)*.]
PAGE 217

[Cd. 2815] *L/C.* HC. 21 Feb., HL. 22 Feb. 1906.

1711 Convention between the United Kingdom and France, respecting the Delimitation of the Frontier between the British and French Possessions to the East of the Niger. Signed at London, May 29, 1906. Ratifications exchanged at London, August 29, 1906. [*Treaty Series No. 14 (1906)*.]
PAGE 223

[Cd. 3158] *L/C.* 23 Oct. 1906.

1712 Convention between the United Kingdom and France, confirming the Protocol signed at London on February 27, 1906, respecting the New Hebrides. [*France No. 1 (1906)*.] PAGE 237

[Cd. 3160] *L/C.* 5 Nov. 1906.

1713 Agreement between the United Kingdom and Germany, respecting the Boundary between the British and German Territories from Yola to Lake Chad. Signed at London, March 19, 1906. [*Treaty Series No. 17 (1906)*.] PAGE 271

[Cd. 3260] *L/C.* 27 Nov. 1906.

1714 Declarations between the United Kingdom and Greece, with respect to Commercial Matters. Signed at Athens, November 10 (23), 1904. May 4 (17), 1905. [*Treaty Series No. 23 (1905)*.]
PAGE 291

[Cd. 2688] *L/C.* 19 Feb. 1906.

VOLUME CXXXVII (1906)

State Papers

SESSION 12 FEBRUARY TO 28 AUGUST 1907

VOLUME L (1907)

Navy Estimates

VOLUME LVI (1907)

Colonies and British Possessions

VOLUME LVII (1907)

Colonies and British Possessions

VOLUME LXXV (1907)

Shipping

VOLUME LXXXVII (1907)

Commercial and General Interests, etc.

1742   Despatch by Lieutenant-Colonel Sir Henry Trotter reporting upon the operations of the European Commission of the Danube, during the Years 1894–1906, with a Résumé of its previous history (with a plan) [*v. supra*, No. 1401]. [*Commercial No. 9 (1907)*.]   PAGE 5
        [Cd. 3646]   L/C.   15 Aug. 1907.

VOLUME XCIX (1907)

State Papers

1743   Accession of British Colonies, etc. to the various Treaty Engagements between the United Kingdom and Foreign Powers. [*Treaty Series No. 11 (1907)*.]   PAGE 1
        [Cd. 3393]   L/C.   HC. 26 Mar., HL. 15 Ap. 1907.

1743*a* International Convention for the Amelioration of the Condition of the Wounded and Sick in Armies in the Field. Signed at Geneva, July 6, 1906. British Ratification deposited at Berne, April 16, 1907. [*Treaty Series No. 15 (1907)*.]   PAGE 5
        [Cd. 3502]   L/C.   12 June 1907.

1744   Protocol for the accession of Non-Signatory Powers to the Convention of July 29, 1899, for the Pacific Settlement of International Disputes, June 14, 1907. [*Treaty Series No. 26 (1907)*.]   PAGE 59
        [Cd. 3649]   L/C.   27 Aug. 1907.

1745   International Agreement respecting the Unification of the Pharmacopoeial formulas for Potent Drugs. Signed at Brussels, November 29, 1906. [*Treaty Series No. 10 (1907)*.]   PAGE 65
        [Cd. 3392]   L/C.   HC. 18 Mar., HL. 19 Mar. 1907.

1746   Agreement between the United Kingdom, France, and Italy, respecting Abyssinia. Signed at London, December 13, 1906. [*Treaty Series No. 1 (1907)*.]   PAGE 89
        [Cd. 3298]   L/C.   12 Feb. 1907.

1760a   do. Convention of Rome, 26th May 1906.   PAGE 353
        [Cd. 3556]   L/C. HL. 11 June, HC. 13 June 1907.

1761   *International Conference at Algeciras:* General Act of the International Conference at Algeciras relating to the Affairs of Morocco, April 7, 1906. Ratifications deposited at Madrid, December 31, 1906. [*Treaty Series No. 4 (1907).*]   PAGE 383
        [Cd. 3302]   L/C. 12 Feb. 1907.

1762   Accession of Nicaragua to the Convention, signed at Geneva, July 6, 1906, for the Amelioration of the Condition of the Wounded and Sick in Armies in the Field. June 17, 1907. [*Treaty Series No. 22 (1907).*]   PAGE 463
        [Cd. 3644]   L/C. 14 Aug. 1907.

1763   Agreement between the United Kingdom and Norway respecting the mutual Surrender of Fugitive Criminals. Signed at Christiania, February 18, 1907. [*Treaty Series No. 19 (1907).*]
        PAGE 467
        [Cd. 3606]   L/C. 16 July 1907.

1764   Accession of Panama to the Convention, signed at Geneva, August 22, 1864, for the Amelioration of the Condition of Wounded in Armies in the Field, July 29, 1907. [*Treaty Series No. 23 (1907).*]   PAGE 471
        [Cd. 3645]   L/C. 14 Aug. 1907.

1764a   Treaty between the United Kingdom...and Panama for the mutual Surrender of Fugitive Criminals. Signed at Panama, August 25, 1906. Ratifications exchanged at Panama, April 15, 1907. [*Treaty Series No. 25 (1907).*]   PAGE 475
        [Cd. 3648]   L/C. 23 Aug. 1907.

1765   Agreement between the Post Office of the United Kingdom... and the Post Office of Peru, for the Exchange of Postal Parcels.
        PAGE 489
        [Cd. 3671]   L/C. HC. 7 Aug., HL. 8 Aug. 1907.

1765a   Treaty between the United Kingdom and Peru for the Mutual Surrender of Fugitive Criminals. Signed at Lima, January 26, 1904. Ratifications exchanged at Lima, November 30, 1906. [*Treaty Series No. 13 (1907).*]   PAGE 509
        [Cd. 3498]   L/C. HC. 23 May, HL. 28 May 1907.

VOLUME C (1907)

State Papers

1772   General Index of Treaty Series, 1902–1906. [*Treaty Series No. 18 (1907)*.]   PAGE 553
        [Cd. 3605]   *L/C.* 15 July 1907.

1773   Correspondence respecting the International Conference on the White Slave Traffic, held in Paris, October 1906. [*Misc. No. 2 (1907)*.]   PAGE 585
        [Cd. 3453]   *L/C.* HC. 3 May, HL. 6 May 1907.

1774   Despatch from the Earl of Cromer respecting proposals of the Egypt General Assembly. [*Egypt No. 3 (1907)*.]   PAGE 605
        [Cd. 3451]   *L/C.* HC. 24 Ap., HL. 25 Ap. 1907.

1774*a*   Reports by His Majesty's Agent and Consul-General on the Finances, Administration, and Condition of Egypt and the Sudan in 1906. [*Egypt No. 1 (1907)*.]   PAGE 617
        [Cd. 3394]   *L/C.* HC. 8 Ap., HL. 15 Ap. 1907.

1774*b*   Despatch from the Earl of Cromer respecting the Water Supply of Egypt. [*Egypt No. 2 (1907)*.]   PAGE 785
        [Cd. 3397]   *L/C.* 17 Ap. 1907.

SESSION 29 JANUARY TO 21 DECEMBER 1908

VOLUME LXV (1908)

Navy Estimates

1775   Return showing the Fleets of Great Britain, France, Russia, Germany, Italy, United States of America, and Japan, on the 31st day of March 1908....   PAGE 779
        277   *Pursuant to Order (HC. 28 Ap.),* HC. 30 July 1908.

VOLUME LXXI (1908)

Colonies and British Possessions

1776   Further Correspondence respecting the Independent State of the Congo. [*Africa No. 1 (1908)*.]   PAGE 1
        [Cd. 3880]   *L/C.* HC. 21 Feb., HL. 24 Feb. 1908.

1776*a*   Further Correspondence [June 1907–April 1908]. [*Africa No. 2 (1908)*.]   PAGE 67
         [Cd. 4079]   *L/C.* 26 May 1908.

1776*b*   Correspondence respecting the Taxation of Natives, and other questions, in the Congo State. [*Africa No. 3 (1908)*.] PAGE 85
         [Cd. 4135]   *L/C.* HC. 15 June, HL. 16 June 1908.

1776*c*   Further Correspondence [June–July 1908]. [*Africa No. 4 (1908)*.]   PAGE 127
         [Cd. 4178]   *L/C.* 12 Oct. 1908.

1776*d*   do. [Nov. 1908]. [*Africa No. 5 (1908)*.]   PAGE 141
         [Cd. 4396]   *L/C.* 23 Nov. 1908.

VOLUME LXXIII (1908)

Colonies and British Possessions

1777   Further Correspondence relative to the Newfoundland Fishery Question.   PAGE 1
         [Cd. 3765]   *L/C.* 29 Jan. 1908.

VOLUME CXXIV (1908)

State Papers

1778   Accessions, etc. of Foreign States to various International Treaty Engagements [i.e. International Conventions (1) for the Pacific Settlement of International Disputes, (2) with respect to the Laws and Customs of War by Land, (3) for adapting to maritime warfare the principles of the Geneva Convention of August 22, 1864, etc.]. [*Treaty Series No. 39 (1907)*.]   PAGE 1
         [Cd. 3783]   *L/C.* 29 Jan. 1908.

1778*a*   Protocol between the United Kingdom, the Independent State of the Congo, France, Germany, Portugal and Spain, prohibiting the Importation of Firearms, Ammunition, etc., within a certain zone in Western Equatorial Africa. Signed at Brussels, July 22, 1908. [*Treaty Series No. 29 (1908)*.]   PAGE 5
         [Cd. 4320]   *L/C.* HC. 17 Nov., HL. 18 Nov. 1908.

1779   *Independence of Norway:* Treaty between the United Kingdom, France, Germany, Norway, and Russia respecting the Independence and Territorial Integrity of Norway. Signed at Christiania, November 2, 1907. Ratifications deposited at Christiania, February 6, 1908. [*Treaty Series No. 4 (1908)*.]
                                         PAGE 11
       [Cd. 3878]   *L/C.* 12 Feb. 1908.

1780   International Convention respecting the Liquor Traffic in Africa. Signed at Brussels, November 3, 1906. [*Treaty Series No. 46 (1907)*.]   PAGE 15
       [Cd. 3856]   *L/C.* 29 Jan. 1908.

1781   *Peace Conference at the Hague:* Protocols of the Eleven Plenary Meetings of the Second Peace Conference held at The Hague in 1907; with the Annexes to the Protocols. [*Misc. No. 4 (1908)*.]   PAGE 27
       [Cd. 4081]   *L/C.* HC. 3 June, HL. 16 June 1908.

1781 *a*   Correspondence respecting the Second Peace Conference held at The Hague in 1907. [*Misc. No. 1 (1908)*.]   PAGE 583
       [Cd. 3857]   *L/C.* 29 Jan. 1908.

1781 *b*   Further Correspondence. [*Misc. No. 5 (1908)*.]   PAGE 765
       [Cd. 4174]   *L/C.* HC. 24 July, HL. 27 July 1908.

1781 *c*   Final Act of the Second Peace Conference held at The Hague in 1907; and Conventions and Declaration Annexed thereto. [*Misc. No. 6 (1908)*.]   PAGE 769
       [Cd. 4175]   *L/C.* HC. 24 July, HL. 27 July 1908.

1782   International Sanitary Convention. Signed at Paris, December 3, 1903. Ratifications deposited at Paris, April 6, 1907. [*Treaty Series No. 27 (1907)*.]   PAGE 921
       [Cd. 3730]   *L/C.* 29 Jan. 1908.

1783   Sick and Wounded in War: Papers relating to the Geneva Convention, 1906.   PAGE 1049
       [Cd. 3933]   *L/C.* HC. 11 June, HL. 16 June 1908.

1784   Additional Act to the International Sugar Convention of March 5, 1902. Signed at Brussels, August 28, 1907. Protocol recording the Accession of Russia to the International Sugar Convention of March 5, 1902, and additional Act of August 28, 1907. Signed at Brussels, December 19, 1907. Procès-verbaux recording Deposit of Ratifications, March 31, 1908. [*Treaty Series No. 12 (1908)*.]   PAGE 1123
       [Cd. 3968]   *L/C.* 11 May 1908.

VOLUME CXXV (1908)

State Papers

1799   Accession of Nicaragua to the Declarations signed at the Hague, July 29, 1899, respecting (1) Expanding Bullets; (2) Asphyxiating Gases. October 11, 1907. [*Treaty Series No. 40 (1907)*.]   PAGE 435

        [Cd. 3819]   *L/C.* 29 Jan. 1908.

1799*a*   Accessions of British Colonies, etc., to the Treaty of Friendship, Commerce, and Navigation between the United Kingdom and Nicaragua. Signed at Managua, July 28, 1905. [*Treaty Series No. 43 (1907)*.]   PAGE 439

        [Cd. 3822]   *L/C.* 29 Jan. 1908.

1800   Parcel Post Agreement between the United Kingdom and Panama. Signed at Panama, April 13, 1908. [*Treaty Series No. 15 (1908)*.]   PAGE 443

        [Cd. 4136]   *L/C.* 17 June 1908.

1801   Declaration between the United Kingdom and Paraguay, amending the Treaty of Commerce of October 16, 1884. Signed at Asuncion, March 14, 1908. [*Treaty Series No. 14 (1908)*.]   PAGE 453

        [Cd. 4134]   *L/C.* HC. 10 June, HL. 16 June 1908.

1802   *British Policy in Persia:* Extract from a Despatch from the Government of India to the Secretary of State for India in Council, dated September 21, 1899, relating to British Policy in Persia, which was referred to in Debate on the Anglo-Russian Convention, which took place in the House of Lords on February 6 and 10, 1908. [*Persia No. 1 (1908)*.]   PAGE 457

        [Cd. 3882]   *L/C.* 25 Feb. 1908.

1803   Declaration between the United Kingdom and Portugal respecting Boundaries in Central Africa (Barotseland). Signed at London, August 12, 1903. [*Treaty Series No. 28 (1907)*.]

        PAGE 469

        [Cd. 3731]   *L/C.* 29 Jan. 1908.

1803*a*   Agreement for the Direct Exchange of Parcels between the United Kingdom...and the Portuguese Colony of Moçambique.

        PAGE 473

        [Cd. 4013]   *L/C.* 25 Mar. 1908.

1804   *Anglo-Russian Convention:* Convention signed on August 31, 1907, between Great Britain and Russia, containing arrangements on the subject of Persia, Afghanistan, and Thibet. [*Russia No. 1 (1907)*.]   PAGE 477

        [Cd. 3750]   *L/C.* 29 Jan. 1908.

1809 *a*   Notes exchanged between the United Kingdom and Sweden
and Norway relative to the Agreement of July 12, 1881, for
the Mutual Relief of Distressed Seamen. November 1907 to
May 1908. [*Treaty Series No. 19 (1908)*.]   PAGE 569
  [Cd. 4140]   *L/C.* 6 July 1908.

1809 *b*   Accession of Sweden to International Sanitary Convention.
Signed at Paris, December 3, 1903, December 20, 1907.
[*Treaty Series No. 6 (1908)*.]   PAGE 575
  [Cd. 3957]   *L/C.* HC. 6 Mar., HL. 9 Mar. 1908.

1810   Accession of the Colony of Trinidad and Tobago to the
Industrial Property Convention of 1883, as modified by the
Additional Act of 1900. May 14, 1908. [*Treaty Series No. 11
(1908)*.]   PAGE 579
  [Cd. 3967]   *L/C.* 5 May 1908.

1811   Accession of Turkey to the Convention signed at Geneva,
July 6, 1906, for the Amelioration of the Condition of Wounded
and Sick in Armies in the Field. August 24, 1907. [*Treaty Series
No. 38 (1907)*.]   PAGE 583
  [Cd. 3781]   *L/C.* 29 Jan. 1908.

1812   Further Correspondence respecting Proposals by His Majesty's
Government for Reforms in Macedonia. [*Turkey No. 1 (1908)*.]
          PAGE 587
  [Cd. 3958]   *L/C.* HC. 27 Mar., HL. 30 Mar. 1908.

1812 *a*   Further Correspondence. [*Turkey No. 2 (1908)*.]   PAGE 597
  [Cd. 3963]   *L/C.* 14 Ap. 1908.

1812 *b*   Further Correspondence respecting Affairs of South-Eastern
Europe. [*Turkey No. 3 (1908)*.]   PAGE 607
  [Cd. 4076]   *L/C.* 11 May 1908.

1813   Accession of the United Kingdom to the Declarations signed at
the Hague, July 29, 1899, respecting (1) Expanding Bullets;
(2) Asphyxiating Gases. August 30, 1907. [*Treaty Series No. 32
(1907)*.]   PAGE 891
  [Cd. 3751]   *L/C.* 29 Jan. 1908.

1814   Arbitration Convention between the United Kingdom and the
United States of America, with an Exchange of Notes as to
the Interpretation of Article 2. Signed at Washington, April 4,
1908. Ratifications exchanged at Washington, June 4, 1908.
[*Treaty Series No. 21 (1908)*.]   PAGE 907
  [Cd. 4179]   *L/C.* 12 Oct. 1908.

1814*a*   Treaty between the United Kingdom and the United States
of America respecting the Demarcation of the International
Boundary between the United States and the Dominion of
Canada. Signed at Washington, April 11, 1908. Ratifications
exchanged at Washington, June 4, 1908. [*Treaty Series No. 18
(1908)*.]   PAGE 911

   [Cd. 4139]   *L/C.* 1 July 1908.

1814*b*   Agreement between the United Kingdom and the United States
of America respecting (1) Commercial Travellers' Samples
entering the United Kingdom; (2) Import Duties on British
Works of Art entering the United States. Signed at London,
November 19, 1907. [*Treaty Series No. 44 (1907)*.]   PAGE 927

   [Cd. 3853]   *L/C.* 29 Jan. 1908.

1814*c*   Treaty between the United Kingdom and the United States of
America, providing (1) For the Conveyance of Persons in
Custody for Trial, either in the Dominion of Canada or the
United States, through the Territory of the other; and (2) For
reciprocal rights in Wrecking and Salvage in the waters con-
tiguous to the Boundary between the Dominion of Canada
and the United States. Signed at Washington, May 18, 1908.
Ratifications exchanged at Washington, June 30, 1908. [*Treaty
Series No. 22 (1908)*.]   PAGE 931

   [Cd. 4247]   *L/C.* 31 July 1908.

1814*d*   Agreement between the United Kingdom and France respecting
Death Duties. Signed at London, November 15, 1907. Rati-
fications exchanged at London, December 9, 1907. [*Treaty
Series No. 10 (1908)*.]   PAGE 935

   [Cd. 3965]   *L/C.* HC. 27 Ap., HL. 5 May 1908.

1814*e*   Notes exchanged with the American Ambassador on the subject
of the Newfoundland Fisheries. [*United States No. 1 (1907)*.]
                                                                            PAGE 939
   [Cd. 3734]   *L/C.* 29 Jan. 1908.

1814*f*   Exchange of Notes establishing a *modus vivendi* between the
United Kingdom and the United States of America with regard
to the Newfoundland Fisheries. September 4 and 6, 1907.
[*Treaty Series No. 35 (1907)*.]   PAGE 943

   [Cd. 3754]   *L/C.* 29 Jan. 1908.

Session 16 February to 3 December 1909

Volume LI (1909)

Army Estimates, etc.

Volume LIII (1909)

Navy Estimates, etc.

VOLUME LIV (1909)

Navy

VOLUME LIX (1909)

Colonies and British Possessions

VOLUME LXXI (1909)

Miscellaneous

1822   Return showing all General Treaties of Arbitration between the United Kingdom and other States. [*Misc. No. 9 (1909)*.]

                                                                     PAGE 1

         [Cd. 4870]   *R–A. (HC. 14 Sept.)*, 22 Sept. 1909.

VOLUME CV (1909)

State Papers

1823   Correspondence respecting the Revised Convention of Berne for the Protection of Literary and Artistic Works. Signed at Berlin, November 13, 1908. [*Misc. No. 2 (1909)*.]   PAGE 1

         [Cd. 4467]   *L/C.* 16 Feb. 1909.

1823*a*   Notes exchanged between the United Kingdom, and Belgium, Italy, Portugal, and Spain respecting Protection of Patents in Morocco. February to December 1907. [*Treaty Series No. 30 (1909)*.]   PAGE 179

         [Cd. 4951]   *L/C.* HL. 19 Nov., HC. 23 Nov. 1909.

1823*b*   International Agreement respecting the creation of an International Office of Public Health. Signed at Rome, December 9, 1907. [*Treaty Series No. 6 (1909)*.]   PAGE 191

         [Cd. 4532]   *L/C.* 10 Mar. 1909.

1823*c*   International Radiotelegraphic Convention. Signed at Berlin, November 3, 1906. [*Treaty Series No. 8 (1909)*.]   PAGE 207

         [Cd. 4559]   *L/C.* HC. 26 Mar., HL. 30 Mar. 1909.

1824   Protocol between the United Kingdom, Austria-Hungary, France, Germany, Italy, Russia, and Turkey respecting Turkish Customs Duties. Signed at Constantinople, April 25, 1907. [*Treaty Series No. 1 (1909)*.]   PAGE 257

         [Cd. 4469]   *L/C.* 18 Feb. 1909.

1825   Accession of United Kingdom to the International Convention, signed at Berne, September 26, 1906, prohibiting the use of White (Yellow) Phosphorus in the Manufacture of Matches. December 28, 1908. [*Treaty Series No. 4 (1909)*.]   PAGE 263

         [Cd. 4530]   *L/C.* 2 Mar. 1909.

1826   Accession of Austria and Hungary to the Industrial Property
Convention 1883, etc. January 1, 1909. [*Treaty Series No. 15
(1909)*.]   PAGE 273

[Cd. 4649]   *L/C.* HC. 14 June, HL. 23 June 1909.

1827   Additional Agreement between the United Kingdom and
Bulgaria modifying the Convention of Commerce, Customs
Duties, and Navigation of December 9, 1905. Signed at Sofia,
February 9, 1909. [*Treaty Series No. 7 (1909)*.]   PAGE 277

[Cd. 4557]   *L/C.* HC. 19 Mar., HL. 22 Mar. 1909.

1828   Despatch from His Majesty's Minister in China, forwarding
a General Report by Sir Alexander Hosie respecting the
Opium Question in China. [*China No. 1 (1909)*.]   PAGE 281

[Cd. 4702]   *L/C.* HC. 23 June, HL. 24 June 1909.

1828a   Correspondence relative to the International Opium Commission at Shanghai, 1909. [*China No. 2 (1909)*.]   PAGE 305

[Cd. 4898]   *L/C.* HC. 4 Nov., HL. 8 Nov. 1909.

1829   Regulations respecting Trade in Tibet (amending those of
December 5, 1893), concluded between the United Kingdom,
China, and Tibet. Signed at Calcutta, April 20, 1908. [*Treaty
Series No. 35 (1908)*.]   PAGE 317

[Cd. 4450]   *L/C.* 16 Feb. 1909.

1830   Agreement between the United Kingdom and Colombia providing for the settlement by Arbitration of certain classes of
Questions which may arise between the two Governments.
Signed at Bogota, December 30, 1908. [*Treaty Series No. 5
(1909)*.]   PAGE 325

[Cd. 4531]   *L/C.* 4 Mar. 1909.

1831   Accession of Cuba to the Convention signed at Geneva,
July 6, 1906, for the Amelioration of the Condition of the
Wounded and Sick in Armies in the Field. [*Treaty Series No. 16
(1909)*.]   PAGE 329

[Cd. 4698]   *L/C.* HC. 17 June, HL. 23 June 1909.

1832   Reports by His Majesty's Agent and Consul-General on the
Finances, Administration, and Condition of Egypt and the
Soudan in 1908. [*Egypt No. 1 (1909)*.]   PAGE 333

[Cd. 4580]   *L/C.* HC. 29 Ap., HL. 3 May 1909.

1833   Despatch from His Majesty's Agent and Consul-General at Cairo, forwarding the Egyptian Law of July 4, 1909, for placing persons under Police Supervision. [*Egypt No. 2 (1909)*.]

PAGE 415

[Cd. 4734]   L/C. HC. 27 Aug., HL. 30 Aug. 1909.

1834   Accessions of British Colonies, etc., to the Commercial Convention between the United Kingdom and Egypt. Signed at Cairo, October 29, 1889. [*Treaty Series No. 18 (1909)*.]

PAGE 425

[Cd. 4700]   L/C. HC. 22 June, HL. 23 June 1909.

1835   Despatch from His Majesty's Ambassador at Paris, forwarding a Convention between Great Britain and France. Signed at Paris, July 3, 1909, in regard to Workmen's Compensation for Accidents. [*Misc. No. 8 (1909)*.]   PAGE 429

[Cd. 4731]   L/C. HC. 18 Aug., HL. 30 Aug. 1909.

1836   Exchange of Notes between the United Kingdom and Germany renewing for a further period of one Year the Arbitration Agreement, signed at London, July 12, 1904. June 7/July 9, 1909. [*Treaty Series No. 20 (1909)*.]   PAGE 435

[Cd. 4729]   L/C. 26 July 1909.

1836a   Declaration between the United Kingdom and Germany, referring the Delimitation of the Southern Boundary of the British Territory of Walfish Bay to Arbitration. Signed at Berlin, January 30, 1909. [*Treaty Series No. 10 (1909)*.]

PAGE 439

[Cd. 4579]   L/C. HC. 23 Ap., HL. 26 Ap. 1909.

1836b   Exchange of Notes between the United Kingdom and Germany, confirming Protocols defining Boundaries between British and German Territories in Africa. With Map. [*Treaty Series No. 17 (1909)*.]   PAGE 445

[Cd. 4699]   L/C. HC. 17 June, HL. 23 June 1909.

1836c   Accession of German Protectorates to the Berne Copyright Convention of September 9, 1886, and to the Additional Act and Declaration, signed at Paris, May 4, 1896. [*Treaty Series No. 36 (1908)*.]   PAGE 453

[Cd. 4451]   L/C. 16 Feb. 1909.

1836*d* Exchange of Notes between the United Kingdom and Germany for the Mutual Protection of British and German Trade Marks in Corea. August 31–October 8, 1909. [*Treaty Series No. 25 (1909)*.]   PAGE 457

[Cd. 4897]   *L/C.* HC. 3 Nov., HL. 8 Nov. 1909.

1837 Abrogation of the Convention between the United Kingdom and Hayti of April 6, 1906, respecting Nationality. April 1, 1909. [*Treaty Series No. 12 (1909)*.]   PAGE 461

[Cd. 4644]   *L/C.* HC. 13 May, HL. 17 May 1909.

1838 Exchange of Notes between the United Kingdom and Italy renewing for a further period of five years the Arbitration Agreement, signed at Rome, February 1, 1904. [*Treaty Series No. 2 (1909)*.]   PAGE 465

[Cd. 4470]   *L/C.* 24 Feb. 1909.

1839 Accession of Mexico to the Declaration respecting Maritime Law, signed at Paris, April 16, 1856. February 13, 1909. [*Treaty Series No. 11 (1909)*.]   PAGE 469

[Cd. 4582]   *L/C.* HC. 10 May, HL. 11 May 1909.

1839*a* Convention between the United Kingdom and Mexico, supplementary to the Parcel Post Convention of February 25, 1897. Signed at Mexico, December 1, 1908. Ratifications exchanged at Mexico, March 13, 1909. [*Treaty Series No. 9 (1909)*.]   PAGE 473

[Cd. 4577]   *L/C.* HC. 20 Ap., HL. 21 Ap. 1909.

1839*b* Accession of Mexico and Sweden to the International Agreement of December 9, 1907, respecting the creation of an International Office of Public Health. [*Treaty Series No. 22 (1909)*.]   PAGE 477

[Cd. 4817]   *L/C.* 22 Sept. 1909.

1840 Agreement between the United Kingdom and the Netherlands respecting the Exchange of Insured Letters and Boxes. Signed at the Hague, December 1, 1908. [*Treaty Series No. 37 (1908)*.]   PAGE 481

[Cd. 4452]   *L/C.* 16 Feb. 1909.

1841 Convention between the United Kingdom and Norway renewing for a further period of five years the Arbitration Convention of August 11, 1904. Signed at London, November 9, 1909. [*Treaty Series No. 27 (1909)*.]   PAGE 485

[Cd. 4900]   *L/C.* HL. 16 Nov., HC. 23 Nov. 1909.

1847a   Treaty between the United Kingdom and Siam. Signed at
         Bangkok, March 10, 1909. (Ratifications exchanged at London,
         July 9, 1909.) With Map. [*Treaty Series No. 19 (1909)*.]
                                                                 PAGE 919
         [Cd. 4703]   *L/C.* 20 July 1909.

1848   Exchange of Notes between the United Kingdom and Spain,
         renewing for a further period of five years the Arbitration
         Agreement, signed at London, February 27, 1904. January 11,
         1909. [*Treaty Series No. 3 (1909)*.]   PAGE 931
         [Cd. 4527]   *L/C.* 24 Feb. 1909.

1849   Convention between the United Kingdom and Sweden,
         renewing for a further period of five years the Arbitration
         Convention of August 11, 1904. Signed at London, November
         9, 1909. [*Treaty Series No. 31 (1909)*.]   PAGE 935
         [Cd. 4952]   *L/C.* 23 Nov. 1909.

1850   Exchange of Notes between the United Kingdom and Switzer-
         land, renewing for a further period of five years the Arbitration
         Convention, signed at London, November 16, 1904. November
         3/12, 1909. [*Treaty Series No. 33 (1909)*.]   PAGE 939
         [Cd. 4957]   *L/C.* 24 Nov. 1909.

1851   Correspondence respecting the Constitutional Movement in
         Turkey, 1908. [*Turkey No. 1 (1909)*.]   PAGE 943
         [Cd. 4529]   *L/C.* 18 Mar. 1909.

1852   Treaty with the United States relating to Boundary Waters
         and Questions arising along the Boundary between Canada
         and the United States. Signed at Washington, January 11,
         1909. [*United States No. 2 (1909)*.]   PAGE 1083
         [Cd. 4558]   *L/C.* 22 Mar. 1909.

1852a   Agreement with the United States for submitting to Arbitra-
         tion the question of the North Atlantic Fisheries. Signed at
         Washington, January 27, 1909; and Notes respecting the same.
         [*United States No. 1 (1909)*.]   PAGE 1091
         [Cd. 4528]   *L/C.* HC. 26 Feb., HL. 2 Mar. 1909.

1852b   Agreement between the United Kingdom and the United
         States of America for the submission to Arbitration of questions
         relating to Fisheries on the North Atlantic Coast. Signed at
         Washington, January 27, 1909. [*Treaty Series No. 21 (1909)*.]
                                                                 PAGE 1099
         [Cd. 4815]   *L/C.* HC. 2 Sept., HL. 10 Sept. 1909.

1852*c* Denunciation of the Agreement of November 19, 1907, between the United Kingdom and the United States of America respecting (1) Commercial Travellers' Samples entering the United Kingdom; (2) Import Duties on British Works of Art entering the United States. May 1, 1909. [*Treaty Series No. 13 (1909)*.]   PAGE 1109

    [Cd. 4645]   *L/C.* 25 May 1909.

1852*d* Denunciation of the Agreement of November 19, 1907, between the United Kingdom and the United States of America respecting (1) Commercial Travellers' Samples entering the United Kingdom; (2) Import Duties on British Works of Art entering the United States. August 7, 1909. [*Treaty Series No. 23 (1909)*.]   PAGE 1113

    [Cd. 4871]   *L/C.* 23 Sept. 1909.

Session 15 February to 28 November 1910

Volume LXI (1910)

Navy

1853 Return showing the Fleets of Great Britain, France, Russia, Germany, Italy, United States of America, and Japan on the 31st day of March 1910....   PAGE 631

    83   *Pursuant to Order (HC. 16 Mar.),* HC. 4 Ap. 1910.

Volume LXVI (1910)

Colonies and British Possessions

1854 Return of the Correspondence between His Majesty's Government and the Governments of the Self-Governing Dominions and Colonies respecting the constitutional position of the latter in the negotiation of Commercial and other Treaties with Foreign Powers, including the letter from His Majesty's Secretary of State for Foreign Affairs, dated Foreign Office, London, 4th July 1907, addressed to the British Ambassador at Paris, and laid upon the Table of the Canadian House of Commons.
    PAGE 25

    129   *R–A. (HC. 13 Ap.),* HC. 27 Ap. 1910.

VOLUME LXVIII (1910)

East India

1855   Further Papers relating to Tibet [*v. supra*, No. 1667].

PAGE 615

[Cd. 5240]   *L/C.*   4 July 1910.

VOLUME LXXIV (1910)

Miscellaneous

1856   Correspondence respecting the Declaration of London [*v. supra*, Nos. 1819 and 1819*a*]. [*Misc. No. 4 (1910)*.]   PAGE 133

[Cd. 5418]   *L/C.*   23 Nov. 1910.

1857   Despatch...enclosing...the Award of the Permanent Court of International Arbitration at the Hague in the North Atlantic Coast Fisheries Arbitration. [*Misc. No. 3 (1910)*.]   PAGE 385

[Cd. 5396]   *L/C.*   18 Nov. 1910.

VOLUME CXII (1910)

State Papers

1858   Accessions to and Withdrawals from various Treaty Engagements between the United Kingdom and Foreign Powers, on the part of British Colonies. [*Treaty Series No. 5 (1910)*.]

PAGE 1

[Cd. 5026]   *L/C.*   4 Ap. 1910.

1858*a*   Accessions, etc., of Foreign States to various International Treaty Engagements. [*Treaty Series No. 6 (1910)*.]   PAGE 7

[Cd. 5027]   *L/C.*   4 Ap. 1910.

1859   International Convention respecting the Limitation of the Employment of Force for the recovery of Contract Debts. Signed at The Hague, October 18, 1907. [*Treaty Series No. 7 (1910)*.]   PAGE 11

[Cd. 5028]   *L/C.*   HC. 12 Ap., HL. 13 Ap. 1910.

1859*a* International Convention relative to the Opening of Hostilities. Signed at the Hague, October 18, 1907. [*Treaty Series No. 8 (1910).*]   PAGE 35

   [Cd. 5029]   L/C. HC. 12 Ap., HL. 13 Ap. 1910.

1859*b* International Convention concerning the Laws and Customs of War on Land. Signed at the Hague, October 18, 1907. [*Treaty Series No. 9 (1910).*]   PAGE 59

   [Cd. 5030]   L/C. HC. 12 Ap., HL. 13 Ap. 1910.

1859*c* International Convention relative to the Status of Enemy Merchant Ships at the outbreak of Hostilities. Signed at the Hague, October 18, 1907. [*Treaty Series No. 10 (1910).*]
                                                     PAGE 101

   [Cd. 5031]   L/C. HC. 12 Ap., HL. 13 Ap. 1910.

1859*d* International Convention relative to the Conversion of Merchant Ships into War Ships. Signed at the Hague, October 18, 1907. [*Treaty Series No. 11 (1910).*]   PAGE 125

   [Cd. 5115]   L/C. HC. 12 Ap., HL. 13 Ap. 1910.

1859*e* International Convention relative to the laying of Automatic Submarine Contact Mines. Signed at the Hague, October 18, 1907. [*Treaty Series No. 12 (1910).*]   PAGE 149

   [Cd. 5116]   L/C. HC. 12 Ap., HL. 13 Ap. 1910.

1859*f* International Convention respecting Bombardments by Naval Forces in Time of War. Signed at the Hague, October 18, 1907. [*Treaty Series No. 13 (1910).*]   PAGE 173

   [Cd. 5117]   L/C. HC. 12 Ap., HL. 13 Ap. 1910.

1859*g* International Convention relative to certain restrictions on the Exercise of the Right of Capture in Maritime War. Signed at the Hague, October 18, 1907. [*Treaty Series No. 14 (1910).*]
                                                     PAGE 199

   [Cd. 5118]   L/C. HC. 12 Ap., HL. 13 Ap. 1910.

1859*h* International Declaration prohibiting the Discharge of Projectiles and Explosives from Balloons. Signed at the Hague, October 18, 1907. [*Treaty Series No. 15 (1910).*]   PAGE 223

   [Cd. 5119]   L/C. HC. 12 Ap., HL. 13 Ap. 1910.

1860   *Integrity of Norway and Sweden:* Declarations between the United
       Kingdom, France, and Norway and between the United
       Kingdom, France, and Sweden concerning the abrogation of
       the Treaty of November 21, 1855, relative to the Integrity of
       Norway and Sweden. Signed at Christiania, November 2,
       1907, Stockholm, April 23, 1908. [*Treaty Series No. 16 (1910)*.]
                                                              PAGE 231
          [Cd. 5123]   L/C. 10 May 1910.

1861   International Convention for the creation of an International
       Agricultural Institute. Signed at Rome, June 7, 1905. [*Treaty
       Series No. 17 (1910)*.]   PAGE 235
          [Cd. 5124]   L/C. 20 June 1910.

1862   Convention with respect to the International Circulation of
       Motor Vehicles. Signed at Paris, October 11, 1909. [*Treaty
       Series No. 18 (1910)*.]   PAGE 251
          [Cd. 5125]   L/C. 5 July 1910.

1862 *a* International Convention respecting the Prohibition of Night
       Work for Women in Industrial Employment. Signed at Berne,
       September 26, 1906. [*Treaty Series No. 21 (1910)*.]   PAGE 275
          [Cd. 5221]   L/C. 15 Nov. 1910.

1863   Accession of Bulgaria to the International Agreement of
       December 9, 1907, respecting the creation of an International
       Office of Public Health. [*Treaty Series No. 1 (1910)*.]
                                                              PAGE 291
          [Cd. 4969]   L/C. 21 Feb. 1910.

1864   Despatches from His Majesty's Minister at Peking forwarding
       Reports respecting the Opium Question in China. [*China
       No. 3 (1909)*.]   PAGE 295
          [Cd. 4967]   L/C. 21 Feb. 1910.

1865   Reports by His Majesty's Agent and Consul-General on the
       Finances, Administration, and Condition of Egypt and the
       Soudan in 1909. [*Egypt No. 1 (1910)*.]   PAGE 347
          [Cd. 5121]   L/C. HC. 22 Ap., HL. 25 Ap. 1910.

1866   Exchange of Notes between the United Kingdom and Ethiopia
       with regard to import duties in Ethiopia. April 13/May 12,
       1909. [*Treaty Series No. 3 (1910)*.]   PAGE 435
          [Cd. 5020]   L/C. 21 Feb. 1910.

SESSION 31 JANUARY TO 16 DECEMBER 1911

VOLUME XLVIII (1911)

Navy

VOLUME LII (1911)

Colonies and British Possessions

1875   Correspondence respecting the Affairs of the Congo. [*Africa No. 2 (1911)*.]   PAGE 601
        [Cd. 5860]   *L/C.* 20 Nov. 1911.

1876   Translation of the Award of Don Joaquin Fernandez Prida, Arbitrator in the matter of the Southern Boundary of the Territory of Walfisch Bay. (With Map.) [*Africa No. 1 (1911)*.]
                                                         PAGE 745

        [Cd. 5857]   *L/C.* 31 Oct. 1911.

VOLUME CIII (1911)

State Papers

1877   Convention of March 5, 1903; Statutes of Imperial Bagdad Railway Company; Specification; Loan Contract, First Series 1903; Loan Contract, Second and Third Series 1908; Additional Convention of June 2, 1908. (With Maps.) [*Bagdad Railway No. 1 (1911)*.]   PAGE 1
        [Cd. 5635]   *L/C.* 11 May 1911.

1878   Conventions for the Unification of certain Rules of Law respecting Collisions, and Assistance and Salvage at Sea. Signed at Brussels, September 23, 1910, and Documents relating thereto. [*Misc. No. 5 (1911)*.]   PAGE 79
        [Cd. 5558]   *L/C.* HC. 25 Ap., HL. 26 Ap. 1911.

1879   Correspondence respecting the Declaration of London [*v. supra*, Nos. 1819, 1819*a* and 1856]. [*Misc. No. 8 (1911)*.]   PAGE 113
        [Cd. 5718]   *L/C.* 26 June 1911.

1880   Correspondence respecting an Additional Protocol to the Convention relative to the Establishment of an International Prize Court of October 18, 1907. [*Misc. No. 4 (1911)*.]
                                                         PAGE 133
        [Cd. 5554]   *L/C.* HC. 17 Mar., HL. 20 Mar. 1911.

1881   International Agreement for the Suppression of obscene publications. Signed at Paris, May 4, 1910. [*Treaty Series No. 11
(1911)*.]   PAGE 141

    [Cd. 5657]   *L/C.* 23 May 1911.

1882   Treaties etc., between the United Kingdom and Foreign States.
Accessions, Withdrawals, etc. [*Treaty Series No. 6 (1911)*.]
                                                          PAGE 151

    [Cd. 5555]   *L/C.* HC. 24 Mar., HL. 27 Mar. 1911.

1882*a* Index to Treaty Series, 1910. [*Treaty Series No. 27 (1910)*.]
                                                          PAGE 161

    [Cd. 5521]   *L/C.* HC. 27 Feb., HL. 28 Feb. 1911.

1883   Convention between the United Kingdom and Austria-
Hungary providing for the settlement by Arbitration of Certain
Classes of Questions which may arise between the two Governments. Signed at London, July 16, 1910. [*Treaty Series No. 1
(1911)*.]   PAGE 167

    [Cd. 5471]   *L/C.* 6 Feb. 1911.

1884   Convention between the United Kingdom and Belgium
amending Article 6 of the Extradition Treaty of October 29,
1901. Signed at London, March 3, 1911. [*Treaty Series No. 21
(1911)*.]   PAGE 173

    [Cd. 5807]   *L/C.* HC. 24 Oct., HL. 25 Oct. 1911.

1885   Belgian Decree of March 22, 1910, relative to the Collection
of the Natural Products of the Soil in the Domain Lands of
the Congo. [*Congo No. 1 (1911)*.]   PAGE 177

    [Cd. 5559]   *L/C.* 1 May 1911.

1886   Arbitration Convention between the United Kingdom and
Brazil. Signed at Petropolis, June 18, 1909. [*Treaty Series
No. 12 (1911)*.]   PAGE 183

    [Cd. 5659]   *L/C.* HC. 13 June, HL. 26 June 1911.

1887   Award pronounced by His Majesty King George V as 'Amiable
Compositeur' between the United States of America and the
Republic of Chile in the matter of the Alsop Claim. [*Chile
No. 1 (1911)*.]   PAGE 187

    [Cd. 5739]   *L/C.* 1 Aug. 1911.

1888   Despatches from Sir A. Hosie forwarding Reports respecting
the Opium Question in China. [*China No. 1 (1911)*.]
                                                          PAGE 205

    [Cd. 5658]   *L/C.* HC. 13 June, HL. 26 June 1911.

1904   Additional Articles to the Convention of August 24, 1889, for the exchange of Money Orders between the United Kingdom and Tunis. Signed at Paris, December 22, 1910. [*Treaty Series No. 3 (1911)*.]   PAGE 647

    [Cd. 5468]   *L/C.* 6 Feb. 1911.

1905   Imperial Ottoman Debt. Decree of 28 Muharrem, 1299 (December 8 (20), 1881). [*Turkey No. 1 (1911)*.]   PAGE 653

    [Cd. 5736]   *L/C.* HL. 14 July, HC. 17 July 1911.

1906   Treaty of Arbitration between the United Kingdom and the United States of America. Signed at Washington, August 3, 1911. [*United States No. 2 (1911)*.]   PAGE 691

    [Cd. 5805]   *L/C.* HC. 24 Oct., HL. 25 Oct. 1911.

1906*a*   Agreement between the United Kingdom and the United States respecting Commercial Travellers' Samples. [*Treaty Series No. 4 (1911)*.]   PAGE 697

    [Cd. 5518]   *L/C.* HC. 24 Feb., HL. 27 Feb. 1911.

1906*b*   Treaty between the United Kingdom and the United States respecting Measures for the preservation and protection of the Fur-Seals. Signed at Washington, February 7, 1911. [*Treaty Series No. 25 (1911)*.]   PAGE 701

    [Cd. 5971]   *L/C.* 4 Dec. 1911.

1906*c*   Agreement between the United Kingdom and the United States of America for the settlement of various pecuniary claims outstanding between the two Governments, with the First Schedule of Claims and terms of submission thereof. [*United States No. 1 (1911)*.]   PAGE 707

    [Cd. 5803]   *L/C.* 8 Aug. 1911.

1907   Treaty between the United Kingdom and Zanzibar abrogating the Treaty of April 30, 1886. Signed at Zanzibar, November 4, 1908. Declaration abrogating, so far as regards Zanzibar, the Treaty of May 31, 1839, between the United Kingdom and Muscat. Signed at Zanzibar, April 3, 1911. [*Treaty Series No. 7 (1911)*.]   PAGE 715

    [Cd. 5636]   *L/C.* 10 May 1911.

VOLUME LX (1912–13)

Colonies and British Possessions

VOLUME LXVIII (1912–13)

Miscellaneous

VOLUME CXXI (1912–13)

State Papers

1915   Declaration modifying paragraph 5 of the declaration annexed to the General Act signed at Brussels, July 2, 1890. Signed at Brussels, June 15, 1910. British Ratification deposited at Brussels, April 27, 1911. [*Treaty Series No. 5 (1912)*.]   PAGE 1

    [Cd. 6037]   *L/C.* 14 Feb. 1912.

1915*a*   International Convention relative to the Protection of Literary and Artistic Works, revising that signed at Berne, September 9, 1886, etc. Signed at Berlin, November 13, 1908. British Ratification deposited at Berne, June 14, 1912. [*Treaty Series No. 19 (1912)*.]   PAGE 9

    [Cd. 6324]   *L/C.* 7 Oct. 1912.

1915*b*   Despatch from His Majesty's Ambassador at Washington containing the text of the Treaty for the preservation and protection of the Fur Seals which frequent the waters of the North Pacific Ocean. Signed at Washington, July 7, 1911. [*Misc. No. 12 (1911)*.]   PAGE 43

    [Cd. 6008]   *L/C.* 14 Feb. 1912.

1915*c*   Convention between the United Kingdom, the United States, Japan, and Russia, respecting measures for the preservation and protection of the Fur Seals in the North Pacific Ocean. Signed at Washington, July 7, 1911. Ratifications deposited at Washington, December 12, 1911. [*Treaty Series No. 2 (1912)*.]

                                              PAGE 51

    [Cd. 6034]   *L/C.* 14 Feb. 1912.

1915*d*   International Opium Convention. Signed at The Hague, January 23, 1912. [*Misc. No. 2 (1912)*.]   PAGE 61

    [Cd. 6038]   *L/C.* 20 Feb. 1912.

1915*e*   Despatches from His Majesty's Minister at Brussels respecting the Signature and Ratification of the Protocol of March 17, 1912, relative to the prolongation of the International Sugar Union. [*Commercial No. 3 (1912)*.]   PAGE 83

    [Cd. 6146]   *L/C.* HC. 9 May, HL. 13 May 1912.

1915*f*   International Convention for the suppression of the White Slave Traffic. Signed at Paris, May 4, 1910. British Ratification deposited at Paris, August 8, 1912. [*Treaty Series No. 20 (1912).*]   PAGE 95

   [Cd. 6326]   *L/C.* HC. 16 Oct., HL. 21 Oct. 1912.

1916   Treaties, etc. between the United Kingdom and Foreign States. Accessions, Withdrawals, etc. [*Treaty Series No. 14 (1912).*]   PAGE 111

   [Cd. 6204]   *L/C.* HC. 10 June, HL. 11 June 1912.

1916*a*   General Index to Treaty Series, 1907–1911. [*Treaty Series No. 4 (1912).*]   PAGE 121

   [Cd. 6036]   *L/C.* 14 Feb. 1912.

1916*b*   Index to Treaty Series, 1911. [*Treaty Series No. 27 (1911).*]   PAGE 175

   [Cd. 6012]   *L/C.* 14 Feb. 1912.

1916*c*   Index to Treaty Series, 1912. [*Treaty Series No. 27 (1912).*]   PAGE 181

   [Cd. 6527]   *L/C.* 16 Jan. 1913.

1917   Agreement between the United Kingdom and Bolivia for the Exchange of Postal Money Orders. Signed at La Paz, February 12, 1912. [*Treaty Series No. 15 (1912).*]   PAGE 187

   [Cd. 6205]   *L/C.* 26 June 1912.

1917*a*   Treaty of Commerce between the United Kingdom and the Republic of Bolivia. Signed at La Paz, August 1, 1911. Ratifications exchanged at London, July 5, 1912. [*Treaty Series No. 17 (1912).*]   PAGE 215

   [Cd. 6267]   *L/C.* 22 July 1912.

1918   Correspondence respecting the Affairs of China. [*China No. 1 (1912).*]   PAGE 227

   [Cd. 6148]   *L/C.* HC. 20 May, HL. 11 June 1912.

1918*a*   Further Correspondence [Nov. 1911–Mar. 1912]. [*China No. 3 (1912).*]   PAGE 363

   [Cd. 6447]   *L/C.* 7 Nov. 1912.

1918*b*   Correspondence respecting Chinese Loan Negotiations. [*China No. 2 (1912).*]   PAGE 591

   [Cd. 6446]   *L/C.* HC. 28 Oct., HL. 29 Oct. 1912.

1918c Despatches from His Majesty's Ambassador at St. Petersburg transmitting the Russo-Mongolian Agreement and Protocol of the 21st October (3rd November) 1912. [*China No. 1 (1913)*.]
PAGE 615

[Cd. 6604]   *L/C.* 5 Feb. 1913.

1919 Protocol between the United Kingdom and Colombia respecting the application of the Treaty of Commerce of February 16, 1866, to certain parts of His Britannic Majesty's Dominions. Signed at Bogota, August 20, 1912. [*Treaty Series No. 24 (1912)*.]
PAGE 623

[Cd. 6523]   *L/C.* HC. 13 Dec. 1912, HL. 14 Jan. 1913.

1920 Ratification by Denmark of the International Copyright Convention signed at Berlin, November 13, 1908. July 1, 1912. [*Treaty Series No. 26 (1912)*.]
PAGE 627

[Cd. 6525]   *L/C.* HC. 3 Jan., HL. 14 Jan. 1913.

1920a Declaration between the United Kingdom and Denmark respecting the application of existing Treaties of Commerce to certain parts of His Britannic Majesty's Dominions. Signed at Copenhagen, May 9, 1912. [*Treaty Series No. 13 (1912)*.]
PAGE 631

[Cd. 6203]   *L/C.* HC. 7 June, HL. 11 June 1912.

1921 Report by His Majesty's Agent and Consul-General on the Finances, Administration, and Condition of Egypt and the Soudan in 1911. [*Egypt No. 1 (1912)*.]   PAGE 635

[Cd. 6149]   *L/C.* HC. 4 June, HL. 11 June 1912.

1922 Exchange of Notes between the United Kingdom and France respecting boundaries between Sierra Leone and French Guinea. London, July 6, 1911, with map. [*Treaty Series No. 9 (1912)*.]   PAGE 709

[Cd. 6101]   *L/C.* 25 Mar. 1912.

1922a Protocol between the United Kingdom and France respecting the application of the Additional Articles of the Commercial Convention of 1826 to certain parts of His Britannic Majesty's Dominions. Signed at Paris, July 6, 1912. [*Treaty Series No. 18 (1912)*.]   PAGE 715

[Cd. 6269]   *L/C.* HC. 26 July, HL. 29 July 1912.

1922*b*   Agreement between the United Kingdom and France regulating the Telephone Service between the two countries. Signed at Paris, February 5, 1912. [*Treaty Series No. 8 (1912)*.]

PAGE 719

[Cd. 6076]   *L/C.* 4 Mar. 1912.

1922*c*   Agreement between the United Kingdom and France respecting Postal Rates between New Zealand and French Oceania. Signed at Paris, December 29, 1911. [*Treaty Series No. 7 (1912)*.]   PAGE 727

[Cd. 6075]   *L/C.* 4 Mar. 1912.

1923   Agreement between the United Kingdom and France respecting the delimitation of the frontier between the British and French Possessions east of the Niger [*v. supra*, No. 1711]. [*Treaty Series No. 1 (1912)*.]   PAGE 731

[Cd. 6013]   *L/C.* 14 Feb. 1912.

VOLUME CXXII (1912–13)

State Papers

1924   Treaty between the United Kingdom and Germany relating to Extradition between certain British Protectorates and Germany. Signed at Berlin, August 17, 1911. Ratifications exchanged at Berlin, January 20, 1912. [*Treaty Series No. 3 (1912)*.]   PAGE 1

[Cd. 6035]   *L/C.* 14 Feb. 1912.

1924*a*   Treaty between the United Kingdom and Greece for the Mutual Surrender of Fugitive Criminals. Signed at Athens, September 24, 1910. Ratifications exchanged at Athens, December 30, 1911. [*Treaty Series No. 6 (1912)*.]   PAGE 7

[Cd. 6074]   *L/C.* HC. 23 Feb., HL. 27 Feb. 1912.

1925   Exchange of Notes between the United Kingdom and Honduras extending until April 6, 1913, the operation of the Treaty of Commerce and Navigation between the two countries of January 21, 1887. April 7/8, 1912. [*Treaty Series No. 12 (1912)*.]

PAGE 21

[Cd. 6202]   *L/C.* HC. 4 June, HL. 11 June 1912.

1926   Exchange of Notes between the United Kingdom and Japan for the reciprocal waiver of Consular Fees on Certificates of Origin relating to Exports. Tokio, October 26/31, 1912. [*Treaty Series No. 23 (1912)*.]   PAGE 25

    [Cd. 6522]   *L/C.* 11 Dec. 1912.

1927   Franco-Spanish Declaration and Convention respecting Morocco (Signed at Paris, October 3, 1904). Exchange of Notes between Great Britain and France, October 6, 1904. Franco-German declaration respecting Morocco (Signed at Berlin, February 8, 1909). Franco-German Convention and Exchange of Notes respecting Morocco (Signed at Berlin, November 4, 1911). [*Morocco No. 4 (1911)*.]   PAGE 29

    [Cd. 6010]   *L/C.* 14 Feb. 1912.

1928   Accession of the Netherlands to the International Copyright Convention, signed at Berlin, November 13, 1908. November 1, 1912. [*Treaty Series No. 25 (1912)*.]   PAGE 47

    [Cd. 6524]   *L/C.* HC. 17 Dec. 1912, HL. 14 Jan. 1913.

1929   Joint Note addressed by the British and Russian Representatives at Tehran to the Persian Government on September 11, 1907. [*Persia No. 1 (1912)*.]   PAGE 51

    [Cd. 6077]   *L/C.* 7 Mar. 1912.

1929 *a*   Notes exchanged between the Persian Government and the British and Russian Ministers at Tehran, February 18–March 20, 1912. [*Persia No. 2 (1912)*.]   PAGE 55

    [Cd. 6103]   *L/C.* 26 Mar. 1912.

1929 *b*   Further Correspondence respecting the Affairs of Persia. [*Persia No. 3 (1912)*.]   PAGE 61

    [Cd. 6104]   *L/C.* 28 Mar. 1912.

1929 *c*   do. [Sept. 1911–Jan. 1912]. [*Persia No. 4 (1912)*.]   PAGE 259

    [Cd. 6105]   *L/C.* HC. 11 Ap., HL. 16 Ap. 1912.

1929 *d*   do. [Dec. 1911–Ap. 1912]. [*Persia No. 5 (1912)*.]   PAGE 429

    [Cd. 6264]   *L/C.* 3 July 1912.

1930   Agreement between the United Kingdom and Portugal respecting the Boundary between the British and Portuguese Possessions North and South of the Zambesi. London, October 21–November 20, 1911. (With Map.) [*Treaty Series No. 16 (1912)*.]   PAGE 583

    [Cd. 6265]   *L/C.* 3 July 1912.

1930*a* Agreement between the United Kingdom and Portugal respecting Boundaries in East Africa. Lisbon, July 22–August 9, 1912. (With Map.) [*Treaty Series No. 21 (1912)*.]
PAGE 595

[Cd. 6449]   L/C. HC. 3 Dec., HL. 5 Dec. 1912.

1930*b* Agreement between the United Kingdom and Portugal respecting the Boundary between the British and Portuguese Possessions on the Ruo and Shire Rivers. Lisbon, November 6/30, 1911. (With Map.) [*Treaty Series No. 10 (1912)*.]
PAGE 603

[Cd. 6147]   L/C. 13 May 1912.

1931 Agreement between the United Kingdom and Siam respecting the rendition of Fugitive Criminals between certain States in the Malay Peninsula and Siam. Signed at Bangkok, November 20, 1912. [*Treaty Series No. 2 (1913)*.]   PAGE 611

[Cd. 6586]   L/C. 28 Jan. 1913.

1932 Declaration between the United Kingdom and Sweden relating to the Amendment of Treaties of Commerce between the two countries. Signed at Stockholm, November 27, 1911. [*Treaty Series No. 26 (1911)*.]   PAGE 615

[Cd. 6009]   L/C. 14 Feb. 1912.

1933 Agreement between the United Kingdom and Turkey respecting Commercial Travellers' Samples. Constantinople, November 6, 1912. [*Treaty Series No. 1 (1913)*.]   PAGE 619

[Cd. 6584]   L/C. 22 Jan. 1913.

1934 Agreement between the United Kingdom and the United States of America for the settlement of certain Pecuniary Claims outstanding between the two countries. Signed at Washington, August 18, 1910. [*Treaty Series No. 11 (1912)*.]   PAGE 627

[Cd. 6201]   L/C. HC. 22 May, HL. 11 June 1912.

1934*a* Agreement between the United Kingdom and the United States of America respecting the North Atlantic Fisheries. Signed at Washington, July 20, 1912. Ratifications exchanged at Washington, November 15, 1912. [*Treaty Series No. 22 (1912)*.]   PAGE 639

[Cd. 6450]   L/C. 9 Dec. 1912.

1934*b* Despatch from His Majesty's Ambassador at Washington respecting the Panama Canal Act. [*Misc. No. 12 (1912)*.]
PAGE 645

[Cd. 6451]   L/C. 9 Dec. 1912.

SESSION 10 MARCH TO 15 AUGUST 1913

VOLUME XIV (1913)

Reports from Committees

VOLUME XLIII (1913)

Navy

Volume XLV (1913)

Colonies and British Possessions

1938   Further Correspondence respecting the Affairs of the Congo.
        [*Africa No. 3 (1913)*.]   PAGE 717
        [Cd. 6802]   *L/C.* 27 May 1913.

Volume LI (1913)

Miscellaneous

1939   *Putumayo:* Report by His Majesty's Consul at Iquitos on his
        tour in the Putumayo District. [*Miscellaneous No. 6 (1913)*.]
                                                                    PAGE 791
        [Cd. 6678]   *L/C.* HC. 2 Ap., HL. 4 Ap. 1913.

Volume LXXXI (1913)

State Papers

1940   International Conventions for the Unification of certain Rules
        of Law respecting Collisions between Vessels, and Assistance
        and Salvage at Sea. Signed at Brussels, September 23, 1910.
        [*Treaty Series No. 4 (1913)*.]   PAGE 1
        [Cd. 6677]   *L/C.* HC. 12 Mar., HL. 28 Mar. 1913.

1940a   International Agreement for the Prevention of False Indications
        of Origin on Goods. Signed at Washington, June 2, 1911.
        [*Treaty Series No. 7 (1913)*.]   PAGE 43
        [Cd. 6804]   *L/C.* HC. 6 June, HL. 9 June 1913.

1940b   International Convention for the Protection of Industrial
        Property. Signed at Washington, June 2, 1911. [*Treaty Series
        No. 8 (1913)*.]   PAGE 51
        [Cd. 6805]   *L/C.* HC. 6 June, HL. 9 June 1913.

1940c   International Radiotelegraph Convention. Signed at London,
        July 5, 1912. [*Treaty Series No. 10 (1913)*.]   PAGE 79
        [Cd. 6873]   *L/C.* HC. 4 July, HL. 7 July 1913.

Session 10 February to 18 September 1914

Volume LIV (1914)

Navy

Volume LX (1914)

Colonies and British Possessions

Volume CI (1914)

State Papers

1950*b* Despatch from His Majesty's Ambassador at Vienna [1 Sept. 1914] respecting the rupture of Diplomatic Relations with the Austro-Hungarian Government. [*Misc. No. 10 (1914)*.]
                                                                PAGE 101
         [Cd. 7596]   *L/C.* 16 Sept. 1914.

1950*c* Correspondence regarding the Naval and Military Assistance afforded to His Majesty's Government by His Majesty's Oversea Dominions.   PAGE 109
         [Cd. 7607]   *L/C.* 14 Sept. 1914.

1950*d* Correspondence relating to Gifts of Foodstuffs and other Supplies to His Majesty's Government from the Oversea Dominions and Colonies.   PAGE 125
         [Cd. 7608]   *L/C.* 14 Sept. 1914.

1951   Additional Protocol to the International Copyright Convention of November 13, 1908. Signed at Berne, March 20, 1914. British Ratification deposited, July 8, 1914. [*Treaty Series No. 11 (1914)*.]   PAGE 143
         [Cd. 7613]   *L/C.* 18 Sept. 1914.

1952   Treaties, etc., between the United Kingdom and Foreign States. Accessions, Withdrawals, etc. [*Treaty Series No. 7 (1914)*.]   PAGE 151
         [Cd. 7359]   *L/C.* 7 May 1914.

1952*a* Index to Treaty Series, 1913. [*Treaty Series No. 20 (1913)*.]
                                                                PAGE 159
         [Cd. 7150]   *L/C.* 10 Feb. 1914.

1953   Further Correspondence respecting the Affairs of China. [*China No. 3 (1913)*.]   PAGE 163
         [Cd. 7054]   *L/C.* 10 Feb. 1914.

1953*a* do. [Dec. 1912–Oct. 1913]. [*China No. 1 (1914)*.]   PAGE 253
         [Cd. 7356]   *L/C.* 29 Ap. 1914.

1954   Protocol between the United Kingdom and Costa Rica respecting the Application of the Treaty of Commerce of 27th November 1849 to certain parts of His Britannic Majesty's Dominions; signed at Panama, August 18, 1913. [*Treaty Series No. 16 (1913)*.]   PAGE 323
         [Cd. 7097]   *L/C.* 10 Feb. 1914.

1955   Reports by His Majesty's Agent and Consul-General on the Finances, Administration, and Condition of Egypt and the Sudan in 1913. [*Egypt No. 1 (1914)*.]   PAGE 327
    [Cd. 7358]   *L/C.* 25 May 1914.

1956   Exchange of Notes between the United Kingdom and France renewing for a further period of Five Years the Arbitration Agreement signed at London, October 14, 1903. October 14, 1913. [*Treaty Series No. 18 (1913)*.]   PAGE 401
    [Cd. 7099]   *L/C.* 10 Feb. 1914.

1956*a*   Agreement between the United Kingdom and France respecting the Boundary between Sierra Leone and French Guinea. London, September 4, 1913. (With Map.) [*Treaty Series No. 19 (1913)*.]   PAGE 405
    [Cd. 7147]   *L/C.* 10 Feb. 1914.

1956*b*   Agreement between the United Kingdom and France respecting the Delimitation of the Frontier between the British and French Possessions from the Gulf of Guinea to the Okpara River. London, February 18, 1914. (With Map.) [*Treaty Series No. 5 (1914)*.]   PAGE 413
    [Cd. 7278]   *L/C.* HC. 16 Ap., HL. 21 Ap. 1914.

1956*c*   Parcel Post Agreement between the United Kingdom and France; signed at Paris, November 22, 1913. [*Treaty Series No. 2 (1914)*.]   PAGE 451
    [Cd. 7152]   *L/C.* 18 Feb. 1914.

1956*d*   Exchange of Notes between His Majesty's Government and the Government of the French Republic respecting the Trade in Arms and Ammunition at Muscat. London, February 4, 1914. [*Treaty Series No. 9 (1914)*.]   PAGE 491
    [Cd. 7361]   *L/C.* HC. 9 June, HL. 15 June 1914.

1957   Agreement between the United Kingdom and Germany respecting the Settlement of the Frontier between Nigeria and the Cameroons from Yola to the Sea; and the Regulation of Navigation on the Cross River; signed at London, March 11, 1913. (With Maps.) [*Treaty Series No. 13 (1913)*.]   PAGE 497
    [Cd. 7056]   *L/C.* 10 Feb. 1914.

1958   Despatches from His Majesty's Ambassador at Berlin respecting an Official German Organisation for influencing the Press of other Countries. [*Misc. No. 9 (1914)*.]   PAGE 515
    [Cd. 7595]   *L/C.* 9 Sept. 1914.

1959　Exchange of Notes between the United Kingdom and Greece recording an Agreement between the respective Governments relating to Commercial Travellers' Samples. [*Treaty Series No. 8 (1914)*.]　　PAGE 523

　　[Cd. 7360]　　*L/C.* HC. 9 June, HL. 15 June 1914.

1960　Arrangement between the United Kingdom and Honduras referring to Arbitration Matters relating to the Masica Incident: signed at Tegucigalpa, April 4, 1914. [*Treaty Series No. 10 (1914)*.]　　PAGE 529

　　[Cd. 7465]　　*L/C.* 25 Aug. 1914.

1960*a*　Exchange of Notes between the United Kingdom and Honduras extending until April 6, 1915, the operation of the Treaty of Commerce and Navigation between the two countries of January 21, 1887. February 13/March 31, 1913. [*Treaty Series No. 12 (1913)*.]　　PAGE 537

　　[Cd. 7055]　　*L/C.* 10 Feb. 1914.

1961　Exchange of Notes between the United Kingdom and Italy renewing for a further Period of Five Years the Arbitration Agreement, signed at Rome, February 1, 1904. London, January 31, 1914. [*Treaty Series No. 4 (1914)*.]　　PAGE 543

　　[Cd. 7275]　　*L/C.* HC. 2 Mar., HL. 3 Mar. 1914.

1962　Notes exchanged with the Netherlands Minister on the Subject of Oil Properties in Mexico. [*Misc. No. 7 (1914)*.]　　PAGE 547

　　[Cd. 7468]　　*L/C.* 25 Aug. 1914.

1963　Convention between the United Kingdom and Norway respecting the Application of the Convention of Commerce and Navigation of March 18, 1826, to certain parts of His Britannic Majesty's Dominions; signed at Christiania, May 16, 1913. [*Treaty Series No. 14 (1913)*.]　　PAGE 551

　　[Cd. 7095]　　*L/C.* 10 Feb. 1914.

1964　Agreement between the United Kingdom and Paraguay relating to Extradition between certain British Protectorates and Paraguay (Supplementary to the Extradition Treaty of September 12, 1908); signed at Asuncion, July 16, 1913. [*Treaty Series No. 15 (1913)*.]　　PAGE 555

　　[Cd. 7096]　　*L/C.* 10 Feb. 1914.

1965　Further Correspondence respecting the Affairs of Persia. [*Persia No. 1 (1914)*.]　　PAGE 559

　　[Cd. 7280]　　*L/C.* 22 Ap. 1914.

1965*a*   Financial Advances made by His Majesty's Government and the Government of India to the Persian Government. [*Persia No. 2 (1913)*.]   PAGE 741
    [Cd. 7053]   *L/C.* 10 Feb. 1914.

1966   Agreement between the United Kingdom and Portugal for the Regulation of the Opium Monopolies in the Colonies of Hong Kong and Macao; signed at London, June 14, 1913. [*Treaty Series No. 11 (1913)*.]   PAGE 745
    [Cd. 7052]   *L/C.* 10 Feb. 1914.

1967   Agreement between the United Kingdom and Siam respecting the Rendition of Fugitive Criminals between the State of North Borneo and Siam; signed at Bangkok, September 18, 1913. [*Treaty Series No. 17 (1913)*.]   PAGE 751
    [Cd. 7098]   *L/C.* 10 Feb. 1914.

1968   Exchange of Notes between the United Kingdom and Spain renewing for a further period of Five Years the Arbitration Agreement signed at London, February 27, 1904. London, February 15, 1914. [*Treaty Series No. 3 (1914)*.]   PAGE 755
    [Cd. 7274]   *L/C.* HC. 2 Mar., HL. 3 Mar. 1914.

1969   Agreement between the United Kingdom and the United States of America renewing for a further period of Five Years the Arbitration Convention signed at Washington on April 4, 1908; signed at Washington, May 31, 1913. [*Treaty Series No. 6 (1914)*.]   PAGE 759
    [Cd. 7357]   *L/C.* HC. 4 May, HL. 5 May 1914.

1969*a*   Exchange of Notes between the United Kingdom and the United States of America respecting the Rendition of Fugitive Criminals between the State of North Borneo and the Philippine Islands or Guam. Washington, September 1/23, 1913. [*Treaty Series No. 1 (1914)*.]   PAGE 763
    [Cd. 7149]   *L/C.* 10 Feb. 1914.

1969*b*   Notes exchanged between His Majesty's Ambassador at Washington and United States Government on the subject of Oil Properties and Mining Rights in Mexico. [*United States No. 1 (1914)*.]   PAGE 767
    [Cd. 7463]   *L/C.* 16 July 1914.

APPENDIX I

NOTES ON CERTAIN ENTRIES IN THE TEXT DEALING WITH PAPERS RELATING TO SPANISH AMERICA (1825); ROME (1849); THE PAPACY (1891); THE CONGO (1894)

i. *Spanish American Colonies (1825)*

No. 141. Note of Mr Secretary Canning to the Chevalier de Los Rios of 25 March 1825.

[This is a good example of how and why a British State Paper was published in *B.F.S.P.* of 1825 and the *Annual Register* and not in Parliamentary Papers. The note of Mr Secretary Canning to the Chevalier de Los Rios of 25 March 1825 is of great importance, as it sums up the British case for recognition of the Spanish American Colonies. This document through leakage of some kind got into the Press. It was first published in the *Argus* at Buenos Ayres. Then on 3 November 1825 it was published in the *Star*. The version published was not accurate, being in fact 'the translation of a translation'. On 9 November the *Star* published a new version stating, 'We are now enabled to publish this remarkable document in its original and authentic form.' The *Star* was in touch with Canning and, though he never seems to have directly communicated with the Press in the first instance, he doubtless authorised the correction of the original version. So far as Canning himself was concerned there is no question that he was not himself responsible for the original leakage. For he thought 'de los Rios' 'the nicest little Minister' he knew, and would undoubtedly have refused to do anything to hurt his feelings. A British Foreign Office clerk may have been indiscreet or there may have been leakage from the Foreign Office at Madrid or the Spanish Legation in London. Though the *Star* announced that the version was 'authentic' on 9 November (*v.* Temperley and Penson, *Foundations of British Foreign Policy*, 77 and *n.*), it was not published in the *London Gazette* nor in Parliamentary Papers. But it appeared in both *B.F.S.P.* and the *Annual Register*.]

ii. *Rome (1849)*

No. 649. Correspondence relating to the Affairs of Rome, 1849.

[This is an important example of a paper laid before the House of Lords alone. In February 1863, Normanby raised questions in a debate in the Lords about the British attitude in 1849 to the occupation of Rome by the French, and was successful in extracting papers on the subject from the Government. Moreover these documents, in contrast to those recently laid before both Houses (*v. supra*, No. 645*a*), expressed approval of the French action.

The debate which produced these documents has a further importance, for Grey asserted the principle that 'Your Lordships ought not to listen to quotations from despatches which have not been laid before Parliament, these quotations being made by a noble Lord formerly a servant of the Crown, and being made without the authority of the Crown'. Later, Russell quoted certain dispatches which had not been laid, and said that he would 'be happy to give the whole or extracts from the despatches' to the House. Normanby complained some days afterwards that the documents had not yet been presented, and stated that 'no Minister of the Crown ought to read extracts from any public document, unless he were prepared at once—he emphatically stated at once—to lay the document upon the table'. Russell acknowledged the principle, although, as he said, it was sometimes broken, and the papers were laid on the following day. *Hans. Deb.* 3rd Ser. CLXIX, 374–93, 790, 17 and 26 February 1863.]

iii. *The Papacy (1891)*

Nos. 1293, 1293 a. Correspondence respecting the Duke of Norfolk's Special Mission to the Pope. Correspondence respecting Monsignor Ruffo-Scilla's Mission.

[These papers provide an example of the practice, followed only rarely, of laying papers in 'dummy'. Although returned to an Address, they were laid only in form, and there was nothing to print. As a result the actual circulation was delayed for over a year, and then only after they had been pressed for in the House of Commons. *Hans. Deb.* 3rd Ser. CCCLIV, 540, 16 June 1891; CCCLV, 1910, 21 July 1891.]

iv. *The Congo (1894)*

P. 417, note. Correspondence relating to the Independent State of the Congo.

[This paper was laid by command on 23 August 1894, and was clearly intended to supplement the meagre Blue Books on the Congo crisis. It was, however, never printed, and there is no evidence available as to its contents. It was probably laid in 'dummy', as it is marked in the index to the *Sessional Papers* of the House of Lords as 'not ready'. In the House of Commons' bound set—Volume LVII of 1894—it is marked as 'not printed'. In view of the fact that by this date Foreign Office Blue Books were always laid in print, the conclusion that no material was in fact presented seems inevitable.]

APPENDIX II

FURTHER ILLUSTRATIONS OF BLUE-BOOK POLICY FROM PALMERSTON (1848, 1857), GLADSTONE (1861), DERBY (1875)*

Pp. 102–6. *Palmerston*. Statement in House of Commons, 1 March 1848. *Hans. Deb.* 3rd Ser. xcvii, 68.

'I may state that with regard to the correspondence generally of Governments, the practice is this—and, I may add, that practice I have invariably followed—the practice and the duty of a Government when diplomatic transactions occur which it is desirable that the House and the country should become acquainted with—the practice is, to lay before Parliament such portions of the diplomatic transactions that have taken place as will convey to Parliament a true and faithful knowledge of all the main and important circumstances that occurred. But it is not the duty of the Government—but on the contrary, it would be a breach of that duty if it did so—to lay before Parliament such portions of that correspondence as contained mere opinions and confidential communications made by the Foreign Minister to our agents abroad concerning other matters, and the publication of which would be injurious to the public service.'

Pp. 127–33. *Palmerston*. Private letter from Palmerston to Clarendon, 9 February 1857. *Pte Clarendon Papers*.

'There is certainly an awkwardness in laying Papers about an affair for the amicable Settlement of which negotiations are in progress, and general Principle is against doing so; at the same time we have begun a war, and Parliament has a Right to know for what reasons we have done so. It would therefore be right to present such Papers as would shew the grounds of Quarrel with Persia leaving out all that are connected with negotiations either at Constantinople or at Paris.' (*v. supra*, No. 536.)

Pp. 162–3. *Gladstone*. Private letter to the Duke of Newcastle, 22 March 1861. *Pte Gladstone Papers*.

'It is commonly a good argument to say that where there have been papers relating to a particular plan or proposal in the nature of a negotiation, and the negotiation has failed, these papers are not to be produced. Or at least, if not generally sound, it is sometimes sound, and always at least available.'

* *Editors' Note.* These extracts were not found in time for incorporation in the text at the appropriate places, but they are given here in view of their intrinsic value.

Pp. 251–7. *Disraeli and Derby*. Statement by Derby in House of Lords, 31 May 1875. *Hans. Deb.* 3rd Ser. CCXXIV, 1095–6.

'As far as Her Majesty's Government are concerned, there is nothing we have said or done which we have the slightest desire to keep from the knowledge of this House or the other House of Parliament or the public. But there is this objection to the production of these documents—that it would be impossible to give anything like such an account of these matters as Parliament and the country would expect without making use of confidential communications as to the opinions and policy of other Governments, and those other Governments would object in the strongest manner to our disclosing this confidential information. We could not in fairness disclose it without their consent; but even if we could, I do not think that in good policy we ought to do so—because the result would be to give other Governments reason to conclude that whatever passed into the hands of British diplomatists would be sure to be published. The consequence of that conviction would be that British diplomatists would receive very little confidential information in future. Therefore, my Lords, the production of the whole of the Correspondence is impossible; and I do not think the production of the Correspondence mutilated or severely edited would answer any useful purpose.'

APPENDIX III

THE EFFECT OF BLUE BOOKS ON NAPOLEON III AND THOUVENEL DURING THE YEARS 1860–1

[Numerous references have been made in the various introductions in this volume to the attitude of Foreign Powers towards the policy of British ministries in the matter of publishing Blue Books. Some additional material is printed here, dealing particularly with the French views on this subject in 1860–1. The first two extracts bear upon the question of Italy and Savoy, on which France might well be supposed to be sensitive; but the third shows that her anxiety about publication was a more general one.]

Private letter from Cowley to Russell, 3 February 1860. *Pte Russell Papers.* G. & D. 22/54.

'I was very glad to get your telegram informing me that you had decided not to give any papers respecting Savoy for the moment, for the publication of any document at this instant, would I think render a satisfactory solution of this question even less likely than it is. If any impression is to be made upon the Emperor, it must be by friendly advice. Any attempt to hold him to previous declarations by showing them up to the public would irritate him and drive him perhaps to commit himself still further in a contrary direction.'

Private letter from Cowley to Russell, 12 April 1861. *Pte Russell Papers.* G. & D. 22/56.

'...He [Thouvenel] remarked...but in perfect good humour, that if you wanted the evacuation, you could not take a better way of preventing it, than by addressing him official remonstrances, to be published hereafter in a Blue Book. Of course he did not mean, he said, to dispute your right to make any observations, which you might deem advisable, but it would never do for France to appear to follow the dictates of England....'

Private letter from Cowley to Russell, 26 April 1861. *Pte Russell Papers.* G. & D. 22/56.

'...Since Thouvenel has had a translation made of your No. 492 (Saïd Jumblatt*) he has taken it very much to heart, and he is going to write privately to Flahault to ask you not to publish it in a Blue Book, as he says he must otherwise answer it and that he does not want to continue the polemic. The truth however is that you have bowled him over so completely he is ashamed of himself and does not want that his disgrace sh[oul]d be made public....'

* This dispatch refers to Saïd Jumblatt, a Druse Chief, who was implicated in massacres of Christians. Russell and Dufferin wished the Turkish Government to acquit, while Thouvenel wished to execute, him. His life was ultimately spared.

INDEX TO BLUE-BOOK POLICIES
OF FOREIGN SECRETARIES

The references in this index are to pages. Italic type is used for dates

INDEX TO LIST OF BLUE BOOKS
(including Conferences, Congresses and Treaties)

The references in this index are all to entry numbers. Italic type is used for dates